D1571288

SEXUAL SELECTION AND REPRODUCTIVE COMPETITION IN INSECTS

Academic Press Rapid Manuscript Reproduction

This volume had its origins in a symposium presented at the 15th International Congress of Entomology, Washington, D.C., chaired by Dr. Daniel Otte.

SEXUAL SELECTION AND REPRODUCTIVE COMPETITION IN INSECTS

edited by

Murray S. Blum
Nancy A. Blum

University of Georgia
Athens, Georgia

1979

Academic Press   New York San Francisco London
A Subsidiary of Harcourt Brace Jovanovich, Publishers

ACADEMIC PRESS, INC.
111 Fifth Avenue, New York, New York 10003

United Kingdom Edition published by
ACADEMIC PRESS, INC. (LONDON) LTD.
24/28 Oval Road, London NW1 7DX

Library of Congress Cataloging in Publication Data

Main entry under title:
Sexual selection and reproductive competition in insects.

Includes index.
1. Insects—Behavior. 2. Sexual selection in
animals. 3. Reproduction. 4. Insects—Evolution.
I. Blum, Murray Sheldon, Date II. Blum, Nancy A.
QL496.S44   591.5′6   78-25967
ISBN 0-12-108750-6

CONTENTS

CONTRIBUTORS

Numbers in parentheses indicate the pages on which the authors' contributions begin.

JOHN ALCOCK (381), Department of Zoology, Arizona State University, Tempe, Arizona 85281

RICHARD D. ALEXANDER (417), Museum of Zoology, The University of Michigan, Ann Arbor, Michigan 48109

ROBERT BARRASS (403), Department of Biology, Sunderland Polytechnic, Chester Road, Sunderland SR1 3SD, England

GERALD BORGIA (19, 417), Museum of Zoology, The University of Michigan, Ann Arbor, Michigan 48109

WILLIAM CADE* (343), Department of Zoology, The University of Texas, Austin, Texas 78712

WILLIAM G. EBERHARD (231), Departamento de Biologia, Universidad de Valle, Cali, Colombia and Smithsonian Tropical Research Institute, P.O. Box 2072, Balboa, Canal Zone

W. D. HAMILTON (167), Museum of Zoology, The University of Michigan, Ann Arbor, Michigan 48109

JAMES E. LLOYD (293), Department of Entomology and Nematology, University of Florida, Gainesville, Florida 32611

DAVID K. McALPINE (221), Department of Entomology, The Australian Museum, Post Office Box A285, Sydney South, 2000 Australia

*Present address: Department of Biological Sciences, Brock University, Region Niagara, St. Catherines, Ontario L2S 3A1, Canada

DANIEL OTTE (1,259), The Academy of Natural Sciences of Philadelphia, Nineteenth and the Parkway, Philadelphia, Pennsylvania 19103

G. A. PARKER (123), Department of Zoology, The University of Liverpool, Brownlow Street, P.O. Box 147, Liverpool L69 3BX, England

KATHARINE STAYMAN (259), The Academy of Natural Sciences of Philadelphia, Nineteenth and the Parkway, Philadelphia, Pennsylvania 19103

RANDY THORNHILL (81), Department of Biology, The University of New Mexico, Albuquerque, New Mexico 87131

PREFACE

Increasing interest in reproductive behavior in insects led to its selection as a symposium topic for the Behavior Section of the 15th International Congress of Entomology in Washington, D.C., in 1976. Daniel Otte was selected to chair and organize the symposium. The overall quality of contributions, as well as interest in the subject, led to the arranging for its publication by Academic Press.

For inclusion in this volume, many of the papers presented at the meeting have been expanded and updated, so that they represent much broader experimental and theoretical treatments than were originally possible. Additional manuscripts were contributed by outstanding evolutionary biologists, resulting in a volume that ranges far and wide over the area of reproductive biology. The final product represents a synthesis of biological concepts that emphasizes intrasexual reproductive competition as a driving force in sexual selection.

It has been more than a century since Darwin explored mating systems in evolutionary terms. Since that time considerable progress has been made in analyzing the multiplicity of factors that affect sexual selection. In particular, the importance of inclusive fitness, operating at the level of the individual genome, has really been appreciated only in the last 15 years. This development has resulted in focusing on the importance of natural selection operating on individuals rather than populations in determining reproductive success.

The papers in this volume address the question of the role of individual fitness in reproductive success as a primary prerequisite to comprehending sexual selection. In so doing, the authors demonstrate that reproductive competition has many evolutionary faces. Their message is perfectly clear—only when these faces are analyzed and their significance understood can we hope to comprehend the subtleties of sexual selection.

ACKNOWLEDGMENTS

We wish to thank all the contributors for their prompt help in dealing with minor editorial problems. We are grateful to Dr. Daniel Otte for his assembling and initial reading of the manuscripts. Special thanks are due to Academic Press for helping with the preparation of this book. Last, but certainly not least, we wish to express our great gratitude to Ms. Kathy Andrews for typing the camera-ready copy of the manuscripts in such an outstandingly accurate manner. The consistently high quality of her work and her patience are greatly appreciated.

HISTORICAL DEVELOPMENT OF SEXUAL SELECTION THEORY

Daniel Otte

The Academy of Natural Sciences of Philadelphia

INTRODUCTION

In 1889 Wallace stated emphatically that some of the agencies which Darwin thought must influence the development of sexual differences would not in general be important, and furthermore that sexual selection was merely a form of natural selection. Huxley (1938) believed that sexual selection subsumed several quite distinct phenomena and suggested that the terms be replaced. Recent writers still disagree on various points concerning sexual selection, even as to whether the terms should be retained.

Progress in this field has throughout been retarded by two distinct problems: The first is that the multifarious modes of reproductive interactions have not been fully explored, mainly, it seems, because the origins of sexual differentiation have not been fully considered. Once this is attempted, the ramifications of reproductive competition and of mutualistic adjustments will probably be shown to be broad indeed. A second problem has been that of making overly rigid definitions of sexual and natural selection and then attempting to attribute sexual differences to one or the other. Whether such an endeavor is worthwhile is debatable. It can be argued either that the connections between natural and sexual selection have been sufficiently clarified to make such attempts worthwhile, or that we now understand the connections well enough to know that it is not. Disagreements on relatively trivial issues will continue as long as there are efforts to pigeonhole selective agencies into mutually exclusive categories when they cannot be so treated.

In this introduction, an attempt is made to expose readers as directly as possible to some of the principal conceptual advances in sexual selection theory. Quotations are used to minimize problems inherent in paraphrasing and in taking statements out of their original context. In the process it is hoped that a broader framework of reproductive competition and of the connections between selective components can be constructed. The papers in this volume, although dealing principally with insects, show the diversity of competitive modes which exist for animals and how these might affect the behavior and morphology of the two sexes differently. In the future, new facts and insights will doubtless necessitate some restructuring of the theoretical and factual framework which this book attempts to construct.

THE ORIGINAL FORMULATION

According to Darwin (1871), a sexual character was a characteristic possessed by only one sex and not the other. Following Hunter, he distinguished between "primary" sexual characters (the organs of reproduction) and "secondary" sexual characters (characters "not directly connected with the act of reproduction; . . . the male (for example) possesses certain organs of sense or locomotion, of which the female is quite destitute, or has them more highly developed, in order that he may readily find or reach her; or again the male has special organs of prehension for holding her securely" [p. 210]). But the dichotomy was for convenience only, for certain characters he could not assign to one category or another with certainty. Some characteristics--such as sex-linked color dimorphisms influenced by predatory pressure, differences in feeding habits between males and females, and differences in vagility--were only indirectly coupled to mating. Other differences were more strongly coupled to securing mates than was at first apparent. He was especially impressed by characteristics in animals which he thought must reduce the survival chances of individuals bearing them, but he saw that such costs could be counterbalanced by gains made in reproduction. Gaudy plumages in birds, immense horns in stags and beetles, and other features must, he reasoned, be maintained only because of their benefit in relation to sexual reproduction. The following passages set forth his concept of sexual selection:

> Sexual selection depends on the success of certain in-
> dividuals over others of the same sex, in relation to the
> propagation of the species; while natural selection depends
> on the success of both sexes, at all ages, in relation to
> the general conditions of life. [Sexual selection is] a
> struggle between individuals of one sex, generally the
> males, for the possession of the other sex. The result is
> not death to the unsuccessful competitor, but few or no
> offspring (Darwin, 1859).

Darwin wrestled with the problem of when a characteristic was to be ascribed to either sexual selection or natural selection, and the problem continues to the present (Mayr,

1972; Ghiselin, 1974). Some recent statements suggest that only characteristics which augment a male's ability to win in fights (for females) or which are the result of female choice can be ascribed to sexual selection. But Darwin clearly indicated that the "struggle" among males for females involved direct as well as indirect forms of competition. He wrote:

. . . if the chief service rendered to the male by his prehensile organs is to prevent the escape of the female before the arrival of other males, or when assaulted by them, these organs will have been perfected through sexual selection, that is by the advantage acquired by certain individuals over their rivals. *But in most cases of this kind it is impossible to distinguish between the effects of natural and sexual selection* (1871, p. 213) (emphasis added).

His discussion of orthopteran sound organs illustrates clearly his belief that female choice or male combat need not be involved for sexual selection to occur:

No one who admits the agency of selection of any kind, will . . . dispute that . . . musical instruments have been acquired through sexual selection . . . the individuals which were able to make the loudest or most continuous noise would gain partners before those which were less noisy, so that these organs have probably been gained through sexual selection.

Some of Darwin's notions now seem false. The notions that natural and sexual selection may act with different degrees of intensity and that natural selection acts mainly through differential survival rather than through differential reproduction now seem unjustified, given that death and a failure to reproduce have equivalent selective effects in nonparental animals.

Darwin perceived that sexual selection could counteract the effects of natural selection, a relationship which Fisher (1958) was later to discuss at length. About bright colors, Darwin said: "Obscure tints have often been developed through natural selection for the sake of protection, and the acquirement through sexual selection of conspicuous colours appear to have been sometimes checked from the danger thus incurred" (p. 230).

The Law of Battle, he believed, did not apply to insects as readily as to higher vertebrate groups. Competition in the former was usually of a different kind--less direct and usually involving efforts by males to increase the probability of encounter with females or of being the first to find the females (1871, p. 233). Darwin also saw that sexual selection operated in monogamous species as well as in polygamous species, although somewhat differently. Thus, in birds:

> There can also be no doubt that the most vigorous, best
> nourished and earliest breeders would on an average succeed
> in rearing the largest number of fine offspring. The
> males . . . are generally ready to breed before the females;
> the strongest, and with some species the best armed, of
> the males drive away the weaker; and the former would then
> unite with the more vigorous and better nourished females,
> because they are the first to breed. Such vigorous pairs
> would surely rear a larger number of offspring . . . .

We can summarize Darwin's main points concerning sexual
selection: (1) The concept was initially devised to account
for striking morphological and behavioral differences between
the sexes which on the face of it appeared unnecessary for
survival. (2) "Primary" and "secondary" sexual characters
were part of a continuum referring to the directness with
which sexual differences were coupled to reproducing. (3)
Although sexual selection operates importantly through the
agencies of male combat and female choice, the so-called
"struggle" by males to gain access to females encompassed
more than fighting. It also referred to indirect, first-come-
first-served forms of competition, which could have selected
for more acute sense organs, more effective locomotory
structures, as well as adult sizes and developmental rates
which would enhance the males' chances of finding females.
(4) Sexual selection operates on females as well as males.
(5) It operates in monogamous as well as polygamous animals,
although somewhat differently in the two. (6) The effects of
sexual selection may be opposed by the effects of natural
selection. (7) It is not always easy to attribute a sexual
character either to sexual or natural selection.

A CHALLENGE TO FEMALE CHOICE

Wallace (1889) did not believe that female choice was an
important agency in the evolution of sexual differences. And
as for male rivalry, he repeatedly considered it to be a form
of natural selection:

> It is to male rivalry [which involves fighting] that Mr.
> Darwin first applied the term "sexual selection." It is
> evidently a real power in nature . . . . But he has extended
> the principle into a totally different field of action,
> which has none of that character of constancy and of
> inevitable result that attaches to natural selection,
> including male rivalry; for by far the larger portion of
> the phenomena, which he endeavors to explain by the direct

action of sexual selection, can only be so explained on
the hypothesis that the immediate agency is female choice
or preference. In this extension of sexual selection to
include the action of female choice or preference and in
the attempt to give to that choice such wide-reaching
effects, I am unable to follow him more than a very little
way . . . (p. 283).

Wallace raised the problem, later tackled by Fisher, of
whether females are normally capable of choosing among a
series of males who might differ only in the slightest degree
from one another:

Anyone who reads [Darwin's] most interesting chapters
[on bird displays] will admit that . . . the display is
demonstrated; and it may also be admitted as highly probable that the female is pleased or excited by the display.
But it by no means follows that slight differences in the
shape, pattern or colours of the ornamental plumes are
what lead a female to give the preference to one male over
another; still less that all the females of a species, or
the great majority of them over a wide area of country,
and for many successive generations, prefer exactly the
same modifications of the colour or ornament (p. 284).

Wallace seems to have minimized the role of female choice
simply because such choice is difficult to detect. He believed that bright colors, ". . . were again and again modified
by natural selection for purposes of warning, recognition,
mimicry, or special protection."

Wallace seems to have been very close to seeing the connection between real fitness (a function of reproductive
potential and survival probability) and the features which
animals might use to advertise that fitness to potential
mates. Not until Fisher (1958) did biologists begin to
understand the connection between the actual physical properties of organisms and the signals which inform potential
recipients of those properties. In his discussion of the
"vital energy," Wallace anticipated the idea of selective
compromises, which Fisher later discussed in more theoretical
terms. Wallace wrote

Natural selection . . . acts perpetually and on an enormous
scale in weeding out the "unfit" at every stage of existence, and preserving only those which are in all respects
the very best. . . . Now this extremely rigid action of
natural selection must render any attempt to select mere
ornament utterly nugatory, unless the most ornamented
always coincide with the "fittest" in every other respect;
while, if they do so coincide, then any selection of
ornament is altogether superfluous. If the most brightly

colored and fullest plumaged males are *not* the most healthy
and vigorous, have *not* the best instincts for the proper
construction and concealment of the nest, and for the care
and protection of the young, they are certainly not the
fittest, and will not survive, or be the parents of survi-
vors. If, on the other hand, there *is* generally this
correlation--if . . . ornament is the natural product and
direct outcome of superabundant health and vigour, then no
other mode of selection is needed to account for the
presence of such ornament . . . . *The term "sexual selection" must . . . be restricted to the direct results of male
struggle and combat. This is really a form of natural
selection,* and is a matter of direct observation; while its
results are as clearly deducible as those of any of the
other modes in which selection acts (p. 296) (emphasis added).

To Wallace, then, elaborate ornaments were not so much signals
as by-products of other processes. Had he seen them as
signals he could well have struck on the modern theories of
ornament evolution.

THE "RUNAWAY PROCESS," SELECTIVE COMPROMISES, AND DECEIT

Fisher (1958) included under sexual selection only male
combat and female preference, perhaps because these two
factors seemed to stand out as the most important ones which
could produce striking sex-related differences.

Fisher's most remarkable contribution to sexual selection
theory was his explanation of how bizarre weaponry and other
ornamental structures could arise and be maintained by
selection, through the so-called "runaway process." He
wrote

. . . the modification of the plumage character in the cock
proceeds under two selective influences, (i) an initial
advantage not due to sexual preference, which advantage
may be quite inconsiderable in magnitude, and (ii) an
additional advantage conferred by female preference which
will be proportional to the intensity of this preference.
The intensity of preference will itself be increased by
selection so long as the sons of hens exercising the
preference most decidedly have any advantage over the sons
of other hens, whether this be due to the first or the
second cause. The importance of this situation lies in
the fact that the further development of the plumage
character will still proceed, by reason of the advantage
gained in sexual selection, even after it has passed the
point in development at which its advantage in Natural
Selection has ceased. The selective agencies other than

sexual preference may be opposed to further development, and yet the further development will proceed, so long as the disadvantage is more than counterbalanced by the advantage in sexual selection. Moreover, as long as there is a net advantage in favor of further plumage development, there will be a net advantage in favor of giving to it a more decided preference (p. 152).[1]

There is thus in any bionomic situation in which sexual selection is capable of conferring a great reproductive advantage . . . the potentiality of a runaway process, which, however small the beginnings from which it arose, must, unless checked, produce great effects, and in the later stages with great rapidity. Such a process must soon run against some check. Two such are obvious. If carried far enough, it is evident that sufficiently severe counter-selection in favour of less ornamented males will be encountered to balance the advantage of sexual preference; at this point both plumage elaboration and the increase in female preference will be brought to a standstill, and a condition of relative stability will be attained. It will be more effective still if the disadvantage to the males of their sexual ornaments so diminishes their numbers surviving to the breeding season, relative to the females, as to cut at the root of the process, by diminishing the reproductive advantage to be conferred by female prefer-ence. . . . In most existing species the runaway process must have been already checked . . . (p. 153).

He introduced the role of deceit in the following passages:

The possibility should perhaps be borne in mind in such studies that the most finely adorned males gain some reproductive advantage without the intervention of female preference, in a manner analogous to that in which advan-tage is conferred by special weapons . . . . As a propagan-dist the cock behaves as though he knew that it was as advantageous to impress the males as the females of his species, and a sprightly bearing with fine feathers and triumphant song are quite as well adapted for war-propa-ganda as for courtship (p. 155).

Appearance of strength and pugnacity is analogous to the possession of these qualities in producing the same effect; but the effect is produced in a different way, and in particular, as in the case of attractive ornaments, by the

---

[1] Excerpts from Ronald Fisher, *The Genetical Theory of Natural Selection,* copyright (c) 1958 by Dover Publications, Inc., New York. Reprinted through permission of the publisher.

emotional reaction of other members of the species. It
involves in fact closely similar mental problems to those
raised by the existence of sexual preference. One difference should be noted; in the case of attractive ornaments
the evolutionary effect upon the female is to fit her to
appreciate more and more highly the display offered, while
the evolutionary reaction of war paint upon those whom it
is intended to impress should be to make them less and
less receptive to all impressions save those arising from
genuine prowess. Male ornaments acquired in this way might
be striking, but could scarcely ever become extravagant
(pp. 155-156).

EPIGAMIC AND INTRASEXUAL SELECTION

Huxley (1938) suggested that Darwin's concept of sexual
selection be replaced by two terms: "epigamic selection,"
selection which one sex exerts on the other, and "intrasexual
selection," selection involving competition between members
of the same sex. These two terms are widely used in current
literature. Insofar as the agencies of sexual selection are
either members of the same sex or members of the other sex,
even in the context of reproductive isolation, Huxley's
classification seems reasonable, but the scheme suffers mainly
because most characters have effects on both male rivals and
females, and it becomes very difficult to tease apart the
epigamic and intrasexual effects. Nevertheless, the terms
remain generally useful.
Huxley was also the first to note that the variance in
reproductive success in males should be greater than in females, at least in polygamous breeders, and that such a
difference would result in greater selective pressures on
males than on females. Furthermore, this variance in reproductive success, or reproductive advantage as he put it, could
be attributed mainly to the competition between males.

ANISOGAMY AND THE NUMBERS OF MALE AND FEMALE GAMETES

Bateman (1948) gave a new perspective by suggesting that
coevolution between and within the sexes is almost as ancient
as sex itself. He suggested that the sizes and therefore
numbers of gametes that males and females produce determine
the different degrees to which the sexes affect one another.
The following passages set forth his principal ideas:

In most animals the fertility of the female is limited by
egg production which causes a severe strain on their

nutrition. In mammals the corresponding limiting factors are uterine nutrition and milk production, which together may be termed the capacity for rearing young. In the male, however, fertility is seldom likely to be limited by sperm production but rather by the number of inseminations or the number of females available to him. In promiscuous species the share of males in the progeny of any female will be proportional to the number of inseminations for which each is responsible. In general, then, the fertility of an individual female will be much more limited than the fertility of a male. The primary cause of intra-masculine selection would thus seem to be that females produce much fewer gametes than males. Consequently there is competition between male gametes for the fertilization of the female gametes. And this competition is vastly more intense than that hitherto considered between zygotes.

The primary feature of sexual reproduction is . . . the fusion of gametes irrespective of their relative size, but the specialization into large immobile gametes and small mobile gametes produced in great excess (the primary sex difference), was a very early evolutionary step. One would therefore expect to find in all but a few very primitive organisms, and those in which monogamy combined with a sex ratio of unity eliminated all intra-sexual selection, that males would show greater intra-sexual selection than females. This would explain why in unisexual organisms there is nearly always a combination of an undiscriminating eagerness in the males and a discriminating passivity in the females. Even in derived monogamous species (e.g., man) this sex difference might be expected to persist as a relic.

If the differentiation into male and female gametes is the basis of intra-masculine selection, there should be signs of this selection in plants as well as in animals. Since plants are usually hermaphrodite and also sedentary, such selection would only be expected to show in the pollen. The greater general tendency for the production of microspores far in excess of the minimum required to produce effective fertilizations is explicable in this way. In dioecious plants or moneocious plants, where the sexes are separated, the results of intra-masculine selection might be more obvious. A possible example here is the insect-pollinated sallow *(Salix caprea)* in which the male catkins are brightly coloured whereas the female catkins are inconspicuous (though both produce nectar) (pp. 365-366).

THE BROADER SCOPE OF ADAPTATION AND PARENTAL INVESTMENT

Williams (1966) ushered in a new era in biological thinking.
Reproduction was now couched in the broadest possible framework. Williams' analysis of the concept of adaptation demonstrated the artificiality of separating sexual and natural
selection as mutually exclusive phenomena and pointed clearly
to the need to view sexual selection as a facet of natural
selection:

> It is possible and often convenient to recognize two cat-
> egories of adaptation, those that relate to the continued
> existence of the individual soma, and those involved in
> reproduction. Basically, however, all adaptation must
> relate to reproduction. Somatic survival is favored by
> selection only when the soma is necessary to reproductive
> survival. Heart failure and mammary failure have exactly
> equivalent effects on the fitness of a female mammal.
> Similarly, all the adaptations of embryonic, larval,
> juvenile, and adult forms have meaning only as mechanisms
> that promote the survival of the genes that direct the
> morphogenetic sequence (p. 160).[2]

Williams also elaborated on Bateman's ideas on investment
patterns in determining how the sexes affect one another:

> It is a common observation that males show a greater
> readiness for reproduction than females. This is under-
> standable as a consequence of the greater physiological
> sacrifice made by females for the production of each
> surviving offspring. A male mammal's essential role may
> end with copulation, which involves a negligible expendi-
> ture of energy and materials on his part, and only a
> momentary lapse of attention from matters of direct concern
> to his safety and well-being. The situation is markedly
> different for the female, for which copulation may mean a
> commitment to a prolonged burden, in both the mechanical
> and physiological sense, and its many attendant stresses
> and dangers. Consequently the male, having little to lose
> in his primary reproductive role, shows an aggressive and
> immediate willingness to mate with as many females as may
> be available. If he undertakes his reproductive role and
> fails, he has lost very little. If he succeeds, he can
> be just as successful for a very minor effort as a female

[2] Excerpts from George C. Williams, *Adaptation and Natural
Selection: A Critique of Some Evolutionary Thought* (copyright
(c) 1966 by Princeton University Press; Princeton Paperback,
1974), pp. 159-184. Reprinted by permission of Princeton
University Press.

could be only after a major somatic sacrifice. Failure
for a female mammal may mean weeks or months of wasted
time. The mechanical and nutritional burden of pregnancy
may mean increased vulnerability to predators, decreased
disease resistance, and other dangers for a long time.
Even if she successfully endures these stresses and hazards
she can still fail completely if her litter is lost before
weaning. Once she starts on her reproductive role she
commits herself to a certain high minimum of reproductive
effort. Natural selection should regulate her reproductive
behavior in such a way that she will assume the burdens of
reproduction only when the probability of success is at
some peak value that is not likely to be exceeded (p. 163).

The traditional coyness of the female is thus easily attributed to adaptive mechanisms by which she can discriminate the ideal moment and circumstances for assuming the
burdens of motherhood. One of the most important circumstances is the inseminating male. It is to the female's
advantage to be able to pick the most fit male available
for fathering her brood. Unusually fit fathers tend to
have unusually fit offspring. One of the functions of
courtship would be the advertisement, by a male, of how
fit he is. A male whose general health and nutrition
enables him to indulge in full development of secondary
sexual characters, especially courtship behavior, is
likely to be reasonably fit genetically (pp. 183-184).

Inevitably there is a kind of evolutionary battle of the
sexes. If a male attempts to reproduce at all in a
certain breeding season, it is to his advantage to pretend
to be highly fit whether he is or not. If a weak and
unresourceful male successfully coaxes a female to mate
with him he has lost nothing, and may have successfully
reproduced. It will be to the female's advantage, however,
to be able to tell the males that are really fit from those
that merely pretend to be. In such a population genic
selection will foster a skilled salesmanship among the
males and an equally well-developed sales resistance and
discrimination among the females (p. 184).

REPRODUCTIVE ISOLATION AND SEXUAL SELECTION

Mayr (1972) draws attention to several kinds of differences
between the sexes which he believed were not the result of
sexual selection. Epigamic selection, he says, is selection
which results in characteristics which facilitate the finding
of one sex by another. As we have seen, Darwin clearly included such pressures under his process of sexual selection.

A second form of selection is that for reproductive isolating
mechanisms, which would take place when hybrids between
previously isolated populations have a relatively low fitness.
Genetic changes which permitted females to be more discriminating or which resulted in male characteristics that reduced
the probability of their being confused with the males of
other species would be selected. Because activities and
behavior of one sex have an effect on the fitness of the other
sex in both of the above cases, it is obvious that they are
forms of Darwinian sexual selection. The degree of incompatibility between the populations developing reproductive
isolation is irrelevant. A third form of selection which
could produce sexual differences is competition within a
species for food, which could result in males and females
evolving different food habits, and subsequently in the
adjustment of their morphological characteristics to their
habits.

THE ROLE OF PARENTAL CARE

A recent influential synthesis of ideas on sexual selection
is that of Trivers (1972). Following Bateman and Williams,
he elaborates on the primary gametic differences between the
sexes and the stages through which different reproductive
investment patterns between males and females might have
evolved. He argues that competition between males will tend
to operate against male parental investment, because parental
care decreases the time and effort available for inseminating
other females. What governs the operation of sexual selection,
he says, is the relative investment of the sexes in their
offspring. Trivers also discusses sexual selection occurring
in largely monogamous breeders. He argues that in species
in which males retain psychological traits consistent with
promiscuous habits, males should be discriminating in their
choice of with whom they will raise young, but they should
not be very discriminating in their choice among females with
whom they will only mate. A male should also have adaptations
which will guarantee that a female's offspring will also be
his own. Females, on the other hand, who are deserted by
males should be adapted to induce another male to help her
raise young. Males, in turn, would be selected to avoid such
a fate through various adaptations. (See paper by Parker
in this volume for a detailed discussion of such issues.)
Trivers also shows how the evolution of reproductive
isolation can be attributed to sexual selection. When two
species which have recently speciated begin to interact,
selection is expected to favor females which can distinguish
between the two species of males, and they are least likely

to make mistakes by preferring the appropriate extreme of an available sample. In the absence of countervailing selection pressures, the differences between males could become far greater than what is necessary for females to discriminate. Some of the bizarre plumage characteristics in birds and complicated courtship rituals in insects may have originated as isolating mechanisms.

FURTHER NOTES ON ANISOGAMY AND ITS ROLE IN SEXUAL SELECTION

The following passages from Parker et al. (1972) outline some possible steps which led to gamete size and number differences between the sexes--differences which seem to be at the root of sexual differentiation and sexual selection:

Assuming that a given gametic mass can be produced in unit time, then individual variations in gamete size may arise either from differences in the production time, or in the number of cell divisions at the time of production. Where zygote fitness is in some way related to zygote volume, relative reproductive rates can be calculated for a range of variants with different gamete productivities (and therefore different gamete sizes). This model yields either drive for small-producing (where the advantage of high productivity exceeds that of increased provisioning for the zygote) or drive for large-producing (in the reverse case). However in certain conditions . . . a marked disruptive effect can be generated in which the two extremes (large and small gamete production) are favoured. . . . As anisogamy is approached, the disadvantageous dominant homozygote is lost leaving two sexes (sperm producers and ovum producers) in a stable 1:1 ratio . . . (pp. 529, 530). Once a difference in reproductive rates is obtainable from a random fusion system, it is likely that selection for non-random fusions would begin to operate. The model suggests that the smaller gametes obtain their advantage by virtue of their fusions with the largest gametes. Because of the relative disadvantage of fusions with the largest gametes, sperm producers would be favoured if their sperm fused selectively with large gametes . . . . Selection would, however, also favour ovum producers whose ova fused selectively with other ova (assortative fusions), since this would yield either fitter zygotes or allow the parental variants an increased productivity for the same zygote fitness. Thus a conflicting situation might be predicted since the favoured variants would produce sperm which fused disassortatively and ova which fused assortatively (p. 547).

How is the conflict of interest resolved?

> The potential source of variation and mutation is proportional to the number of germ cells and therefore differs in the two sexes .... Where sperm are in a competitive situation for fusion of ova, it seems reasonable to argue that sperm producers have more available mutants for sperm-ovum fusions than the ovum producers have to avoid and prevent this. The result might be a greater rate of incorporation of advantageous sperm mutants .... These effects (possible stronger selection, more potential variance and competition of sperm for the fertilization of ova) would give a much higher rate of adaptation in sperm than in ova. Thus any move towards assortative fusions on the part of the ovum producers would be quickly offset by counter adaptations in the sperm .... The only possible way a population would prevent dimorphic drive should be by constant maintenance of a faster rate of counter adaptation to renewed sperm drives--this seems rather against the odds in view of a predictably higher rate of adaptation in sperm than in ova. Ovum producers are forced into an evolutionary impasse--they must adapt the gamete size which gives the maximum reproductive rate as the product of productivity and zygote fitness, and since most of their fusion will be with sperm, the ovum size must be maintained accordingly large. The relationship between sperm and ova is not dissimilar from the relationship between parasite and host--the parasitic sperm are dependent upon and propagating at the expense of the host ovum (p. 549).

> Once this step has occurred, a further stage might be predicted which further commits ova to disassortative fusions with sperm. It is assumed that the initial isogametes would have been motile; this would be necessary to ensure encounter and fusion. Selection would operate differently in a system of dimorphic gametes. Because of the numerical predominance of sperm and selection favouring their fusing disassortatively with ova, ovum producers could afford to lose the motility of their gametes without affecting the time taken to achieve a fusion. This would allow them a greater productivity for the same gamete size and fitness. For sperm producers, however, increased motility would be highly favourable since it would yield gametes which would fare better in competition with other sperm by virtue of increased encounter and ovum penetration possibilities. Then when ovum-ovum encounters become very rare and the possible advantage in ovum-ovum fusions relatively small, the optimum strategy for ovum producers may lie in total commitment to disassortative fusions ....

Sperm excess may not reflect inadequacies at fertilization; rather it may represent an adaptation towards maximization of reproductive success in response to competition between sperm producers and the fertilization of ova (pp. 549-550).

THE AGENCIES OF SEXUAL SELECTION

Ghiselin (1974) provides a comprehensive discussion of the various forms of competition which exist in relation to reproduction. Table 1 is a modified version of his scheme.

CONCLUSIONS

The components of natural selection. I believe that the tendency to view sexual selection as something distinct from natural selection is basically without merit. Certainly Darwin never set up the mutually exclusive categories which some authors attribute to him. If one views everything in the life of a particular individual as part of that individual's environment, then, aside from man-made agencies, all such elements are "natural." In this light, sexual selection is conveniently viewed as one of many components of natural selection. Since the various components do not operate independently of one another, any attempts to rigidly categorize selective agents or to raise one component to the same rank as natural selection is bound to be confusing.

Biological compromise. Much has been made of the countervailing effects of sexual and natural selection. This is perhaps natural since the effects of mating are so pervasive. But it should be stressed that such countervailing effects are the rule among many components of selection. The major distinguishing characteristic of sexual selection appears to be that female choice (and, perhaps in fewer cases, male choice) may result in a runaway process, which one would not expect to see in the establishment of other forms of compromise.

Reproductive isolation. Sexual selection and selection for reproductive isolating mechanisms are closely connected phenomena. In either case, the members of one sex effect the evolution of preferences in the other. The degree of incompatibility has no bearing on whether selection is natural or sexual.

Hard and soft selection. Wallace (1968) distinguished between two general forms of selection, and this distinction can suitably be applied to selection as it occurs in the context of reproduction. Soft selection leads to a probability of survival and reproduction for one genotype

TABLE 1

Various forms of competition existing in relation to reproduction (modified from Ghiselin (1974)).

A. Combat for access to the opposite sex
   1. between males (common)
   2. between females (rare)
B. Mate choice
   1. by males (common in species displaying high parental investment)
   2. by females (common in all species; less common in species in which males fight intensively to produce clear winners and losers; most intense in monogamous species with considerable male parental care)
C. Mate sequestering
   1. by males (common--includes usurping of females, carrying them off and hiding them or monopolizing them, thereby reducing the effects of sperm competition)
   2. by females (rare or does not exist)
D. Mate finding (pair formation; scrambling; dispersal)
   1. by males (common, especially in insects and more solitary species--selection for species recognition, for high degree of dispersal or locomotion and for acute sensory apparatus)
   2. by females (less common; selection less for dispersal than for recognizing potential mates)
E. Mate attracting
   1. by males (common; more common in males than in females?)
   2. by females (common, especially when signaling entails few risks)
F. Cooperation between the sexes in raising offspring (selection for the ability by both sexes to choose genetically or behaviorally compatible mates)

---

that depends upon the presence or absence of individuals of other genotypes. Hard selection leads to a probability of survival and reproduction independent of other individuals. In the latter form, the selective coefficient for a particular genotype is fixed. Most sexual differences usually attributed to the action of sexual selection would therefore seem to be due to soft selection, while many, though not all, characters attributed to natural selection would seem to be due to hard selection.

Sexual conflicts of interest. A problem of great importance in socioecology concerns the conflicts of interest which arise

between males and females. Specifically, when the optimal
breeding mode for females differs from that of males, how
is the conflict of interest resolved? If, to take one
example, it is in the best interest of a female to have her
mate help her raise offspring, but at the same time it is in
the male's best interest to mate with many females and not to
help, what kind of breeding system will emerge? As suggested
by Parker et al. (1972), an equilibrium point must be reached
where the selective forces on males just equal the selective
forces on females. The factors which determine where such a
point will come to lie are in need of further investigation
(see Parker, this volume).

Deception. Deception is particularly likely to occur when
conflicts of interest exist between members of the same or
different sexes, but it happens more commonly when phenotypic
states of the contestants or potential sexual partners are
communicated through signals, i.e., when the condition of the
contestant or sexual partner must be *assessed* or *estimated*
rather than directly *determined*. Sexual selection arising
through combat between contestants is not likely to result in
deceit if no signals are involved in the interaction. Direct
physical interactions preclude the propaganda which is likely
to arise through signaling. Likewise, propaganda by males
directed toward females is less likely if the fitness of males
is determined in physical contests between males, i.e., when
females mate with winners. For the most part, deceit is less
likely to occur in insects than in vertebrates, mainly because
fitness advertising is less likely to be prevalent in animals
in which distance sensory structures are poorly suited for
accurately assessing the quality of one's opponents or mates
(see Hamilton and Otte and Stayman, this volume).

REFERENCES

Bateman, A.J. 1948. Intra-sexual selection in *Drosophila*.
    Heredity 2:349-368.
Darwin, C. 1859. *On the Origin of Species by Means of Natural
    Selection*. John Murray, London.
Darwin, C. 1871. *The Descent of Man and Selection in Relation
    to Sex*. 2nd ed., rev. (1898). D. Appleton and Co., New York.
Fisher, R.A. 1958. *The Genetical Theory of Natural Selection*.
    Dover Publ., Inc., New York.
Ghiselin, M.T. 1974. *The Economy of Nature and the Evolution
    of Sex*. Univ. California Press, Berkeley.
Huxley, J. 1938. Darwin's theory of sexual selection. *Amer.
    Nat.* 72:416-433.
Mayr, E. 1972. Sexual selection and natural selection. *In*

Campbell, B. (ed.), *Sexual Selection and the Descent of Man, 1871-1971*. Aldine, Chicago.

Parker, G.A., R.R. Baker, and V.G.F. Smith. 1972. The origin and evolution of gamete dimorphism and the male-female phenomenon. *J. Theor. Biol.* 36:529-553.

Trivers, R.L. 1972. Parental investment and sexual selection. *In* Campbell, B. (ed.), *Sexual Selection and the Descent of Man, 1871-1971*. Aldine, Chicago.

Wallace, A.R. 1889. *Darwinism*. Macmillan and Co., London.

Wallace, B. 1968. *Topics in Population Genetics*. W.W. Norton and Company, New York.

Williams, G.C. 1966. *Adaptation and Natural Selection*. Princeton Univ. Press, Princeton.

SEXUAL SELECTION AND THE EVOLUTION

OF MATING SYSTEMS

Gerald Borgia

The University of Michigan

INTRODUCTION

A precise understanding of the manner in which mating
associations between individuals develop is essential for
generating a comprehensive model of social interactions. Not
only is mating behavior a key social event in any species,
but it may have important effects on patterns of parental
behavior (Trivers, 1972), parent-offspring interaction
(Trivers, 1974; Alexander, 1974), the evolution of sociality
(Trivers and Hare, 1976), sex ratios (Fisher, 1958; Hamilton,
1967), and the population genetics of breeding units (Williams, 1975). In spite of the central role of mating behavior, our ability to predict patterns of matings in any
population is relatively limited.

Darwin (1871) noted two patterns by which mating associations are formed. He considered (1) "a constantly recurrent
struggle between males for the possession of females" (p. 213)
and (2) choice by females in which they "select those (males)
which are vigorous and well armed, and in other respects most
attractive" (p. 214). He also recognized the relationship of
extreme sexual dimorphism to high variance in male reproductive success or "polygamous marriages." However, he did not
explicitly relate patterns of mate choice to sexual dimorphism
and variance in reproductive success. From his discussion of
male elephant seals physically controlling harems of females
(p. 523), he seemed aware of the relationship of large male
size to success in controlling females, but this idea was not
developed further.

For some time after Darwin's work, mating systems were
classified into types without concern for how natural selection might cause observed differences. Various criteria for
classification have been used (see Selander, 1972, for review),
but the significance of these factors as causes of observed
variation in mating type has seldom been considered in
detail.

   Important departures from this kind of analysis were provided in salient papers by Orians (1969) and Trivers (1972).
These authors refocused analysis of mating systems on fundamental problems of mate selection and placed particular
emphasis on individual behaviors designed to maximize reproductive gain. However, models developed in each case tended
to minimize differences in types of male-female mating
relationships and gave little detail relating how such variation might evolve.
   The approach taken here is to emphasize differences in
patterns of sexual selection. Four different types of male-
female mating relationships are considered in relation to
(1) how each pattern influences reproductive success of
individuals and (2) what conditions are likely to cause each
of the different patterns of mate selection. A critical part
of this analysis is to evaluate genetic and material, or nongenetic, benefits described by Orians (1969) as an important
criterion for mate choice by females.

PREDICTING PATTERNS OF MATING SUCCESS

Types of Male-Female Interactions

   Bateman (1948) provided both experimental and logical bases
for an understanding of the operation of mating systems. In
a series of experiments with *Drosophila,* he showed that males'
reproductive success varied over a wider range than that of
females. Males were able to gain added reproduction with
increased numbers of matings, but similar opportunities for
multiple matings by females led to no increase in the output
of offspring. Two important conclusions from the results of
these experiments seem to apply to most mobile outbreeding
species. First, female gametes are rare relative to those of
males. Under all but lowest density conditions, females
should have little difficulty in obtaining sufficient sperm
to fertilize eggs. Second, under no conditions should all
males (who provide only sperm) realize their reproductive
potential. High levels of mating success of some males necessarily come at the expense of other males. Low reproductive
variance simply describes a situation where all males have
unsatisfied reproductive capabilities.
   These relationships have been used in constructing various
mating system models (Maynard Smith, 1958; Orians, 1969;
Trivers, 1972). Each of these models suggests that the relative shortage of gametes produced by females places the female
in control of the mating circumstance. It is stated or implied that the ability of females to control male access to

gametes allows them to choose mates who give them or their offspring the highest return on investment in calorically expensive eggs.

Criteria females use in selecting mates may be exclusively based on the *genetic quality of mates* (Fisher, 1958; Williams, 1966; Orians, 1969; Alexander, 1975; Ghiselin, 1974; Trivers, 1972; but see Williams, 1975; Davis and O'Donald, 1976). Presumably, female choice of some males leads to advantageous heritable differences in offspring. Males may use energy and effort not spent or not likely to be spent in producing sperm to demonstrate their relative genetic quality. (See section below on the mechanism of "genetic choice.")

Males may spend available reproductive effort on other types of behavior which may be effective in attracting females. Such effort may include attempts by individual males to enhance their prospects for reproduction by *providing females and their young with material benefits,* such as food, nests, or protection, in exchange for the opportunity to mate. Such alternative types of mate attraction are especially important to individual males who are otherwise not likely to mate successfully because of the relatively low quality of genetic benefits that they offer. Genetic benefits such males can offer are fixed, and their ability to provide material benefits can serve as the only effective inducement to alter female mating decisions in their favor.

In many situations, unrestricted female choice is the primary mechanism for determining male-female mating relationships. However, males may evolve to remove some degree of freedom for females in their mating decisions and, in some cases, completely dominate females in determining viable patterns of reproduction. A male may *make genetic representation in a female's offspring a prerequisite for the use of resources that he controls.* The female tendency to invest heavily in gametes often commits females to a strategy of high levels of resource utilization. Such a commitment may allow males to use resources that are otherwise abundant and easily exploitable to force female mating decisions in their favor. Females are then forced to choose a particular male as their mate, whereas another male would have been chosen had the females been unconstrained in their access to resources.

It is worthwhile to contrast this pattern of mate choice with one in which males collect needed resources and offer them to females in exchange for matings. If *collected* resources are used as inducements, a female may choose to forego contributions offered by a male, as she may be able to rear some offspring by herself. However, if one male should *control* all available resources, every successfully reproducing female would have to choose him as a mate, regardless of the qualities of other males. Control and collection also differ

in their effect on the reproductive output of females. Male
delivery of material benefits should result in a net increase
in absolute reproductive output of offspring by a female.

Control of resources needed by females may lead to reduced
output, since females may be forced to sacrifice genetic gain
from choosing males in order to gain access to resources
controlled by other males. Male ability to attract mates
through either the control or collection of resources will be
considered in terms of individual ability to provide material
benefits. In initial considerations, differences in the
quantity of offspring produced through the use of these
different types of benefits will not be important because
comparisons are restricted to males using similar means for
attracting females.

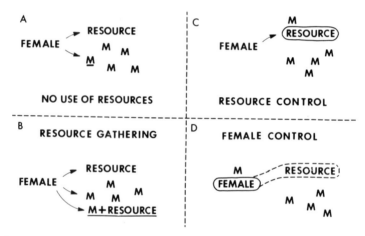

Fig. 1. Four male strategies in mate procurement and the use
of resources by males to enhance mating prospects. (A) Females
have free access to resources and presumably choose among
males on the basis of differences in genetic benefits that
they offer. (B) Males gather resources to enhance their
attractiveness to females. The female is free to choose among
all males, but may compromise gain from genetic benefits in
order to obtain needed material benefits in excess of those
she can collect herself. (C) If males control resources,
female options for mate choice may be severely limited. To
obtain needed resources, she mates with a male who has established control over resources. (D) Males who directly control
females deny them the opportunity to freely choose a mate.
Although resources are not a necessary ingredient in the
capture of females, they may serve as a focus for capture; in
addition, success of the capture strategy depends on male a-
bility to allow females unmolested access to needed resources.

Direct control of females by individual males represents
a fourth pattern for determining male-female mating interactions. A male may capture a female and prevent her from
mating with individuals other than himself (Darwin, 1871;
Ghiselin, 1974; Emlen and Oring, 1977). Such capture denies
females the opportunity to demand material and genetic benefits as a prerequisite for mating. As in the case of resource
control, such capture may be most easily accomplished near
limited resources required by females. Male control may not
be complete, since a female may exert some level of choice in
mates by selecting her own capture site. The relation of each
of these patterns of establishing male-female matings and the
value of resources in determining these associations are
described in Fig. 1.

The very different patterns discussed here suggest that in
order to develop a predictive model of mating systems, two
questions must be answered:

1. How can individual and "populational" patterns of reproductive success be predicted within each system of mate
choice?

2. Under what conditions is each of the four patterns of
male-female interaction likely to occur?

Predicting Variance in Male Reproductive Success

Patterns of male reproductive success for conditions in
which females choose their mates only on the basis of the
genetic benefits that they offer have been described by
Williams (1975). He predicts high levels of variance in
success among males. This may occur for two reasons. First,
females are likely to use the same criteria in choosing males.
If females are unimpeded in their ability to choose, this
should lead them to a small set of males who have been able
to demonstrate fitness in some significant way. Second,
Orians (1969) points out that males offering high quality
genetic benefits should rarely be limited in their ability to
fill female needs. Males provide rapidly renewable sperm at
a relatively low caloric investment, and a male should be
able to mate with as many females as choose him.

Material benefits offered by males typically differ from
genetic benefits in that they may be used up as males mate
successively with different females. Matings in which males
use material benefits to attract females reduce the residual
value of benefits that they can offer to other females. Devalu-
ation of the amount of benefits held by some males increases
the opportunity for other individuals to father offspring.
The high variance in mating success, typical in genetic choice

systems, may be rare where material benefits are the primary basis for mate choice and may be restricted to conditions in which one or a few males hold all or nearly all material benefits.

The allocation of benefits a female is likely to receive is determined by her value to males as a mate when compared to other females. Similarly, males must compete to attract females. In each case, depletion of a male's benefits with successive matings is a key element in understanding patterns of individual success. Males who offer too few benefits may not successfully attract mates; those who offer too many rapidly exhaust their supply of expendable benefits and allow other males, who spend less per female, an opportunity to attract mates. If material benefits limit female reproduction, then female demands may be fashioned around an equilibrium value as they shop among males for those who offer the best deal. Those females making excessive demands are passed over by males in favor of other females who require a guarantee of fewer benefits as a precondition for mating. Females demanding too few benefits may be very attractive to some males, particularly when the number of benefits a male contributes only partially determines the number and quality of offspring he fathers. Even so, these females reproduce at a lower than average rate over their lifetime because of the more limited assistance they receive from males.

If material benefits are the sole basis for mate choice by females, then male reproductive success should be proportional to the share of all material benefits that an individual male can defend or deliver. This prediction follows the pattern of mate choice outlined by Orians (1969). The relationship may not be exact in all cases because female benefits, and male gain derived from them, come in discrete packages which may not exactly match the amount of benefits that individual males have to offer. In large populations it is more likely that males and females of nearly equal value can find each other and mate. Females may also split broods, allowing several males--each with a probability of leaving offspring in proportion to the amount of benefits he delivers--to father their offspring.

Female Compromise and Patterns of Mate Selection

The delivery of genetic and material benefits and their effect on mating patterns have been considered in cases where males provide each kind of benefit separately. Genetic benefits may be offered where they are the sole basis for mate choice. However, in cases where males offer material benefits, it is unlikely that males selected as mates are

identical in genetic quality. Females who gain most in mating
decisions are those who discriminate among males on the basis
of differences in genetic quality, in addition to evaluating
the material benefits offered by these males. The need for
females to simultaneously consider two kinds of benefits may
force them to compromise gain through one or the other of the
types in order to maximize the number of descendants that they
can produce. For example, males of highest genetic quality
may be somewhat limited in their ability to provide material
benefits. Females choosing males other than the one offering
the highest level of genetic benefits may be sacrificing some
prospects for genetic gain in order to secure material benefits which may be more valuable to them.

Placing females in situations where they must compromise
gain from different sources suggests that they may develop
some means of evaluating each kind of benefit a prospective
mate may offer. Patterns of female mating decisions and male
reproductive success are then based on (1) the relative value
females assign to the two kinds of benefits and (2) the degree
of correlation in the quality of benefits a male may offer
(that is, are males who have high levels of genetic benefits
likely to hold high levels of material benefits?). These two
factors, combined with variance in genetic quality and
distribution of material benefits among males, should be
sufficient to develop a simple model of mating systems in
which females have the opportunity to compare and choose among
males who offer varying levels of material and genetic benefits.

The Equilibrium Model of Mate Choice

A mating system model can be developed which applies to
conditions in which males collect or control resources.
Consider the case involving two males and F_t females who are
of equal quality and who mate once with the male offering
them the greatest share of benefits. These matings invariably
lead to the production of offspring. For the nth male, G_n
represents the value of genetic benefits he is able to offer
prospective mates, $\emptyset_n$, the fraction of all material benefits
he controls of the total controlled or collected by all males,
and F_n, the equilibrium number of matings received by the nth
male. A constant, R, describes for each mating system the
absolute value of material benefits males can offer to females. Females are assumed to value resources at a constant
rate not dependent on the value of R. Where males attempt to
control resources, R is proportional to the fraction of all
resources controlled by males. If males provide resources,
R is proportional to the level of assistance given to females

or their offspring relative to that given by females.

Patterns of matings can be approximated using the following set of relationships:

$$G_1 + \frac{\emptyset_1 R}{F_1} = G_2 + \frac{\emptyset_2 R}{F_2}. \qquad (1a)$$

And if $\Delta G = G_1 - G_2$, Equation 1a can be reduced to

$$\Delta G + \frac{\emptyset_1 R}{F_1} = \frac{\emptyset_2 R}{F_2}. \qquad (1b)$$

This relationship compares the genetic and material benefits offered by the two males. Material benefits are devalued by the number of matings a male accomplishes, while the genetic benefits he can offer a female remain constant. If the number of females and quantitative relationships between material and genetic benefits are specified, predictions can be made about the distribution of matings among males. The number of variables does not permit an analytic solution, but by restricting the level of genetic benefits to low values (see below) and by considering end points in the range in variation in material benefits, a picture of mating patterns in different situations involving two males and two females can be developed. These results then will be generalized for large numbers of males and females.

Consider the case in which each male has equal amounts of material benefits, $\emptyset_1 = \emptyset_2$; Equation 1b will reduce to

$$\frac{2 \Delta G}{R} + \frac{1}{F_1} = \frac{1}{F_2}.$$

The number of matings obtained by male #1, F_1, can be graphed as a function of R and ΔG, a constant (Fig. 2a). At low R, male #1 gets all of the matings due to differences in genetic quality. As R increases and becomes more important in female decisions, male #2 gains opportunities for matings.

In systems where resources are not distributed equally among males, there are two limiting cases in which one or the other of the males controls all resources. Genetic and material benefits may be negatively correlated between males or held by different males. In this case $\emptyset_1 \to 0$, $\emptyset_2 \to 1$, and $G_1 > G_2$, Equation 1b reduces to

$$\frac{R}{\Delta G} \approx F_2$$

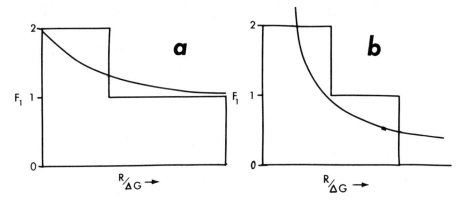

Fig. 2. (a) Pattern of male mating success with changing male ability to provide material benefits. In this case, both males have equal ability to provide the available material benefits. (b) Same as a, but males have unequal ability to provide benefits. Here, male ability to provide material and genetic benefits shows an extreme negative correlation.

and F_1 is directly related to R, so that when R is large, so is F_2, and vice versa (Fig. 2b).

If material and genetic benefits are held by the same individual or are positively correlated ($\emptyset_1 \to 1$, $\emptyset_2 \to 0$, and $G_1 > G_2$), male #1 will win at all values of R since $F_2 \to 0$.

Having shown patterns of mating success under changing conditions of R for three different relationships of $\emptyset_1$ and $\emptyset_2$, these results can be combined in order to develop a more general model for predicting patterns of mating success. Cases in which one or the other of the males receives all or nearly all of the resources represent end points on a scale of changing levels of evenness in apportionment of material benefits among males. Using these two end points as limiting values, together with results from the case in which $\emptyset$s are equal, and assuming simple relationships with changing levels of evenness, patterns of mating success can be predicted for conditions where resources are positively and negatively correlated with male genetic quality (Fig. 3).

Increasing unevenness in resource distribution has, not unexpectedly, the same effect in both cases--increasing differences in the level of success among males. In the case in which genetic and material benefits show a strong positive correlation, a consistently high level of success for male #1 is maintained for all values of R. In the case in which the two types of benefits are negatively correlated, there is a reversal in the type of male which wins. Male #1 wins at low values of R and male #2 wins at high values. The significance

GERALD BORGIA

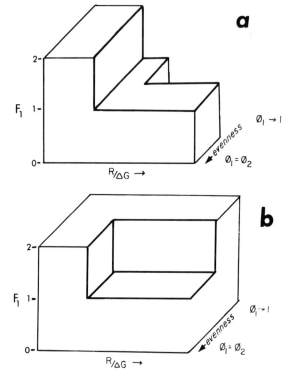

Fig. 3. (a) Pattern of male mating success determined by differences in the ability of individuals to collect from or control resources and differences in the relative importance of genetic and material benefits. There is a positive correlation between ability to deliver material and genetic benefits. (b) Same as a, but with a negative correlation between male ability to deliver material benefits and the genetic benefits offered by that male.

of differences between these two cases lessens if variance in reproductive success is considered instead of which male wins. The depression in variance at intermediate levels of R in cases in which benefits are negatively correlated is likely to disappear when mating systems involving multiple males and females are considered. This occurs because transitions in success of particular individuals may have little effect on population-wide variation in mating success, and distinctions between male success based on the different benefits they provide may be difficult to establish.

The two-male equilibrium model can be extended to deal with n males and varying conditions of R and distributions of resources. Such an equilibrium relationship for multiple mates might appear in the form

$$\Delta G + \frac{\emptyset_1 R}{F_1} = \frac{\emptyset_2 R}{F_2} = \cdots = \frac{\emptyset_n R}{F_n} ,$$

when it is assumed that $G_2 = G_3 = \cdots = G_n$. The pattern of matings under these conditions with equal sex ratios might appear as in Fig. 4. Increased proportions of females will

tend to enhance the importance of differences in genetic
quality. The degree of change in male mating success with
variation in the value of R depends on the pattern of differences in the values of genetic quality among males. Where
all differences in genetic quality of males involve one male
who is better by an equal amount over all other males, a
sudden steep change in variance in mating success at some
intermediate level of R is expected. More variable differences
in quality among males allow a more gradual response.

Patterns of variance in reproductive success shown in Fig.
4 can be related to mating systems in different species. High
variance in mating success at low values of $R/\Delta G$ is related
to the use of male genetic quality as a primary criterion in
female mating decisions. This may be common in typical breeding leks of birds (Snow, 1962; Robel, 1966, 1969; Scott, 1942).
In these leks males apparently give no material benefits to
females. Territories may exist, but there is no necessary
relationship between territory size and male mating success;
relative position seems more important.

High variance in ability of males to control resources
leads to a second type of polygyny. Resources held by a male
may be present in such abundance that use by one female does
not strongly affect the residual value of benefits a male can
offer to subsequent mates. In such cases, females choose
males primarily for the material benefits they provide. This
pattern of choice may be independent of the genetic quality
of males who control available resources, although in most
circumstances it is likely that these two male qualities are
positively correlated. These types of polygyny really represent end points on the high variance plateau in which genetic
and material benefits are both important in allowing high
variance in success.

High levels of success due to high variance in the quality
of material benefits a male can offer are likely restricted
to situations in which males control resources. Success of

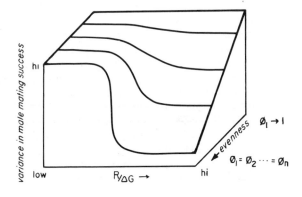

Fig. 4. Changes in
patterns of male
reproductive success
due to variation in
the value of mater-
ial benefits and in
individual male
ability to provide
these benefits. See
text for further
explanation.

an individual male in collecting from resources is extremely
time and energy dependent. Time and energy constraints seem
to limit even the most able individuals from collecting more
than a few times the amount of benefits gathered by the
average male.

Review of Assumptions of the Equilibrium Model

Constancy in Value of Benefits

   In the preceding model, it was assumed that the two types
of benefits maintained a constant value to females independent
of the amount they had already received. However, females may
often be limited in their ability to utilize benefits. Given
the choice of two males, one of whom offers material benefits
in excess of her needs, a female may choose the male of higher
genetic quality, even though he may be able to provide fewer
total benefits. The effect of placing limits on female needs,
especially if females mate only once, is to lower the value
of material benefits and shift choice in favor of males of
high genetic quality, even when resources are distributed
equally among males. Male gain from offering genetic benefits
faces no parallel limitation since relative and not absolute
value of benefits is important to females. In other instances,
females may require a minimum commitment of material benefits
in order to successfully reproduce. The only source of such
benefits may be males offering overall fewer benefits than
high quality individuals. Effect of such limits will be to
lower the value to females of differences in male genetic
quality.

Are Females Always Limiting?

   Male-female patterns of interactions in the pattern of
resource utilization are generally based on male interest in
maximizing the number of matings they achieve with females.
Assuming this behavior in males generally leads to an accurate
description of mating patterns because males commonly profit
from exploiting high levels of investment already made by
females in eggs. However, a strategy of attracting as many
females as possible onto a territory may not be effective in
cases in which males control, but do not directly provide, a
resource that limits the overall reproduction of females. In
these cases, a female's success depends on getting onto breeding areas that are controlled by males. When pairing takes
place, a female may have little investment in gametes. All
investment on her part must come from exploiting limiting
resources controlled by a male. The territorial male is

essentially "hiring" the female to turn resources he owns into offspring. A shortage of resources may present a condition in which there are more females than can effectively convert resources into offspring. Males may limit the number of females on their territories to that which yields the highest output of offspring, even though this may be below the maximum number of mates the individual males could attract. Such relationships may be common in marmots (Downhower and Armitage, 1971) and in species in which nonreproducing females are common in the breeding season.

Availability of females and their eggs in excess of resources needed to mature these eggs may be important in the development of polyandry as a dominant reproductive mode in some birds. Females in these populations may evolve to control resources in order to guarantee for themselves access to suitable sites where young can be raised. In jacanas, Jenni (1974) describes not only resource control by polyandrous females but also large numbers of nonreproducing females during the breeding season. This is a relatively uncommon occurrence in most species and suggests that suitable habitats for raising young are in short supply. Ability to relate polyandry and female territoriality to the shortage of resources seems important since a pathway for the evolution of high variance in female reproductive success, which may even surpass that of males, is not apparent from Bateman's (1948) model and its more recent derivatives.

Effects of Variance in Female Quality

The assumption of equal value of females in the equilibrium model may not be realistic in most situations and, in certain cases, may strongly influence predictions relating to the pattern of mating success. Such incongruities may commonly occur in cases where individuals pair with mates of their own relative quality, as was considered by Darwin (1871), Fisher (1958), and O'Donald (1974). They point out that where such pairings occur, nearly all males may be able to obtain matings, but there still may be high levels of variance in reproductive success. For the equilibrium model, prediction of patterns of mating success depends on the assumption of equal quality among females. However, ability of males to discriminate among females suggests that, under most conditions, variance in the quality of females should have little effect on patterns of male reproductive success, since gain through choice of a few very good females or many poor females should generally give similar levels of genetic gain for males.

Variation in the quality of females may also influence mating patterns if a significant interaction between male and female quality effects the quality of their offspring. A

multiplicative relationship between the quality of parents
and offspring will lead to selection for females who seek out
high quality males and forego possible gain derived from
paternal investment in offspring. High quality males should
certainly be able to supply receptive females with contributions of sperm. Males need only choose among females if it is
likely that they might run out of sperm. It is unclear if
this kind of multiplicative relationship exists. The preva-
lence of monogamous pairs in situations in which it is possible for females to rear their broods alone suggests that, at
least in some instances, this is not the case.

   Females who vary in quality may not be able to demand
benefits according to the relative quality of offspring that
they produce--the expected basis for determining an individual's market value. Consider the case in which one of two
males who offer material benefits if of high relative genetic
value. The male of high genetic value may favor mating with
low value females. Selective matings with low quality females
allow him to utilize his entire complement of genetic benefits
to attract females while using only a small amount of his
material benefits. His ability to secure additional matings
is thereby only slightly reduced. Preference for low value
females by these males may allow selected females to bargain
for higher levels of material benefits than they might otherwise expect to obtain.

Male Commitment To Deliver Benefits

   In the equilibrium model, males were assumed to be able to
deliver material and genetic benefits to females with equal
ease. Trivers (1972) points out some of the problems associated with the transfer of material benefits in relation to
mating. The model he develops focuses on apparent instances
of deception, such as "desertion" of females by males and
cuckoldry of males by females. In this analysis, the relative
likelihood of "desertion" is considered important in determining patterns of male-female interactions. He argues that
desertion becomes a theoretical temptation for the partner
that has made the lesser investment, particularly if the
difference is great. Later, in discussing the profitability
of the desertion strategy, he states, "The balance between
these opposing forces should depend on the exact form of the
cumulative investment curves as well as opportunities for
further matings." This view has been criticized by Dawkins
and Carlisle (1976), who note correctly that parents are
concerned with maximizing gain from their future opportunities
to invest, and, in some cases, the past history of investment
in individuals may be of little importance in influencing
future patterns of parental contribution. However, situations

in which past investment and future ability to invest are correlated must be common. Under these conditions, past investment may define opportunities for further investment by both parents.

Another, and perhaps more important, problem common to both of these explanations of male-female behavior in benefit transfer comes from the attempts of Trivers, and Dawkins and Carlisle, to describe patterns of parental investment in terms of desertion by one or the other of the parents, usually the male. Desertion is defined as "abandonment without consent or legal justification of a person, post, or relationship and duties and obligations therewith" (*Webster's Third International Dictionary*). Obviously, most animal species have no legal system, but opportunities to make agreements and for partners to develop expectations about levels of benefit a partner will contribute seem to exist. In the equilibrium model discussed above, choice of a mate based on his expected delivery of benefits that are not at hand may be interpreted as requiring the development of an obligation or agreement supported by some guarantees. However, that model and the one offered by Trivers differ in the manner by which females develop expectations about the amount of material benefits they can demand. The amount of benefits demanded by females and delivered by males in the equilibrium model depends on the market value of each individual at the time of mating. By contrast, Trivers assumes that each sex's obligation to its mate should be equivalent to the amount that its partner contributes, and he thus calls individuals who contribute less to offspring than their partners "deserters." Similarly, Dawkins and Carlisle do not seem to view commitments made near the time of mating as having any significant role in mate choice.

The definition of desertion suggests deception of the nondeserting parent by its mate. The common tendency for one parent to leave the other with their offspring, and the suggestion of these authors that attributes all bias in parental commitment to desertion, leads to the prediction that deception occurs on a large scale. By contrast, in the equilibrium model I assume that males meet female expectations for the delivery of material benefits in the great majority of cases. Female tendencies to choose among males offering different levels of benefits suggest that long-term success in deception by males is rare. In cases where successful tendencies to deceive females spread, selection may favor females who devalue material benefits according to the level of deception and favor males who provide high quality genetic benefits. Deception in benefit transfer is unlikely among males chosen for their ability to provide genetic benefits, since such males will rarely lose in supplying females with

sperm that they are likely to use. Females might also select
males who offer the best assurances for the delivery of
material benefits. The ability of males to offer material
benefits may allow many males their only means of attracting
a mate. Shifts in female preference toward choice based on
genetic characters would strongly reduce these males' prospects for mating. Such shifts in preference should cause
selection among these males so that they strive to provide
the best possible assurance that obligations established at
the time of mating will be met.

Females must commonly adjust their expectations for receiving benefits according to their own quality, the availability of benefits, and the likelihood that benefits will be
delivered. Successful deception by males, although important
in determining the amount of benefits delivered through its
effect on male ability to guarantee benefits, is likely to
exist for only short periods, i.e., up to the time when a
female adjusts mate choice patterns so as to maximize gain
from her alternatives for choosing mates.

Other than desertion, there are several reasons why males
may commonly contribute fewer material benefits than females
to raise a brood. These might include: (1) lower confidence
of genetic relationship for males than females to offspring,
which may lead males to alternative investment patterns with
higher payoff (Alexander, 1974); (2) females may prefer
genetic benefits offered by some males over material benefits
offered by others; and (3) males may be unable to collect
and/or guarantee material benefits at the time of mating.
Consistent lower investment by males, resulting from the
operation of one or more of these factors, may give the
appearance of deception or desertion when, in fact, males are
satisfying all commitments they are able to make at the time
of mating. For example, in instances when females appear to
prefer genetic benefits offered by males, behavior in which
the male leaves before the female's contribution to the brood
is complete may not result from "maltreatment at the hands of
one's mate" (Trivers, 1972), but because females are victims
of their own decisions. The "deserted" female may have passed
up the opportunity to mate with a male who offered a full
complement of material benefits and who would have stayed with
her through the whole nesting period. In his place she may
choose a male who offers higher levels of genetic benefits
but who is likely to contribute fewer material benefits to
offspring. Presumably the choice of this second male leads
to an overall higher payoff in descendants even though her
selected mate will leave before she finishes rearing her
brood.

The importance of understanding behaviors effecting the
transfer of material benefits is underlined by the treatment

of mating patterns in fish by Dawkins and Carlisle. They
invoke Trivers' notion of the "cruel bind" to explain typical
male behavior in guarding eggs and sometimes hatchlings.
Using this concept, they suggest that males are stuck in the
parental role because females who lay externally fertilized
eggs have the opportunity to "desert first." The cruel bind
these males find themselves in is one in which any tendency
for them to leave after the female has departed would lower
their reproduction to below what it would be if they stay.
It is suggested that the deserting female gains from having
her eggs guarded at a much lower cost than if she tended them
herself.

In fishes in which males are parental, the pattern of
mating and investment by parents seems to be less haphazard
and largely determined before the eggs are laid. Male protection of eggs is preceded by nest building and territorial
defense (sticklebacks: Assem, 1967; sunfish: Keenleyside,
1972). The territorial behavior of males commits them to stay
with eggs, since territories are important in attracting
future mates and may be difficult to reestablish (J. Taylor,
pers. comm.). Protection of eggs probably adds little cost
to the male if considered in relation to his other reproductive activities, but it may be important to the female in
allowing her to leave the oviposition site to feed and produce
more eggs. The ability of males to guarantee some level of
protection to eggs is probably a key element in allowing males
who are inferior in genetic quality the opportunity to attract mates.

Reliance on an individual's relative opportunity to abandon
its mate to predict patterns for the transfer of benefits
ignores (1) the effect of one sex's consistent failure to
contribute benefits to their mates in long-term mating patterns, and (2) the importance of limiting investment, usually
controlled by females, in influencing the amount of postmating
benefits delivered by a prospective mate.

If males are consistently left by females, there should
soon be a shortage of unmated males, since most are committed
to the care of offspring. In response to these conditions,
females may either start a new brood, for which they provide
all necessary benefits, or forego reproduction until males
become available. In either case, females may be forced to
compete for opportunities to mate with rare, available males.
The latters' rarity gives them leverage to make demands on
females which in turn enhance the reproduction of the individual male.

The material benefits that males offer in exchange for
matings may be of little value in affecting mating decisions
unless females can be assured of their delivery. A female
can only value male commitments to deliver benefits if they

occur before fertilization of the eggs--in which she has made
a large investment, or commitment of parental effort. Assurance of delivery is most certain in cases of nuptial feeding
(reviewed by Thornhill, 1976a) in which males provide benefits
as a precondition to mating. Probably, males most often provide guarantees which give the female a high degree of confidence that promised benefits will be delivered.

Several means exist by which males might guarantee delivery
of benefits to females after they have mated. A male may
commit himself to a situation which would lead to a net loss
in offspring if he were to attempt to deliver to other females
benefits his mate expected to receive. As suggested, a high
quality territory may be difficult to reestablish; even when
new territories can be formed, all or most females may have
already mated. Trivers (1972) recognizes that the male's
investment after copulation may be increased by the
indirect force of female choice exerted before copulation.
While this statement agrees with the views suggested here, it
is inconsistent with his attempts to relate the amount of
committed parental investment to tendencies to desert. Pre-
fertilization indices of aid-giving behavior and actual
contributions of benefits directly to the female may have no
direct effect on individuals' tendencies to leave their mates,
since, according to Trivers' definition, neither represents
parental investment. His notion of the cruel bind, if generally applied (as by Dawkins and Carlisle, 1976), further
complicates the development of a clearcut view of male-female
relationships, since its operation allows for no important
premating agreements.

Females often must recognize tendencies to give benefits
by simple contextual cues. After some point in the reproductive season, it may be difficult for a male to obtain a high
quality mate, so with limited alternatives for reproduction,
a female is guaranteed her mate's assistance. Prolonged
courtship could function to force males in seasonal mating
systems to wait until the critical point at which their
interest in leaving has passed (Wiley, 1976). If this is so,
females who have lost a courting male should mate rapidly
after spending reduced time in courtship with a new male.
These females would be expected to mate at approximately the
same time as other females of the same quality. High quality
females may also mate first, since male expectation of subsequently finding a better female is low. Waiting need not
occur if females cannot raise offspring without male assistance. Under these conditions, males should not begin matings
unless it is likely that they will remain with their first
mate, since all effort devoted to abandoned females is ultimately lost.

Installment mating may be important in some species in

which females allow a male to mate repeatedly. Each mating gives that male a low probability of paternity of a female's offspring. Between matings, the male may provide benefits. The sum of benefits may equal that contributed by a single parental male, and total copulations lead to a high probability of success for some males (see Cronin and Sherman, 1977).

Female Promise of Paternity

Successful reproduction by males involves not only mating with females but successfully fertilizing eggs. Males chosen primarily on the basis of genetic characters are assured of some level of success if females control matings, since benefits to females are only gained when sperm from these males is used to fertilize eggs. By contrast, males who provide material benefits face the possibility of reduced or even no reproduction if they are unable to tie the delivery of benefits and sperm to females with a high confidence of paternity.

Cuckoldry is most likely to be profitable for females when they are forced into conflicts resulting from their attempts to maximize gain in benefits from different sources. One such conflict arises from choosing among mates who differ in the material and genetic benefits they are able to offer. Females who mate exclusively with males who deliver material benefits may outgain those who mate with males who provide only genetic benefits. However, increased material gain from these matings comes at the cost of reduced gain in the genetic quality of offspring. If females can deceive males into providing a full complement of material benefits, but use the sperm of males providing genetic benefits, they can simultaneously enjoy the benefits of both types of matings. For males who rely on material benefits to attract mates, this female behavior will lead to severe reductions in fitness and possibly complete loss of reproduction. We must ask whether females commonly are able to deceive benefit-providing males, or if selection will work on males to suppress apparent instances of deception.

Existence of females who vary in detectable levels of confidence offered may allow males the opportunity to bargain for high confidence by offering extra material benefits to females who offer high levels of confidence. Competition among males for high confidence matings gives truthful females the ability to demand and receive material benefits at levels above those that would occur if there were no attempts to deceive males. Increased levels of offerings to these females come at the expense of females who attempt to cuckold. If material benefits are highly valued, as indicated by female tendencies to include them in mate-choice decisions,

preferential treatment of truthful females by males should
lead to an increase in the proportion of females who assure
high levels of confidence. Selection by males should favor
rewarding demonstrations of confidence by females to levels
approaching (but usually below) those in which material benefits are accorded their true value (the value if males had
complete confidence) relative to genetic benefits. In cases
where males can bargain for higher confidence, reduction in
the value of material benefits may come from costs in determining variations in confidence and rewards to pay off truthful females.

Male success in offering benefits to females in return for
higher confidence of paternity depends on (1) how females
value added benefits relative to the amount they have already
received from males, and (2) ability of individuals to evaluate differences in benefits provided by members of the
opposite sex. If females value new benefits as much as those
received when they had less, the prospects for male success
in bargaining for high confidence in offspring are quite good.
Competition among females for these added benefits may be
strong, and females would be expected to guarantee high levels
of confidence at relatively low cost. However, if female
interest in benefits diminishes in relation to the level of
material benefits already received, then added contribution
of material benefits in exchange for higher confidence will
have little effect on female decisions to share paternity of
a brood with other males.

In cases where males have evolved to contribute material
benefits, there are two reasons to suspect that males providing valued benefits may often win in conflicts over confidence
in paternity of offspring. First, the material benefits they
offer outweigh the value of the genetic benefits, and, as I
have attempted to show, they are often in a position to use
them to control female mating decisions. Second, males suffer
a greater loss in being cuckolded. Under the best conditions,
females gain only the difference between the genetic quality
of the male who provides them with material benefits and that
of the male who eventually fathers their offspring. A
deceived male loses his entire reproduction. This asymmetry
in the potential for gain suggests that benefit-providing
males will be more inclined to invest effort and resources in
preventing cuckoldry than females will in attempting to carry
it out. For these reasons it is suggested that cuckoldry may
be rare, but other factors must be considered in determining
its actual level of occurrence. In the model which discussed
males exchanging benefits for increased confidence of paternity, it is assumed that females can demonstrate high male
confidence at a low real cost. However, if these costs are
high, as may occur when females must forage over large areas

for food, it may be impossible for males economically to
provide sufficient benefits to cause females to raise the
guaranteed level of confidence beyond very low levels.
Selection should work to reduce these costs where possible,
since females would stand to gain increased shares of resources. But there may be limits to how far this type of
selection can go, and where these limits appear, the real
value of material benefits to a male in attracting mates shows
a related decrease.

In cases where females are not able to demonstrate differences in levels of confidence in paternity, there may be
several outcomes. The simplest of these may involve males
not changing their behavior. Reductions in confidence given
by females may leave those benefit-providing males who offer
less than the highest level of genetic benefits with few
options but to continue to provide their benefits, even if
these are severely devalued in their effectiveness for
attracting females as mates. Formerly benefit-providing males
may adopt entirely new strategies, including devoting energies
to the direct control of females. Even if these only generate
a low payoff, they may be more profitable than collecting and
providing resources and getting little or no return on genetic
representation in offspring. Alexander (1974, 1977) has
pointed out that if male confidence in paternity is low,
individuals may contribute to full sisters' and even half-
sibs' offspring, related to them by 1/4 and by 1/8, instead
of to those who, on average, may be related by a lower fraction.

Several males may be involved in the fathering of offspring
in one brood in blackbirds (Bray et al., 1975), but it is
unclear whether this results from deception or female attempts
to balance benefits received from males with some expected
level of confidence in offspring. Multiple matings by females
with males who provide different amounts of material benefits
do not necessarily mean that males are being deceived. For
instance, a female may have only limited need for material
benefits that males contribute. Such a female may compromise
when confronted with the choice of mating with the highest
genetic quality male, who offers no material benefits, or with
a male offering material benefits important to her reproduction. She may mate with both males, apportioning confidence
among them according to the relative worth of the benefits
they provide. One male would be offered fractional confidence
of parenthood in her brood for his supply of material benefits, while sperm derived from the male of highest genetic
quality was used for the remaining eggs. If there is a population-wide change in the rate of female gain from material
benefits per unit of confidence delivered to a male, the
material benefits would be revalued according to this change

in need. Fractions of females won in the equilibrium model
are significant in this context. The payment to males in
probability of fathering offspring relative to the value of
benefits they provide may give a false appearance of deception. Such opportunities to split broods may allow males of
low genetic quality their only opportunity to gain any offspring.

Splitting paternity of broods between males who contribute
material benefits at different rates, e.g., one male contributes all material benefits and other none, may complicate a
male's problems of assessing a female's relative value. In
these cases, benefits of resources contributed by males are
shared by all offspring. No problem exists if males are
utilizing only previous female investment, as apparently occurs in Mecoptera (Thornhill, 1976b) in which a male's
contribution is not directly associated with his offspring.
If the quality of offspring is dependent on the level of male
contribution, then males contributing material benefits may
suffer a relative loss in mixed broods. The genetic benefits
females acquire go only into specific offspring, but material
benefits go to all and perhaps even more to those of high
genetic quality; therefore, males of high genetic quality
enjoy the gain in their offspring though they contribute no
benefits of their own.

Because a male's interest in the disbursement of benefits
differs from that of his multiple-mated mate, males should
avoid direct contribution to her. One strategy may be for
males to deliver material benefits directly to their offspring, provided they can discern those likely to be their
own. Another may be for males to place a premium on females
who mate exclusively with them.

MALE CONTROL OF FEMALES

Up to this point I have focused attention on systems in
which choice by females, although sometimes restricted, is the
key element in determining patterns of mating associations.
Male capture of females, or sequestering or otherwise denying
them access to other males in order to force copulations or
severely restrict their reproductive alternatives, provides an
interesting contrast. Since males who embark on a female
control strategy commonly have much more uncommitted reproductive effort available than females, presumably, this effort
can be directed to capture of females.

For females, effort to avoid capture must be deducted from
investment in offspring. Differences in quality between males
chosen by a female and those who might capture and inseminate
her must be sufficiently large so that costs of avoidance,

paid in reduced reproductive output, are justified. It might appear that males have a distinct advantage over females, but female proximity to eggs and differences in difficulty of capture and escape suggest that there is no simple way to compare male effort spent in attempts to capture females and the effectiveness of females in avoiding capture. At best, situations can be noted in which such capture and control are more or less likely.

Male success in control must be most common when differences in the genetic quality of the male an uncontrolled female might choose and the male who actually controls her are small. In harems of sea lions (Gentry, 1970) or ungulates (Jarman, 1974), successful males gain their position by winning many intense fights, and these triumphs are probably a good indicator of genetic quality. Since in these cases it appears that males have not been able to provide or control any valued material benefits, the real cost to females of establishment of control by males may be small. In some cases such control may actually enhance female reproduction. If males who are unlikely to attract females even occasionally are successful in "stealing" a copulation, females may submit to control and protection by a male of their choice. Cox and Le Boeuf (1977) point out that harem females often call out when sexually harassed by an invading male. The harem master recognizes the call and responds by chasing away the invader. In the dung fly *Scatophaga stercoraria,* Parker (1970b, c) has suggested that a female may gain from a male's postcopulatory guarding, since he fends off would-be copulators while she oviposits. Female *Scatophaga* actively choose large males with whom they are most likely to rapidly complete copulation and oviposition (Borgia, in prep.). In addition, females begin to display rocking motions when held away from the oviposition site by males for more time than is commonly required for copulation. These rocking motions cause an increase in attack rate and increase the probability of male replacement. Notably, it is generally small males who hold females for long durations, up to three times the average copula duration. The female signal and consequent replacement of the guarding male may reduce the time needed to place her eggs into the oviposition site, which decays rapidly in quality as it ages.

In a variety of insect groups, females fly into aggregations of males, are grasped, and the pair falls to the ground where they mate (see Downes, 1969). Choice of timing and pattern of approach may give females a high degree of control over which males capture them. Differences in genetic gain lost between this pattern of choice and one in which females can more facilely reject males may be minimal.

High costs to females in resisting control in some contexts seem the most common basis for establishment of this mating

strategy. In ungulates and other mammals, group formation by
females is considered predominantly a defensive response
against predators (Hamilton, 1971; Alexander, 1974). However,
such an adaptation may restrict the ability of herd members
to freely express mate choice, since attempts to leave the
herd are likely to severely increase the risk of predation.
Grouping by females may not be as costly as being captured by
random males, since females in groups are commonly controlled
by a dominant male who has "earned" his position and may,
therefore, be considered to be a good choice as a mate in most
contexts.

Male control may also be effective when the time and space
in which reproductive functions are carried out are restricted. Male *Scatophaga* (Hammer, 1941; Parker, 1970a) capture
females as they attempt to oviposit on restricted sites. Male
dragonflies also capture females and then guard them from
above as they oviposit (Campanella and Wolf, 1973). As Parker
(1970c) has suggested, male control may simplify and speed the
mating and oviposition process for females, but initial tendencies to control must have been encouraged by female tendencies to group around oviposition sites.

Long-term success of a strategy in which males attempt to
control females is dependent on male ability to limit access
of sperm from other males to a female's eggs between ovulation
and fertilization. Without this extended control, internally
fertilized females who are captured and then released may move
to a preferred male and mate with him. Selection on females
should work to increase their control over which male's sperm
actually fertilize their eggs.

Males able to directly control females save on expenses
associated with collecting and/or defending resources in order
to obtain benefits to exchange for matings. However, the
absence of a tendency to contribute resource-based benefits
removes the leverage males might have in rewarding females who
offer high confidence of paternity with extra material benefits. This may not often be a problem for highly successful
males if ability to control females and gene quality are
highly correlated. However, if there is no bias in terms of
which males can control females and consequently no correlation between control and gene quality, some investment in
avoidance of males and attempts to choose controlling males
is likely.

Female tendencies to clump may strongly affect the variance
in male reproductive success in cases where males capture
females. In these instances, females can be treated as resources controlled by males, and the analysis below can be
used to predict patterns of male mating success if the relationship between timing of copulation and its effect on mate
success in fertilizing eggs is understood.

HIERARCHY IN TYPES OF MATING ASSOCIATIONS

Predicting which of the four mate selection strategies will occur in a given instance requires knowledge of (1) habitat conditions sufficient for each of the patterns of mate procurement and (2) some means of specifying outcomes in cases where sufficient conditions exist for more than one of the four patterns. Conditions necessary for establishment of each mating pattern have been discussed, and relationships among resource control, resource collection, and genetic choice strategies mentioned. This discussion suggests that a hierarchy exists among strategies which defines which is likely to prevail for cases in which more than one might occur.

A strategy in which males can control the resources which females must have to reproduce would seem to be dominant over those in which males either collect resources or provide high quality genetic benefits. Arguments presented earlier which suggest a low expected value of genetic benefits can be used to define typical relationships among the remaining subordinate strategies. Low value of genetic benefits implies that whenever material benefits are available, they will be the primary criteria used in mate choice decisions by females. Pure genetic choice systems can then occur only where males are unable to collect any substantial amount of items from the habitat that are of value to females. Choice involving males offering material benefits might then be considered dominant over a pure strategy in which mate selection is based only on genetic benefits offered. However, consideration of genetic benefits offered by a prospective mate is involved in both of the strategies discussed here.

Strategies involving male capture of females also dominate over some other mate selection patterns. The other types of mate choice generally involve a high level of control by females over which males will be their mate. However, any demands a female might make in the mate selection process are voided if a male offering no material benefits can force a female to use his sperm to fertilize her eggs. Therefore, when males can control females, strategies involving collection of benefits and pure genetic choice by females are likely to be ineffective. The relationship between female control and resource control is less clear, since both females and limiting resources may be necessary for successful reproduction. Males who capture and release females away from oviposition sites may be able to fertilize the eggs of a female in a way which cannot be detected by a resource-controlling male. Males using a resource control strategy will likely lose in sexual competition if these female-controlling males capture a sufficiently large share of females who have not yet reached areas where males hold territories. Alternatively, a mate-capturing

male may only be able to insure successful fertilization of
eggs with his sperm by guarding a female after copulation
(Parker, 1970d). Success in mating may demand males capable
of both controlling resources and of capturing and holding
females who come to utilize these resources.

In the hierarchy of mating strategies, male control of
resources and ability to capture females share the highest
rank; male contribution of collected benefits, a lower position; and when no other strategy is effective, a pure strategy
of genetic choice by females will occur. The hierarchy
system can be used for determining the likelihood of a strategy in a given context by asking if sufficient conditions
exist for the highest ranking strategy to occur. If so, that
strategy should characterize the behavior of individuals
fertilizing the majority of eggs in the population. If not,
then the same procedure is carried out for the strategy of
next highest rank. This testing is continued until genetic
choice represents the only remaining strategy. If this type
of selection is limited, as by a high density of predators,
then we might add an even lower level of "choice" onto the
hierarchy. This new level would involve a tendency for females to mate with the first male that they encounter.

It is implicit in the categorization of strategies presented here that the last male to attempt to mate with a gravid
female fertilizes the largest share of her eggs. This relationship is typical of cases in which a female's eggs are
fertilized externally. Development of internal fertilization,
particularly in cases in which females store sperm, allows
females more control over the process of mate selection. As
discussed above, control of sperm by females may reduce the
rank of some strategies, particularly those involving direct
control of females.

Interspecific comparisons of breeding systems in Central
American hummingbirds illustrate dominance effects in patterns
of mate selection (Stiles and Wolf, 1977). Males of large
species commonly hold territories around inflorescences where
females feed; acceptance of copulations from controlling males
is apparently a precondition for feeding by the females.
Males of smaller species are effectively excluded from holding
territories around flowers by males of the larger species.
In these excluded species leks are the common type of breeding
systems.

Dominance relationships also occur in the mating systems
of flies which use cow dung as oviposition sites (Borgia, in
prep.). *Scatophaga stercoraria* is a predator on adult flies
of other species and is the only one of at least ten large
species in which males come to the oviposition site and control this resource to influence mating decisions. Costs of
predation on males from other species by *Scatophaga* may have

prevented them from evolving and maintaining a resource control strategy. In two small dipterous species, males do come to the oviposition site. Males of one species cannot be held and eaten by *Scatophaga,* and those of the other, which are eaten but do not appear to be a preferred food source, mate in crevices underneath the dung when *Scatophaga* is present in abundance.

GENETIC CHOICE

The Lek Paradox

Understanding mechanisms of genetic choice is critical to developing mating system models if, as I have suggested, genetic choice consistently forms an alternative to mate choice systems based on other criteria. However, Williams (1975) has pointed out a problem in assuming that variance in genetic quality is a likely basis for mate choice. He states, "High heritability of fitness from father to son must be maintained in order to explain mate choice based only on genetic criteria." The problem Williams (pers. comm.; see also Davis and O'Donald, 1976) alludes to is that of maintaining the levels of genetic variation necessary to form the basis for mate choice if only a small fraction of males breed successfully. Though this criticism appears valid, there should be an explanation for those behaviors of animals which suggest that differences in genetic quality are sufficient to provide the basis for mate selection. Perhaps the most convincing evidence for genetic choice occurs in what Alexander (1975) calls nonresource-based leks. These have been studied in greatest detail in birds (Robel and Ballard, 1974; Lill, 1974a, b, 1976; Wiley, 1973) and in some mammals (Buechner and Roth, 1974) in which single males achieve large proportions of observed matings. Several aspects of the behavior of animals in these systems characterize the pattern of mate choice: (1) no vehicle for female benefit appears to be transferred other than sperm, (2) females reject numerous males capable and seemingly willing to fertilize them, (3) females seem to exhibit unrestricted choice which is directed at particular males, (4) males fight for positions which affect their success, (5) no obvious postcopulatory assistance is given by males. Although the gene-quality hypothesis may have problems, no alternative appears to explain lek behavior better. It is the unique behavior associated with lek-breeding systems which causes the separation of what appears to be pure genetic choice systems from the continuum of systems that rely on material benefits and perhaps other male attributes.

In what might be called the lek paradox, there is apparent contradiction in theoretical predictions about (1) disappearance of genetic variance, the necessary basis for heritable variation in mate choice, and (2) suggested advantage to females in choosing males of high genetic quality in the lek system. Resolution of this paradox is important if we are to understand the operation of nonresource-based leks and related systems.

Alternative explanations for the selective basis of leks have been proposed, but none seems to fully explain the very specific behavior which occurs in breeding leks. For example, Lack (1968) and Trivers (1972) suggested that breeding leks in birds speed mating by females. Abundant data suggest that females may spend much more time around the lek, displaying to and surveying different males, than one might expect if females were attempting to minimize time devoted to mating (Lill, 1976; Brandler, 1967). Lack (1968) also suggested that lek behavior may reduce predation. Although he provides no specific mechanism, we might assume systems similar to those described by Hamilton (1971) in which individuals who join groups enjoy reduced likelihood of attack or, as suggested by Pulliam (1973), are capable of enhanced detection of predators. By itself, this hypothesis seems inadequate to explain complex displays by both sexes; repeated female displays with different males (Lill, 1976; Robel and Ballard, 1974); and behavior likely to attract predators, including the bright coloration, loud calls, and odors that invariably accompany male lek behavior.

As might be expected if predators were unimportant in lek evolution, reports of behavior near leks either scarcely mention activities of potential predators or suggest that they are only infrequent visitors. For example, Lill (1976), having observed manakin leks, states, "During nearly 2000 hours of observations made from partially enclosed blinds at arenas, I saw neither actual nor attempted predation." However, if leks have been effective in predator defense, it may be improper to eliminate the predation hypothesis only on the basis of this type of observation.

The lek paradox might be resolved in several ways that would allow females to base their mating decisions primarily on the quality of genetic benefits that a male might provide. One way is to consider the actual levels of polygyny in populations where genetic choice appears to occur. Supposed reductions in fitness in lek-breeding populations are based on assumptions of high levels of polygyny. However, in many cases, these supposed levels of variance in male success are not achieved; therefore, expected reductions in genetic variance may not occur. Lill's (1976) work on the manakin *Pipra erythrocephala* provides some of the rare data on behavior of

marked males and females on leks. On the four leks he
observed, my calculations, using his data, show that 39.8%
of the males copulated more than the average. In addition,
45.7% of the males on leks copulated with the average number,
or more, different females.

Large numbers of leks provide an additional barrier to the
rapid depletion of genetic variance. Snow (1962) estimated
approximately 1,700 individuals of *Pipra erythrocephala* on
Trinidad, and using Lill's data on sex ratio of adult males
and mean lek size, I calculate that there may be approximately
45 leks on the island. Similar results appear to characterize
other lekking birds (e.g., Patterson, 1952).

Levels of genetic variation are probably maintained at or
near some equilibrium value, and variance in male mating
success is only one of several factors likely to affect this
equilibrium. Shifts in selection patterns may provide the
main source of genetic variation. In eukaryots, which contain
large numbers of loci, it is probable that changes in selective coefficients which affect the relative success of alleles
at the same locus occur at the rate of one such shift per
generation. With some slowdown in the loss of variance, as
occurs in manakins, it may be possible for males to offer
females significant levels of genetic benefits. Linkage
disequilibrium may act as another barrier to the rapid loss
of variability.

Another, but not exclusive, explanation for the maintenance
of heritable gain from mate choice based on genetic characteristics is dependent on advantage for heterozygotes. Heritable
advantage for females can be maintained even when there are
extreme levels of polygyny if it is assumed (1) that females
have no effective means of assessing the type of alleles that
they carry and (2) that a substantial number of male characteristics which affect male vigor are dependent on heterosis.
Dominance on the lek of males possessing the greatest level
of heterotic loci should cause females to favor whatever
pattern of mate choice yields offspring with the highest
probability of having high levels of heterozygosity. Denying
females information about their own genetic make-up prevents
potential advantage from complementation by matching specific
alleles that they carry with alternatives that occur in males.
Even with information about their own genetic qualities,
difficulties in attempts to complement large numbers of loci
should make such behavior ineffective (Alexander and Borgia,
1978; and see below).

Choice of the dominant/heterozygous males offers one route
to greater than average expectation of producing heterozygous
offspring. At any one locus, all matings involving heterozygous males or females will produce one-half heterozygous
offspring, regardless of the genotype of the female. However,

probability of homozygotes producing heterozygotes depends
on the frequency of alleles in the population. If two alleles
are present in equal frequency among potential mates, a
female's success in producing heterozygous offspring will be
the same whether she picks randomly among homozygotes or
heterozygotes. But, if the two alleles are not present in
equal frequency and are unequal by relatively constant proportions in both sexes, there is a payoff in choosing dominant
males. Most matings in which females mate with males other
than those showing high levels of heterozygosity will lead
to a greater than average expectation of producing only homo-
zygous offspring; frequency of the common allele in one sex is
correlated with a high frequency of the same allele in the
other sex. Some matings will lead to whole broods of heterozygous offspring, but these will occur at a lower rate than
those producing only homozygotes.

The success of this pattern of mate selection is dependent
on overdominance as a common pattern in genetic systems. High
levels of genetic variation are known to occur in a wide
variety of species (see Powell, 1975), and heterozygous
advantage has been suggested (Fincham, 1972; Johnson, 1976)
to account for much of this observed intraspecific variability.
Even in overdominant systems, deviation of allelic frequencies
from equality should be common because of unequal fitness in
homozygotes. In fact, the fitness values of homozygotes must
rarely be exactly equal. Females' ability to base mate choice
only on relative dominance of males presents them with an
opportunity to pick genetic characters without any need to
identify particular alleles in males. While dominant males
will probably rarely come near to being heterozygous at every
overdominant locus, the dominant male presents the best
average choice, considering all loci, for females.

I have suggested that genetic choice by females is most
likely directed at some genome-wide indication of gene quality. Three reasons for this view are (1) difficulties may
arise in carrying out assessment of individuals where several
favored alleles may occur, but not in the same individuals;
(2) females who use generalized characters in choosing mates
have the greatest opportunity for gain in mate choice because
they can take advantage of variation at each locus; and (3)
selection on genomic elements is likely to oppose consistent
patterns of identification and control of choice by individual
alleles when these deny the full potential for success in
reproduction to other alleles (Hamilton, 1967; Alexander and
Borgia, 1978).

The notion of genome-wide selection of characters in males
by females might be questioned because of results of mate
choice experiments with *Drosophila* (reviewed by Petit and
Ehrman, 1969). Females show convincing tendencies to choose

males of rare phenotypes in laboratory experiments in which
differences in traits are based on differences of single
mutation or chromosomal inversion. This type of experiment
commonly has been cited as strong evidence for genetic choice
in which females are programmed to select males based on a
difference of a single gene, which is suggested to complement
alleles in their gametes (Sheppard, 1953; Anderson, 1969;
Ford, 1971; Trivers, 1972; Charlesworth and Charlesworth,
1975; Ehrman and Parsons, 1976; and many others). Surprisingly, in more recent publications these interpretations have
not taken into account experiments by Ehrman (1970) which show
that by introducing the odor from a colony of the rare type
into the mating chamber, the pattern of mate selection can be
regularly reversed so that common alleles are favored. This
suggests that characters used in mate choice by females are
not those initially selected by investigators. Biases favoring rare types apparently occur because these types are
correlated with odors derived from the different genetic
backgrounds of the test animals or nongenetic differences
related to the different growth conditions. Females may have
evolved to prefer "rare-smelling" males because, on average,
these males are from different habitats and are not close
genetic relatives. Maynard Smith (1956) has described the
severe costs associated with inbreeding which females commonly
appear to be programmed to avoid. Males from different
habitats may also offer females the opportunity for gain from
genome-wide complementation, which is quite different from
hypothesized gain based on complementation of individual
alleles. Even if foreignness is indicated by differences in
single genes, odor may be only the first element in a hierarchy of criteria used in mating decisions. There appears to
be ample evidence for the importance of other criteria in mate
selection by *Drosophila* (Ewing and Manning, 1967), and these
may give better indications of genome-wide differences in
male quality.

Sheppard (1953) points out that olfactory cues may also
provide a basis for instances of supposed complementation in
the moth *Panaxia dominula*. He describes experiments in which
when the characters he used to separate moths of different
genotypes were concealed, females were able to maintain a
biased pattern of mate choice. Since we are not told of the
procedures for collecting and rearing moths for these experiments, the possibility of inbreeding avoidance patterns must
be considered. These might occur if tests were carried out
using adults reared from a small number of broods or from
larvae which developed proximate to each other in the labora-
tory--as might occur in nature among siblings. Interestingly,
the calculations of Haldane (1954) from field data on these
moths suggest that in natural populations moths mate randomly

with regard to the characters investigated by Sheppard. The
choice based on the presumed gain from complementation of
single alleles appears to be less common than Sheppard (1953)
predicted would occur.

Mechanisms for Genetic Choice

Male-Male Fights

Direct interactions between males provide perhaps the best
composite indication of relative overall quality. Male success in fights summarizes lifetime success in collecting food,
resisting disease, and avoiding predators and injury. Conspecific males perform the most rigorous tests when matched head-
to-head, and even small differences in performance are likely
to be significant. These tests are always of considerable
relevance since males tend to evolve together, and it is often
in their interest to challenge attempts at deception by other
males. In cases in which there is extensive maternal care,
fights are likely to indicate not only quality of the chosen
individual male in development and fighting ability, but the
quality of those genes carried by the male which affect
maternal parental care, as Alexander (1975) points out.
Fighting by males, especially in systems in which structured
dominance relations exist, leads to unambiguous results.
Females with even limited abilities are likely to quickly and
inexpensively discern differences among males based on fighting ability, especially if the loser is chased away or leaves.
For lek organisms, fighting has been associated with obtaining
central positions (Ballard and Robel, 1974; Wiley, 1974;
Buechner and Roth, 1974), which are generally correlated with
mating preference by females.
   Large mating leks should be most common when females are
able to move freely through the habitat and are not forced to
compromise choice in the genetic quality of males to gain
material benefits or to avoid predation. Females may generally favor mating with males in aggregations because such
groupings (1) allow inexpensive, direct comparisons of physical attributes of many males, (2) facilitate tests by males
of competitors because of nearness of potential opponents,
and (3) provide indicators which females may use to judge the
outcomes of past aggressive encounters. Each of these conditions should cause females to generally favor males in groups.
If females can fully control sexual access of mates, then
males must respond to female demands to mate successfully.
Alexander (1975) pointed out that acoustical displays, luminescence, olfactory signals, and other cues generated by females,
which have been considered to have the exclusive function of

attracting males to insure fertilization, may often be important in assisting females to institute "private leks" at which·
a female may encourage aggressive interactions among males,
the outcomes of which may aid her in mate choice (see also
Cox and Le Boeuf, 1977).

Lek-like aggregations are common in insects as well as
vertebrates. Instances occur in a wide variety of groups
(Lepidoptera: Shields, 1967; Scott, 1972; Hymenoptera:
Zmarlecki and Morse, 1963; Diptera: Downes, 1969; Spieth,
1974a, b; Coleoptera: Lloyd, 1971). Among mammals (Le Boeuf,
1974; Gentry, 1970; Jarman, 1974) and some insects (Lin,
1963; Alcock, 1975; Alcock et al., 1976; Parker, 1970b-e,
1974a), males commonly control females. Even so, their behavior may strongly resemble a lek situation in that males
commonly fight for access to females or places where females
can be controlled (see discussion of *Scatophaga* behavior
below).

Alexander (1975) has also suggested that fighting is
important in mate choice as an indicator of the "prowess" of
males (see also Waage, 1973); and on this basis, he explains
lek formation. Alexander's argument differs from the one
proposed here in that he suggests that females choose males
because of the males' ability to fight. The suggested gain
from this mate choice pattern arises from the assumption that
females have been selected to choose fighting males as mates
in order to have sons who fight well and are preferred in
mate choice. Although it is clear how such a system might be
maintained once started, this explanation does not provide a
mechanism to explain why females who are unconstrained in
mate choice are initially programmed to choose fighting males.
No such problem exists if male fighting ability is correlated
with greater average genetic quality among offspring of both
sexes; then a net genetic gain should be expected among
females who initially tend to choose aggressive males.

"War Propaganda" and Courtship Patterns

On "true" leks, private leks, or even when males are
offering benefits derived from a territory, females are expected to test males through courtship displays. In some
instances, females may encourage males to send out highly
developed signals, which are often associated with aggressive
interactions among males. Here I suggest that males willing
to advertise their presence are either dominant and winners
in previous combat or will soon be tested if they have not
established such dominance. The greater the commotion a
female can force a prospective mate to raise, the more effective is his advertisement to other potential suitors with
whom she might mate. Males who can develop extravagant

displays from a particular mating territory or perch, yet
remain undisturbed through the whole courtship bout to be
dominant over other nearby males. Such displays evince that
the courting male is not a short-term intruder temporarily
occupying a position or territory of a higher ranking male.
If courtship is interrupted, a female's interests may be best
served by leaving that male and searching for another who can
maintain his position even after having provided a high
quality display. Courting queen butterflies may leave the
territory of a displaying male if chased by more than one
male (Brower et al., 1965). Robel and Ballard (1974) describe
female tendencies to avoid matings with males in leks without
stable dominance relationships.

Most courtship structure and behavior has been commonly
related to interspecific recognition of males by females.
However, these characters may have a primary function in
intraspecific communication among males. Fisher (1958) hinted
at the relationship between characters which influence other
males' aggressive tendencies and those which attract females.
He stated, "As a propagandist, the cock behaves as though he
knew that it was advantageous to impress the males as well as
the females of his species, and a sprightly bearing with fine
feathers and a triumphant song are quite as well adapted for
war propaganda as for courtship." Wynne-Edwards (1962), in
considering a very different hypothesis, recognized the same
relationship when he noted, ". . . adornments used in epidectic
(which includes fights among males) and amatory displays are
frequently the same." He continues, "The converse development
of adornments used solely for courtship and never for aggressive display seems at best to be relatively uncommon: examples
probably exist, though I have not succeeded in finding a clear
case among birds." In general, vivid and active displays
which most accurately show a male's dominance should be
favored by females not seriously threatened by predators
during the mating process. I will refer to structures and
behaviors which evolve in this context as products of selection under the war propaganda model.

Evolution of "Extravagant" Characters

Zahavi (1975) recognizes the need for female choice of
males to be based on a wide array of genetic characters.
However, the mechanism he proposes for how females might make
these decisions has received extensive criticism (Dawkins,
1976; Davis and O'Donald, 1976; Maynard Smith, 1976). Based
on Zahavi's "handicap" principle, females are expected to
choose males based on the existence of characters likely to
decrease males' fitness. Zahavi reasons that males who survive despite these recognizable handicaps are likely to

otherwise carry a better overall genetic complement than those
who have failed or have not carried the handicap. He maintains that this model provides an alternative to the "runaway
selection" model suggested by Fisher (1958) to explain the
evolution of what Fisher called "extravagant" characters.

However, both Maynard Smith (1976) and Davis and O'Donald
(1976) develop genetic models which suggest that the type of
mechanism described by Zahavi is not effective. (A simulation by Maynard Smith showed no condition where genes responsible for the handicap and others for its selection by females
could be favored. In their model, Davis and O'Donald found
that handicaps could be favored only under extremely high
intensity of selection against the handicap, a condition they
considered extremely unlikely.)

It is my view that the structure of male characters used
by females in mate selection does not correspond to what might
be expected if the "handicap" principle were operative. Characters in species in which mate location is not difficult appear
to be of two types--those of high signal value and those which
are effective weapons. In each case, they seem extremely
effective at carrying out specific functions. Deer antlers
(Lincoln, 1972) and beetle horns (see Eberhard, this volume)
realistically cannot be considered handicaps since they have
a very apparent role in helping males to directly control
conspecifics of both sexes. Exaggerated characters, such as
brightly colored feathers and scales, acoustical signals, and
odors, appear almost invariably to function in signaling male
dominance both to females and to other males. According to
the "war propaganda" hypothesis, a female who chooses a displaying male is choosing one who has earned his right to display.
Nondominant males who attempt to court through displaying are
promptly interrupted by dominant males. A female's encouragement of behavior which tests a male's dominance should include
not only extravagant displays but sufficiently long courtship
to insure that the behavior of her prospective mate has not
gone unnoticed by other males.

Gilliard (1969) describes behavior among birds with the
most extravagant displays, such as the Greater Bird of
Paradise, which has dominance territories. Males of the
Magnificent Bird of Paradise also appear to hold territories
in trees (Rand, 1940). Most of the species described in
detail by Gilliard have "loud, police whistle calls" and, in
some cases, plumes are raised when a male approaches a
territory-holding male's space. Male courtship displays
commonly involve extension of plumes and loud noises from
wing flapping.

Peacocks, which provide perhaps the most exaggerated
display, are identified by Zahavi as an example of handicap.
They also use their feathers primarily as a signal device.

Beebe (1926) states that

> Cockbirds, before they begin to fight, will often erect
> their tails about one another, although when the first
> actual threat is made these ornaments are folded away as
> compactly as possible . . . .

> There is no doubt about severe battles taking place, how-
> ever, judging from the circumstantial evidence of sturdy
> legs and sharp spines, and actual evidence of fierce
> encounters between captive birds. As I said these are
> usually preceded by the display on the part of both birds.

In domestic fowl (Lill, 1966) and wild grouse (Kruijt et
al., 1972; Kruijt and Hogan, 1967), frequency of display
correlates with mating success. Ballard and Robel (1974)
found that prairie chickens show the same trend. In addition,
they present evidence that dominant males prevent subdominants
from giving displays associated with courting.

Audubon (1831) says that male turkeys

> immediately fly towards the spot when a female calls from
> the ground. [Males then erect their tails, strut, quiver,
> and vocalize.] While thus occupied, the males often
> encounter each other, in which case desperate battles take
> place, ending in bloodshed, and often the loss of many
> lives, the weaker falling under the repeated blows inflict-
> ed on their head by the stronger.

While it is clear that displays used by males fit the "war-
propaganda" function described by Fisher, they seem inappropriate in the role of handicaps, as suggested by Zahavi. In
most cases, most or all of the plumage can be folded and
concealed from the view of predators outside the mating
season. Such structures seem designed to maximize signal
value for a minimum of caloric cost. A true handicap needs
to be demonstrably expensive to its bearer. Females should be
generally unimpressed by males with the ability to conceal the
handicap, as is common for most secondary sexual characters
which are not weapons. Contrary to this prediction, display
of such ornaments seems to strongly influence female mate
choice.

Davis and O'Donald (1976) present several additional
criticisms of the "handicap" principle which not only are
relevant to that model, but also to the analysis of selection
based on female preference for males able to demonstrate
dominance. They suggest that models in which females are
presumed to gain by choosing males of high genetic quality
are ineffective in explaining long-term patterns of mate
selection. Using an argument similar to the one attributed
to Williams (1975, see above), they state that "When the

combination of characters is as near the optimum as it can
get, there can be no advantage in mating with a more highly
selected male since no benefits can be received in an increase
in fitness in offspring." Davis and O'Donald imply that the
disappearance of genetic variability and associated benefits
in mate choice are the expected condition. This conclusion
is predictable considering their reaction to Zahavi's insist-
ence that selection is based on the composite of characters
in the whole genotype. They state, "The number of characters
that are being selected as a result of mating preferences
appears quite irrelevant to us, for different phases in a
polymorphism are being selected, each phenotype of which is
usually a combination of several characters." The apparent
disregard for the female's need to consider effects of
selection on alleles throughout the genome calls into question
their assertion that genetic variance and consequent gain from
mate choice are unimportant. Models relating to this problem
have already been discussed. These, considered together with
changes in selective coefficients likely to involve some of
the vast number of alleles in the genome in each generation,
suggest that gain is available for females from choice among
males of a given generation. In addition, long-term gain
from even occasional substitution of beneficial alleles may
be sufficient to maintain a constant mate selection pattern
among females.

The concluding remark made by Davis and O'Donald is that
"Zahavi offers no substantive criticisms of Fisher's theory
of evolution of mating preferences." These authors consider
the absence of such criticism important since "This theory
provides a sufficient explanation for difficulties that led
Zahavi to put forward his own theory." Even though Zahavi
has failed to put forward any suggestion of problems with the
"runaway process," as it is called by Fisher (1958), important
difficulties do exist with it. The general acceptance of this
model (O'Donald, 1967, 1973; Brown, 1975) suggests that
further discussion is warranted.

Generally unstated implicit assumptions in Fisher's model
are necessary for the pattern of character development he
describes, e.g., females must employ an open-ended preference
whereby the greatest extreme in a character present in a group
of males is favored. This requirement leads to problems with
the model. Fisher and later O'Donald (1967, 1973) suggest
that the "runaway process" will continue until balanced by
disadvantage, presumably through male mortality. However,
they do not state exactly how this equilibrium is established.

Two types of "equilibrium" outcomes might occur. One type
is stable and is expected when male mortality due to the
development of an exaggerated character is constant or nearly
constant between generations. Under these conditions,

directional selection should produce a situation in which
only one or a few males survive to breed in each generation.
If, for example, tail length is the character of concern,
males with shorter tails never reproduce so there is little
value in producing them.

The other "equilibrium" condition often may be unstable
and is associated with variable male mortality between
reproductive periods. Under this condition, short-tailed
males may reproduce in seasons when all of the long-tailed
males die. If mortality is unpredictable, there may be
disruptive selection for the character of concern. However,
this may also affect the pattern of female choice. Since
tail length of males is heritable, females who choose short-
tailed mates will produce sons that are more likely to live
under all conditions. These females who choose short-tailed
males will not lose, even in years when long-tailed males are
available, since they may mate within their own type and,
barring any differences in female mortality associated with
type and/or random events, should persist to the same degree
as females who have chosen long-tailed males. In bad years,
short-tail-choosing females have an advantage. Sons of long-
tail-choosing females die, and these females are forced to
mate with short-tailed males. The relative frequency of
short-tailed males and females who choose them should increase. If choice of short-tailed males is open-ended, as
was choice of long-tailed males, then selection for the
"runaway" character should be reversed. This will be fueled
not only by the open-ended selection process as described by
both Fisher and O'Donald, but by added gain for females who
produce males with a greater than average life expectancy.

It can be argued that within-type mating may lead to
inbreeding and consequent reductions in fitness (Maynard
Smith, 1956) and may cause such lines to decrease in frequency. However, when the limits of male survival are reached
under variable conditions, many females are likely to produce
short-tailed males; hence, inbreeding may be avoided.

Two kinds of information suggest that the "runaway process"
may be of limited significance. First, outbreeding populations with extreme shortages of males in which polygyny is
common do not exist. For example, Selander (1965) describes
biases of 2.42 females per male in the great-tailed grackle,
but even at these levels many more males are present than
females need in order to be effectively fertilized. In this
instance, the "runaway process" appears not to have stabilized
at a condition in which available males are limiting female
reproduction. Second, the "runaway process" suggests that
females would choose males based only on physical characteristics. Typical lek behavior, in which females appear to
choose males based on their position, would only be predicted

from the "runaway selection" model if differences in tail
length could account for male position on the lek.   However,
males fight for position, and since there is no *a priori*
reason to suspect that fighting ability is enhanced by exaggerated characters, it appears that female choice based
ultimately on male fighting ability does not support the "runaway selection" model.   One might argue that dominant males
keep other males from displaying and thereby limit female
ability to survey other males.   However, if females were only
interested in the size or intensity of display, subordinate
males with high quality displays should leave the lek and
females should seek them out.   Lill (1976) describes male and
female manakins feeding together during the mating season with
little suggestion of attempts by males to display off the lek.
This also seems to be true for other lekking species in which
males show more highly developed dimorphism.

Mate choice based on selection of dominant males, according
to the "war propaganda" hypothesis, provides perhaps the most
likely explanation for the evolution of Fisher's "extravagant
characters."   This model also may have some significance in
territorial species in which males control material benefits.
A display, perhaps not as well developed as might occur in a
genetic choice system, could show that a male present on a
territory is the true owner and not simply visiting while the
owner is temporarily away.   Certainly, various modes of
signaling are well known for most species with resource-based
territories (crickets: Alexander, 1961; grasshoppers: Otte
and Joern, 1975; birds: Howard, 1974; fish: Assem, 1967;
lizards: Evans, 1938).   Even in these cases, the signal may
not only indicate possession of resources and consequent
ability to disburse material benefits, but may also serve as
an indicator of the genetic quality of an individual male.

Although Fisher (1958) recognized the essence of the "war-
propagandist" model, he clearly did not intend for it to be
used to describe the wide variety of characters outlined here.
This is shown in the sentence concluding the discussion of
this model: "Male ornaments acquired in this way might be
striking, but could scarcely ever become extravagant."
Information presented on the behavior of cocks who display
"extravagant" characters, as well as problems with the
"runaway" model he apparently favored in explaining these
cases, suggest that a revision in thinking of how sexual
selection operates may be in order.

RESOURCE STRUCTURE AND MALE ABILITY TO INFLUENCE FEMALE MATE
CHOICE

The Effect of Resource Structure on Male Control of Resources

In the equilibrium model presented above, knowledge of
male variation in ability to control resources appears as a
key element in predicting patterns of mating success. Two
factors are important in determining this ability: (1) success
of an individual male in dominating conspecifics in aggressive
encounters and (2) structure of resources used by males to
influence mating decisions by females. Brown (1964) considered variation in aggressive ability of individuals as central
to their ability to hold territories. Trivers (1972) discussed
the evolution of male size and provided data to show its
relation to reproductive success. A more general model which
discusses strategies of individual males in holding resources
has been discussed by Parker (1974b). He models male decisions to fight in a habitat in which resources are subdivided
into units of equal quality. Differences in male ability to
win fights are considered in terms of varying physical
characteristics, which are valued according to their ability
to confer "resource holding power."

Resource structure, defined as the spatial pattern and
richness of resources along spatial and temporal axes, has
been considered to a more limited extent. Verner (1964)
discussed the relationship of male territoriality and actual
levels of benefits males could provide and thereby affect
female mating decisions. He compared his own and Kale's
(1965) work with marsh wrens and suggested that the different
degrees of polygyny enjoyed by males in the two studies would
be related to territory shape. Kale's birds bred along a
canal and territories had long, lateral dimensions. The
territories of Verner's birds were in swamps and were more
nearly circular. It was suggested that the oblong shape of
territories belonging to Kale's birds limited the effective
area a male could defend (see review by Emlen and Oring, 1977).

Fretwell and Lucas (1969) developed a model which related
aspects of resource structure to male ability to control
resources. Male success from aggressive behavior was tied to
variance in the quality of habitats occupied by males. They
predicted that males fill various levels of habitat quality
in accordance with their ability to displace lower-ranking
males. The best males gain the best habitat sites, while
males of lowest ability obtain low quality sites which would
otherwise be unoccupied.

An attempt is made here to develop a more general model.
However, predicting patterns of male control of resources
directly from resource structure is difficult because of the

large number of spatial configurations possible under conditions where resources are unevenly dispersed. It is unlikely
that each specific configuration could be conveniently described. In addition, males with differing abilities to move
may react differently to a given pattern of resource distribution. Classification of resource structures into types thus
appears as the only feasible approach to using resource
characteristics and predicting how they affect male ability
to set territories. The approach used here is not to consider
resource structure directly, but to deal with resources as
seen by males who control them. Changes in structure can be
viewed in terms of their relevance to males. Aside from
reducing the number of resource configurations which must be
considered, this approach avoids variations in level of male
control due to interspecific differences in males' abilities.
With minimal knowledge of the physical capabilities of males
attempting to control resources, resource structure can be
used to predict the distribution of material benefits among
males.

Consider a situation in which all resources available for
females of a population for successful rearing of offspring
are condensed into a minute clump. A dominant male exists who
is able to exclude other males and unreceptive females from
these resources. If females are fully dependent on the
resources he controls, such a male would father most, if not
all, offspring of the next generation. Expanding the area
over which resources are distributed is likely to handicap the
dominant male in his attempts to control resources. Defense
of a larger perimeter results in increased energetic costs and,
together with physical limitations on movements, should lead
to a maximum *defense perimeter*. A spread of resources beyond
the maximum perimeter which a male can effectively defend
leads to an automatic increase in prospects for matings by
subdominant males.

Males who have escaped the influence of the dominant can
establish their own territories and influence the pattern of
female mating decisions in their favor. Where strong dominance relationships exist between males, an increase in the
area over which resources are distributed should cause a
reduction in population-wide variation in reproductive success. High levels of dispersion may allow all males some
access to resources and may even reduce variance in success
to zero, especially under conditions in which mating decisions
are based solely on the amount of resources controlled by an
individual.

A similar shift in resource structure can be considered
under conditions in which males are more nearly equal in their
ability to control resources. Inability of any one male to
control all resources will lead to either temporal or spatial

subdivision of the resource. Although males may have equal
overall ability, males may focus risk and energetic expenditure into a small time segment so they can control the resource and gain exclusive matings over a short period.
Alternatively, males may subdivide the resource into small
territories, all contained within the perimeter of one individual, since, over long periods, it is unlikely that a male
can be continuously excluded by another of equal ability.

Effects of changes in the degree of dispersion of resources
can also be considered in cases in which an increase in the
variance in the pattern of resource distribution accompanies
the spread of resources. The initial condition may be similar
to the first case in which the dominant male controls all
matings. As resources spread, the situation becomes identical
to the one described by Fretwell and Lucas (1969) and the same
results are predicted. The aggressive ability of males is
correlated with the quality of the position they win.

If resources vary in quality, but males are of constant
ability, prediction is more difficult. Males in good habitats
are likely to be challenged at various intervals by others of
very similar aggressive ability. If movement between territories and fights are low cost, and owners of good territories
do not have a consistent advantage, then replacement should
be common. Individual males may spend nearly equal amounts of
time in the various quality habitats.

These models involve three of four variables important in
determining patterns of male control. Two of these deal with
resources and are defined by the limits of male ability to
control resources. By assuming that males have a maximum
diameter that they can defend, the *number of defense perimeters* can be used as a measure of the total area over which
resources are spread. *Variance in quality among perimeters*
can be used to measure the degree of clumping of resources
relative to a male's ability to cover some limited area. An
accurate measure of resource clumping requires several parameters, among which is *variance among perimeters*. However,
by assuming homogeneity of resource quality within perimeters
and by establishing a protocol to standardize the positioning
of perimeters on resources, e.g., establishing the first
perimeter so that it covers the richest area and successively
placing subsequent perimeters on the highest quality area
that remains uncovered, this one measure may give reasonable
estimates of variance in resource distribution.

Males competing for control of resources are rated in terms
of *variance in aggressive ability* as measured by differences
between individuals in their ability to win conflicts over
resources valued by females. *Number of males* has not been
dealt with, but changes in this variable parallel those in
which the number of resource perimeters changes. Increase in

the number of males is equivalent to reducing the number of perimeters if in each case variance in quality of resources among perimeters and in aggressive abilities among males remains unchanged.

Resource Structure and Resource Defense

The variables which describe the proportion of individually held resources are also important in determining the value of the resource control strategy. If the number of defense perimeters in which resources occur exceeds the number of territorial males, then females and nonterritorial males are free to use uncontrolled resources. Females not limited to controlled resources can avoid compromises based on the need for resources in choosing a male. The presence of resources outside the control of males allows other males the option of collecting on resources when benefits derived from this behavior represent an effective attractant to potential mates.

The success of both females and nonterritorial males in using these unprotected resources is also affected by variation in resource quality. High variance in resource quality will allow territorial males to concentrate resource defense efforts on high quality areas. These hot spots reduce the rate at which males lose control of resources as the resources become spread over an increasingly wide area (see Fig. 5).

A decrease in the percent of all resources controlled by all males may lead some individuals to abandon resource control as a strategy for attracting mates. Alternatives for these males include (1) collecting on resources and then using the items collected to attract mates or (2) abandoning efforts to use resources in mate attraction and becoming subject to genetic-based evaluation by females. Transition from resource control or resource collection was dealt with in the equilibrium model above. The first of these two kinds of transitions is most likely if the formerly defended resource is not easily collected, at least in terms of the immediate physical abilities of the animal being considered. Examples of such noncollectable resources are oviposition sites of odonates and nest sites for birds. Alternatively, food--or time and energy to obtain it--is commonly a limiting resource (Lack, 1954) for which collection and control may be important in determining male success in attracting mates.

Successful initiation of resource collection must be related to conditions where some male-female pairs are able to collect more resources useful to the female than she can obtain being paired to a territorial male and using resources collected and defended by him. At least six variables are likely to affect the value of collection and control strategies

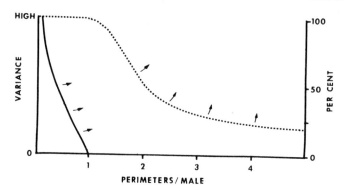

Fig. 5. Change in number of defense perimeters per male and
its effect on variance in the proportion of resources held by
individuals (solid line) and the percent of resources controlled
by all males (dotted line). Spreading males out over the
available resources reduces the effects of dominant males on
individual ability to hold resources. Consequently, variation
among males in the share of resources held by individuals
decreases. This spreading may also reduce overall male ability to control available resources. Some variation in the
aggressive abilities of males is assumed; lines in the figure
show relationships when all perimeters are equal in value.
Increased variation in the quality of perimeters causes a
shift in curves resulting from a higher variance among males
in the proportion of resources controlled and a smaller percent of any uncontrolled resources.

to males. These include (1) variation in control of resources
among males, (2) percent resources controlled by all males,
(3) ability of males to guarantee benefits, (4) correlation
of control with genetic quality, (5) efficiency of resource
collection both on and off territories by both sexes, and
(6) the degree of contribution of collected benefits by
territorial males.

A decrease in the proportion of resources controlled by
males is likely to favor attempts at resource collection, but
predicting the level at which such a transition is likely to
begin is difficult. If females are very inefficient in
collecting resources that are valuable to them and there is
low variance in the quality of resources, then collection may
become an important strategy with only a small fraction of
the resources beyond the control of males. However, if
females need as much foraging space as possible and are very
efficient in collecting available resources, then males need
to control only a little more than 50% of all resources for
resource control to remain as a dominant strategy. Additional
difficulties for prediction of the relative importance of

resource control and collection strategies come from our
inability to evaluate the effect of high levels of variance
in the amount of resources controlled by individual males.
High variance may suggest a decreased tendency for territory-
holding males to assist individual mates in resource collection, especially since such efforts by these males might
detract from their ability to hold territories needed to
attract additional females. However, high variance in control
implies clumping of resources within a few defense perimeters
and perhaps greater efficiency for females in collecting
resources in these defended areas. The first effect would
tend to devalue the controlling male, while the second is
likely to enhance his attractiveness.

Resource Structure and Male Fighting Ability

In dealing with the evolution of characters in males which
enhance their aggressive ability, Trivers (1972) identified
two primary patterns for the expenditure of reproductive
effort by males--those involving "appreciable male parental
investment" and those in which males have "little or no
parental investment." Individual success among noninvesting
males is suggested to be strongly dependent on the level of
effort made by other males. Males who are able to dominate
others are more likely to enjoy frequent matings. Success in
male-male encounters is correlated with the amount of effort
spent by males on characters which enhance their ability to
dominate others. In systems in which some males gain from
heavy investment in characters which enhance their ability to
win fights, Trivers (1972) predicts that the mating success
of individual males remains low until there are very high
levels of effort in reproduction. A sharp increase in success
is expected to follow this effort (see also Gadgil, 1972).
Trivers suggests that competition in "investing" males is
likely to be less severe. As a result, no escalation of
effort is predicted to occur; expenditure of effort by males
is not directed toward the high degree of development of
specialized structures common in males who frequently engage
in combat. Although Trivers did not tie the evolution of
these characters to resource structure, these relationships
are easily developed.

Although the suggested dichotomy in reproductive competition by investing and noninvesting males is often true,
exceptions occur which make a more detailed understanding of
evolution of patterns for expending reproductive effort
important. Among noninvesting males, those who do not use
resources to influence female mating decisions may commonly
be involved in direct physical encounters with other males

(but see below). Dominance in such conflicts was understood by Darwin (1871) to be important in determining levels of mating success and selection of males for development of structures which aid in winning sex-related combat. However, use of resources by males may cause expenditure-of-effort patterns to be most closely tied to resource structure. Resources distributed in a small number of clumps, relative to the number of males, provide dominant males with the opportunity to gain from their ability to exclude nearby competitors. Areas which individuals might defend overlap, and males successful in excluding sexual competitors within the contested area gain control of a large share of the available resources. The potential to achieve control provides strong selection for increased expenditure of effort in resource control. Spreading out resources leads to a reduction in male opportunity to gain from extreme investment in characters required for success in aggression; there is a smaller payoff from winning which does not justify diversion of parental investment or added risk to the developing juvenile. Reduced prospects for gain from winning fights favor adjustment of potential investment, which may be devoted to characters useful in allowing some males to dominate other males.

Benefits delivered to females before mating may serve to attract mates and detract from a male's ability to provide investment. In some cases, these contributions may constitute the total items delivered by males to either females or their offspring and reduce male ability to invest directly in offspring. Although such contributions are not considered parental investment by Trivers, their effect on female success and male ability to attract mates is quite similar. By considering patterns of male effort which include premating contributions of benefits by males (see Alexander and Borgia, this volume), the suggested dichotomy in male strategies can be extended to explain most common patterns of male behavior.

In examples discussed so far, only two real alternatives have been considered for spending reproductive effort. Another context in which noninvesting males are not likely to devote effort to activities or structures related to combat may occur at extremely low population densities. In this context males searching for females may exhaust themselves in the search for mates. Scarcity of competitors suggests very limited need to commit effort to the development of fighting ability and little residual ability to invest in mates when they are found.

Resource Structure and Male Mating Success: Experimental Support

Other studies besides that of wrens (Verner, 1964) correlate polygyny with the quality of male territories (Zimmerman,
1966, 1971; Haartman, 1969; Verner and Willson, 1966; Verner
and Engelsen, 1970). Although these studies support suggested
relationships between resource structure and variance in male
success, they do not correlate characteristics of males with
the ability to supply females with items from the habitat that
they need. Also, the correlative nature of these data leaves
some question as to the true nature of cause and effect in
these relationships.

Experiments involving changes in availability of resources
used by females as oviposition sites have allowed me to test
the effect of these changes on the mating success of males of
various size classes in the fly *Scatophaga stercoraria*. In
these experiments, cow dung, which is used as an oviposition
site by females, was placed in two levels of abundance under
conditions of high and low fly density in an isolated cow
pasture. Male *Scatophaga,* which are highly variable in size,
hold territories and/or patrol oviposition sites. These
behaviors enhance their ability to capture females who come
to the dung pat to oviposit. After males capture females,
they copulate and then guard them during oviposition (see
Parker, 1970b). Availability of oviposition sites was
controlled by removing all fresh dung pats deposited by
grazing cattle. Fresh dung of constant quality was put out
under two conditions--high (two hundred pats) and low (six
pats) availability. Each pat was 15 cm in diameter. Fly
density was controlled by running experiments at times during
the mating season when numbers of breeding flies are known to
differ (see Hammer, 1941; Parker, 1970a). Mating success of
males was measured by counting frequency of copulations by
males in each size class. Results suggest that under conditions of both low and high fly density, an increase in resource
availability lowers the mean size of the copulating male. In
addition, the mean size of males who can obtain positions on
the dung pat shows a similar decrease (Fig. 6).

These data support the notion that the spreading of males
over a resource tends to reduce variance in mating success, a
prediction one might make if females used only resources in
mating decisions. Observations suggest that females choose
pats for reasons other than the males who occupy them and that
males capture the majority of females in the vicinity of the
pats.

Large males influenced the mating success of small males
in at least two ways. Attacks by large males caused small
males to move off fresh dung pats. Large males also successfully stole females from copulating or guarding smaller males.

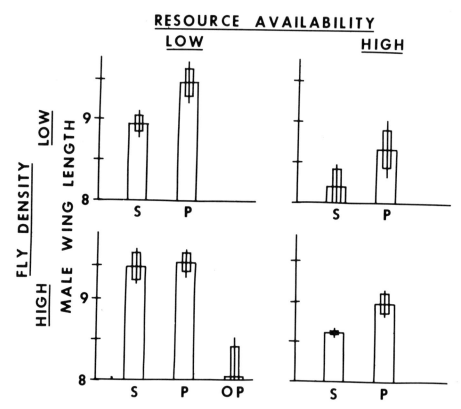

Fig. 6. Results of resource manipulation experiments performed at high and low male density conditions. S represents the mean size of unpaired males who are on pats, P is the mean size of males paired to copulating or ovipositing females, and OP is the mean size of males not in the immediate vicinity of pats. Bars and lines represent 95% and 99% confidence intervals, respectively. Under both conditions of male density, shifts in resource availability appear to cause significant changes in the mean size of copulating males.

At low densities of males per pat, small males chased from pats by large males could move to unoccupied pats and capture any females that came to these pats. As the number of pats was decreased, males were forced onto fewer resources and interactions with large males caused smaller males to leave the dung pats.

Territories were common at low male densities per pat, but as density increased, males scrambled to capture females without obvious attempts to remove conspecifics from the dung. Small males apparently avoided these pats because of (1) the

high probability of being replaced by larger males while
guarding females, and (2) costs from being attacked by large
males searching for females in the vicinity of the pat.

In the models presented above, it was assumed that females
choose males on the basis of the resources that they offer.
Increasing the males per unit area of resource was predicted
to cause a reduction in territory size, much like the model
proposed by Huxley (1934). In *Scatophaga,* females have
limited ability to choose mates, and it appears that the
primary function of male territories is to aid males in
capturing females. As male density increases, defense of
small areas becomes ineffective if, as appears to happen,
nonterritorial males can capture females before they reach
areas where males' territories are formed at low density.
Ability of large males to control females during and after
copulation, and their inability to effectively remove other
large males from the available resources, eliminate opportunities for gain through attempted resource control at high
male densities per pat.

The relationship of sexual dimorphism to resource structure
and the effect of each on male-male combat are supported by
these experiments with dung flies. If males are forced onto
a few pats, advantage to large males is shown by their
increased mating success. The spreading of resources and
increased relative success of small males suggest a reduction
in the advantage gained from large size. Maintaining low
density conditions should commonly cause selection for reduced average size among males. Apparently, increased size
comes at some cost in terms of mortality, and when it provides no net gain in reproduction, selection would favor
individuals who avoided additional growth.

A convincing comparative study also points out the relationship between resource structure and the development of
sexual dimorphisms. Alexander et al. (1978) correlate the
degree of sexual dimorphism with harem size for four mammalian groups. In this case, groups of females may be considered
resources, and harem size a direct measure of the number of
females per diameter containing resources.

Variation in Male Ability To Control Resources

Variability in adaptations related to defense of resources
might be best considered by comparing growth strategies of
individuals placed in habitats of different quality. Considering size as a typical sexually selected character, males
must make a "decision" as to how much risk of mortality to
take in order to reach a size which enables them to most
effectively compete with other males. Particularly in

organisms in which growth is restricted to larval habitats,
and which receive no parental assistance, risk due to mortality during growth can be related to the length of time an
individual spends in its larval habitat (Wilbur and Collins,
1973). Larger adult size also results from a longer larval
growth period. Male gain from large size must be weighed
against increased risks (Williams, 1966; Wiley, 1974) to
determine the best size at which to leave the larval habitat.
In cases in which parents are the primary source of resources
needed for growth, there may be a similar time-dependent
growth rate. However, the decision lies with both parent and
offspring. For both parent and offspring, increased commitment must be considered primarily in terms of decreased
parental ability to contribute to other offspring (Trivers,
1974).

Such relationships are considered in Fig. 7, in which gain
from the male decision to grow to a larger size is compared
to the cost derived from increased mortality and delayed or
lost reproduction. Slope of the benefit curve is determined
by the added payoff in reproductive success for a mature male
about to reproduce who shows an infinitesimal increase in
size. He competes in a population in which all other males
are the same size and have not experienced this same tendency
to grow. The cost curve shows the effect on mortality and
reproductive rate related to the same change in male size.
Successive instances of directional change in size are predicted to occur until the difference between costs and
benefits reaches a maximum.

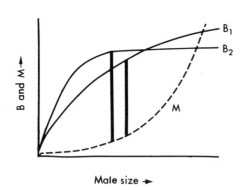

Male size →

Fig. 7. The effect of
increased male size on
costs of growth (M) and
associated benefits of
increased size. B_1
shows a relatively con-
stant increase in gain
for males·with addition-
al size, which could be
related to conditions
in which resources are
clumped. Males under
conditions which show
the B_2 pattern of gain
probably occur where
resources are spread
far apart and increased
size leads to little
measurable gain in
mating success.

The pattern of gain from changes in male size depends upon resource structure. Extreme clumping of resources allows a consistent gain from increased size, particularly in populations with many males. Spreading of resources causes a limit in gain from size and a flattening of the gain curve. Assuming the same association of mortality with size, the predicted size for males when resources are spread is much smaller than when resources are clumped.

Populations in which equilibrium male size occurs in a flat portion of the gain curve may be considered to have realized the full potential for developing dimorphism as determined by the structure of resources. In other cases in which males can only control territories smaller than they can effectively cover, limits on the development of characters needed for defense are, at least theoretically, determined by conditions of growth.

The growth conditions for all individuals within a population may not be identical. This is likely to have important effects on male patterns of competition. Insects which develop in suboptimal host plants, or in ponds of different temperatures or prey density, must adjust accepted levels of risk to reach a competitively successful adult size. Parents may also differ in the amount of effort they are able to devote to sons (Trivers and Willard, 1973). Open sexual competition among adult males will force growth "decisions" of a developing male in any habitat to be weighed against those made under the best prevailing conditions for juvenile development.

Developmental strategies of growing males in three habitats that differ in quality are considered in Fig. 8. Those that grow in the lowest quality habitat, even when taking maximum risks, may not be able to attain the level of aggressive ability of males who grow up in the best habitat. Males in the habitat of intermediate quality can equal the quality of males produced under the best conditions, but only with high levels of risk. Under conditions in which there is little predictable variance in the quality of resources controlled by adults, there may be few, if any, opportunities for reproduction by males who develop in low quality habitats. However, variance in resource quality, the number of males, and the spread of resources may allow males who develop in low quality habitats to occasionally hold resources. In a system with two states of resource dispersion, males who grow in low quality habitats may only be able to gain access to resources under conditions of high resource dispersion. All growth and behavior of males in low quality habitats are keyed to success under conditions in which resources are highly dispersed when these individuals are adults. If there is some possibility of added reproduction by these males when

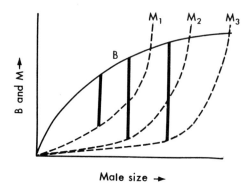

Fig. 8. Variable growth conditions lead to different costs to
males in obtaining a sufficient size for effective sexual
competition. Males growing under the worst conditions (M_1)
cannot, with any level of risk, equal the optimal size of
males who grow in the best habitat (M_3). Males growing under
intermediate conditions (M_2) can reach that size, but only
with high levels of risk. Decisions about size for males
who grow under the best conditions may change with an increase in the number of males from other habitats who attain
what might otherwise be their optimal size.

resources are condensed, individuals may evolve to take added
risks so as to exploit the preferred habitat. Males' strategies for development will generally depend on the commonness
of each condition of sexual competition and the costs to
males of each of the growth strategies. Developmental models
discussed here are designed for organisms, such as insects,
in which growth is complete before sexual maturity. Similar
kinds of decisions must be made by vertebrates and other
organisms with less determinate patterns of growth if growth
is less efficient at different stages of the life cycle, such
as after sexual maturity.

   A constant pattern of variation in resource structure may
allow the development of genetically determined polymorphisms
for male size and other sexually selected attributes.
Genetic variation in males necessary to cause polymorphisms
is most likely maintained in a frequency-dependent fashion.
The balance of genetic alternatives is adjusted in relation
to (1) the proportion of resources to which morphs are best
adapted and (2) the relative cost of growth to produce the
ideal phenotype for each condition of sexual competition.
This form of polymorphism may be most likely where there is
little variation in juvenile growth conditions which might
predispose individuals to certain strategies of resource

acquisition. Despite the plausibility of these genetically
determined polymorphisms associated with resource structure,
their occurrence seems limited (Charlesworth and Charlesworth,
1975; but see Gadgil, 1972; Gadgil and Taylor, 1975), while
there is abundant evidence for occurrence of polymorphisms
apparently based on varying growth conditions (Wynne-Edwards,
1962).

SUMMARY

   It is unlikely that a single model of sexual selection
can be developed which is sufficient to explain all mating
associations. Four typical patterns of male-female pairing
are discussed. These show varying degrees of participation
by members of each sex in mating decisions. Differences
apparently result from variation in the relative ability of
members of each sex to gain control of conditions in which
mating occurs. Outcomes of intrasexual shifts in control may
be largely determined by ecological conditions.
   Of the different types of mating associations, female
choice based on male ability to generate both material and
genetic benefits is given special attention. This is done
because of difficulties in (1) female attempts to weight the
value of each type of benefit and (2) effective transfer of
benefits between the sexes. A model is developed in which
females shop among males to maximize gain from the combination of benefits received. Patterns of male mating success
are predicted on the basis of (1) distribution of each type
of benefit among males, (2) female need of the two types of
benefits, and (3) the effect of previous matings on male
ability to discharge both types of benefits. Transfer of
material benefits in this model assumes that members of each
sex can effectively guarantee delivery of benefits before
mating. Such an approach implies that (1) the use of the term
"desertion" by Trivers (1972) and others is inappropriate for
most conditions in which males leave before nesting is
complete, and (2) males may often be able to bargain through
the control of benefits to avoid instances of cuckoldry.
   The four patterns of male-female interactions can be
organized into a dominance hierarchy. If conditions are
sufficient for the development of more than one of these
strategies, then the relative position of the strategies
involved in this hierarchy predicts which one will occur.
Strategies in which males have the highest relative influence
in mate choice tend to be more dominant.
   Strategies and implications resulting from the use of
genetic and material benefits in mate attraction are considered in detail. In apparent genetic choice systems, the "war

propaganda" model is developed to consider the evolution of
what Fisher (1958) called "exaggerated characters" and
common patterns of courtship. Success in fights among males
(Alexander, 1975) is seen as a key character for females in
making appropriate mating decisions about the genome-wide
quality of their prospective mate. Fisher's "runaway selection" model is criticized and suggested to be inferior to the
"war propaganda" model. The key elements of the "war propaganda" model are extended to explain courtship patterns,
particularly in species in which males generally transfer
only genetic benefits.

Problems of the genetic choice model are discussed and
plausible explanations consistent with the effective function-
ing of that model are presented. Two models for the maintenance of genetic variation at levels sufficient to allow for
females using genetic criteria to gain through nonrandom
mating are presented. Interpretations of experiments on mate
choice which suggest selection of mates based on single
alleles are questioned.

Aspects of male population and resource structure are used
to describe (1) the overall importance of material benefits
to females and (2) the relative ability of individuals to
provide benefits. Experimental data are provided which support the hypothesis that changes in resource structure can
have important effects on patterns of resource control by
males and on male reproductive success. The relationship of
resource structure to the ability of males to control versus
provide benefits derived from resources is related to patterns
of male population and resource structure. Factors affecting
variation in male ability are also considered and these are
reviewed in Fig. 9.

ACKNOWLEDGMENTS

I thank the following people whose helpful discussions
aided me in developing this paper: M. Feaver, M. Hirschfield,
J.L. Hoogland, R.D. Howard, C. Kagarise, L. Kirkendall, K.
Noonan, R.B. Payne, D. Ruby, P. Sherman, R.W. Storer, R.
Thornhill, D.W. Tinkle, and, especially, R.D. Alexander.
J.L. Hoogland, L. Blumer, and R.D. Alexander read the paper
and improved it in many ways. Support for field research
has been provided by the following groups: Theodore Roosevelt
Memorial Fund, Sigma Xi, The University of Michigan, and the
National Science Foundation (BM575-17806). Diane B. de
Forest gave technical and financial support. This paper is
dedicated to the late Jasper Loftus-Hills, who greatly
stimulated my interest in problems relating to sexual
selection.

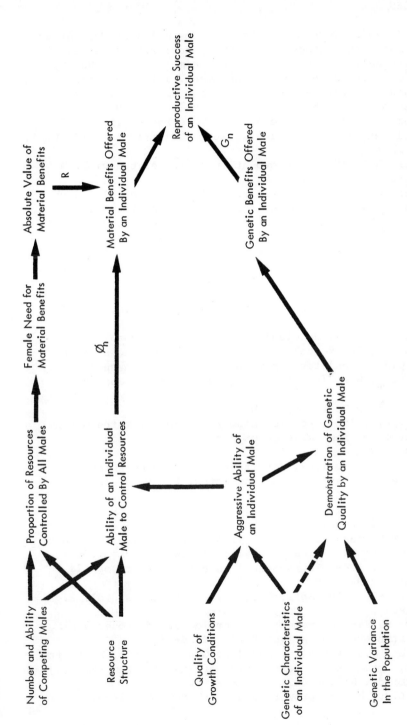

Fig. 9. Summary of relationships among variables influencing male reproductive success in situations where benefits males offer originate from defended resources.

REFERENCES

Alcock, J. 1975. Territorial behavior by males of *Philanthus multimaculatus* (Hymenoptera: Sphecidae) with a review of territoriality in male Sphecids. *Anim. Behav.* 23:889-895.

Alcock, J., C.E. Jones, and S. Buchmann. 1976. Location before emergence of the female bee, *Centris pallida,* by its male (Hymenoptera: Anthophoridae). *J. Zool.* 179:189-199.

Alexander, R.D. 1961. Aggressiveness, territoriality, and sexual behaviour in field crickets (Orthoptera: Gryllidae). *Behaviour* 17:130-223.

Alexander, R.D. 1974. The evolution of social behavior. *Ann. Rev. Ecol. Syst.* 5:325-383.

Alexander, R.D. 1975. Natural selection and specialized chorusing behavior in acoustical insects. *In* Pimentel, D. (ed.), *Insects, Science, and Society*. Academic Press, New York.

Alexander, R.D. 1977. Natural selection and the analysis of human sociality. *In* Goulden, C.E. (ed.), *Changing Scenes in Natural Sciences*. Bicentennial symposium monograph, Philadelphia Academy of Natural Sciences. 283-377.

Alexander, R.D., and G. Borgia. 1978. Group selection, altruism, and the hierarchical organization of life. *Ann. Rev. Ecol. Syst.* (in press).

Alexander, R.D., J. Hoogland, R. Howard, K. Noonan, and P.W. Sherman. 1978. Sexual dimorphisms and breeding systems in Pinnepids, Ungulates, Primates and Man. *In* Chagnon, N.A., and Irons, W.G. (eds.), *Evolutionary Biology and Human Social Behavior: An Anthropological Perspective*. Duxbury Press, North Scituate, Mass. (in press).

Anderson, W.W. 1969. Polymorphism resulting from the mating advantage of rare male genotypes. *Proc. Nat. Acad. Sci.* 64:190-197.

Assem, J. van den. 1967. Territory in the three-spined stickleback, *Gasterosteus aculeatus*. *Behaviour* (Suppl.) 16:i-viii,1-164.

Audubon, J.J. 1831. *Ornithological Bibliography*. Vol. 1. Black, Edinburgh.

Ballard, W.B., and R.J. Robel. 1974. Reproductive importance of dominant male greater prairie chickens. *Auk* 91:75-85.

Bateman, A.J. 1948. Intra-sexual selection in *Drosophila*. *Heredity* 2:349-368.

Beebe, W. 1926. *Pheasants: Their Lives and Homes*. Vol. 2. Doubleday, Page and Co., New York.

Brandler, R. 1967. Movements of female ruffed grouse during the mating season. *Wilson Bull.* 79:28-36.

Bray, O.E., J.J. Kennelly, and J.L. Guarino. 1975. Fertility of eggs produced on territories of vasectomized red-wing blackbirds. *Wilson Bull.* 87:187-195.

Brower, L.P., J.V.Z. Brower, and F.P. Cranston. 1965.

Courtship behavior in the queen butterfly, *Danaus gilippus berenice* (Cramer). *Zoologica* 50:1-39.

Brown, J.L. 1964. The evolution of diversity in avian territorial systems. *Wilson Bull.* 76:161-169.

Brown, J.L. 1975. *The Evolution of Behavior*. Norton, New York.

Buechner, H.K., and D.H. Roth. 1974. The lek system in the Uganda kob antelope. *Amer. Zool.* 14:145-162.

Campanella, P.J., and L.L. Wolf. 1973. Temporal leks as a mating system in a temperate zone dragonfly (Odonata: Anisoptera), I: *Plathemis lydia* (Drury). *Behaviour* 47:4-87.

Charlesworth, D., and B. Charlesworth. 1975. Sexual selection and polymorphism. *Amer. Nat.* 109:465-469.

Cox, C., and B. Le Boeuf. 1977. Female incitation in the northern elephant seal. *Amer. Nat.* 111:317-355.

Cronin, E.W., and P.W. Sherman. 1977. A resource-based mating system: the orange-rumped honeyguide. *Living Bird* 15:5-32.

Darwin, C. 1871. *The Descent of Man and Selection in Relation to Sex*. John Murray, London.

Davis, J.W.F., and P. O'Donald. 1976. Sexual selection for a handicap: a critical analysis of Zahavi's model. *J. Theor. Biol.* 57:345-354.

Dawkins, R. 1976. *The Selfish Gene*. Oxford Press, New York.

Dawkins, R., and T.R. Carlisle. 1976. Parental investment, mate desertion and a fallacy. *Nature* 262:131-133.

Downes, J.A. 1969. The swarming and mating flight of Diptera. *Ann. Rev. Ent.* 14:271-298.

Downhower, J.F., and K.B. Armitage. 1971. The yellow-bellied marmot and the evolution of polygamy. *Amer. Nat.* 105:355-370.

Ehrman, L. 1970. Simulation of the mating advantage in mating of rare *Drosophila* males. *Science* 167:905-906.

Ehrman, L., and P.A. Parsons. 1976. *The Genetics of Behavior*. Sinauer, Sunderland, Mass.

Emlen, S.T., and L.W. Oring. 1977. Ecology, sexual selection, and the evolution of mating systems. *Science* 197:215-223.

Evans, L.T. 1938. Cuban field studies on territoriality of the lizard, *Anolis sagrei*. *J. Comp. Psych.* 25:97-125.

Ewing, A.W., and A. Manning. 1967. The evolution and genetics of insect behavior. *Ann. Rev. Ent.* 12:471-494.

Fincham, J. 1972. Heterozygous advantage as a likely basis for enzyme polymorphism. *Heredity* 28:387-391.

Fisher, R. 1958. *The Genetical Theory of Natural Selection*. 2nd ed. Dover, New York.

Ford, E.B. 1971. *Ecological Genetics*. 3rd ed. Chapman and Hall, London.

Fretwell, S.D., and H.L. Lucas, Jr. 1969. On territorial behavior and other factors influencing habitat distribution in birds. *Acta Biotheoret.* 19:16-36.

Gadgil, M. 1972. Male dimorphism as a consequence of sexual

selection. *Amer. Nat.* 106:574-580.

Gadgil, M., and C. Taylor. 1975. Plausible models of sexual selection and polymorphism. *Amer. Nat.* 109:470-471.

Gentry, R.L. 1970. *Social Behavior of the Stellar Sea Lion.* Ph.D. Thesis, Univ. California, Santa Cruz.

Ghiselin, M. 1974. *The Economy of Nature and the Evolution of Sex.* Univ. California Press, Berkeley.

Gilliard, E.T. 1969. *Birds of Paradise and Bower Birds.* Weidenfield and Nicolson, London.

Haartman, L. von. 1969. Nest site selection and evolution of polygamy in European passerine birds. *Ornis Fennica* 46:1-12.

Haldane, J.B. 1954. An exact test for randomness of mating. *J. Genet.* 52:631-635.

Hamilton, W.D. 1967. Extraordinary sex ratios. *Science* 156:477-488.

Hamilton, W.D. 1971. Geometry for the selfish herd. *J. Theor. Biol.* 31:295-311.

Hammer, O. 1941. *Biological and Ecological Investigations of Flies Associated with Pasturing Cattle and Their Excrement.* Bianco Lunos Bogtrykkeri, Copenhagen.

Howard, R.D. 1974. The influence of sexual selection and interspecific competition on mockingbird song. *Evolution* 28:428-438.

Huxley, J.S. 1934. A natural experiment on territorial instinct. *British Birds* 27:270-277.

Jarman, P.J. 1974. The social organization of antelope in relation to their ecology. *Behaviour* 48:215-266.

Jenni, D. 1974. Evolution of polyandry in birds. *Amer. Zool.* 14:129-144.

Johnson, G.B. 1976. Genetic polymorphism and enzyme function. *In* Ayala, F.J. (ed.), *Molecular Evolution.* Sinaurer, Sunderland, Mass.

Kale, H. 1965. Ecology and bioenergetics of the long-billed marsh wren in Georgia salt marshes. *Publ. Nuttall Ornith. Club,* No. 5.

Keenleyside, M.H.A. 1972. Intraspecific intrusions into nests of spawning long-ear sunfish (Pices: Centrarchidae). *Copeia* 1972:272-278.

Kruijt, J., G. de Vos, and I. Bossema. 1972. The arena system of black grouse *Lyrurus tetrix tetrix* (L.). *Proc. XV Ornith. Congr.* 339-423.

Kruijt, J., and J. Hogan. 1967. Social behavior of the lek in black grouse, *Lyrurus tetrix tetrix* (L.). *Ardea* 55:203-240.

Lack, D. 1954. *The Natural Regulation of Animal Numbers.* Oxford Univ. Press, New York.

Lack, D. 1968. *Ecological Adaptations in Breeding Birds.* Methuen, London.

Le Boeuf, B. 1974. Male-male competition and reproductive success in elephant seals. *Amer. Zool.* 14:163-177.

Lill, A. 1966. Some observations on social organization and non-random mating in captive Burmese red jungle fowl *(Gallus gallus spadiceus)*. *Behaviour* 26:228-242.

Lill, A. 1974a. Sexual behavior of the lek-forming white-bearded manakin *(Manacus manacus trinitatis* Hartert). *Z. Tierpsychol.* 36:1-36.

Lill, A. 1974b. Social organization and space utilization in the lek-forming white-bearded manakin, *M. manacus trinitatis* Hartert. *Z. Tierpsychol.* 36:513-530.

Lill, A. 1976. *Lek Behavior in the Golden-headed Manakin,* Pipra erythrocephala *in Trinidad (West Indies).* Verlag Paul Parey, Berlin.

Lin, N. 1963. Territorial behavior in the cicada killer wasp, *Sphecius speciosus* (Drury) (Hymenoptera: Sphecidae). *Behaviour* 20:115-133.

Lincoln, G.A. 1972. The role of antlers in the behavior of red deer. *J. Exptl. Zool.* 182:233-250.

Lloyd, J.E. 1971. Bioluminescent communication in insects. *Ann. Rev. Ent.* 16:97-122.

Maynard Smith, J. 1956. Fertility, mating behavior, and sexual selection in *Drosophila subobscura. J. Gen.* 54:261-279.

Maynard Smith, J. 1958. *The Theory of Evolution.* Pelican Books, Baltimore.

Maynard Smith, J. 1976. Sexual selection and the handicap principle. *J. Theor. Biol.* 57:239-242.

O'Donald, P. 1967. A general model for sexual and natural selection. *Heredity* 22:499-518.

O'Donald, P. 1973. Models of sexual and natural selection in polygynous species. *Heredity* 31:145-156.

O'Donald, P. 1974. Mating preferences and sexual selection in the arctic skua. *Heredity* 33:1-16.

Orians, G. 1969. On the evolution of mating systems in birds and mammals. *Amer. Nat.* 103:589-603.

Otte, D., and A. Joern. 1975. Insect territoriality and its evolution: Population studies of desert grasshoppers on creosote bushes. *J. Anim. Ecol.* 44:29-54.

Parker, G.A. 1970a. The reproductive behaviour and the nature of sexual selection in *Scatophaga stercoraria* L. (Diptera: Scatophagidae). II. The fertilization rate and the spatial and temporal relationships of each sex around the site of mating and oviposition. *J. Anim. Ecol.* 39:205-228.

Parker, G.A. 1970b. The reproductive behaviour and the nature of sexual selection in *Scatophaga stercoraria* L. (Diptera: Scatophagidae). IV. Epigamic recognition and competition between males for the possession of females. *Behaviour* 37:113-139.

Parker, G.A. 1970c. The reproductive behaviour and the nature
    of sexual selection in *Scatophaga stercoraria* L. (Diptera:
    Scatophagidae). V. The female's behaviour at the oviposi-
    tion site. *Behaviour* 37:140–168.
Parker, G.A. 1970d. Sperm competition and its evolutionary
    consequences in the insects. *Biol. Rev.* 45:525–567.
Parker, G.A. 1970e. Sperm competition and its evolutionary ef-
    fect on copula duration in the fly *Scatophaga stercoraria*.
    J. Insect Physiol. 16:1301–1328.
Parker, G.A. 1974a. Courtship persistence and female-guarding
    as male time investment strategies. *Behaviour* 48:157–184.
Parker, G.A. 1974b. Assessment strategy and the evolution of
    fighting behaviour. *J. Theor. Biol.* 47:223–243.
Patterson, R.L. 1952. *The Sage Grouse in Wyoming*. Wyoming Game
    and Fish Commission, Cheyenne.
Petit, C., and L. Ehrman. 1969. Sexual selection in *Droso-
    phila*. *In* Dobzhansky, T., Hecht, M.K., and Steere, W.C.
    (eds.), *Evolutionary Biology*. Appleton-Century-Crofts,
    New York.
Powell, J. 1975. Protein variation in natural populations of
    animals. *Evol. Biol.* 8:79–119.
Pulliam, H.R. 1973. The advantages of flocking. *J. Theor.
    Biol.* 38:419–422.
Rand, A.S. 1940. Breeding habits of the birds of paradise
    Macgregoria and *Diphyllodes*. Results of the Archbold
    expeditions. No 26. *Amer. Mus. Novitates*, No. 1073:1–14.
Robel, R.J. 1966. Booming territory size and mating success
    of the greater prairie chicken *(Tympanuchus cupido
    pinnatus)*. *Anim. Behav.* 14:328–331.
Robel, R.J. 1969. Movements and flock stratification within
    a population of blackcocks in Scotland. *J. Anim. Ecol.*
    38:755–763.
Robel, R.J., and W.B. Ballard. 1974. Lek social organization
    and reproductive success in the greater prairie chicken.
    Amer. Zool. 14:121–128.
Scott, J. 1972. Mating of butterflies. *J. Res. Lepid.*
    11:99–127.
Scott, J.W. 1942. Mating behavior of the Sage Grouse. *Auk*
    59:477–498.
Selander, R.K. 1965. On mating systems and sexual selection.
    Amer. Nat. 99:129–141.
Selander, R.K. 1972. Sexual selection and dimorphism in birds.
    In Campbell, B. (ed.), *Sexual Selection and the Descent of
    Man 1871–1971*. Aldine, Chicago.
Sheppard, P.M. 1953. A note on non-random mating in the moth
    Panaxia dominula (L.). *Heredity* 6:239–241.
Shields, O. 1967. Hilltopping. *J. Res. Lepid.* 6:69–178.
Snow, D.W. 1962. A field study of the Black and White Manakin,
    Manacus manacus, in Trinidad. *Zoologica* 47:65–104.

Spieth, H. 1974a. Mating behavior and evolution of the
    Hawaiian *Drosophila*. *In* White, M.J.D. (ed.), *Genetic
    Mechanisms of Speciation in Insects*. Australia and New
    Zealand Book Company, Sydney.

Spieth, H. 1974b. Courtship behavior in *Drosophila*. *Ann. Rev.
    Ent*. 19:385-405.

Stiles, G., and L. Wolf. 1977. Mating systems in Central
    American hummingbirds. (ms).

Thornhill, R. 1976a. Sexual selection and paternal investment
    in insects. *Amer. Nat*. 110:153-163.

Thornhill, R. 1976b. Sexual selection and feeding behavior in
    Bittacus apicalis (Insecta: Mecoptera). *Amer. Nat*.
    110:529-548.

Trivers, R.L. 1972. Parental investment and sexual selection.
    In Campbell, B. (ed.), *Sexual Selection and the Descent
    of Man 1871-1971*. Aldine, Chicago.

Trivers, R.L. 1974. Parent-offspring conflict. *Amer. Zool*.
    14:249-264.

Trivers, R.L., and H. Hare. 1976. Haplodiploidy and the
    evolution of social insects. *Science* 191:249-263.

Trivers, R.L., and D. Willard. 1973. Natural selection of
    parental ability to vary the sex ratio of offspring.
    Science 179:90-92.

Verner, J. 1964. Evolution of polygamy in the long-billed
    marsh wren. *Evolution* 18:252-261.

Verner, J., and G.H. Engelsen. 1970. Territories, multiple
    nest building, and polygyny in the long-billed marsh wren.
    Auk 87:557-567.

Verner, J., and M. Willson. 1966. Influence of habitats on
    mating systems of North American passerine birds. *Ecology*
    47:143-147.

Waage, J.K. 1973. Reproductive behavior and its relation to
    territoriality in *Calopteryx maculata* (Beauvois) (Odonata:
    Calopterygidae). *Behaviour* 47:240-256.

Wilbur, H., and J. Collins. 1973. Ecological aspects of
    amphibian metamorphosis. *Science* 182:1305-1314.

Wiley, R.H. 1973. Territoriality and non-random mating in sage
    grouse, *Centrocercus urophasianus*. *Anim. Behav. Monogr*.
    6:87-169.

Wiley, R.H. 1974. Evolution of social organization and life-
    history patterns among grouse. *Quart. Rev. Biol*. 49:201-227.

Wiley, R.H. 1976. Affiliation between the sexes in common
    grackles. I. Specificity and seasonal progression. *Z.
    Tierpsychol*. 40:59-79.

Williams, G.C. 1966. *Adaptation and Natural Selection*.
    Princeton Univ. Press, Princeton.

Williams, G.C. 1975. *Sex and Evolution*. Princeton Univ. Press,
    Princeton.

Wynne-Edwards, V.C. 1962. *Animal Dispersion in Relation to*

Social Behavior. Oliver and Boyd, Edinburgh.

Zahavi, A. 1975. Mate selection--a selection for a handicap. *J. Theor. Biol.* 53:205-214.

Zimmerman, J.L. 1966. Polygyny in the dickcissel. *Auk* 83:534-546.

Zimmerman, J.L. 1971. The territory and its density-dependent effect in *Spiza americana*. *Auk* 88:591-612.

Zmarlecki, C., and R.A. Morse. 1963. Drone congregation areas. *J. Apicult. Res.* 2:64-66.

MALE AND FEMALE SEXUAL SELECTION

AND THE EVOLUTION OF

MATING STRATEGIES IN INSECTS

Randy Thornhill

The University of New Mexico

INTRODUCTION

The concept of sexual selection, formulated originally by
Darwin (1871, 1874) in *The Descent of Man, and Selection in
Relation to Sex,* has received less attention from evolutionary
biologists than the concept of natural selection. Early
opposition to some of Darwin's ideas on sexual selection
(e.g., Huxley, 1938; Grant, 1963) probably discouraged investigators. Also, some authors writing on the subject of
sexual selection seem to have difficulty in distinguishing
between natural selection and sexual selection as envisioned
by Darwin (e.g., Richards, 1927; Mayr, 1972). Recently, however, there has been a reevaluation of the importance of
sexual selection as shown by the increasing number of publications on the subject (e.g., see papers in Campbell, 1972).
Part of the change in attitude must be attributed to a
relatively recent realization by evolutionary biologists of
the potency of selection acting at the level of the individual
organism rather than at a supraorganismal level (Lewontin,
1970; Williams, 1966, 1971; Wilson, 1975; Alexander, 1974,
1975). An investigator must consider the severe reproductive
competition between individuals of the same species in order
to understand sexually selected attributes.
   Darwin proposed his theory of sexual selection to explain
certain characteristics of organisms not explicable in terms
of survival or natural selection. Sexually dimorphic attributes in insects played a prominent role in the development of
Darwin's ideas on sexual selection. He cited numerous insect
examples to support his ideas on how such attributes might be
favored by selection even though they increased the chances of
individual mortality. For example, the elaborate and cumber-
some mandibles of male stag beetles and dobsonflies were cited
as characteristics that primarily function in sexual combat

or in the sequestering of females, but impair locomotion and
feeding (Darwin, 1874).

Richards (1927) reviewed numerous sexually selected attributes in insects. Group selection is implied in some of his
interpretations of the functions of certain characteristics
supposedly acquired through sexual selection. He speaks of
certain displays and complex morphological structures as being
of value to the species rather than the individual. Recent
investigators of sexual selection in insects have concentrated
on interpretations based on the reproductive advantage to
individuals, i.e., the strategies by which individuals maximize their genetic contribution to future generations by
their behavior in the context of reproduction (e.g., Alexander, 1975; Campanella and Wolf, 1974; Parker, 1970a-f,
1972a, b; Petit and Ehrman, 1969; Smith, 1976; Spieth, 1968;
Thornhill, 1974, 1976a-c). I use the word "strategy" in the
sense of Wilbur et al. (1974): the adaptive responses of an
organism accumulated over evolutionary time, without any
teleological implications.

In this paper, I have tried to bring together current
sexual selection theory and the literature on sexual selection
in insects. Throughout, I adhere to the evolutionary philosophy that all attributes I consider can be understood from
the standpoint of selection favoring some individuals over
others through differential reproduction. I will not delve
into alternative explanations based on selection operating at
the level of the group and resulting in adaptations for group
rather than individual benefit. It is unfortunate that in
biology one must still specify a selective philosophy to the
reader. However, I feel this is necessary because many biologists feel (knowingly or unknowingly) that organisms behave
in such a way as to benefit the group rather than in a genetically selfish manner. Uncritical thinking as to the level
at which selection operates most effectively is apparent in
every issue of every biological publication I receive and
in many of the presentations at every biological meeting I
attend.

BACKGROUND SEXUAL SELECTION THEORY

Darwin (1871) first pointed out the distinction between
adaptations enhancing survival and those enhancing reproduction. He called the selective forces operating to promote
reproduction "sexual selection" and those operating to promote
survival "natural selection." Both types of selective forces
are naturally imposed by Darwin's "hostile forces" as opposed
to being artificially imposed by man, and the inevitable
consequence of both forces is differential reproduction by the

units being selected. More recently, sexual selection has
been regarded as the natural selective forces working in the
context of reproduction as well as how these forces work
differently on the sexes in this context (Selander, 1972;
Thornhill, 1976a; Trivers, 1972). Thus, sexual selection is
felt to be the context responsible for most adaptations of
reproductive biology, including attributes that facilitate
copulation and fertilization and those involved in parental
care. An understanding of sexual selection is therefore
critical in dealing with many of the important general questions in biology: (1) Why is there an initial disparity in the
parental care placed in individual gametes by the two sexes?
(2) Why are sex ratios usually 1:1?   (3) Why do sex ratios
sometimes deviate from 1:1?   (4) Why do most organisms have
two sexes?   (5) Why do mating systems vary, i.e., why are some
organisms monogamous, some polygynous, and others polyandrous?
(6) Why do parental care patterns vary among species?

     Darwin (1871) stressed that two types of selective forces
come into play during reproduction. The distinction between
selective forces during reproduction was also recognized by
Fisher (1958) and Huxley (1938). The two selective forces
may be called intrasexual selection, or competition within one
sex for individuals of the opposite sex, and intersexual selection, or preferential choice for mating partners by one sex
relative to the other. Intrasexual selection is most pronounced in males (male sexual selection), whereas discrimination in the choice of mating partners is primarily an
attribute of females (female sexual selection). The major
problem in understanding adaptations attributed to sexual
selection is the difficulty involved in separation of the
contexts of male and female sexual selection. These two
selective forces are often inseparable because of the ubiqui-
ty of male sexual selection. The best one can do in most
cases is to determine the relative importance of these two
phenomena in the evolution of the adaptations under consideration. This is discussed further in the section on female
choice.

     Selective forces during reproduction operate differently on
the sexes because of the disparity in parental investment by
the sexes (Bateman, 1948; Trivers, 1972). Trivers (1972)
defined parental investment as "any investment by the parent
in an individual offspring that increases the offspring's
chance of surviving (and hence reproductive success) at the
cost of the parent's ability to invest in other offspring."
Using the sex-ratio premise of Fisher (1958) that each offspring in a sexually reproducing species must have a mother
and father, he showed that the sex which makes the greatest
parental investment will become a limited resource for the
opposite sex, and the members of the sex investing the least

will compete among themselves in order to mate with individuals of the sex investing the most. In general, female
organisms make a greater parental investment than males.
This greater investment begins with the production of large
gametes, relative to the smaller male gametes. In many
organisms, the male's investment ends with fertilization, but
the female's investment may continue through each developmental period of the propagule. The reproductive success of the
female is thus limited to a far greater extent by parental
investment than the reproductive success of the male. These
circumstances result in intense competition among males for
mates and discriminatory behavior in females as to which
male(s) will secure her investment.

PARENTAL INVESTMENT PATTERNS IN INSECTS

    Parental investment patterns in insects vary from invest-
ment only in gametes by both sexes, through situations where
the female provides postgametic parental care, to circumstances where both sexes provide some parental care. The
extent of parental contribution by both the male and female
determines the relative importance of male and female sexual
selection in the evolution of mating behavior in insects as
well as in other organisms. When a male makes a parental
investment greater than that placed in the sperm, a male's
willingness and ability to invest parentally become a major
criteria used by a female in her assessment of male quality.
When a male's investment is nothing but genes, all aspects of
his reproductive effort (one of which is parental investment)
should be channeled into direct competition with other males
for females, and females may be selected to judge males (1)
in terms of attributes related to frequency of copulation
and/or (2) possibly in terms of non-sex-linked characters
that insure survival of a female's daughters (Trivers, 1976).
Criteria of female choice are discussed in a later section.
    In the vast majority of insects there is no parental in-
vestment beyond what is placed in the gametes. The size and
number of gametes produced by the female in these species is
an indication of maternal investment. Another level of maternal investment which has independently evolved numerous times
in insects involves the retention of developing young internally. In ovoviviparity the nourishment that the progeny receives comes from the egg. The nourishment in viviparity, in
addition to that in the egg, is provided by the mother. With
the evolution of increased maternal care in terms of larger
eggs or internal nourishment of the young, there is presumably
a concomitant decrease in fecundity. As the number of gametes
and subsequent progeny that a female can produce decreases as

a result of increased maternal investment per gamete or offspring, the female should be selected to show greater discrimination of mating partners because her potential re- productive success becomes more and more dependent on the genetic contribution of the male and/or on male parental care.

Insect reproductive strategies involving further parental investment per offspring come under the broad topic of pre- social behavior. Wilson (1971) defined presocial behavior as any type of social behavior beyond the interaction of the sexes during mating, short of eusociality. The most common type of presocial behavior in insects involves parental care of eggs or young for some period of time. This type of be- havior is known in Blattoidea (Liechti and Bell, 1975; Roth and Willis, 1960), crickets (West and Alexander, 1963), earwigs (Fulton, 1924; Lamb and Wellington, 1974; Shepard et al. 1973), mantids (Faure, 1940), psocids (Mockford, 1957), web-spinners (Ledoux, 1958), hemipterans (Odhiambo, 1960), homopterans (Wood, 1976), thrips (Mani and Rao, 1950), beetles (Hinton, 1944), bees (Michener, 1969), and wasps (Evans, 1958). In the majority of the cases, the presocial behavior involves the female guarding the young and/or eggs, but in some cases the mother feeds the developing young, e.g., bury- ing beetles of the genus *Necrophorus* (Pukowski, 1933). The amount of parental care displayed by eusocial insects varies greatly (Wilson, 1971). In some there is almost no contact between the queen and workers and the immatures. In others, the care contributed by the mother is extensive. In at least one case involving bumble bees, in addition to care provided by the queens and workers, the drones exhibit parental care by brooding the young (B. Heinrich, pers. comm.).

The occurrence of paternal investment is much less frequent and usually lower in intensity than female investment. Pater- nal investment in insects may be direct, through feeding the offspring, or indirect, through feeding the female during courtship or copulation. The former investment is uncommon in insects. It occurs most notably in certain species of *Necrophorus* beetles (Pukowski, 1933). In these beetles the female still contributes most of the nourishment for the larvae. Indirect feeding of the eggs or young by the male through nuptial feeding of the female may be viewed as a form of paternal investment (Thornhill, 1976a). The feeding of the female before, during, or after copulation by the male is fairly common in insects and has evolved independently several times (Thornhill, 1976a). Nuptial feeding may be of three types in insects: (1) females may receive nourishment from a glandular product of the male, (2) females may receive nour- ishment from food captured or collected by the male, or (3) females may cannibalize males during or after mating. Types

2 and 3 are easy to conceive, but type 1 applies to certain
behaviors that are not normally thought of as feeding. Glandular secretions from dorsal and salivary glands, spermatophores, and mating plugs from which females may receive
nourishment fall in this category.

Male investment may take the form of protective behavior
directed toward the eggs or nymphs. For example, males of
certain species of water bugs (Belostomatidae) allow the
females to attach eggs to their backs where they remain until
the eggs hatch (Smith, 1976). Bequaert (1935) and Odhiambo
(1959) describe egg-brooding behavior by the males of the
reduviid genus *Rhinocoris*.

SELECTIVE FORCES FAVORING INCREASED PARENTAL INVESTMENT
IN INSECTS

Wilson (1975) discusses some of the ecological circumstances that may result in the evolution of increased parental
investment in the form of parental care. He mentions
K-selection, parasitism or predation, scarce or specialized
food sources, and stressful physical environments. Odhiambo
(1959), for example, feels that the subsocial behavior of
egg- or nymph-guarding in the Hemiptera was selected because
it protected the immature stages from parasites. Harsh
physical environment may have been important in the evolution
of parental care in the staphylinid beetle *Bledius,* which
lives in intertidal mud flats (Bro Larsen, 1952). Egg mortality due to fungal invasion may have selected for brooding
behavior in earwigs (Fulton, 1924).

The above selective forces may operate on both males and
females to favor greater parental investment and thus reduce
offspring mortality. Trivers (1972) pointed out that the
initially large investment in gametes is more likely to commit
the female to further investment than is the relatively small
male investment in gametes. Dawkins and Carlisle (1976)
correctly pointed out, however, that both father and mother
are equally related to each offspring, and, no matter which
sex contributed most of the previous investment, either
parent's decision to continue investment is related to the
quantity of investment still needed to produce a sexually
mature offspring. As discussed above, female reproductive
success is limited by the number of gametes that a female can
produce, whereas male reproductive success is primarily limited by the number of copulations that a male can secure.
Thus, sexual selection, all other things being equal, will
operate against increasing paternal investment because the
more a male invests in the young of each female he mates with,
the fewer copulations he will obtain.

Another important consideration in understanding investment patterns is the relative uncertainty of parenthood of the
sexes. Internal fertilization, sperm storage, the overlap of
ejaculates from different males, and multiple mating by females result in high levels of sperm competition in insects
(Parker, 1970a). This reduces the certainty of paternity
to a very low level. Everything else equal, uncertainty of
paternity alone should select against increased male parental
investment in insects as well as in other organisms with
internal fertilization. Male adaptations to increase the
certainty of paternity should exist in those species which
show large paternal investment, and these adaptations should
be very elaborate in monogamous animals in which the amount of
male investment is similar to the female's. A monogamous male
that raises offspring fathered by another male has failed to
reproduce (unless he does so through nepotism). Adaptations
that help insure paternity in insects might involve mating
plugs or female-guarding behavior. Intense male sexual
selection in the form of sperm competition has apparently
selected for female-guarding behavior in dung flies (Parker,
1970e).

Insects in which the male makes some significant investment
should show adaptations to insure paternity. Two insect
groups in which the male invests significantly have been
studied in some detail. In hangingflies of the genus *Bittacus*
(Mecoptera), the male invests in terms of a nuptial offering
that the female feeds on during copulations. Females prefer
males with certain sizes of prey as mating partners (Thornhill, 1974, 1976a, b). Certainty of paternity may be assured
in bittacids by sperm displacement and male-induced nonreceptivity in females. Sperm displacement is defined by Parker
(1970a) as "the displacement of previously stored sperm and
its replacement with sperm from the last male to mate."
Parker cites evidence from the literature and from his own
work suggesting that sperm displacement may occur in multiple
matings in *Drosophila* and dung flies (Scatophagidae). Economopoulos and Gordon (1972) have shown that in *Oncopeltus
fasciatus* (Hemiptera: Lygaeidae), a species in which the male
places semen directly into the spermatheca of the female
through a long penile tube (Bonhag and Wick, 1953), the sperm
of the first male is replaced by a "washing out" of the
spermathecal contents by the flow of the semen of the second
male to mate. The lengths of the aedeagi in the species of
Bittacus I studied *(B. apicalis, B. pilicornis, B. strigosus,
B. stigmaterus)* correspond to the lengths of the spermathecal
ducts in each species. This suggests that the aedeagus is
extended all the way into the spermatheca for sperm transfer
during copulation, and it is tempting to infer that a replacement of stored sperm by the copulating male may take place.

In *B. apicalis* an apparently male-induced female mating
refractory period of 3-4 hr. follows male-terminated copulations (i.e., copulations of 20 min. or more). During the
mating refractory period, oviposition is initiated if the
female was a virgin and accelerated if the female was a
nonvirgin. Females lay about three eggs during each refractory period. The female mating refractory period probably
maximizes the number of eggs that a copulating male fertilizes
by reducing sperm competition that would result if additional
matings took place during that time (Thornhill, 1976b).

The males of certain belostomatids (Hemiptera) allow conspecific females to deposit eggs on their backs, which the
males carry around until the nymphs hatch. Smith (1976) has
studied this behavior in some detail. He found a sex reversal
in courtship behavior to some degree: the female is very
active in courtship. Female courtship is expected in species
in which the male makes a large investment. In strictly
monogamous species with equal investment by both sexes, the
male should be as discriminating in terms of his mating partner as the female. As pointed out by Trivers (1972) and
discussed above, the relative parental investment by the sexes
determines the operation of both male and female sexual selection. Before a male will allow a female to oviposit on his
back, he requires that she copulate with him. In fact, a male
copulates with a female before each egg is deposited on his
back. In most cases in insects, the last male to mate with a
female in a multiple mating sequence fertilizes most of the
eggs laid until the female mates again (see review by Parker,
1970a). The behavior of the male water bug insures that the
eggs carried by a male have been fertilized by his own sperm.
The observations of Odhiambo (1959) on the egg-brooding behavior of the male of *Rhinocoris albopilosus* (Reduviidae) suggest
that the male copulates with the female each time she adds
eggs to the clutch he is brooding.

VARIANCE IN MALE AND FEMALE REPRODUCTIVE SUCCESS

Any study of sexual selection could include a detailed
study of variance in reproductive success. The sex that invests the least parentally (i.e., usually the male) should
show greater variance in reproductive success than the other
sex, according to theory (Bateman, 1948; Trivers, 1972). Data
for females are easy to obtain in many organisms, at least in
terms of the number of eggs laid by or number of young born
to a sample of females. On the other hand, data for males,
especially field data, are difficult to obtain because it is
very difficult to determine which males are mating and which
matings are effective. Few studies have been conducted on

variance in reproductive success in insects. Bateman (1948)
conducted a detailed laboratory study of variance in reproductive success in *Drosophila*. Parker (1970b-f) has accumulated
a large body of information on variance in reproductive
success of male and female dung flies under field conditions.
Jacobs (1955) and Campanella and Wolf (1974) have reported
less detailed data on dragonflies in nature. Bateman's
results are based on the appearance of genetic markers in the
progeny. In the dragonfly work the investigators used frequency of copulation as a means of measuring male reproductive
success. Parker's work is based on both frequency of copulation and a thorough understanding of the effectiveness of
copulations of different durations in terms of sperm competition. These investigations strongly support the theory that
variance in male reproductive success exceeds variance in
female reproductive success.

Since there is a paucity of information on variance in
male reproductive success in insects (as well as in other
animals), I will summarize here the results of a study I
conducted on *Bittacus apicalis* (Mecoptera), the black-
tipped hangingfly (Thornhill, 1977). During the mating
refractory period in *B. apicalis* (discussed in the last
section), a male gains all the eggs laid if he mates with a
virgin and probably most of the eggs if he mates with a nonvirgin. That the male fertilizes most of the eggs laid during
the refractory period subsequent to mating with a nonvirgin
is, of course, an assumption, which is, however, based on data
from studies on other insect groups (see review by Parker,
1970a). In most insects that have been studied, the last male
to inseminate a female in a multiple mating sequence fertilized most (50% to 95%) of the subsequent eggs prior to
another mating, at which time the sperm of the last male takes
precedence in fertilization. In multiple insemination of
females, sperm competition is an important factor in determining a male's reproductive success and sperm from matings
prior to the last may compete for the percentage of eggs not
fertilized by the last male to mate. For example, Parker
(1970b) has shown that in dung flies the last male to mate
fertilizes about 80% of the succeeding batch of eggs irrespective of the number of previous matings. Also, sperm from
previous matings compete for the remaining 20% of the batch
in the same proportionate relationship as they did for the
previous batch. I presume that a somewhat similar situation
exists in bittacids; however, if sperm replacement exists and
is complete in *B. apicalis,* the last male to mate would fertilize all the eggs of a female during her refractory period.

Forty-two individually marked males of *B. apicalis* were
followed through four successive copulations, and all copulatory and intercopulatory events were timed and recorded. This

procedure provides a means of assessing the variance in male
reproductive success. I make two assumptions: (1) The last
male to mate for 20 min. with a female in a multiple mating
sequence fertilizes most of the eggs laid until she copulates
with another male. In quantifying egg gains, I use 85% as
the percentage of eggs fertilized by a male until another
mating takes place. The remaining 15% of the eggs are fertilized by the sperm of the male(s) which copulated with the
female prior to the last copulation. (2) Copulations of
durations less than 20 min., resulting from interruptions by
intruding males or from premature termination by the female,
lead to no egg gain for a male. It was shown that copulations
of less than 20 min. do not initiate nonreceptivity and oviposition in females and that those females immediately seek
out another male to mate with (Thornhill, 1976b).

The first assumption is very reasonable because of the
information available from studies on sperm competition in
insects. However, in *B. apicalis,* 85% may be much too conservative an estimate of the last male's egg gain, especially
if complete sperm replacement by the last male to mate takes
place. Of course, 85% egg gain by a male in the refractory
period following mating is too low when a male mates with a
virgin, in which case the male would presumably fertilize all
the eggs during the refractory period of 3 hr. Eighty-five
percent of this is 2.98 or three eggs gained by a male copulating with a female 20 min. or more.

The second assumption will probably not be substantiated
unless complete sperm replacement takes place during copulations of 20 min. or more. Despite the problems with these
assumptions, I believe that male reproductive success can be
more meaningfully measured this way than merely by the number
of copulations. Male reproductive success undoubtedly varies
as a function of the number of copulations that a male obtains, but in *B. apicalis* copulations of less than 5 min.
duration result in the transfer of very few or no sperm
and therefore cannot be considered to increase a male's
reproductive success (Thornhill, 1976b).

Variance in male reproductive success in *B. apicalis* is
primarily influenced by four factors: (1) interrupted copulations by intruding males, (2) the time necessary for nuptial
prey location and capture by males, (3) prey-piracy by males
between copulations, and (4) mistakes in prey selection and
evaluation by males (Thornhill, 1974, 1976b, 1977). The
frequencies of interrupted copulations and prey-piracy are
directly related to population density. Interrupted copulations reduce a male's time *in copulo* and therefore the number
of sperm transferred. The number of times a male is robbed of
his prey between copulations is positively correlated with
intercopulatory duration; therefore, more time is required by

robbed males for prey acquisition, resulting in less copulatory time. Mistakes in prey selection and evaluation result
in time wasted by males because the females either refuse to
copulate or copulate for a short duration.

The egg gains for 20 males that were followed through four
copulations, and in which none of the four copulations was
interrupted by intruding males, reveal relatively little
variation: egg gain, 9 or 12; eggs gained per minute, 0.046 to
0.080. These observations were recorded under conditions of
low population densities in the last portions of the seasonal
flight periods of *B. apicalis*. A better estimate of the
variation in egg gain by males was obtained by recording 22
males through four successive copulations under moderate to
high population densities. Sixty-one percent of the 88
copulations recorded for these 22 males were interrupted by
intruding hangingflies. The egg gains of the 22 males in
four copulations ranged from 1 to 12, and the eggs gained per
minute ranged from 0 to 0.064. Five males (22.7%) had egg
gains of zero since they were unable during any of their four
copulations to remain coupled for 20 min. because of intruding males. One male had an egg gain of 12, thus being
more than twelve times as successful as those five males with
zero egg gains. If the egg gain per minute is extrapolated
to egg gain per day, assuming a 12-hr. day of activity and
that the male's reproductive success would not change during
the day, egg gains per day vary from zero to 46 eggs. Copulations and time between copulations require on the average
about 23 and 25 min., respectively. A male under these
average conditions might be expected to effect 15 successful
copulations per 12-hr. day. If a male fertilized 85% of the
eggs that the 15 females laid during their refractory periods
(i.e., three eggs per mating), he would fertilize 45 eggs per
12-hr. day. One male had an egg gain of 0.080 per minute
during four copulations. This would be an egg gain of 57.6
per 12-hr. day if the male maintained this egg gain all day.

Thus, there appears to be considerable variation in the
reproductive success of males if measured in terms of egg
gain in four copulations or in egg gain per minute. Females,
on the other hand, do not exhibit this degree of variation in
the number of eggs they produce. Females lay about 3.5 eggs
per 4-hr. mating refractory period and experience four
matings and four refractory periods per day under average
conditions. The only factor that was observed to significantly influence variance in the number of eggs a female laid in
nature was interrupted copulations by intruding males, which
delay the insemination of a female and delay the acceleration
of oviposition. However, these delays are short because a
female occasionally resumes copulation with the original male,
or she copulates with the intruding male, or she rapidly

locates another male ($\bar{x}$ = 2.5 min. in nature) (Thornhill, 1974, 1976b).

FEMALE CHOICE

    A great deal of laboratory research on animals other than insects has revealed that females are capable of subtle choices of conspecific males. For example, female preferences have been demonstrated in dogs (Beach and Le Boeuf, 1967), house mice (Mainardi et al., 1965), monkeys (Herbert, 1968), domestic chickens (Lill and Wood-Gush, 1965), and canaries (Kroodsma, 1976). Most of the laboratory studies of female choice in insects have been conducted with *Drosophila* (Bateman, 1948; Maynard Smith, 1956; Petit and Ehrman, 1969). Bateman's study was primarily directed at male-male competition for females. He demonstrated that variance in male reproductive success greatly exceeded variance in female reproductive success. Petit and Ehrman have demonstrated that females of several species of *Drosophila* prefer mates of the rare type in choice experiments. Maynard Smith's study of *D. subobscura* provided insight into how female choice might affect male sexual behavior. He found that female *Drosophila* prefer outbred over inbred males, apparently because only the outbred males could perform the proper courtship dance. He also found that females that preferred outbred males left four times the number of viable offspring as those females that did not discriminate in mate choice. Although Maynard Smith's study was conducted under the artificial conditions of the laboratory, he did demonstrate an adaptive value for the preference of the females.
    The importance of female choice in the evolution of male reproductive behavior in nature is poorly understood because (1) the other contexts in which females may be selected to discriminate between mating partners are seldom separated from the context of sexual selection; (2) it is often impossible to separate the effects of male sexual selection from those of female sexual selection; (3) male sexual selection is intense in most mating systems, so investigators tend to attribute all male sexual behavior to this context; and (4) the cues that females use in their choice of mating partners are very difficult to determine for most species.
    For the most part, studies of female choice have involved investigations of choices made in the contexts of reproductive isolation or sexual discrimination. Aspects of male sexual behavior in numerous animals, including insects, apparently evolved in these contexts. Any study of sexually selected behavior of males must first deal with the other contexts in which the behavior may have evolved. In my study

of sexually selected behavior in two genera of mecopterous insects *(Bittacus* and *Panorpa),* I first gained an understanding of the behavioral reproductive isolating mechanisms in these insects. I demonstrated that the species of both genera primarily employ species-specific pheromones that function as reproductive isolators over distances of about 12 m (Thornhill, 1974). Vision over distances in most mecopterans is precluded by the nature of their habitats, i.e., the dense herb strata of forests. Thus two individuals must be in close proximity for sexual recognition and for the female to evaluate the male in terms of relative fitness.

A female that arrives in the proximity of a male by following a pheromone gradient can probably be sure that the individual with which she is about to interact is a male; however, the male can not be certain that the individual in front of him is a female, at least not in the genus *Bittacus* because of prey-piracy by males. In *B. apicalis* males and females are monomorphic and monochromatic. The typical pattern is for a female to lower her wings when she reaches the immediate vicinity of a male. In this species the male feeds the female a prey arthropod during copulation. When a female arrives in the immediate vicinity of a male and lowers her wings, the male presents his nuptial gift to her, but retains a grasp on the prey as the female feeds. Piracy of the prey of males by other males is common, and males have been observed to mimic the behavior of females in order to increase the likelihood of successful prey theft. The pirating male under these circumstances lowers his wings when he flies up to a male in the "calling" posture (i.e., dispersing pheromone and holding a nuptial prey item), and the calling male presents the prey to the female-mimicking male. The calling male then tries to couple his genitalia with those of the transvestite male in the same way he would with a female. The transvestite male keeps his abdomen out of reach of the other male.

Within a couple of minutes ($\bar{x}$ = 2.2 min., N = 38 observations), the male that presented the prey tries to retrieve it by wrestling it from the grasp of the intruder. About 50% of the time (20 of 38 field observations), however, the female-mimicking male has secured a strong hold on the prey and flies off with it. I have shown (Thornhill, 1977), by following individually marked males of *B. apicalis* in nature, that a male that steals a prey arthropod from another male rather than catching it on his own reduces intercopulatory time significantly (from means of 25 min. to 17 min.) and experiences more copulations over any given period of time. Thus, the adaptive advantage to a male of assuming the behavior of a female is clear in this system.

Observations of marked males between copulations indicate that males display a mixed hunting strategy (Thornhill, 1974,

1977). If a hunting male first encounters another male with
prey, he usually attempts to steal the prey. However, if the
same hunting male encounters a prey arthropod before seeing
another male with prey, it becomes his victim. An individual
male may employ three prey-piracy strategies: (1) he may fly
directly into another male possessing prey with some force
(this behavior probably increases the efficiency of prey-
piracy by males); (2) he may merely fly up to the male with
prey and struggle with him; or (3) he may fly up to the male
with prey and assume the behavior of a female. The incidence
of prey-piracy is dependent on the size of the population of
B. apicalis (Thornhill, 1974, 1977). A mixed strategy of
prey theft and hunting has been favored by selection because
the success of a male in prey theft depends on the availability of other males with prey.

The behavioral sequence in the evolution of transvestite
behavior of males may have been as follows. Originally females probably held their wings up when they interacted with
a male possessing a prey item. Males then evolved behavior
associated with prey theft. This resulted in males being
frequently robbed because they could not distinguish the sex
of the individual to which they presented their prey. Females
that could indicate their sex unambiguously to a male holding
a nuptial prey item were favored because this saved the
female time and energy that otherwise would be spent wrestling
with a male over the prey. A lowering of the wings was an
unambiguous signal of sex because this species normally keeps
its wings lifted. Males were favored that responded only to
the lowered-wing posture because this reduced the likelihood
of prey theft. The more times a male is prey-pirated between
copulations, the longer the intercopulatory period and the
fewer copulations he obtains (Thornhill, 1977). The interaction of males and females at this point was still subject to
parasitism by males. The ability of a male to mimic the
wing-lowering behavior of females was then favored because it
reduced intercopulatory time and increased copulatory success
of the mimic, as the behavior does at present in natural populations of *B. apicalis*. The evolution of wing lowering in
females can clearly be viewed as a means of communication to
the male that she is a female.

Aspects of sexual behavior in *B. apicalis* that evolved in
the contexts of reproductive isolation (i.e., pheromone dispersing behavior) and sexual recognition (i.e., wing lowering)
are easily separated from behaviors evolved in the context of
sexual selection. The two contexts of sexual selection, however, are difficult to separate, but I feel they can be separated in the *B. apicalis* system, allowing a better evaluation
of the role of female choice in the evolution of male behavior
in this species. Intrasexual selection occurs in *B. apicalis*

in two forms (Thornhill, 1974, 1977): (1) theft among males of prey of a certain size range and (2) disrupted copulations. The incidence of both forms of male sexual selection is higher at high population density. Males typically use prey in the size range of 19 mm^2 to about 50 mm^2 to feed females during copulation. (Prey size here refers to length times width of prey in millimeters.) Prey arthropods smaller than 19 mm^2 are captured by males, but then normally discarded after a brief feeding and not used by a male to feed a female during copulation. A male may be robbed of his prey by another male in four contexts (Thornhill, 1977): (1) while feeding upon a prey item, (2) while flying through the vegetation holding a prey item, (3) while dispersing pheromone, and (4) during copulation. An attempted disruption of a copulating pair results in the intruder copulating with the female 15% (8 of 54 observations) of the time. The intruder succeeds in robbing the copulating pair of the prey 57% (31 of 54 observations) of the time (Thornhill, 1977).

Female choice has apparently dictated the prey size preferences of males (Thornhill, 1976b). I have shown that females discriminate against males with prey smaller than 19 mm^2 at two levels by either refusing to mate entirely or mating for only a short duration. Females prefer males possessing prey in the size range 19 mm^2-50 mm^2. Copulations, involving prey in this size range, range in duration from 20 to 29 min. ($\bar{x}$ = 23 min.) and result in maximal sperm transfer, increased oviposition, and a female mating refractory period of 3-4 hr. Copulations of durations less than 20 min. result in small numbers of sperm being transferred, no increase in oviposition, and no female mating refractory period.

Maynard Smith (1966) pointed out that adaptive female choice has not been demonstrated in a natural population. He added that this is not surprising since two criteria, the latter of which is very difficult to obtain under natural conditions, are necessary for a demonstration of intersexual selection: (1) it is necessary to show that females are selecting as mates some kinds of males in preference to others and (2) that by so choosing, females are increasing their own reproductive success. I have shown that female preference of males with nuptial prey in the size range 19 mm^2-50 mm^2 is probably adaptive since females with this preference exhibit increased fecundity.

The extent to which females hunt on their own depends on the abundance of males in the population (Thornhill, 1976, 1977). If males are abundant, females depend entirely on nuptial feeding. The feeding of 20 min. or longer associated with a copulation involving prey between 19 mm^2 and 50 mm^2 apparently supplies a female with enough nourishment for

maintenance during the intercopulatory period of 3-4 hr.
This provides another possible advantage to females preferring
males with large nuptial prey: nonhunting females may be
subject to less predation than hunting females. Also, if
hunting is risky for females, this may explain why nuptial
feeding by males was initially favored by selection.

In most insects the last male to mate fertilizes most or
all the eggs until a female mates again (Parker, 1970a); this
is almost surely the case in B. apicalis (Thornhill, 1974,
1977). A male, by feeding a female during copulation, may
reduce the amount of risk-taking activity, in this case hunting, that a female engages in. This hypothesis is reasonable
because females of B. apicalis become sexually nonreceptive
for 3-4 hr. following mating with males possessing large
prey, and oviposition is increased during this period
only. The male then may gain because he is reducing the
risk-taking activity of his mate during the time that she is
laying eggs fertilized by his sperm. Hunting for prey probably exposes females to greater predation than males, since
females are slower and more awkward flyers because of the
weight burden of eggs (Thornhill, 1974). Web-building spiders
are an important cause of mortality for B. apicalis (Thornhill, 1974), and surely the more both males and females move
around in search of food, the greater the likelihood of their
ending up in a spider web. Adult mortality in the mecopterous
genus Panorpa is related to increased movement associated with
increased competition for food (Thornhill, 1974, 1975). Manipulation of sex ratios, food availability, and number of
web-building spiders in the field and in large enclosures in
the laboratory will provide a precise evaluation of the risks
of hunting for both males and females. If nuptial feeding is
found to reduce predation pressures on the female, this will
suggest that hunting is more risky than finding mates and
copulating for females. Copulation is often thought to be
dangerous behavior for both male and female because it is felt
that it makes them more conspicuous to visual predators
(Dewsbury, 1975).

A male of B. apicalis probably gains an advantage by
nuptial feeding because it reduces the likelihood that his
mate will copulate again during her mating refractory period
of 3-4 hr., i.e., nuptial feeding reduces sperm competition.
This is also the time when her oviposition rate is accelerated.
The male may be guarding the female in absentia from other
males. This is different from postmating guarding behavior
that involves the presence of the male described in some
other insects (Parker, 1970a). However, strong direct selection for increased time that a male spends with each female
he mates with to insure paternity will probably be uncovered
only in species in which males are densely aggregated. In

this situation the chance of any one male securing a successful copulation is low, as in the mating system of scatophagid
dung flies (Parker, 1970b; Borgia, this volume). Under
these circumstances increased time spent with a female would
be of little cost because of the small chance of a male
missing a copulation while remaining with a female he has
already mated with. In dung flies it is clear how postmating
guarding by males increases male reproductive success. The
last male to mate fertilizes about 80% of the eggs until a
female mates again (Parker, 1970a, b). The male guards the
female until she lays a batch of eggs and then he departs.
Thus, he can be 80% certain of his paternity in the egg batch.

Nuptial feeding behavior of males of *B. apicalis* was probably not originally favored because this increased the certainty of a male's paternity. Adaptations that insure a
male's paternity should coevolve with adaptations associated
with greater male parental investment in each female mated
with. The sequence of selective forces in the history of
nuptial feeding in *B. apicalis* may have first involved an
advantage to a male that fed a female because this increased
the likelihood of the female's living long enough for her to
lay some eggs fertilized by the male's sperm. Males that did
not feed females would find fewer mates and thus fertilize
fewer eggs because their mates would be exposed to greater
predation during hunting. After the evolution of primitive
nuptial feeding behavior in this context came selection for
paternity insurance. A study of *B. strigosus* Hagen by James
B. Johnson (unpublished) suggests that a factor produced in
the accessory gland of the male and passed from the male to
the female late in copulation inhibits female sexual receptivity and accelerates oviposition. If the male ancestors of
B. apicalis could control the oviposition and receptivity
patterns of females in the same way, and thus help insure
their paternity, this would have increased the likelihood of
selection having favored males with more sophisticated nuptial
feeding behavior, resulting in the type of nuptial feeding
seen in *B. apicalis* today.

In most animal species that have been studied in nature
from the standpoint of intersexual selection, females apparently choose males on the basis of complex criteria such as
territory size (Verner, 1964; Willson, 1966), or quality
(Howard, 1968; Kluyver, 1955; Zimmerman, 1966), or age, size,
or position in a lek (Robel, 1966; Hogan-Warburg, 1966; Wiley,
1973). In these studies and others it is difficult to determine the precise cues females are using in mate choice. In
B. apicalis, as well as in some other *Bittacus* species (Thornhill, 1974, 1977), the exact criteria used by a female in her
evaluation of potential mating partners are readily visible
to the researcher. This is convenient because it allows one

to assign a general fitness value to males based on their
nuptial gift. Males with prey in the size range preferred by
females will probably copulate successfully, whereas those
with small prey will not.

Zahavi (1975) suggested that (1) females should prefer
males that have demonstrated their ability to survive despite
risks because this is a reliable cue that females can use to
test male quality, and (2) males should evolve means of com-
municating to the female that they have undergone considerable
risks and survived. The more elaborate morphological structures (e.g., tail plumes of peacocks) of many male animals
relative to females of the same species are cited as examples
explained by this hypothesis. Initially, Zahavi's idea seems
plausible because it provides a criterion for female choice
that seems reliable (i.e., male survival despite risks) despite inevitable shifts in the fitness of male types due to
fluctuating ecological conditions. Zahavi's idea, however,
probably has little potential for explaining general criteria
that females will use to determine male quality because the
model requires females to constantly assess the relative risks
incurred by males that use different courtship and display
strategies to coax females to mate. This type of choice
system would be difficult for a female to monitor constantly
and would be hazardous if risks changed with time, because
it would often result in a female choosing a male that
produced sons genetically programmed to take greater than
the optimal risks.

It is clear that males that possess prey over a certain
size range are preferred by females of *B. apicalis*, but the
details of preferences within this range are not understood.
If movement associated with hunting is risky in terms of
exposure to predators for *B. apicalis,* Zahavi's hypothesis
leads to the following prediction: Females should prefer males
possessing nuptial prey sizes within the preferred range of
sizes that reflect the risks involved in capturing the prey.
Thus, males would not be expected to feed females prey that
are very abundant and within the preferred size range, and
females would not be expected to prefer males using such
nuptial gifts, because little risk would be involved in capturing such prey. A negative correlation between abundance
of prey of different sizes within the preferred size range
and frequency of the prey sizes used by males would support
Zahavi's idea.

The intense competition among males of *B. apicalis* for
nuptial prey, manifested as prey-piracy behavior, suggests
that food is limiting and thus a male that has found and
captured a prey item indicates his abilities to do so to a
female when he presents the prey to her. If food is limiting,
then the female has little chance of making a mistake when

she chooses a male possessing any prey in the size range
that provides enough nutriment to sustain her during her
mating refractory period of 3-4 hr. A positive correlation or no correlation between availability of prey sizes
within the suitable size range for nuptial feeding and the
frequency of the prey sizes used by males would support the
idea that food is limiting and females do not discriminate
against a male with a suitable size prey just because the male
incurred little risk in obtaining the prey. In *Panorpa*
(discussed below) food is limiting and the nature of male-male
competition and female choice have apparently evolved around
the availability of food.

It is important to determine the degree to which sexually
selected behavior is heritable. Male prey selection in *B.
apicalis* apparently has a genetic component. Males collected
in the field and isolated immediately after eclosion from the
pupae, before they begin feeding and before they see other
individuals feeding, discard insects smaller than the size
range preferred by females and only use larger insects to feed
females under laboratory conditions (Thornhill, 1974, 1976b).
Also, males which make a mistake in prey selection (i.e.,
attempt to use prey that are unpalatable or too small to feed
females) are more likely to make another mistake than males
that never make such mistakes (Thornhill, 1974, 1977). Female
preference of mates also apparently has a genetic basis.
Adult females field collected immediately after eclosion show
the same preferences for males shown by older field-collected
females (Thornhill, 1974).

In species with little or no male parental investment, as
is the case with most insects, most of a female's investment
in male offspring will be lost each generation because the
variance in male reproductive success is very large compared
to that of females. Trivers (1976) suggested that in such
species females may choose males on the basis of a male's
genetic abilities associated with the production of fit
daughters. That is, females may choose males on the basis
of a phenotypic character(s) that has a non-sex-linked genetic
association and which is an indication that the male will
father exceptionally fit daughters. It follows from Trivers'
hypothesis that females should choose males on the basis of
non-sex-linked criteria that are associated with the survival
and reproductive success of both sons and daughters. In
species with low male parental investment that are food limited, females should choose males in some way related to a
male's ability to acquire this resource. Males should also
compete among themselves in a manner that indicates to females
their ability to acquire food. Male-male competition and
female choice in both *Bittacus* and *Panorpa* seem to support these
ideas on how sexual selection should operate in such a system.

In *B. apicalis,* if food is limiting, as is known to be the case in some species of *Panorpa* (Thornhill, 1974, 1975; the ecology of sexual selection in *Panorpa* is discussed in detail later in this paper), then intrasexual selection favors males that can effectively compete for this resource through prey location and capture, as well as through prey-piracy. Females of *B. apicalis* also choose males on the basis of their predatory abilities. In *B. apicalis* the survival and reproduction of both a male and a female probably depend to a great extent on predatory ability. This is obvious for the male, but perhaps not so obvious from what has been indicated already about the biology of the female. Females in *B. apicalis* feed on their own a few days after pupal emergence. After this period, if males are abundant, they depend entirely on the nuptial meals provided by males. Predatory ability then is critical to a female right after adult emergence and in situations where males are not always available because of small population numbers.

Females of *B. apicalis* collected in the field in the teneral state are all virgins (Thornhill, 1974, 1976b). All eggs obtained from a mating of a virgin female with a male of known behavior with regard to frequencies at which he makes mistakes in prey selection will be fertilized by that male. If the sons of males that make mistakes also make mistakes, and the sons of males that do not make mistakes make fewer mistakes, this would indicate inheritance of the sexually selected predatory behavior of males. The extent to which an individual male of *B. apicalis* makes mistakes in prey selection is easily quantified in the field or laboratory by observations of a male's selection of prey sizes over consecutive copulations in choice experiments (Thornhill, 1974, 1977). The degree to which a male's predatory abilities are inherited by his female offspring can be determined in the laboratory in terms of (1) prey sizes selected outside the context of copulation by daughters, (2) handling of prey by daughters, and (3) time between prey captures by daughters.

I will briefly describe the results of my three-year study of ecological competition and mating behavior in the genus *Panorpa* in southeastern Michigan (Thornhill, 1974) because this information is critical to an understanding of sexual selection in the genus. Panorpas typically live in the herb strata of moist forests. In such habitats they may be the most abundant large insects. Adults of several species of *Panorpa* may occur together, often in large numbers, in the same woods. My study of seven species of *Panorpa* in southeastern Michigan reveals that the species overlap almost completely in their feeding ecology and that food in the form of dead or moribund arthropods is a limiting resource.

Interacting species are not separated with respect to habitat utilization, feeding location or time, or food type; however, the season of adult emergence reduces species overlap to some extent. The species investigated compete primarily in an interference manner through intense intra- and interspecific aggression around food. Panorpas also compete for food with other scavenging arthropods such as phalangids, ants, and some beetles. Interference competition in *Panorpa* results in reduced adult longevity under natural conditions. The reduction in longevity is apparently a result of increased dispersal and movement into less desirable and more risky habitats in terms of exposure to predators, especially web-building spiders. A selective history involving intense competition for food has apparently resulted in the evolution of klepto-parasitism of web-building spiders by panorpas (Thornhill, 1975). Panorpas feed on insects entrapped in spider webs about 25% of the time. This is a dangerous feeding strategy and results in 60% of observed panorpa mortality.

The Michigan study (Thornhill, 1974) revealed that male panorpas have three ways of copulating with females. First, males may secrete salivary material that solidifies as it is formed. This is secreted as pillars and attached to the substrate by males of all seven species studied, but males of *P. banksi* Hine may also secrete a solidified coil of saliva that is carried around in the mandibles. After secretion of the salivary material, males begin dispersing species-specific pheromones, and females attracted to the pheromones feed on the salivary mass during copulation. The salivary glands in the genus *Panorpa* are sexually dimorphic (Potter, 1938; Thornhill, unpublished), with those of the male being large and comprising up to one-third of his total dry weight (Thornhill, unpublished). Another method seen in most of the Michigan species involves dispersing sex pheromones from around a dead arthropod. A third method, which does not involve nuptial feeding, occurs with varying frequency in all the Michigan species. A male walks up to a female, lashes out his mobile abdomen, and clasps her leg or wing with his genital forceps. He then clamps the female's wings down in an organ on the dorsum of his abdomen and eventually couples with her. This behavior appears to be a form of rape (Thornhill, 1974).

Males are aggressive toward other males that try to steal salivary masses or dead insects. Aggressive interactions may involve noncontact wing-lifting behavior, or more commonly butting an opponent with the head or body, or lashing out the mobile abdomen and clasping an opponent's wing or leg with the genital forceps. Wings may be torn and legs broken by the genital forceps. The large genital bulb and mobile abdomen are often used in a ball-and-chain fashion to strike another male.

The availability of food over both ecological and evolutionary time is probably the major factor determining mating
behavior in *Panorpa*. I tested this hypothesis by comparing
two Mexican species of *Panorpa* which do not cooccur and which
live under different ecological situations with regard to the
availability of food. One species, *P. penicillata* Byers,
lives at elevations from 1,525-2,135 m on the west slopes of
the Sierra Madre Occidental Mountains. The habitat of this
species is characterized by dominant evergreen pine and oak
trees with deciduous trees in small numbers. The understory
is comprised of knee-high grass and dense patches of broad-
leaf herbs. A second species inhabits relatively dry oak
forest with a sparse understory of poison oak at 2,135-2,745 m
on the western side of the Sierra Madre Oriental Mountains.
This species (hereafter referred to as *P. sp.*) will be described by Dr. George W. Byers, Dept. of Entomology, University of Kansas, in a forthcoming taxonomic paper on the
Mexican Mecoptera.

The habitats of the two species of Mexican *Panorpa* differ
in ways other than vegetation. Five study sites for each of
the two species were sampled over a one-week period. Two-
hundred sweeps with a 30 cm diameter insect net per study
site revealed a significant difference in arthropod abundance
(i.e., potential food for panorpas) between the habitats of
the two species ($\bar{x}$ = 732.2 ± 165 arthropods, pine-oak forests;
$\bar{x}$ = 168.6 ± 70 arthropods, dry oak forests; two-tailed t =
18.04, p < 0.001). All eastern North American *Panorpa* species
eat primarily soft-bodied dead arthropods (Thornhill, 1974).
Beetles and other highly sclerotized arthropods were removed
from the sweep samples and the data were reanalyzed. The
habitats of the two species were still found to be significantly different with regard to arthropod abundance: $\bar{x}$ =
529 ± 82 soft-bodied arthropods in pine-oak forests; $\bar{x}$ =
98 ± 48 soft-bodied arthropods in dry oak forests; two-tailed
t = 11.7, p < 0.001. A ½ hr. count at each of the
ten study sites revealed no significant difference in the
numbers of adults of the two species of *Panorpa* ($\bar{x}$ = 34 ± 15.5
P. sp.; $\bar{x}$ = 39 ± 6.25 *P. penicillata*; two-tailed t = 1.79,
p > 0.10). One-hundred sweep samples in the low vegetation
at each of the ten study sites were used to determine the
numbers of potential competitors (i.e., phalangids and ants)
in the habitats of the two species. The numbers of phalangids
in the habitats of the two species were not significantly
different ($\bar{x}$ = 26 ± 7.52 for the *P. penicillata* sites; $\bar{x}$ =
20.4 ± 5.31 for the *P. sp.* sites; two-tailed t = 2.04,
p > 0.05). The number of ants in the habitat of *P. penicillata* ($\bar{x}$ = 28 ± 10.3) was significantly greater (t = 3.37,
0.05 < p < 0.01) than the number in the habitat of *P. sp.*

($\bar{x}$ = 12.5 ± 5.52). An idea of relative predation pressures
on the two species was obtained by counting the numbers of
active spiders seen in a half hour at each of the ten study
sites. A highly significant difference in the number of web-
building spiders in the two habitats was found: $\bar{x}$ = 19.1 ± 4.21
P. penicillata; $\bar{x}$ = 7.8 ± 3.52 *P.* sp.; two-tailed t = 5.91,
0.01 < p < 0.001.

P. penicillata is a large species (body length 18 mm) with
a large genital bulb (15% of total dry weight), whereas *P.*
sp. is small (body length 10 mm) with a relatively small
genital bulb (6.3% of total dry weight). I found that large
species of Michigan *Panorpa* are better able to deter attack
by being aggressive when approached by a spider while feeding
in a web (Thornhill, 1974, 1975). I also found a significant
positive correlation between the size of contestants and
dominance around food in interspecific aggressive interactions
in the Michigan species of *Panorpa*. Because of its large
body and genitalia size, *P. penicillata* probably experiences
less competition from other scavenging arthropods as well as
less predation from web-building spiders. If this is reasonable, a situation results where potential food (insects and
other arthropods) is abundant for *P. penicillata* compared to *P.*
sp. This circumstance may have had a major influence on the
evolution of mating behavior of these two species of *Panorpa*.

I have made behavioral observations on almost 50% of the
North American species of *Panorpa*. Males of all species I
have investigated (twelve species in Michigan, four in the
southern Appalachian Mountains, and two in Mexico), except *P.*
penicillata, have well-developed salivary glands and secrete
salivary masses as part of their mating behavior. Males of
several North American species that I have not studied are
also known to produce salivary masses (Byers, 1963; Gassner,
1963; Mampe and Nuenzig, 1965). Sexual dimorphism of salivary
glands is known in some European species of *Panorpa* (Potter,
1938). The nature and extent of usage of salivary masses by
the species I have studied vary greatly (Thornhill, 1974,
and unpublished). Relative to the Mexican *P.* sp., *P. penicil-*
lata lives in a food-rich environment. This, coupled with
large body and genitalia size, may account for the loss of
salivary mass secretion behavior in *P. penicillata*.

The extent to which the availability of food determines
how males compete among themselves for females and how females
choose males was tested with *P. penicillata* and *P.* sp. The
experiments were conducted in Mexican hotel rooms in 21 liter
aquaria at temperatures ranging from 21° to 28°C. and under
varying conditions of room light.

Initially, I designed experiments with *P. penicillata* to
determine how males compete for different types of dead arthropods and how females assess males possessing different

types of dead arthropods. Ten males, individually marked with
airplane dope on the thorax or wings, were placed in each of
three aquaria with five freshly dead arthropods of different
sizes. The numbers and types of aggressive interactions observed in 1 hr. around each size arthropod were counted. The
five types of aggressive actions displayed by *P. penicillata*
increase in intensity from Type 1 to Type 5 as follows:

Type 1. Wing fluttering. A characteristic wing movement
whereby both pairs of wings are raised and lowered at a
relatively slow rate while the actor is in a stationary
position.

Type 2. Abdominal lashing without contact. A male lashed
out his abdomen in the direction of another male, but
without contact.

Type 3. Rushing and wing fluttering. Rapid movement of the
aggressor in the direction of another male, while simultaneously fluttering the wings.

Type 4. Butting. The aggressor rushes toward another male
and butts the intruder with his snout.

Type 5. Abdominal striking. A male strikes an intruder with
his genital bulb. The strike is performed simultaneously

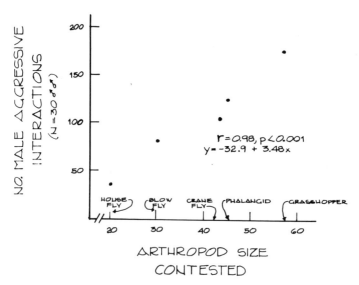

*Fig. 1. Correlation between the size of the dead arthropod
contested and the number of aggressive interactions between
males of* P. penicillata.

TABLE 1

Numbers of aggressive interactions in 1 hr. of
30 males of P. penicillata
around different sizes of prey arthropods

Mean size	No. of each type of aggression					Total
arthropod, contested	1	2	3	4	5	
20 mm^2 (house fly)	15	18	3	0	0	36
30 mm^2 (blow fly)	6	21	20	24	10	81
43.5 mm^2 (crane fly)	0	24	23	37	18	102
45.2 mm^2 (phalangid)	0	10	50	17	36	123
57 mm^2 (grasshopper)	1	0	51	57	65	174

NOTE: The type of aggressive act scored was that which resulted in a termination of the aggressive interaction
between two males.

with an opening and closing of the genital forceps. The
forceps are strong and may damage a leg or a wing of
another male. Occasionally, intruding males may be lifted
off the substrate and thrown through the air by the back-
swing of the abdomen.

Fig. 1 shows a highly significant positive correlation
between the size (length x width in millimeters) of the
arthropod contested over and the number of aggressive interactions. The types of aggressive interactions were of greater
intensity around the larger arthropods (Table 1). These data
strongly suggest that males can distinguish size or something
probably related to size in dead arthropods.

After 1 hr. in the test aquaria, male aggression around
the dead arthropods had almost completely ceased. This left
five males guarding dead arthropods and five males without
prey in each of the three aquaria. Ten females were placed
in each aquarium and watched for 1 hr. Each female had a
choice of ten males. One hour later 87% (13 of 15) of the
males in possession of dead arthropods were copulating, but
only 13% (2 of 15) of those without dead arthropods had copulated. This difference is highly significant (p = 0.01) with
Fisher's Exact Test. All the males not possessing dead arthropods were sexually active and attempted to grasp passing
females. The mean copulation duration for males without dead
arthropods was shorter ($\bar{x}$ = 0.8 ± 0.23 hr.) than that for males
possessing dead arthropods ($\bar{x}$ = 2.41 ± 1.25 hr.). The possible

significance of copulation duration in this species is discussed in connection with the next experiment.

The number of interactions of females with males that
possessed nuptial food vs. the number with males that did not
was counted. Females interacted significantly more ($\bar{x}$ = 11.8,
p. < 0.002) with males possessing food (63 interactions) than
with males that had been excluded from food through aggression
with other males (29 interactions). Also, all interactions
of females with food-possessing males were female initiated,
whereas all interactions of females with males without food
were male initiated. These data indicate that females prefer
males that possess dead arthropods over males that do not.
The choice on the part of the females apparently depends on
the male's ability to secure a dead arthropod through aggression.

An experiment was designed in which the size, shape, and
color of dead arthropods contested by males were held constant, but their quality was manipulated. Blow flies (Calli-
phoridae: *Phaenicia*), apparently of the same species and of
similar size, were collected and killed by chilling in ice
water. One batch of flies was air dried for 24 hr., another
for 12 hr., and another was kept on ice without drying. The
internal organs and tissues of the flies dried 24 hr. were
collapsed and desiccated, those of the flies dried 12 hr.
were also visibly drier than those of the flies kept on ice
without drying. I placed 12 individually marked males of
P. penicillata and 12 blow flies (four of each treatment) in
each of three aquaria. I counted aggressive interactions of

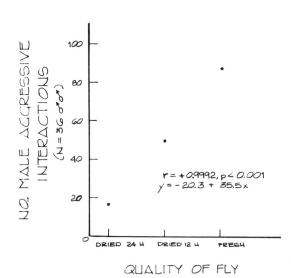

$r = +0.9992, p < 0.001$
$y = -20.3 + 35.5x$

Fig. 2. Correlation
between the quality
of the dead fly con-
tested and the number
of aggressive inter-
actions between males
of P. penicillata.

the males around each of the three types of flies in 1 hr.
Fig. 2 shows a highly significant positive correlation between
the food quality of the dead flies contested by males and
the number of aggressive interactions around them. Also,
more interactions were terminated by high intensity types of
aggression around the flies that had been kept on ice.

I have shown that panorpas find dead arthropods by olfaction over distances of about 1 m (Thornhill, 1974). The
positive correlation between food quality and aggression
indicates that males can distinguish food quality in a dead
arthropod by olfaction and/or vision, since interactions between a male guarding a dead fly and an intruding male took
place without the intruder touching the fly with its mouthparts.

After the continuation of the experiment for 1 hr., aggression had ceased, and the number of males guarding each type of
fly was counted. All the fresh flies and the flies dried 12
hr. were possessed by males at this time, but only 50% (6 of
12) of the flies dried 24 hr. This suggests that males are
not as likely to guard dry arthropods. Thus, there would be
intense selection for finding dead arthropods soon after they
die and before they desiccate to the point of being of little
food value. The rate at which dead arthropods desiccate may be
an important factor limiting the amount of food for panorpas.

Twelve females were added to each aquarium after male
aggression around the flies had ceased. Each of the three
aquaria contained 12 females and 12 males, and in each aquarium some males did not possess flies at all and those that possessed dead flies had flies of different quality. The panorpas were watched continuously for an hour after the addition
of females. The number of each type of male in copulation or

TABLE 2

Copulatory success of males of P. penicillata *possessing*
flies of different food value
as well as males that do not possess flies

% Copulatory success	No. males		Quality of fly in possession of male
	In cop.	Not in cop.	
33.3	2	4	No fly in possession
50	3	3	Fly dried 24 hrs.
100	12	0	Fly dried 12 hrs.
100	12	0	Fresh dead fly
	29	7	

that had copulated by one hour after the introduction of
females is shown in Table 2. Approximately equal numbers of
males not possessing flies at all and males possessing flies
dried 24 hr. copulated. However, all the males copulated
that possessed fresh dead flies and flies dried 12 hr. All
the males that possessed fresh dead flies were in copulation
sooner ($\bar{x}$ = 1.32 ± 4.94 min.) after the introduction of
the females than males that possessed flies dried 12 hr.
($\bar{x}$ = 27.9 ± 8.6 min.). A two-tailed t-test indicates a highly
significant difference (t = 5.81, p < 0.001) in the times
for copulation to be initiated by these two types of males.
If males in nature obtain mates faster when they possess high
quality food, this could offset the time lost in stealing the
prey of another male or time lost in defending prey against
other males. Too few data are available to test for a difference between the time of introduction of females and copulation for males in possession of flies dried 24 hr. and males
not in possession of flies. However, none of the males in
these two categories initiated copulations with females in
less than 22 min.

   Fig. 3 shows a significant positive correlation between
mean copulation duration and the quality of fly guarded by
males. In *B. apicalis* sperm transfer is positively correlated
with copulation duration (Thornhill, 1976b). Also, in *B.
strigosus* a sexual inhibitory agent is apparently passed from
the male to the female late in copulation (J. B. Johnson,
unpublished). If these things occur in *Panorpa*, females are
discriminating against males without nuptial offerings or with
poor quality nuptial offerings at two levels: first, by preferring mates with better nuptial offerings; second, by copu-

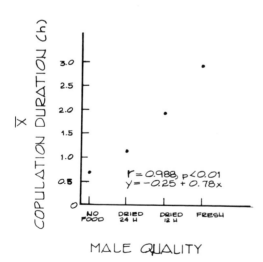

Fig. 3. Correlation be-
tween male quality and
mean copulation duration
in P. penicillata. Male
quality is in terms of
whether or not a male is
guarding a dead fly, and,
if so, the quality of
the fly guarded. N=2
for male not guarding a
fly. N=3, R=0.8-2.0 for
males guarding flies
dried 24 hr. N=12,
R=1.5-2.6 for males
guarding flies dried 12
hr. N=12, R=1.5-3.0 for
males guarding fresh
dead flies.

lating for longer durations with males with better nuptial
offerings.

The results of the experiments on *P. penicillata* using blow
flies indicate that a male's copulatory success depends on the
quality of the nuptial offering that he is able to find and
defend from other males. There is also strong indication that
females prefer males with higher quality nuptial offerings and
that the criterion of female choice is a male's ability to
find and defend a high quality food item.

The males of the undescribed Mexican species of *Panorpa*
(*P. sp.*), unlike *P. penicillata,* have well-developed salivary
glands and secrete salivary masses that are attached to the
substrate. I found a significant negative correlation ($r =
-0.999$, $p < 0.01$) between the numbers of salivary secretions
deposited by males of *P. sp.* and the availability of fresh
dead blow flies (see Table 3). This indicates that when food
is available males refrain from secreting saliva and instead
disperse pheromone from around a dead arthropod. Data presented later further support this interpretation.

An experiment was designed to determine if a male's salivary secreting abilities are related to his reproductive
success. Ten individually marked males were placed in each
of three aquaria without food. Twenty-five of the males
(83.3%) secreted a salivary mass in 1 hr., and ten females
were added to each aquarium. All 25 males that had secreted
salivary masses were copulating 1 hr. after addition of
females, but none of the five males that had not secreted
masses had initiated copulations. The males that did not

TABLE 3

*Relationship between amount of food available for males to
defend and the number of salivary
secretions deposited by males of* P. sp.

No. house flies/ aquarium	No. salivary masses after 12 hrs.								Totals (both nights)
	Rep 1	Rep 2	Rep 3	Total	Rep 1	Rep 2	Rep 3	Total	
0	10	7	9	26	8	8	7	23	49
5	5	3	5	13	3	5	2	10	23
10	0	0	0	0	0	0	0	0	0
Totals	15	10	14	39	11	13	9	33	72

NOTE: Each rep. 10 males.

secrete saliva tried to grasp females, but the females
avoided these attempts.

The copulation duration for *P.* sp. is 4 hr. ($\bar{x}$ = 3.97 ±
0.81, N = 25). An additional salivary mass was secreted by
20 of the 25 males (80%) halfway through the 4 hr. copulation
(mean time of secretion of second mass from beginning of
first copulation = 1.95 ± 0.25 hr.). Two hours of copulation
corresponded to the time necessary for a female to consume
the first mass. Upon secretion of the second mass, a male
repositions the female in such a way as to allow her to
resume feeding. The five males that did not secrete an
additional mass after the female consumed the first copulated
for shortest durations ($\bar{x}$ = 2.08 ± 0.20 hr.).

At the termination of copulation after 4 hr., the 25
males were placed in aquaria (10/aquarium) without food to
determine if they could or would secrete more salivary masses.
In 1 hr., only eight of the 25 males secreted saliva. Ten
females were then added to each aquarium. One hour later 100%
(8 of 8) of the saliva-secreting males were in copulation,
but none of the 17 males that did not secrete saliva had
initiated copulations. The 17 nonsecreting males were sexually active, but their attempts to grasp females were unsuccessful. The eight copulating males did not secrete an
additional mass after the first was eaten by the female.
The copulation duration for these males was about 2 hr. ($\bar{x}$ =
2.5 ± 0.52), which corresponds with the durations of copulations for the males in the previous test that did not secrete
an additional salivary mass when the first was consumed by
the female. The 17 males that did not secrete saliva in this
test had apparently exhausted their ability to do so by their
secretory activities in the previous test. Also, none of the
males in this test secreted an additional mass after the first
was consumed, suggesting that the salivary secreting ability
of these males was exhausted.

The experiments with *P.* sp. indicate that females prefer
males that secrete salivary masses over ones that do not.
The males that did not secrete saliva in the experiments were
sexually active and tried to couple with passing females but
were discriminated against. I designed an experiment to test
whether females prefer males guarding arthropods over males
that are guarding salivary masses. Ten individually marked
males and five fresh dead blow flies were placed in each of
three aquaria. After 1 hr., aggression around the flies
had ceased and each male that did not secure a fly by aggression secreted a salivary mass. After an additional hour, five
females were added per aquarium to determine the copulatory
success of males guarding salivary masses and males guarding
dead flies. In each aquarium each female had a choice of ten
males, five guarding salivary masses and five guarding dead

flies. Eighty-seven percent (13 of 15) of fly-guarding males
but only 13% (2 of 15) of saliva-guarding males were in
copulation 1 hr. after the introduction of the females.
This difference is highly significant (p = 0.01) with Fisher's
Exact Test. Thus, while all the females copulated, they
preferred males guarding flies over males guarding saliva.
This preference was expected since I found an indication in
the first test with *P.* sp. that males refrain from secreting
saliva when dead insects are available for guarding.

The adaptive value of female preference of certain males
in *Panorpa* can be inferred from the experiments with the two
Mexican species of *Panorpa*. It is necessary to show conclu-
sively, however, that females increase their own reproductive
success by their choice of mating partners in order to demonstrate adaptive female choice. In some experiments females
preferred males that provided them with nuptial gifts over
males that did not, and in other experiments males were preferred that provided nuptial gifts of high quality over males
that provided nuptial gifts of poor quality. More food or
higher quality food received by a *Panorpa* female during nuptial feeding may be related directly to increased fecundity,
as in *B. apicalis,* but this must be demonstrated. Feeding on
a male's nuptial offering probably increases the chances of
survival of a female *Panorpa* because it reduces the amount of
feeding that she must do on her own. Increased competition
for food in *Panorpa* was found to increase mortality, apparently because of increased exposure to web-building spiders
(Thornhill, 1974, 1975).

The criterion of female choice in both species of Mexican
Panorpa appears to be related to a male's success at finding
and defending the critical resource food. This is especially
apparent in the preference of females of *P. penicillata* for
males guarding high quality food and in the preference of
females of *P.* sp. for males guarding food over males guarding
salivary masses. It is reasonable that males, which are
securing and maintaining possession of high quality food, will
be challenged more often by males that have similar aggressive
abilities. If the salivary secreting abilities of males are
fairly easily exhausted, as indicated by the tests with *P.*
sp., and a male's ability to secrete saliva depends on his
recent history of feeding, the females of *P.* sp. that preferred males with salivary secretions over males without them
may also be choosing males on the basis of their ability to
find and aggressively dominate food items.

Females are also very aggressive (Thornhill, 1974). Fe-
male-female aggression is intense around oviposition sites,
and females defend food against heterospecific panorpas of
both sexes and conspecific females. Aggression toward conspecific males around food is also shown by sexually nonreceptive

females between matings or when a receptive female locates a
dead arthropod before a male does. Females frequently hunt
and feed on their own (Thornhill, 1974). Thus, the male
behaviors that females evaluate are critical to their own
survival and reproduction. The types of aggressive actions
of females are similar to those listed earlier for males.
Therefore, general aggressive behavior of panorpas is not sex-
linked. Rearing studies will determine the extent to which
a male's aggressive abilities are inherited by both his sons
and daughters.

SEXUAL SELECTION AND THE SEX RATIO

     Trivers and Willard (1973) proposed a model based on
natural selection theory to explain data on sex ratio biases
in mammals. The authors reasoned that in mammals with low
male parental investment, females in good condition (nutri-
tionally and otherwise) should bias their sex ratio toward
sons because their sons, also assumed to be in good condition
as a result of the condition of the mother, would experience
greater reproductive success than daughters in similar condition. Daughters should outreproduce sons if both are in poor
condition, and mothers should bias their sex ratios toward
daughters if they find themselves in a less than optimum condition at the time of reproduction. Sexual selection is
another context in which a female might be selected to bias
her sex ratio. Because of high variance in male reproductive
success in species with no or little paternal investment, a
female mating with a genetically superior male, regardless of
her nutritional state, might experience greater genetic success
by biasing her sex ratio toward males. A female mating with
a less than superior male under these circumstances would pass
on more genes to subsequent generations by producing more
female offspring. Both models, in theory, should apply to all
animal groups, including insects, where male parental investment is low compared to female investment.
     Data are not available from the insect literature to test
the hypothesis of Trivers and Willard or the sexual selection
hypothesis. Both hypotheses assume that only the female is
in control of biasing the sex ratio. However, one could
reason that in a species with low male investment, an unusually fit male might be selected to bias the sperm he transfers
in copulation in favor of male-determining sperm and thus
experience increased genetic success. Conversely, one could
argue that an inferior male might bias sperm in his ejaculate
toward female-determining sperm. A mechanism for this could
involve differential production or mortality of one type sperm
or the other. These circumstances, if real, would explain sex

ratio biases when viewed in terms of either the nutritional or sexual selection hypothesis. To rule out the male as the sex which biases sex ratios of offspring, one ideally needs to work with a species in which the female is the heterogametic sex (birds and the Lepidoptera). The hypotheses on sex ratio manipulation by mothers will be tested with *Panorpa*, in which the male apparently controls sex determination. Females will be reared under different regimes varying in quantity and quality of food. Virgin females so raised will be mated with males of different quality in terms of their abilities to locate food and to defend it in the laboratory.

DISTANCE SIGNALING AND SEXUAL SELECTION

We are naturally led to enquire why the male, in so many and such distinct cases, has become more eager than the female, so that he searches for her and plays the more active role in courtship. It would be no advantage and some loss of power if each sex searched for the other; but why should the male almost always be the seeker (Darwin, 1871).

Sexual communication over distances in animals primarily involves pheromonal and acoustical signals. Everything else equal, selection should be stronger on males than on females to respond to any cue over a distance that indicates the presence and location of a sexually receptive member of the opposite sex. This is because of greater sexual competition among males than among females. A male that could smell and orient to a metabolic byproduct of a female, especially of a sexually receptive female, would have an intrasexual selective advantage. Kittredge and Takahashi (1972) found that male crabs (*Cancer* spp.) respond over distances to the molting hormone of females. In *Cancer* spp. and many other Crustacea, copulation takes place after the molting of the female. Selection has favored males that responded initially to a chemical cue without a sexual function that was produced by females in a state of sexual readiness. Similar selection pressures may have resulted in the intense male aggression around pharate females in *Tetranychus* mites because females are only sexually receptive after molting and while still virgin (Potter et al., 1976). In other animals in which pheromones are important in pair formation over distances and not in territory marking, the female usually emits the pheromone (nematodes [Anya, 1976; Roche, 1966], insects [Jacobson, 1972], mammals of various orders [see Eisenberg and Kleiman, 1972], primates [references in Michael et al., 1974]).

In Jacobson's (1972) review of sex pheromones in insects,

he states that distance sex attractants are usually characteristic of females, and male pheromones where they exist
usually function at close range as part of male courtship.
The relatively few cases where females respond to a male
distance pheromone may be explicable in terms of sexual selection. In *Panorpa* (Thornhill, 1973, 1974) and *Bittacus*
(Thornhill, 1974) as well as in *Harpobittacus* (Bornemissza,
1964, 1966), males produce sex pheromones that attract conspecific females from a distance. In these genera the male
provides the attracted female with a nuptial gift of food.
Perhaps when a male has a nuptial offering, or is in possession of some other resource critical to female fitness such
as a territory or oviposition site, selection is stronger on
females for response to any male odor than vice versa.

It would be of interest to investigate the occurrence of
male-emitted distance sex pheromones within the Lepidoptera
and certain other insect groups in light of this idea. The
nuptial gift in some Lepidoptera consists of a large protein-
aceous spermatophore that the male transfers to the female
during copulation (Thornhill, 1976a). The spermatophore can
be considered a paternal nutritional investment in offspring
because, at least in some butterflies (*Heliconius* and the
monarch), the protein in the spermatophore is important in
enhancing early egg production (L. Gilbert and C. Norris,
unpublished).

Another consideration in understanding patterns of distance signaling by the sexes is the risks involved in
signaling. It is interesting that there are few known cases
of parasites or predators locating prey by following a sex
pheromone trail (e.g., Sternlicht, 1973). A few arthropods
that are commensals in ant nests have been shown to have the
ability to follow odor trails of their hosts (Moser, 1964;
Rettenmeyer, 1963). The rarity of such a phenomenon may be
significant in explaining the predominance of sex pheromone
emission by females. Males should be more strongly selected
than females to participate in risky activities associated
with mate acquisition if the benefits in terms of genetic
representation in future generations offset costs in terms of
exposure to predation. If prey location by olfactory detection of a distance sex pheromone is "evolutionarily infeasi-
ble" for a predator for some reason, this would make pheromone
production less risky for females. Perhaps the ease in which
a pheromone molecule's specificity can be changed allows the
pheromone-emitting prey to stay one step ahead of a predator
in the process of evolving the ability to track prey by
following a pheromone trail.

The risks of calling and/or resources provided to the
female by the male at pair formation may explain the predominance of male distance signaling in the Orthoptera.

Distance acoustical signals in some Orthoptera are risky in
terms of predator detection. Singing males of *Gryllus
integer* are located by a parasitic tachinid fly by acoustical
orientation (Cade, 1976). Males that do not sing but attempt
to intercept and copulate with females attracted to calling
males experience less parasitism. Walker (1964) demonstrated
that domestic cats can orient acoustically to some singing
Orthoptera. Walker (1974) suggested that predators may be a
major selective force in the loss of calling behavior in some
Orthoptera. Resources provided to the female by a male in
the Orthoptera are in the form of an oviposition site and a
place to rear young (see West and Alexander, 1963), protein-
aceous spermatophores that may be of nutritional value
to the female and/or used by the female in egg production
(see Thornhill, 1976b), or the male may allow the female to
consume his body after copulation (see Alexander and Otte,
1967).

CONCLUSIONS

   The role of sexual selection in the evolution of insect
reproductive behavior is poorly understood. Sexual selection
involves the major selective forces acting on the sexes in
the context of reproduction. The importance of male sexual
selection (male-male competition for females) in nature is
better understood than the importance of female sexual selection (female choice) despite considerable theoretical
development as to how females should choose. Our lack of
understanding of sexual selection stems from (1) a failure
to separate sexual selection from other selective contexts
operating during reproduction (i.e., selection for reproductive isolation and sex identification), (2) the difficulty in
separation of the two contexts of sexual selection, and (3)
the difficulty in understanding the criteria that females use
in mate choice.

REFERENCES

Alexander, R.D. 1974. The evolution of social behavior. *Ann.
   Rev. Ecol. Syst.* 5:325-383.
Alexander, R.D. 1975. Natural selection and specialized
   chorusing behavior in acoustical insects. *In* D. Pimentel
   (ed.), *Insects, Science and Society*. Academic Press,
   New York.
Alexander, R.D., and D. Otte. 1967. The evolution of genitalia
   and mating behavior in crickets (Gryllidae) and other

Orthoptera. *Mus. Zool. Misc. Publ. Univ. Mich.* 133:1-62.

Anya, A.O. 1976. Studies on the reproductive physiology of nematodes: The phenomenon of sexual attraction and the origin of the attractants in *Aspiculuris tetraptera*. *Int'l. J. Parasit.* 6:173-177.

Bateman, A.J. 1948. Intra-sexual selection in *Drosophila*. *Heredity* 2:349-368.

Beach, F.A., and B.J. Le Boeuf. 1967. Coital behavior in dogs. I. Preferential mating in the bitch. *Anim. Behav.* 15:546-558.

Bequaert, J. 1935. Presocial behavior among the Hemiptera. *Bull. Brooklyn Ent. Soc.* 30:117-191.

Bonhag, P.F., and J.R. Wick. 1953. The functional anatomy of the male and female reproductive systems of the milkweed bug, *Oncopeltus fasciatus* (Dallas) (Heteroptera: Lygaeidae). *J. Morph.* 93:177-284.

Bornemissza, G.F. 1964. Sex attractant of male scorpion flies. *Nature* 203:786.

Bornemissza, G.F. 1966. Specificity of male sex attractants in some Australian scorpion flies. *Nature* 209:732.

Bro Larsen, E. 1952. On subsocial beetles from the saltmarsh, their care of progeny and adaptation to salt and tide. *Trans. 11th Int'l. Cong. Ent., Amsterdam, 1951* 1:502-506.

Byers, G.W. 1963. The life history of *P. nuptialis* (Mecoptera: Panorpidae). *Ann. Ent. Soc. Amer.* 56:142-149.

Cade, W. 1976. Acoustically orienting parasitoids: fly phonotaxis to cricket song. *Science* 190:1312-1313.

Campanella, P.J., and L.L. Wolf. 1974. Temporal leks as a mating system in a temperate zone dragonfly (Odonata: Anisoptera) I. *Plathemis lydia* (Drury). *Behaviour* 51:4-87.

Campbell, B. (ed.) 1972. *Sexual Selection and the Descent of Man, 1871-1971*. Aldine, Chicago.

Darwin, C. 1871. *The Descent of Man, and Selection in Relation to Sex*. 1st ed. John Murray, London.

Darwin, C. 1874. *The Descent of Man, and Selection in Relation to Sex*. 2nd ed. John Murray, London.

Dawkins, R., and T.R. Carlisle. 1976. Parental investment, mate desertion and a fallacy. *Nature* 262:131-132.

Dewsbury, D. 1975. Diversity and adaptation in rodent copulatory behavior. *Science* 190:947-954.

Economopoulos, A.P., and H.T. Gordon. 1972. Sperm replacement and depletion in the spermatheca of the S and CS strains of *Oncopeltus fasciatus*. *Ent. Exp. Appl.* 15:1-12.

Eisenberg, J.F., and D.G. Kleiman. 1972. Olfactory communication in mammals. *Ann. Rev. Ecol. Syst.* 3:1-32.

Evans, H.E. 1958. The evolution of social life in wasps. *Proc. 10th Int'l. Cong. Ent., Montreal, 1956* 2:449-457.

Faure, J.C. 1940. Maternal care displayed by mantids (Orthoptera). *Ent. Soc. South. Africa* 3:139-150.

Fisher, R.A. 1958. *The Genetical Theory of Natural Selection*. 2nd rev. ed. Dover, New York.

Fulton, B.B. 1924. Some habits of earwigs. *Ann. Ent. Soc. Amer.* 17:357-367.

Gassner III, G. 1963. Notes on the biology and immature stages of *Panorpa nuptialis* Gerstaecker (Mecoptera: Panorpidae). *Texas J. Sci.* 55:142-154.

Grant, V. 1963. *The Origin of Adaptations*. Columbia Univ. Press, New York.

Herbert, J. 1968. Sexual preference in the rhesus monkey *(Macaca mulatta)* in the laboratory. *Anim. Behav.* 16:120-128.

Hinton, H.E. 1944. Some general remarks on sub-social beetles, with notes on the biology of the staphylinid, *Platystethus arenarius* (Fourcroy). *Proc. Roy. Ent. Soc. London* 19:115-128.

Hogan-Warburg, A.J. 1966. Social behavior of the ruff *Philomachus pugnax* (L.) *Ardea* 54:109-229.

Howard, E. 1968. *Territory in Bird Life*. Atheneum, New York. (First published in 1920.)

Huxley, J.S. 1938. The present standing of the theory of sexual selection. *In* G.R. de Beer (ed.), *Evolution: Essays on Aspects of Evolutionary Biology Presented to Professor E.S. Goodrich on his 70th Birthday*. Clarendon Press, Oxford.

Jacobs, M. 1955. Studies in territorialism and sexual selection in dragonflies. *Ecology* 36:566-586.

Jacobson, M. 1972. *Insect Sex Pheromones*. Academic Press, New York.

Kittredge, J.S., and F.T. Takahashi. 1972. The evolution of sex pheromone communication in the Arthropoda. *J. Theor. Biol.* 35:467-471.

Kluyver, H.N. 1955. Das Verhalten des Drosselrohrsängers, *Acrocephalus arundinaceus* (L.), am Brutplatz, mit besonderer Berucksichtigung der Nestbautechnik und der Revierbehauptung. *Ardea* 43:1-50.

Kroodsma, D.E. 1976. Reproductive development in a female songbird: differential stimulation by quality of male song. *Science* 192:574-575.

Lamb, R.J., and W.G. Wellington. 1974. Techniques for studying the behavior and ecology of the European earwig, *Forficula auricularia* (Dermaptera: Forficulidae). *Can. Ent.* 106: 881-888.

Ledoux, A. 1958. Biologie et comportement de l'Embioptère *Monotylota ramburi* Rims.-Kors. *Ann. Sci. Naturelles* 20:515-532.

Lewontin, R.C. 1970. The units of selection. *Ann. Rev. Ecol. Syst.* 1:1-18.

Liechti, P.M., and W.J. Bell. 1975. Brooding behavior of the Cuban burrowing cockroach *Byrsotria fumigata* (Blaberidae: Blattaria). *Insectes Soc.* 22:35-46.

Lill, A., and D.G.M. Wood-Gush. 1965. Potential ethological

isolating mechanisms and assortative mating in the domestic fowl. *Behaviour* 25:16-44.

Mainardi, D., F.M. Scuds, and D. Barbieri. 1965. Assortative mating based on early learning: population genetics. *L'Atenes Parmense* 36:583-605.

Mampe, C.D., and H.H. Neunzig. 1965. Larval descriptions of two species of *Panorpa* (Mecoptera: Panorpidae) with notes on their biology. *Ann. Ent. Soc. Amer.* 58:843-849.

Mani, M.S., and S.N. Rao. 1950. A remarkable example of maternal solicitude in a thrips from India. *Current Sci.* 19:217.

Maynard Smith, J. 1956. Fertility, mating behavior and sexual selection in *Drosophila subobscura*. *J. Genetics* 54:261-279.

Maynard Smith, J. 1966. *The Theory of Evolution*. Penguin Books, Inc., Baltimore.

Mayr, E. 1972. Sexual selection and natural selection. *In* B. Campbell (ed.), *Sexual Selection and the Descent of Man, 1871-1971*. Aldine, Chicago.

Michael, R.P., R.W. Bonsall, and P. Warner. 1974. Human vaginal secretions: volatile fatty acid content. *Science* 186: 1217-1219.

Michener, C.D. 1969. Comparative social behavior of bees. *Ann. Rev. Ent.* 14:299-342.

Mockford, E.L. 1957. Life history studies of some Florida insects of the genus *Archipsocus* (Psocoptera). *Bull. Fla. St. Mus. Biol. Sci.* 1:253-274.

Moser, J.C. 1964. Inquiline roach responds to trail-marking substance of leaf-cutting ants. *Science* 143:1048-1049.

Odhiambo, T.R. 1959. An account of parental care in *Rhinocoris albopilosus* Signoret (Hemiptera-Heteroptera: Reduviidae), with notes on its life history. *Proc. Roy. Ent. Soc. London* 34:175-185.

Odhiambo, T.R. 1960. Parental care in bugs and non-social insects. *New Scientist* 8:449-451.

Parker, G.A. 1970a. Sperm competition and its evolutionary consequences in the insects. *Biol. Rev.* 45:525-567.

Parker, G.A. 1970b. The reproductive behaviour and the nature of sexual selection in *Scatophaga stercoraria* (L.) (Diptera: Scatophagidae) II. The fertilization rate and the spatial and temporal relationships of each sex around the site of mating and oviposition. *J. Anim. Ecol.* 39: 205-228.

Parker, G.A. 1970c. The reproductive behaviour and the nature of sexual selection in *Scatophaga stercoraria* (L.) (Diptera: Scatophagidae) IV. Epigamic recognition and competition between males for the possession of females. *Behaviour* 37:8-39.

Parker, G.A. 1970d. The reproductive behaviour and the nature of sexual selection in *Scatophaga stercoraria* (L.) (Diptera: Scatophagidae) V. The female's behaviour at the oviposition site. *Behaviour* 37:140-168.

Parker, G.A. 1970e. The reproductive behaviour and the nature of sexual selection in *Scatophaga stercoraria* (L.) (Diptera: Scatophagidae) VII. The origin and evolution of the passive phase. *Evolution* 24:791-805.

Parker, G.A. 1970f. Sperm competition and its evolutionary effect on copula duration in the fly *Scatophaga stercoraria*. *J. Insect Physiol*. 16:1303-1328.

Parker, G.A. 1972a. Reproductive behaviour of *Sepsis cynipsea* (L.) (Diptera: Sepsidae) I. A preliminary analysis of the reproductive strategy and its associated behaviour patterns. *Behaviour* 41:172-206.

Parker, G.A. 1972b. Reproductive behaviour of *Sepsis cynipsea* (L.) (Diptera: Sepsidae) II. The significance of the precopulatory passive phase and emigration. *Behaviour* 41:207-215.

Petit, C., and L. Ehrman. 1969. Sexual selection in *Drosophila*. *In* T. Dobzhansky, M. Hect, and Wm. Steere (eds.), *Evolutionary Biology III*. Appleton-Century-Crofts, New York.

Potter, D.A., D.L. Wrensch, and D.E. Johnston. 1976. Aggression and mating success in male spider mites. *Science* 193:160-161.

Potter, E. 1938. The internal anatomy of the order Mecoptera. *Trans. Roy. Ent. Soc. London* 87:467-502.

Pukowski, E. 1933. Ökologische untersuchungen an *Necrophorus* (F.) *Z. Morph. Ökol. Tiere* 27:518-586.

Rettenmeyer, C.W. 1963. The behavior of Thysanura found with army ants. *Ann. Ent. Soc. Amer*. 56:170-174.

Richards, O.W. 1927. Sexual selection and allied problems in the insects. *Biol. Rev*. 2:298-364.

Robel, R.J. 1966. Booming territory size and mating success of the greater prairie chicken *(Tympanuchus cupido pinnatus)*. *Anim. Behav*. 14:328-331.

Roche, M. 1966. Influence of male and female *Ancylostoma caninum* on each other's distribution in the intestine of the dog. *Exp. Parasit*. 19:327-331.

Roth, L.M., and E.R. Willis. 1960. The biotic associations of cockroaches. *Smithsonian Misc. Coll. No. 141*. 470 pp.

Selander, R.K. 1972. Sexual selection and dimorphism in birds. *In* B. Campbell (ed.), *Sexual Selection and the Descent of Man, 1871-1971*. Aldine, Chicago.

Shepard, M., V. Waddill, and W. Kloft. 1973. Biology of the predaceous earwig *Labidura riparia* (Dermaptera: Labiduridae). *Ann. Ent. Soc. Amer*. 66:837-841.

Smith, R.L. 1976. Brooding behavior of a male water bug *Belostoma flumineum* (Hemiptera: Belostomatidae). *J. Kans. Ent. Soc*. 49:333-343.

Spieth, H.T. 1968. Evolutionary implications of sexual

behavior in *Drosophila*. *Evol. Biol.* 2:157–193.

Sternlicht, M. 1973. Parasitic wasps attracted by the sex pheromone of their coccid host. *Entomophaga* 18:339–342.

Thornhill, R. 1973. The morphology and histology of new sex pheromone glands in male scorpionflies, *Panorpa* and *Brachypanorpa* (Mecoptera: Panorpidae and Panorpodidae). *Great Lakes Ent.* 6:47–55.

Thornhill, R. 1974. Evolutionary ecology of Mecoptera (Insecta). Vols. 1, 2. Ph.D. Thesis, Univ. Mich.

Thornhill, R. 1975. Scorpionflies as kleptoparasites of web-building spiders. *Nature* 258:709–711.

Thornhill, R. 1976a. Sexual selection and paternal investment in insects. *Amer. Nat.* 110:153–163.

Thornhill, R. 1976b. Sexual selection and nuptial feeding behavior in *Bittacus apicalis* (Insecta: Mecoptera). *Amer. Nat.* 110:529–547.

Thornhill, R. 1976c. Reproductive behavior of the lovebug, *Plecia nearctica* (Diptera: Bibionidae). *Ann. Ent. Soc. Amer.* 69:843–847.

Thornhill, R. 1977. The comparative predatory and sexual behavior of hanging-flies (Mecoptera: Bittacidae). *Univ. Mich. Mus. Zool. Misc. Publ.* No. 69:1–49.

Trivers, R.L. 1972. Parental investment and sexual selection. *In* B. Campbell (ed.), *Sexual Selection and the Descent of Man, 1871–1971.* Aldine, Chicago.

Trivers, R.L. 1976. Sexual selection and resource-accruing abilities in *Anolis garmani*. *Evolution* 30:253–269.

Trivers, R.L., and D.E. Willard. 1973. Natural selection of parental ability to vary the sex ratio of offspring. *Science* 179:90–92.

Verner, J. 1964. Evolution of polygyny in the long-billed marsh wren. *Evolution* 18:252–261.

Walker, T.J. 1964. Experimental demonstration of a cat locating orthopteran prey by the prey's calling song. *Fla. Ent.* 47:163–165.

Walker, T.J. 1974. *Gryllus ovisopis* n. sp.: a taciturn cricket with a life cycle suggesting allochronic speciation. *Fla. Ent.* 57:13–22.

West, M.J., and R.D. Alexander. 1963. Sub-social behavior in a burrowing cricket *Anurogryllus muticus* (De Geer). Orthoptera: Gryllidae. *Ohio J. Sci.* 63:19–24.

Wilbur, H.M., D.W. Tinkle, and J.P. Collins. 1974. Environmental certainty, trophic level, and resource availability in life history evolution. *Amer. Nat.* 108:805–817.

Wiley, R.H. 1973. Territoriality and non-random mating in sage grouse, *Centrocercus urophasianus*. *Anim. Behav. Monogr.* 6:87–169.

Williams, G.C. 1966. *Adaptation and Natural Selection.* Princeton Univ. Press, Princeton.

Williams, G.C. (ed.). 1971. *Group selection*. Aldine, Chicago.

Willson, M.F. 1966. Breeding ecology of the yellow-headed blackbird. *Ecol. Monogr.* 36:51-77.

Wilson, E.O. 1971. *The Insect Societies*. Harvard Univ. Press, Cambridge.

Wilson, E.O. 1975. *Sociobiology: The New Synthesis*. Harvard Univ. Press, Cambridge.

Wood, T.K. 1976. Alarm behavior of brooding female *Umbonia crassicornis* (Homoptera: Membracidae). *Ann. Ent. Soc. Amer.* 69:340-344.

Zahavi, A. 1975. Mate selection--a selection for a handicap. *J. Theor. Biol.* 53:205-214.

Zimmerman, J.L. 1966. Polygyny in the dickcissel. *Auk* 83: 534-546.

SEXUAL SELECTION AND SEXUAL CONFLICT

G.A. Parker

University of Liverpool

INTRODUCTION

After Darwin's (1871) original insight into the process of
sexual selection, there followed some early discussions and
investigations, but probably largely due to Huxley (1938),
the phenomenon received rather restrained attention until
comparatively recently. Sexual selection can be divided into
two major aspects: (1) direct intramale competition for
females and (2) female choice. "Direct competition" implies
the sort of adaptation by which males may directly outcompete
their rivals for mating opportunities with females. Examples
include optimization of search strategies, development of
direct guarding behavior of females, fighting between males
for mating opportunities, and so on; the possibilities are
legion. By "female choice" it is understood that the major
sexual selective force on the male is determined by the
female--she exerts some form of preference over which one out
of a series of males she will accept for mating. Huxley
doubted that sexually selected adaptations of the "direct
competition" type could evolve if they had any ancillary
selective costs to the male in terms of decreased survival
chances, and he would not accept that any features of males
could arise through "female choice." Since Huxley's rather
dampening effect on the theory of sexual selection, there
have been several insights which suggest that the extent of
sexual selection may be intense and dramatic. Perhaps two of
the most vital milestones are the papers of Bateman (1948)
and Trivers (1972), which extended Fisher's (1930) concept of
parental expenditure into a theorem for the operation of
sexual selection. The sex whose relative parental investment
(PI) (see Trivers, 1972) is highest will be under the most
intense sexual selection (intrasexual competition). There
has been over the past decade a considerable volume of evidence from field and laboratory studies that both aspects of
sexual selection can operate.

It seems reasonable to argue (see Fisher, 1930) that a

characteristic giving increased male reproductive success will
spread if it has less cost (in terms of enhanced mortality or
energy expenditure) than benefits. This problem is generally
simple in that it often resolves into a simple optimization
procedure for male strategy; selection adjusting allocations
of male effort in such a way that the winning strategy--the
one which will fixate--is that which maximizes the ratio of
benefits/costs. However, one must be extremely cautious about
predictions that the outcome of selection will be a single
optimal strategy. In particular, the recent pioneering work
of Maynard Smith (1974) has done most to demonstrate that,
when an individual's benefits depend on what strategy is likely to be played by other members of the population, the end
product of selection may often be a mixed strategy. For
example, if males display over females, and the one that wins
is the one which will display the longest, then the evolutionarily stable strategy (ESS) is for the male population to show
a negative exponential distribution of display costs (Maynard
Smith, 1974).

The topic I wish to emphasize in the present paper parallels that of the conflicting costs and benefits on the male
(mentioned above). What happens when a characteristic of
sexual selection advantage (benefit) to the male conveys a
selective disadvantage (cost) to genes in the female? Many
features of sexual selection may involve near neutral or
beneficial selective effects on the female. For instance,
female choice is often explained in terms of female benefits--
she picks the best male for her offspring (Orians, 1969; see
also Trivers, 1972, for a very clear presentation of the case).
But female reproductive success must sometimes be reduced if
certain features of sexual selection advantageous to males
manage to fixate. I use the term "sexual conflict" here to
imply a conflict between the evolutionary interests of individuals of the two sexes; it is thus equivalent to Trivers'
(1974) usage of "parent offspring conflict." It is extremely
difficult to prove that sexual conflict occurs in animal
species because of the difficulty of measuring costs and benefits. Now consider a case in which a characteristic yielding
a mating advantage to males causes some disadvantage (cost)
to the females with which they mate. The female will always
benefit from a mating with a male possessing the characteristic, provided that the cost is infinitessimal, if this means
that some of her sons will inherit the advantage (see Fisher,
1930; O'Donald, 1962; Maynard Smith, 1956). Similarly for
the male, if the costs are felt by his own progeny via the
damage to his mate, then his mating advantage must be correspondingly greater than for zero costs. Hence as the cost
increases there will be two thresholds of cost, one for the
male and one for the female, beyond which the male character-

istic (or a mating with a male possessing the characteristic)
becomes disadvantageous. If these thresholds differ, then
sexual conflict exists when conditions lie between the two,
for example, when the characteristic is favorable to males but
not to females.

I can make no claim to originality for the suggestion that
this asymmetry can occur commonly in animals; the idea of
sexual conflict is implicit in the works of several authors
since Darwin. The present time seems appropriate for a
reemphasis and for a more analytical survey of the phenomenon.
In one of the most fascinating and stimulating books to be
written in the last decade, Dawkins (1976) has included a
very readable and original discussion of sexual conflict,
which he terms a "battle of the sexes."

A GENERAL GENETIC MODEL FOR CONFLICT THRESHOLDS

This section of the paper will attempt to estimate the
thresholds for each sex, mentioned in the Introduction. There
are two important conditions to be examined: (1) the dominance
characteristics of the male character and (2) whether the
gene for the character occurs as a rare mutant in a population
without the character or whether the gene for the character
has fixed in the population. It is clearly possible to construct a model which considers intermediate gene frequencies,
though this will not be attempted here.

Dominant Allele for Male Mating Advantage

We will first examine benefits of a character to males.
Consider a dominant mutant allele A (in a population fixed for
a) which confers a mating advantage on a male carrying it; he
increases his matings by a factor of B relative to aa males.
The characteristic is sex-limited, not sex-linked. The A
allele causes him to inflict some cost to a female he mates
with, which affects his own offspring produced via that
female. Let this cost be C so that the mutant male will produce $(1 - C)$ offspring from a mating, not 1. To establish the
fitness of the A allele, we carry the analysis to include
the number of replicas of A in grandchildren. First consider
the fate of the A allele in the progeny of a male grandparent.
For spread of A into the aa population, the important condition is how A fares in Aa x aa matings. A male Aa heterozy-
gote mates with an aa female to produce ½ Aa and ½ aa progeny;
each type has a probability of ½ of being male or being female, and there will be $B(1 - C)$ total progeny at the first
generation. There will be then $B^2(1 - C)^2$ x ¼ replicas of A
in grandchildren via sons, but only $B(1 - C)$ x ¼ replicas via

daughters. The corresponding calculations for the fate of
the A gene starting in a female grandparent suggest that
there will be $B(1-C) \times \frac{1}{4}$ replicas via sons and $1 \times \frac{1}{4}$
replicas via daughters. Hence A will spread if

$$\frac{1}{4} \{B^2(1-C)^2 + 2B(1-C) + 1\} > 1$$

$$\therefore \{B(1-C) + 1\}^2 > 4$$

$$\therefore B > \frac{1}{1-C}. \tag{1}$$

Equation 1 gives the condition for the spread of the sex-
limited gene A. What we now need to consider is how this
gene affects the spread of a given gene in a female. Remember
that she may experience an overall gain by mating with the
male carrying the A allele (via her sons) provided that the
cost C_f she experiences is not too great. Note that C_f need
not $= C$, because in a promiscuous mating system any damage
felt by the female may affect *all* the rest of her progeny,
and without on future occasions being associated with any
mating advantage, whereas the cost is always associated with
a mating advantage to the male.

Thus consider the fate of a given "labeled" gene in the
female which mates with the Aa male. The gene could be one
which affects the female's choice of male type. We need to
know under what conditions of B the labeled gene sustains an
increased number of replicas in the female's grandchildren,
relative to a similar gene in a female which mates only with
the common aa type males. Let there be m matings (leading to
conceptions) per lifetime. On proportion $(m-1)/m$ occasions
then, a female mates with a normal male and thus $1/m$ matings
are with the Aa male. Suppose that a proportion p of broods
that are progeny of normal males sustain the cost C inflicted
by the Aa male. There will be an increased number of replicas of the "labeled" gene in the grandchildren provided that

$$\underbrace{\frac{m-1}{m} \times \frac{1}{2} \times \{(1-p) \times 1 + p(1-C)\}}_{\text{replicas via aa x aa matings}}$$

$$\underbrace{+ \frac{1}{m} \times \frac{1}{4} \times (1-C) \underbrace{\{\tfrac{1}{2} \times B(1-C) + \tfrac{1}{2}\}}_{\substack{\text{via Aa sons}}} + \underbrace{\frac{1}{m} \times \frac{1}{4} \times (1-C)}_{\substack{\text{via aa progeny}}} > \frac{1}{2}}_{\text{replicas via the Aa x aa mating}}$$

via Aa sons   via Aa daughters   via aa progeny

$$\therefore \quad \frac{m-1}{2m}(1-pC) + \frac{B}{8m}(1-C)^2 + \frac{3}{8}(1-C) > \frac{1}{2},$$

which resolves to

$$B > \frac{4pC(m-1) + 3C + 1}{(1-C)^2}. \qquad (2)$$

Note that both conditions (1) and (2) require only that B > 1 if the cost C = 0. However, also as expected, condition (1) is always easier to satisfy--which depends on RHS (2) > RHS (1), i.e., that

$$\frac{4pC(m-1) + 3C + 1}{(1-C)^2} > \frac{1}{1-C}$$

$$m + 1 > p$$

--which is always true. Sexual conflict over the initial spread of a mutant allele--which confers a mating advantage B on males, but a cost of C on at least the products of the mating involving the mutant--will thus occur if

$$\frac{4pC(m-1) + 3C + 1}{(1-C)^2} > B > \frac{1}{1-C}.$$

We can set limits for p as follows. If the costs affect only his own progeny, then p = 0. If, however, the cost affects equally all the subsequent progeny of the female, then

$$P_{max} = \frac{(m-1) + (m-2) + (m-3) \ldots (m-m)}{m^2}$$

$$= 1 - \sum_{n=1}^{m} \frac{n}{m^2} .$$

(3)

We can apply exactly the same technique to examine the conflict when A has fixated and a is rare. Let us assume that an aa male has a mating disadvantage against the AA males in the ratio $1/B':1$, as before. It is very unlikely that the mating advantage will remain independent of the frequency of A; the most likely contingency is that the relative advantage experienced by the initial mutant will be considerably smaller than the relative disadvantage experienced by a male not possessing the character once it has fixated (Charlesworth and Charlesworth, 1975; but also see Gadgil and Taylor, 1975). A mating between an aa male and an AA female (the likely partner if AA has fixated) yields all Aa progeny which sustain no cost at that mating. This time the cost C' is the average extra cost felt by the progeny of a given brood when their father is AA rather than aa, hence C is not equivalent to C'. At the next generation all Aa sons show the cost characteristic, and thus the condition for reestablishment of a is that

$$\frac{1}{B'} (1 - C') > (1 - C')^2$$

$$\therefore \quad B' < \frac{1}{(1 - C')} .$$

(4)

There can be a polymorphism between A and a only if for a given benefit, $kB = B'$, the RHS (4)/k > RHS (1) where k is a positive constant. Hence a polymorphism can exist only if

$$\frac{1}{k} > \frac{1-C'}{1-C}; \quad \text{i.e., if } \frac{B}{B'} > \frac{1-C'}{1-C} .$$

If costs are simply additive (e.g., the female loses $-C$ progeny for each conflict mating sustained), then RHS = 1 and the condition for polymorphism is that the mating disadvantage of aa at fixation of AA must be smaller than the mating advantage of Aa when spreading into the aa population. Whether such polymorphisms could occur may be controversial (see Charlesworth and Charlesworth, 1975; Gadgil and Taylor, 1975).

Consider now the female's interests in mating with an aa

male in an AA population. Applying the "labeled allele"
technique to the female (AA) which mates with an aa male, we
can see that her sons will be heterozygotes and hence will all
show the cost character. Thus the labeled gene will always
have more replicas in grandchildren as a result of the mating
with the aa male than through matings with AA males if
$(1 - C') < 1$. The equation corresponding to that leading to
(2) becomes

$$\frac{1}{m} \times \frac{1}{2} \times 1 \times (1 - C') + \frac{m-1}{m} \times \frac{1}{2} (1 - C') \times \{p' + (1 - p)(1 - C')\}$$

$$> \frac{1}{2} (1 - C')^2 , \qquad\qquad (5)$$

where p is this time the proportion of other broods (having
AA fathers) that feel the benefit of the reduced cost arising
from the mating with the aa male. As before, $P'_{min} = 0$ and
$P'_{max} = (3)$. It is clear from (5) and (4) that there will
now *always* be conflict between the interests of the two
sexes if $B' > 1/(1 - C')$, since (5) is always satisfied.

Recessive Allele for Male Mating Advantage

Using similar procedures, it can be shown that the recessive allele d will spread as a rare mutant through its sex-
limited advantage B in males if condition (1) holds, exactly
as for the dominant case. In a population which is fixed
for dd, then D cannot invade unless $B' < 1/(1 - C')$, as
expected from (4). From the female's point of view, there
is no benefit whatever at the start of the spread of d,
because to achieve an advantage from the mating:

$$\frac{1}{m} \times \frac{1}{2} (1 - C) + \frac{m-1}{m} \times \frac{1}{2} \times (1 - C) \{(1 - p) + p(1 - C)\} > \frac{1}{2}, \quad (6)$$

which cannot be true. But at fixation of dd, the "labeled
allele" in the female will have more replicas in the grandchildren through a mating with a Dd male if

$$B' \quad < \quad \frac{1}{(1 - C)(1 - 4C - 4pmC + 4pC)} . \qquad (7)$$

Discussion

The equations in the preceding section define whether (1)
selection is positive or negative on a given gene which acts
in males to cause a certain behavior, and (2) the similar
selective outcome received by another gene in a female which

mates with males having the behavior. Because of the asymmetries in costs and benefits, conditions will exist where the selective coefficient is positive for the male gene but negative for the female gene. Benefits of the male character are always either weaker for the female (arising only via sons) or zero.

Assuming that the characteristic is favored in males, then in summary:

1. When the gene is dominant, there will *sometimes* be sexual conflict at the start of its spread and *always* conflict once the gene has fixated.

2. When the gene is recessive, there will *always* be sexual conflict at the start of its spread and *sometimes* conflict at fixation.

These effects are demonstrated in Fig. 1, which shows the conflict thresholds B_m or B'_m for males and B_f or B'_f for females. These thresholds are determined as the B value that has neither advantage nor disadvantage from the preceding equations. For a given B and C, the least probability of conflict occurs at the start of spread of a dominant gene for mating advantage. At fixation of a recessive gene there will always be conflict if $C' > .25$, and commonly if C' is less than this (see Fig. 1). This is because a female loses from the mating only via the $\frac{1}{4}$ Dd sons; even if these are virtually incapable of mating (B' approaching ∞), then provided the advantages to other sibs exceed $\frac{1}{4}$, she always benefits from a mating with a male lacking the mating advantage.

Suppose that the "labeled" gene we have considered in the female is one which exerts a choice over the male type preferred for mating. Because of the fact that a given male mating allele will always cause conflict when its frequency is 1 or 0, but only sometimes when the frequency is 0 or 1, then provided that there is *no* conflict at the indeterminate extreme, polymorphisms theoretically may exist for female choice and mating behavior in males. That polymorphisms in male types may be maintained by female choice has been demonstrated by O'Donald (1974).

I have looked in some detail at the possible benefits which accrue to females via sons which inherit the sexual selection advantages of their fathers. In the models which will follow, this effect will be omitted to keep the analyses simple; it may however reduce the extent of the conflict suggested by some of the later models.

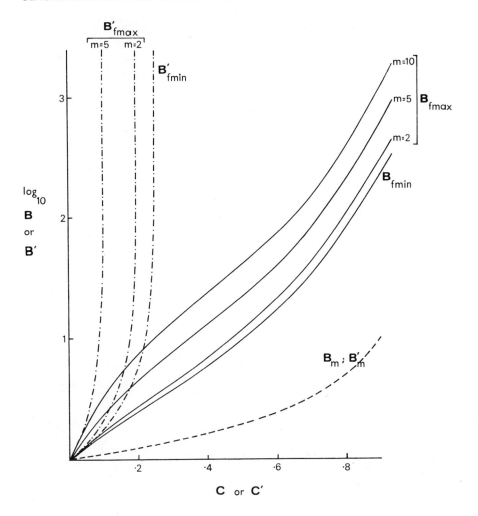

Fig. 1. Conflict thresholds for the two sexes. Sexual
conflict occurs at the start of spread of a dominant
mutant gene conferring a mating advantage to males of
B, but a cost C to offspring if $B_m < B < B_f$, or at
fixation of a recessive gene conferring a mating advantage B' and a cost C' to offspring if $B'_m < B' < B'_f$
(see text). There is always conflict at the start of
spread of a recessive gene or at fixation of a dominant
gene, if $B_m < B$ or $B'_m < B'$. Female thresholds are
dependent on the number of matings affected by cost C
or C'; the plots show B_{fmin}, or B'_{fmin} (where the cost
affects only one brood), and B_{fmax} and B'_{fmax} (where
the cost affects all subsequent progeny) for various
numbers of matings per lifetime.

DIRECT CONFLICT IN NATURE

Cases where males appear directly to harm females as a
result of behaviors which must relate to intramale selection
seem to be quite common. In insects, fights between males for
the possession of females are commonplace, and the result is
often that the female becomes enmeshed in a cluster of pulling
and struggling males. Fig. 2 shows this sort of battle in
the yellow dung fly, *Scatophaga stercoraria* (Parker, 1970b).
If an attacking male touches the female while she is already
paired, the attacker usually attempts to force the original
male away and to mate with the female himself. This can
itself attract further attackers, and so the problem intensifies. Alternatively, a female just arriving at the fresh
dropping (the site of mating and oviposition) may attract
more than one male so that a struggle begins immediately.
Such behavior is very common and the dispute may be lengthy;

*Fig. 2. Struggle for the possession of a female in the yellow
dung fly,* Scatophaga stercoraria *L. The female is at the center of the cluster of males (from* Behaviour, *vol. 37, 1970).*

the female can sometimes become severely contaminated with liquid dung and even drowned or badly torn during the process (see also Hammer, 1941). Most often the female involved in a struggle has already been mated at a previous oviposition site and will contain enough sperm to lay her egg batch (with normal fertility) without needing any further mating. This type of behavior seems to fit fairly exactly with the sort of model just developed. Though common in insects (reviewed by Parker, 1970d), analogous behavior is also found in most other groups. Rape would seem to fit just as well as competitive struggles for female possession.

Another (possibly less direct) form of conflict in insects and other arthropods may occur when the male moves around paired to a female, but without genital contact, in what can be termed a "passive phase" (see Parker, 1970d, 1974). Fig. 3a shows a passive phase in *Cicindela maritima*; every so often the male makes attempts to inseminate the female (Fig. 3b). Passive phases can be of two types, pre- or postcopulatory or both (see Williamson, 1951, for *Orchestia*). On the one hand, the male gains by monopolizing a female close to receptivity until she becomes receptive; on the other, he guards his own sperm against the possibility that they may be displaced by a competitor before being used for fertilization. On *a priori* grounds, it seems that the female must at least incur some energetic costs, if nothing else, as a result of this sexually selected adaptation in males. As with competitive struggles and rape, the cost would probably be passed on to the offspring of both the male and the female in the sort of way envisaged in the model.

Given that the direct fighting and persistence behavior of males is likely to evolve, then allowing males to adopt passive phases may become advantageous to the female if there is nothing she can do to avoid persistent time and energy expenditure on deflecting male attentions. There is evidence that this is true for the *Scatophaga* passive phase (Parker, 1970c). Thus as we shall see, sexual conflict is sometimes resolvable into a simple problem; if there is nothing one sex can do to avoid disadvantages inflicted by the other, then evolution simply favors making the best of things. Alternatively, there appear to be some instances where each sex can "retaliate" against the other and where benefits become conditional on the strategy of one's opponent. This can lead to complex and sometimes apparently unresolvable "evolutionary chases" (see section on the "Opponent-Independent Costs" Game).

Fig. 3.

a. Passive phase in Cicindela maritima *Dj.*

*b. Attempt by male to inseminate female during
the* Cicindela maritima *passive phase.*

EARLY CONFLICTS IN THE DEVELOPMENT OF SEXUAL SELECTION

    Males and females are what they are because of the type
of gamete they carry, i.e., ultimately because of anisogamy.
Very early in the development of multicellular forms from
protistan stock, extra expenditure on provisioning the zygote
would have become increasingly valuable. Benefits of the
enhanced provisioning would include increased survival, but
would accrue to the multicellular adult perhaps mainly from

an increased rate of development. At the origin of anisogamy,
fertilization would almost certainly have been external, with
gametes released into a liquid medium such as sea water. As
zygote provisioning became relatively more important, around
the time that multicellularity was establishing, then isogamy
would have become evolutionarily unstable. It can be shown
by computer simulation that anisogamy will develop by disruptive selection for two gamete-producing morphs (Parker et
al., 1972; Parker, 1977) provided that the zygote's size has
an important influence on its success. Though there are
theories for the establishment of anisogamy through group or
inter-population selection (Kalmus, 1932; Kalmus and Smith,
1960; Scudo, 1967), the "anisogamy via disruptive selection"
theory relies entirely on immediate forms of selection. It
suggests that females are favored because they produce gametes
with the high level of provisioning to confer advantages on
the zygote, and also that males are simultaneously favored
because they can "parasitize" the female investment. Males
can produce so many gametes (from an equivalent expenditure)
that with random gamete fusion, male parents obtain by far
the highest number of fusions with the scarce but highly
provisioned ova.

The more sperm a male produces (and thus the *less* he
contributes to the zygote provisioning), the more ova he will
fertilize in competition with other males. Hence, in males
selection favors an increased gamete productivity at the cost
of a reduction in contribution to zygotic resources, and in
females an optimal ovum size which yields the maximum contribution rate to subsequent generations. As drive for increased
sperm productivity continues, the sperm's contribution to the
zygote tends to zero and the optimization of ovum size becomes
independent of the sperm.

This drive for smaller and smaller sperm is the most primitive form of sexual selection and also the primordial sexual
conflict. As selection forces males to invest less and less
on each gamete's resources, it is simultaneously forcing females to spend more and more. An incidental result here is
that selection is halving the reproductive output for the
species (measured as number of zygotes produced with the
necessary reserve). More important, since selection upon
individuals is generally likely to be much more powerful than
selection upon groups of individuals, are the immediate ways
in which females might "retaliate" against the parasitization
of their PI. There seem to be two possible solutions. First,
she may reproduce parthenogenetically and hence "refuse" to
share her investment in the ovum with the genome of another
individual. This is the familiar "cost of sex" (Maynard
Smith, 1971) or, more strictly, the "cost of anisogamy"
(Williams, 1975; Manning, 1976). But if the benefits of

sexual outcrossing still outweigh the "cost of anisogamy"--
and current models show that this can be so without invoking
group selection (see Williams, 1975; Maynard Smith, 1976;
Felsenstein, 1974)--then there is still a second solution.
Selection may act on females to produce ova which fuse assortatively with other ova and reject sperm. This way the female
benefits from an increased zygote provisioning (via the shared
resource of the two fusing ova). Of course, simultaneously,
sperm which fuse only disassortatively are generally favored
because they "save" themselves for fusions with ova rather
than "wasting" themselves in lethal or near-lethal sperm-
sperm fusions. It is difficult to speculate on the outcome
of this conflict without resorting to computer simulation
(see Parker, 1978). From simulations with two loci, one with
alleles controlling gamete size and the other with alleles
determining gamete fusion behavior (random, assortative, or
disassortative), it becomes clear that mutant genes for assortative fusion of ova will not spread in a random-fusing
population provided that anisogamy has become sufficiently
advanced (i.e., there is a high enough disparity between the
sizes of the largest and the smallest gametes). This effect
arises because there are so many sperm in the gamete pool
that assortatively fusing ova fare very badly in competition
against them for fusions with randomly fusing ova. Hence if
assortative ova survive long enough to fuse, they are usually
forced to fuse with other assortative ova, assuming that the
local spawning population releases its gametes synchronously
into the gamete pool. If such mutants occur as rare events,
the odds are that such fusions are equivalent to selfing,
i.e., automictic parthenogenesis.

In contrast, males which have genes for disassortative
fusion for sperm experience a relatively enormous selective
advantage, and such genes quickly spread, especially where
there is asynchronous or continuous spawning. The best that
the female can do is retain her capacity for random fusion
so that ova are able to fuse with other ova should they
(occasionally) meet. Thus the ESS for this particular sexual
conflict appears to be the strategy: when male, produce dis-
assortative-fusing sperm in maximum numbers; when female,
produce random-fusing ova of optimal size. However, this sex-
limited dual strategy has only an infinitessimal advantage at
high degrees of anisogamy over one which shows disassortative
fusion in the gametes of both sexes. Hence females may do
better by producing ova which are obligatorily disassortative
than by retaining their capacity for random fusion, if this
means that the energy and expenditure saved by losing motility, etc., can be used to better effect in the production of
more ova.

Suppose that the success of a zygote from an ovum-ovum

fusion = α, relative to one for a zygote from a sperm–ovum fusion ($\alpha > 1$). Let the number of sperm produced to every ovum = N (the anisogamy ratio), and let β = the number of ova which could be produced by a female which spends nothing on motility relative to one that does ($\beta > 1$). A mutant female which reallocates her gamete-motility expenditure into provisioning further ova will spread if

$$\underbrace{\beta}_{\substack{\text{(always fuses} \\ \text{with sperm)}}} \quad > \quad \underbrace{\alpha \frac{1}{N+1}}_{\substack{\text{(from ovum–} \\ \text{ovum fusions)}}} \quad + \quad \underbrace{\frac{N}{N+1}}_{\substack{\text{(from sperm–} \\ \text{ovum fusions)}}}$$

$$\beta \quad > \quad \frac{\alpha + N}{N + 1}. \tag{8}$$

Bearing in mind that the anisogamy ratio can often become extremely high (e.g., $N > 10^6$), it is easy to see from (8) how obligatory disassortative fusion for ova may have been favored. For ovum size to be optimized requires (when ovum-ovum fusions are rare) a law of diminishing returns for the increase in success with increase in provisioning. This requires that $\alpha < 2$, and hence a conservative condition for spread is that $\beta > (N+2)/(N+1)$. For an anisogamy ratio of 10^6, all that is required for the loss of motility is that $\beta > 1 + 10^{-6}$. Once motility was lost, the unambiguous refusal by ova to accept other ova may have been favored because of the dangers of selfing.

Thus males were generally likely to have won the primordial sexual conflict--the one over anisogamy itself. The best evidence for this is that most multicellular forms exist as two gamete-producing morphs: males and females. Given that sexual outcrossing has a greater than twofold advantage to a female which has the "alternative" strategy of automictic parthenogenesis, then it is not easy to see how females can win the anisogamy conflict (maintain isogamy) unless zygote provisioning is always rather unimportant in relation to zygote fitness. In Protozoa there is commonly isogamy. There is little to suggest that for most forms an increased size would be advantageous; the fact that they have the size they have implies optimality. Gamete size is presumably set by the selective pressure of survival *before* fusion. Knowlton (1974) has shown that in the Volvocidae those genera with the smallest number of cells/colony and in which zygote provisioning will be least important (*Gonium, Stephanosphaera*) show isogamy. *Pandorina*, which tends to be intermediate in colony size, shows slight anisogamy, and several genera (including *Volvox*) which have large colonies show anisogamy with disassortative fusion.

CONFLICT AND MATE CHOICE

When males and females encounter, there is always some
degree of choice exerted (and by each sex) about whether or
not to mate, even if in males this merely concerns withdrawing
without further interaction when the female encountered is
from some rather distantly related species. Many authors
(particularly Bateman, 1948; Trivers, 1972) stress that selection acts predominantly on the female to be discriminate
and much less so on the male. This is because the female
investment in ova exceeds the male investment in sperm, and
hence the losses to the female (in terms of replacement costs)
far exceed those of the male for a given degree of inviability
of the progeny. Though often implicit, it is less often
stressed that selection can act in opposition on the two
sexes. Commonly, for a given type of encounter, males will
be favored if they do mate and females if they don't. Certainly many insect species show, as Bateman predicted, a
"discriminating passivity" in their females and an "indiscriminate eagerness" in males. Also, there is good evidence that
the choice exerted by a female can be one which fits best
with her evolutionary interests (e.g., Maynard Smith, 1956).
The sort of criteria in males which females might be expected
to monitor have been discussed and reviewed by Trivers (1972).
Suppose that males and females in reproductive condition
are able on encounter to make some sort of assessment of the
suitability as a mate of the encountered individual. No
conscious assessment is implied here, but we shall seek the
evolutionary rules which determine the "mating decision
threshold" for each sex. This is a theoretical threshold at
which there is an equality in terms of selection between the
decision to mate and that not to mate. Sexual conflict and
sexual selection will both be greatest when male PI << female
PI. I shall consider a model which is developed mainly with
insects in mind, but which should be readily modifiable to
suit other cases. Let the time taken for a male to gather
enough energy via food to maintain himself and replenish his
gametes = g_m. For females, the corresponding $g_f > g_m$ because
female PI > male PI. Searching for mates and investing in
gametes are assumed to be mutually exclusive activities. I
shall assume a 1:1 ratio, and that the time taken for a receptive female to be found is an inverse function of the
number of searching males. If a total time of t is taken by
a female to invest her PI and to encounter a male, then

$$t = g_f + kg_m/t.$$

Where the value kg_m/t stipulates the mean search cost for the
female, k is a positive constant which indicates the "aptitude

for encounter." (In time t, t/g_m males per female become
available for searching; thus the search time per female
becomes kg_m/t). Note that g_f may be distributed in time in
any fashion around kg_m/t; it is not necessary that all g_f
occurs before mate searching. The mean search time s_m for a
male to find a female is thus found from

$$g_m + s_m = g_f + kg_m/t; \quad (s_f = kg_m/t)$$

$$\therefore \quad s_m = g_f - g_m + kg_m/t.$$

When two reproductive individuals of opposite sex encounter,
selection favors mating if the mean fitness of offspring
produced from the mating is high enough to make the alternative strategy (withdraw to search for a better mate) disadvantageous. Suppose that there is iteroparity with continuous
breeding during the adult stage. Selection favors the strategy for maximizing the number of surviving progeny per lifetime; for continuous breeding this is equivalent to saying
that it favors decisions which at any time yield the highest
expected "gain rate" of production of surviving progeny.
(For a more complete explanation of this principle, see
Parker, 1974, and Parker and Stuart, 1976).

First consider a rather simplistic case which may be
relevant to rare meetings between nonconspecific males and
females of closely related sympatric species, or to local
races or ecotypes which occasionally overlap. Let the mean
fitness of offspring from a mating with a conspecific be 1,
and the mean fitness of a mating with the closely related
species or race be $1 - d$, where d expresses the hybrid disadvantage. For simplicity, we shall assume initially that the
aptitude for encounter and PI patterns of the two ecotypes is
identical; this helps to establish the rules of the model
without resorting to undue complexity. We can determine the
decision thresholds d_m and d_f for the male and female; these
are the thresholds at which the decision to mate is as good
(evolutionarily speaking) as the decision not to mate. For
the male, selection favors mating if the gain rate due to
mating exceeds that due to withdrawing to search for a conspecific female, i.e., if

$$(1 - d_m)/g_m > 1/(g_m + s_m),$$

and the threshold $$d_m = 1 - \frac{g_m}{g_f + kg_m/t}, \qquad (9)$$

and by a similar method

$$d_f = 1 - \frac{g_f}{g_f + kg_m/t} , \qquad (10)$$

and the difference between the thresholds (a measure of the probability of conflict)

$$d_m - d_f = \frac{g_f - g_m}{g_f + kg_m/t} . \qquad (11)$$

The following conclusions are obvious from (11):

1. The higher the disparity between g_f and g_m ($g_f \gg g_m$), the higher the probability of conflict concerning mating.

2. The lower the cost to the female of encounter relative to her PI cost ($g_f \gg kg_m/t$), the higher the probability of conflict.

Insects seem likely to maximize the probability of conflict because there is generally very little male PI so that g_f/g_m will be extremely high. They are also often highly mobile and it seems likely that s_f will be low relative to g_f (g_f/s_f high). Cost s_f may not be merely encounter time; it could be a measure, say, of the cost of pheromone production. Also females can store sperm for fertilization of several egg batches in many species, a feature which must inevitably reduce s_f. (It is usually inconceivable for most species that $s_f > g_f$, and when it is, then selection may favor hermaphroditism [see Charnov et al., 1976].)

Some estimate can be made of the benefit/cost ratios to measure the intensity of selection on each sex when faced with a conflict of this sort. Selective pressure on males toward attempting to mate with a female which would then have offspring of fitness $1 - d_x$ is proportional to LHS(9) - RHS(9), and selective pressure on females favoring rejection of mating attempts is proportional to RHS(10) - LHS(10). The intensity of selection on males to persist will be greater than that on females to reject if LHS(9) - RHS(9) > RHS(10) - LHS(10), i.e., if

$$d_x < 1 - \frac{2g_m \cdot g_f}{(g_m + g_f)(g_f + kg_m/t)} . \qquad (12)$$

If the sign is reversed, then obviously selection is greater on the female to reject than it is on the male to persist. Does the threshold value of d_x (where selection is equal on the two sexes) always lie within the limits of d_m to d_f? $d_m > d_x$ if

$$\frac{1 - g_m}{(g_f + kg_m/t)} > 1 - \frac{2g_m \, g_f}{(g_m + g_f)(g_f + kg_m/t)}$$

$$\therefore \quad g_m + g_f < 2g_f \, ,$$

which is always true if $g_m < g_f$. But is $d_x > d_f$? A similar examination shows that this requires that $g_f + g_m > 2g_m$, which again is always true if $g_m < g_f$. Hence for any given case of sexual conflict, selection may be stronger on the male to persist than on the female to resist or vice-versa. Fig. 4 shows the "conflict zone" and indicates which sex is under the stronger selective pressure for any given value d in relation to g_m/g_f the ratio of the two gametic investments. Fig. 4a indicates the conflict when searching costs are relatively expensive ($k = 1$, $g_f = 1$) so that when $g_m = g_f$, the relative search time = .618 (calculated from $kg_m = t^2 - t$; $g_f = 1$). Fig. 4b shows the conflict zone when searching is relatively inexpensive ($k = .01$, $g_f = 1$). These graphs support the conclusions suggested by (11), i.e., that the probability of conflict is greatest if $g_f >> g_m$ and where meeting of the sexes is relatively inexpensive. The graphs also indicate that within the conflict zone there is a greater probability that selection will be greater on the male to persist than on- the female to resist. Threshold d_x was calculated from (12).

Of course, a more realistic model would take into account differences between the ecotypes in relation to the parameters important in determining d_f and d_m. Thus, in reality, when the parameters differ, there are two conditions to be considered. For ecotypes A and B, these are (1) male A x female B, and (2) male B x female A. It would be theoretically possible, say, for there to be no conflict in case (1) but conflict in case (2). The implications of such asymmeties for the probability of sympatric speciation, or for the maintenance of separate gene pools, deserve further consideration. However the preceding analysis outlines the general properties of this type of model, and the probability of conflict for asymmetric cases can be guessed from Fig. 4. For instance, if ecotype A has $k = 1$, and B has $k = .01$, then condition (1) above is described by replacing curve d_f in Fig. 4a with d_f from 4b. Conflict is highly probably here. Condition (2) is

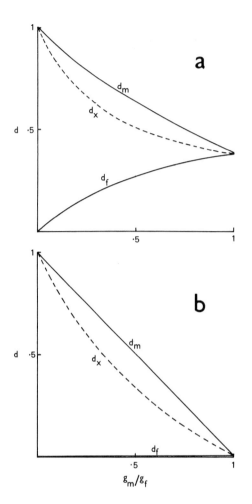

Fig. 4. Conflict thresh-
olds for the two sexes
concerning mating deci-
sion in a rare encounter
between, say, two eco-
types or races which have
similar densities and
parental investment pat-
terns. Sexual conflict
occurs when the reduction
in offspring fitness (d)
is such that $d_m > d > d_f$.
When $d_m > d > d_x$, selection is greater on the
female to reject than on
the male to persist; when
$d_x > d > d_f$, selection is
greater on male persist-
ence than on female re-
jection. (For further
explanation, see text.)
(a) search costs rela-
tively expensive; $k = 1$,
$g_f = 1$.   (b) search costs
relatively inexpensive;
$k = .01$, $g_f = 1$.

described by replacing d_f in Fig. 4b with d_f from Fig. 4a:
this has strange implications. At low male PI, there is still
a high probability of conflict in the direction of males
wanting to mate and females to reject, but as male PI increases, the interests of the sexes can be reversed. Though
males may not be in danger of being raped by females, they
could perhaps be cheated (at least temporarily) if selection
favors A-type females which mimic the B-type females.

In general, where the biology of the two races is not rad-
ically different (in terms of aptitude for encounter and
relative PI of the two sexes), then the model can be left as
stated. Especially where male PI is low, sexual conflict is
highly likely, and selection is likely to be more intense on
the male to persist than on the female to reject.

The model can be extended to cover intraspecific decisions
concerning mating thresholds, but the conclusions remain
rather similar. Here we wish to determine what proportion
of conspecifics of opposite sex should be "acceptable" as
mates. Whether animals can make decisions concerning the
probable goodness of genes carried by a potential mate is
controversial, at least at the level of "fine grained" intraspecific choice (see later); let us however proceed with
faith. Suppose that each sex could make decisions to discard
all but the "best" 50%, or "best" 25%, say, of mates encountered. The search costs are thus doubled or quadrupled.
Hence we can seek an "optimal selectivity" for each sex in
terms of the mean number of search costs which selection
favors sustaining so as to increase the fitness of one's
progeny. Let b = this number of search costs; if an individual plays an optimal selectivity b*, it will accept proportion 1/b* of potential mates it encounters.

The optimal selectivity will depend on the way in which
the offspring fitness increases by increased mate selectivity,
i.e., on $G(b)$. Suppose we make the assumption that mate
choice affects the progeny of each sex equally, i.e., that
$G_m(b) = G_f(b)$. (It should be noted that this assumption is
not necessarily true because of sex-limited genes.) The form
of $G(b)$ is difficult to guess because it depends on the distribution and heritability of fitness. However, let us assume
that $G(bs_f)$ and $G(bs_m)$ eventually obey laws of diminishing
returns (see Figs. 5 and 6). Provided that $g_f > g_m$, then it
is clear that $s_f < s_m$ and hence $G(bs_f)$ will rise to its
asymptote G_{max} much more steeply than $G(bs_m)$, as shown in Figs.
5 and 6. The optimal selectivity for each sex is given by
the tangents to the curves $G(bs_f)$ and $G(bs_m)$, following the
method used by several authors (e.g., Smith and Fretwell,
1974; Parker, 1974; Charnov, 1973; Parker and Stuart, 1976).

Thus the "optimal selectivity" for a female to apply is
determined by the value b* which satisfies

$$\left. \frac{dG(bs_f)}{d(bs_f)} \right|_{b = b* > 1} = \frac{G(bs_f)}{g_f + bs_f} , \qquad (13)$$

and the corresponding equation for the male has

$$\left. \frac{dG(bs_m)}{d(bs_m)} \right|_{b = b* > 1} = \frac{G(bs_m)}{g_m + bs_m} . \qquad (14)$$

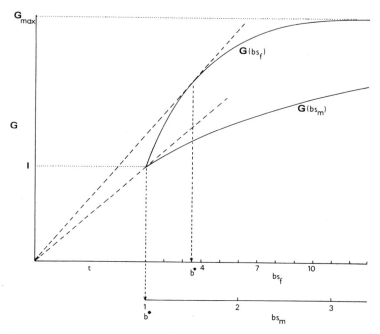

Fig. 5. "Optimal selectivity" concerning mate choice when $G(bs_f)$ rises relatively slowly, where I/G_{max} is relatively high (i.e., fitness variation small), and where the male PI is small relative to female PI. The "optimal selectivity" is given as $b*s_f$ for females' choice of males and $b*s_m$ for males' choice of females. This $b*$ indicates the mean number of search costs which should be sustained to maximize the fitness of the choosing individual ($b > 1$), hence only the "best" $1/b*$ of the opposite sex should be accepted, and the rest $(1-1/b*)$ should be rejected. For the case shown, males should be indiscriminate ($b* = 1$) and females "optimally selective."*

Provided that in both (13) and (14) the LHS (13 or 14) > RHS (13 or 14) at b = 1 (indiscriminateness), then for monotonic decreasing dG(bs)/d(bs), there should always be an optimal selectivity (b* > 1) rather than zero mate choice. Whether or not this will be true depends on I, the offspring fitness of an indiscriminate individual relative to G_{max} (the asymptotic value), and also on the shape constant (determining the starting gradient) of G(bs). From Figs. 5 and 6, it is clear that there are three possible outcomes to this type of problem:

1. Both sexes indiscriminate--both tangents hit the G(bs) curves at b = 1.

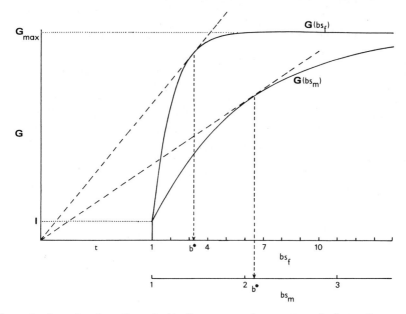

Fig. 6. "Optimal selectivity" concerning mate choice when $G(bs_f)$ rises relatively steeply, where I/G_{max} is relatively low (i.e., fitness variation high), and where male PI is small relative to female PI. Convention as in Fig. 5. Here both sexes should be "optimally selective"($b > 1$), but the lower-investing sex (males) should reject fewer potential mates than the higher-investing sex (females).*

2. Sexual conflict: selection favors males being indiscriminate, but females which make assessments in accordance with "optimal selectivity." This is the case shown in Fig. 5. Where the male search costs s_m >> female search costs s_f (i.e., male PI << female PI), then this is perhaps the most likely outcome.

3. Both sexes discriminate to some degree (see Fig. 6). This can occur when I is small relative to G_{max} and where the starting gradient for both sexes is greater than the slope of the tangent to G(bs) at b = 1. When this occurs, as one might expect, the sex with the higher PI should be the more discriminate (see Fig. 6).

In summary, features which are likely to favor discriminateness are:

1. I/G_{max} low.

2. $\dfrac{dG(bs)}{d(bs)}\ \Bigg|_{\ b\ =\ 1}$ high.

3. Searching cost low relative to PI (follows from 2).

Obviously 3 above means that male discriminateness is not
likely to occur when male PI is high (g_m approaching g_f).
As male PI increases, then for any given aptitude k for
encounter, the female's search cost (s_f) is likely to increase
(because of the dependence of s_f on g_m) and her optimal
selectivity (b*) will decrease. In contrast, as male PI
decreases, then again at any given value of k, s_m will increase and s_f decrease. Thus female discriminateness is
increased by high PI disparity, and the male's discriminateness reduced. The higher the PI disparity, the higher the
chances that males should demonstrate b* = 1, "an indiscriminate eagerness" (Bateman, 1948) and that the female should
show an optimal selectivity b* > 1.

Perhaps the major difficulty with theories which depend
on mate choice in terms of "good genes" (e.g., Zahavi, 1975;
Trivers, 1976) is that if the environment is uniform, males
with "bad genes" always have bad genes and are selected
against both by the female choice *and* the selective agent
which causes them to be less fit in the first place. Hence
male genes should quickly fixate towards the best type,
leaving the females indiscriminate: there being no heritable
basis for the discrimination. Most theories for the maintenance of sex by individual selection (e.g., Williams, 1975;
Maynard Smith, 1976) rely on a fluctuating environment, hence
certain genes are bad only at certain times and in certain
environments. The problem now becomes not one of maintaining
genetic variability, but of how the female could predict
which genotype is likely to be favored in the next generation.
Thus, if the environment is stable, choice can be favored
initially, but the opportunity for the choice will eventually
be lost; if the environment is unpredictable, there is little
basis for choice even if one could be made. This argument
becomes less powerful if the environmental fluctuations are
nonrandom so that the choice is exerted in relation to
predictable future conditions. The models are, of course,
directly applicable to cases of nonheritable variation in
mate quality.

SEXUAL CONFLICT AND INBREEDING

There is little doubt that inbreeding can have severe
effects on fitness (e.g., Maynard Smith, 1956), and the dispersal patterns of the sexes of various species have been
interpreted in terms of adaptations to avoid or reduce the

probability of inbreeding (Greenwood and Harvey, 1976). It
is interesting to consider how selection will operate on each
sex in relation to a mating decision concerning inbreeding.

I shall examine inbreeding decisions in which the two
individuals concerned have half their genes in common, i.e.,
they are full sibs or parents and offspring in species with
diploidy and sexual reproduction. It is easy to extend this
analysis to cover other forms of inbreeding (e.g., cousin
mating, etc.).

Male decision. Selection over whether or not to mate with
a sister, mother, or daughter (assuming that evolution can
favor such "decisions") will depend on how many genes the
male might expect in the next generation if he does or doesn't
perform the mating under question. Since he has one-half
his genes in common with the female, if he "allows" her to
outcross rather than inbreed with him, the number of additional replicas of a given allele (of the male) in the next generation will be $\frac{1}{4}N$, where N is the number of progeny from
each mating. Now suppose that the inbreeding depression is
such that matings between full sibs (or the corresponding
cases) have a fitness of $(1-D)$, relative to 1 for outcrossing. Let c = cost to a male of a mating (plus any other
parental costs he may have) relative to that of the female.
Thus c is roughly male PI/female PI. Selection favors
incestuous mating if

$$\underbrace{\frac{1}{2}N(1-D)}_{\substack{\text{genes}\\\text{from}\\\text{male}}} + \underbrace{\frac{1}{4}N(1-D)}_{\substack{\text{genes}\\\text{shared}\\\text{with}\\\text{female}}} - \underbrace{c\frac{N}{2}}_{\substack{\text{genes which}\\\text{would have been}\\\text{transmitted via}\\\text{outcrossing}}} > \underbrace{\frac{1}{4}N}_{\substack{\text{net gain via}\\\text{refusing incest}\\\text{and allowing}\\\text{the female to}\\\text{outcross}}}$$

$$\underbrace{\phantom{\frac{1}{2}N(1-D) + \frac{1}{4}N(1-D) - c\frac{N}{2}}}_{\text{net gain via incest}}$$

$$\therefore \quad 3(1-D) - 2c > 1, \tag{15}$$

if male PI << female PI

$$\therefore \quad 3(1-D) > 1, \text{ which can be satisfied.}$$

If male PI = female PI, c = 1

$$\therefore \quad 3(1-D) > 3, \text{ which can't be satisfied.}$$

The "decision" to mate depends on: if $c < 3/2(1 - D) - 1/2$, mate; if inequality is reversed, then refuse mating and allow the female to outcross.

Female decision. Applying similar techniques, the female should choose to mate incestuously if

$$\underbrace{\frac{1}{2} N (1 - D) + \frac{1}{4} N (1 - D) - c \frac{N}{4}}_{\text{female's net gain from incest}} > \underbrace{\frac{1}{2} N}_{\substack{\text{female's} \\ \text{gain from} \\ \text{outcrossing.}}}$$

$$\therefore \quad \text{mate if } 3(1 - D) - c > 2 \tag{16}$$

and if male PI is insignificant,

$$3(1 - D) > 2,$$

which can be satisfied, but less easily than the corresponding case for the male; if male and female PI are equal,

$$3(1 - D) > 3, \text{ as before.}$$

Here the "decision" to mate depends on: if $c < 3(1 - D) - 2$, mate; if $c > 3(1 - D) - 2$, then refuse mating.

Conflict over the mating decision for incest can occur if

$$3 - 2c - 1 > \frac{D}{3} > 3 - c - 2, \qquad \begin{array}{l}\text{from (15)} \\ \text{and (16)}\end{array}$$

in which case the male wants to mate incestuously but the female doesn't. Obviously, as with other cases, the probability of conflict is greatest when male PI << female PI (where c approaches zero).
Here:

$$\frac{2}{3} > D > \frac{1}{3}.$$

If sexual reproduction is to be favored rather than parthenogenesis, it is necessary that $N(1 - D_s) > N/2$, where D_s = the cost of selfing; hence $D_s > 1/2$. However, it is fallacious to equate D_s and D; this would assume the inbreeding costs to be equal for selfing and sib mating. One might make a (very) shaky case that $3D_s/4 \simeq D$, thus for sexuality $D4/3 > 1/2$; i.e., $D > 3/8$. If this has any validity, it means that females should always avoid incestuous matings. So too should males if male PI = female

PI, but not if equation (15) can be satisfied, i.e., if male PI is small enough.

That females may have more to lose than males in incestuous matings has been stated (independently) by Dawkins (1976). It seems likely in species with low male PI, that incest may commonly be a case of true sexual conflict in which the interests of the two sexes are opposed.

SEXUAL CONFLICT OVER MATING DECISIONS--WHO WINS?

Throughout this paper we have shown how conflict over mating decisions can arise and have examined its probable extent. It is extremely difficult to make predictions about which sex will win the conflict. For instance, though selection may be much stronger on the male to persist than on the female to reject, one mutation towards increased unreceptivity by females may be far more effective in preventing mating than the effectiveness of ten mutations for male persistence in enhancing the male's mating chances. Circumstances in which the outcome of an evolutionary "game" depend on

1. the rates of evolutionary adaptation (i.e., on selection intensity) in the two "opponents," and

2. the relative effectivenesses of each quantum of adaptation against the opponent's current level of adaptation

seem to be very common in animals and must occur in all interspecific conflicts (e.g., prey-predator and parasite-host interactions). They will be no less common in intraspecific conflicts where there is some asymmetry between the two contestants (male-female, parent-offspring, etc.) or between the aims of the two contestants. For instance, two male insects fighting over a female may have equal aims and abilities to achieve them. A male and a female insect of equal sizes and strengths in a sexual conflict over mating will commonly have strongly asymmetrical gains, and the objectives of the two opponents are also widely different (one is attempting to prevent mating, the other to mate). As mentioned, the asymmetry of aims may ultimately be a much more important determinant of the evolutionary outcome than selection intensity, though the result must depend on the interaction between the two. Parent-offspring conflict (Trivers, 1974) will be very similar to sexual conflict in this respect; it may be far harder (or far easier) for an offspring to solicit extra PI from its parent than for the parent to remain undeceived and to withold its PI.

Some idea of the difficulties can be shown by devising a simple model based on games theory and ESS lines similar to

that used by Maynard Smith (1977) and Maynard Smith and
Parker (1976). Suppose that the value of a mating to a male
(measured in terms of Darwinian fitness) is M. If the female
allows the mating, she loses R units of fitness. Now suppose
also that a female can attempt to prevent a mating, say with
probability q, and that the cost of this rejection is -S
fitness units if the male shows persistence. Males persist
with probability p, and the cost of their persistence is -U.
Thus we allow females two choices (passivity or rejection)
and males two choices (withdrawal if female rejects or persistence). The final parameter we shall use is r, which is the
probability that a mating occurs when a female rejects and a
male persists.

Making the assumption that each outcome (mating:not mating)
is equally possible when a "passive" female meets a "non-
persistent" male, the payoff matrix is:

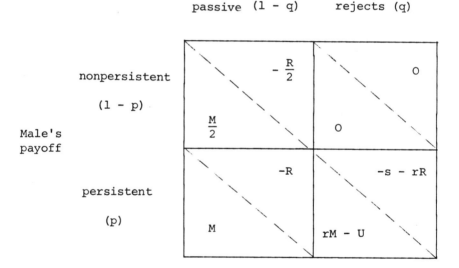

Female's payoff

First consider the male. If

$$(1 - q) \frac{M}{2} < (1 - q) M + q (rM - U),$$

then selection will act to increase the frequency p for
persisting. Obviously if q = 0, persistence will increase
due to the advantage M/2. If q ≠ 0, then selection increases
p only if

$$q < \frac{1}{1 - 2r + \frac{2U}{M}}. \tag{17}$$

For the female, selection will act to increase the frequency q for rejecting if

$$- \frac{R}{2} (1 - p) - Rp < - pS - prR ,$$

and again if $p = 0$, then q increases because of its gain $\frac{R}{2}$. If $p \neq 0$,

$$p < \frac{1}{\frac{2S}{R} + 2r - 1} \tag{18}$$

for q to increase.

Hence, if at the start, $p = q = 0$, then both persistence and rejection will increase. From (17) and (18) it follows that both p and q will become 1 (sex-limited genes for persistence and rejection both proceed to fixation) if

$$1 - \frac{S}{R} > r > \frac{U}{M} , \tag{19}$$

which requires that both S/R (costs of rejection) and U/M (costs of persistence) < 1. This is the equivalent outcome to the "hawks and doves" game for fighting behavior (Maynard Smith and Parker, 1976).

However if condition (19) is not satisfied, then the eventual outcome will be $p = 1$, $q = 0$ if $1 - S/R < r > U/M$, and $q = 1$ and $p = 0$ if $1 - S/R > r < U/M$. If $1 - S/R < r < U/M$, then it is rather more difficult to predict the outcome. The sex that "wins" will be that which first causes inequality (17) or (18) for the other sex to be reversed. For instance, if q rises to $1/(1 - 2r + 2U/M)$ before $p = 1/(2S/R + 2r - 1)$, then p will begin to decrease, causing q to accelerate towards fixation.

This sort of "evolutionary chase" to an ESS must in reality be even more complex. For instance, the male might increase r by increasing the costs of persistence (U/M), and the female might decrease r by increasing the costs of rejection (S/R). Given the particular functions r(U/M) and r(S/R), then it should be possible analytically to predict the eventual outcome of the "chase" from a knowledge of the starting conditions. This proved difficult, but the following computer simulations give some ideas about the dynamics of this type of game. Two models were simulated:

1. Sexual "War of Attrition"

This is the equivalent of the "war of attrition" for
symmetric contests analyzed by Maynard Smith (1974), but
here the values (payoffs) to the two contestants can be asymmetric ($M \neq R$) and also the cost or penalty functions can be
asymmetric (see Maynard Smith and Parker, 1976). There are
six strategies for each sex: P_0, P_1, P_2 .....P_5 for males and
Q_0, Q_1, Q_2 .....Q_5 for females. Strategy P_0 plays zero persistence and Q_0 zero rejection, hence they achieve positive
payoffs ($M/2$ and $R/2$, respectively) only when they meet. They
also achieve zero costs in meetings with all other strategies,
but always lose the payoff since all other strategies are
willing to persist or to reject. Strategies P_1 - P_5 are willing to persist to a cost $-KM$, $-2KM$ .....$-5KM$, where K is a
positive constant; and similarly female strategies Q_1 - Q_5
will reject to a cost of $-LR$, $-2LR$ .....$-5LR$. There is no
particular significance in the choice of linear cost functions. P_5 beats all Q_0 - Q_4 (gains M) and incurs a cost of
0, $-KM$ .....$-4KM$, respectively, and gains $M/2$ with Q_5 for a
cost of $-5KM$. Other outcomes were arranged after the same
logic. Strategies were fed into each generation in probabilities proportional to their relative gains in the previous
generation. This is equivalent to haploidy. It avoids the
complexities posed by dominance for diploidy, and outcomes
should be similar.
  An important condition in the "war of attrition" game is
that the costs to each opponent are set by the opponent
willing to persist least. Thus the game could relate to a
pair of insects in which the male courts vigorously until
time t_m, incurring, say, much higher costs than the female
who is willing to reject effectively, but undemandingly, until
time t_f. The male mates if $t_m > t_f$.
  In the simulations, the numbers of each sex going through
to the next generation were regulated independently. The
computations showed the proportions p_0, p_1 ..... p_5 of male
strategies P_0, P_1 ..... P_5 and proportions q_0, q_1 ..... q_5 of
female strategies Q_0, Q_1 ..... Q_5 after various numbers of
generations. Since starting conditions are important in
determining the ESS, I arranged that the distribution of costs
for the populations of each sex could start as "low cost,"
i.e., for males:

$$p_0 = 32/63, \ p_1 = 16/63, \ p_2 = 8/63 \ ..... \ p_5 = 1/63$$

or "high cost," i.e.,

$$p_0 = 1/63, \ p_1 = 2/63, \ p_2 = 4/63 \ ..... \ p_5 = 32/63.$$

TABLE 1

Outcome of "sexual war of attrition" simulations after 10,000 generations

Costs:	Starting condition:							
	MLFL		MLFH		MHFL		MHFH	
	p	q	p	q	p	q	p	q
K = L = .1 (symmetric cost functions)	-	.479	-	.006	-	.741	-	.023
	-	-	-	-	-	-	-	-
	-	-	-	-	-	-	-	-
	-	-	-	-	-	-	-	-
	-	-	-	-	-	-	-	-
	1.000	.521	1.000	.994	1.000	.259	1.000	.977
K = L = .25 (symmetric cost functions)	-	.999[a]	1.000	-	-	.999[a]	1.000	-
	.001[a]	.001[a]	-	-	.001[a]	.001[a]	-	-
	.076[a]	-	-	.062	.021[a]	-	-	.095
	.166[a]	-	-	.131	.095[a]	-	-	.122
	.249[a]	-	-	.266	.256[a]	-	-	.171
	.508[a]	-	-	.541	.628[a]	-	-	.612
K = .25 L = .1 (male costs relatively higher than female)	1.000	-	1.0	-	1.0	-	1.0	-
	-	-	-	-	-	-	-	-
	-	.001	-	.061	-	-	-	.047
	-	.010	-	.130	-	.001	-	.088
	-	.004	-	.285	-	.000	-	.172
	-	.985	-	.524	-	.999	-	.693
K = .1 L = .25 (female costs relatively higher than male)	-	1.000	-	1.000	-	1.000	-	1.000
	-	-	-	-	-	-	-	-
	.062	-	-	-	.025	-	-	-
	.161	-	-	-	.100	-	-	-
	.272	-	-	-	.260	-	.001	-
	.505	-	1.00	-	.615	-	.999	-

NOTE: In each group of data, the frequencies of male strategies are listed in the LHS column in order $P_0, P_1, P_2 \ldots P_5$ and the female strategies in the RHS column $(q_0, q_1, q_2 \ldots q_5)$. A – indicates that a strategy is eliminated. $N = 10$, $R = 2$.

[a] Frequencies still changing.

With similar cost distributions for females, there are four possible starting conditions: male low cost, female low cost (MLFL); male low, female high (MLFH); male high, female low (MHFL); and male high, female high (MHFH). Payoff M = 10 and R = 2 throughout the simulations. In order to avoid negative total gains for a given strategy, a constant equivalent to twice the maximum male cost (i.e., = 10KM) was added to all payoffs at each generation.

Frequencies of each strategy after 10,000 generations are shown in Table 1. Consider first the case where the cost functions are symmetric, and K = L = .1. This means that there are never any negative payoffs from an encounter. All starting conditions yield fixation of P_5. The reason p_5 changes most rapidly is that it is under more intense selection, although the benefit/cost functions are symmetrical. Once $p_5 = 1$, then there is no further selection on Q_0 and Q_5 since both have equal payoffs against P_5: other $Q_{1 \text{ to } 4}$ are lost. The polymorphism for Q_0 and Q_5 is thus trivial.

When payoffs can be negative, but benefit/cost functions are again symmetric (K = L = .25), then the outcome is the "conventional ESS" suggested by Maynard Smith for asymmetric contests; as expected both ESSs can exist so that either sex can win. When the female starts low, then, because selection is strongest on the male, the ESS tends to be that the male "wins." When the female starts high, the male tends to lose.

Two further conditions were examined in which the benefit/cost functions were asymmetric. When males can lose most (K = .25, L = .1), then females win, and males win when conditions are reversed (K = .1, L = .25). These are thus "commonsense" ESSs (Maynard Smith and Parker, 1976).

These results add little, if anything, to Maynard Smith's analyses and are presented mainly for comparison with the results of the next section. They also serve to indicate the way in which selection intensity and starting conditions can interact with effectiveness of a strategy (benefit/cost) in determining the eventual ESS.

2. The "Opponent-Independent Costs" Game

Here the cost functions are independent of the other players. All other rules are the same, e.g., P_4 beats $Q_0 - Q_3$ and wins and loses with equal probability with Q_4. But throughout life, P_4 always incurs a cost of -4KM. Thus, say a male might have an anatomical feature (possibly just equivalent to size) which causes enhanced success against female rejection, and vice versa. The cost of the morphological specialization is thus constant and independent of conflicts, though *gains* from conflicts do depend on the level of cost "chosen." This sort of game could be fundamentally a rather important one, espe-

TABLE 2

Outcome of "opponent-independent costs game" during the first 10,000 generations

Costs:	Starting condition:							
	MLFL		MLFH		MHFL		MHFH	
	p	q	p	q	p	q	p	q
K = L = .1 (symmetric cost functions)	-	.001	.014	-	-	.170	-	.024
	-	-	-	-	-	-	-	-
	-	-	-	-	-	-	-	-
	-	-	-	-	-	-	-	-
	1.000	.854	.986	1.000	1.000	.830	1.000	.976
K = L = .25 (symmetric cost functions)	+	•	•	•	•	•	•	•
	+	+	+	+	+	+	+	+
	+	+	+	•	+	•	+	+
	+	+	•	+	•	+	+	+
	-	-	-	-	-	-	-	-
K = .25 L = .1 (male costs relatively higher than female)	+	-	+	-	+	-	+	-
	•	•	•	•	•	•	•	•
	+	+	+	+	+	+	+	+
	+	+	+	+	-	+	+	+
	-	-	-	-	-	-	-	-
K = .1 L = .25 (female costs relatively higher than male)	-	+	-	+	?	+	-	+
	+	+	+	+	+	+	+	+
	+	•	+	•	+	•	+	•
	•	+	•	+	•	+	•	+
	-	-	-	-	-	-	-	-

NOTE: Convention as in Table 1 except that where there was an unresolvable evolutionary chase, the most frequently occupied strategies are indicated with a + and less frequent ones with a dot. M = 10, R = 2.

cially for prey-predator systems as well as sexual conflicts.
The totals $p_0 + p_1 \ldots\ldots + p_5$ and $q_0 + q_1 \ldots\ldots + q_5$ are again
set independently at 1 each generation. In all respects,
apart from the opponent independent costs, the simulations
were exactly identical to those for Table 1.

Results are given in Table 2. The first thing to note is
that if either of the cost constants (K and L) is .25, then
the two highest playing strategies for that sex must be lost.
This is either because a win cannot offset the cost (payoff
always negative) or the sum of cost and benefit is zero for
specific cases but otherwise negative. Hence the game will
always be restricted to a zone in which positive payoffs can
occur (always true if K or L = .1). Consider now the case,
say, where K = .1 and L = .25, i.e., female costs are relatively higher. If the females play Q_3, then males are favored
which play P_4. If P_4 fixates, this immediately favors fixation of Q_0 because it offers the same (zero) benefit at zero
cost. This in turn favors fixation of P_1 for the same reason.
Since it now offers a positive payoff, Q_2 becomes favorable.
There is thus an escalation up towards Q_3 and P_4, and so the
cycle repeats. The essential difference between the "opponent-independent costs" game and the "war of attrition" is that
a conventional ESS (in which one opponent is prepared to play
a greater cost than the benefit) is impossible to maintain.
Apart from the case where K = L = .1, the "opponent-independent costs" game never gave any stable solution; as predicted,
the frequencies of the various strategies yielding positive
payoffs fluctuated throughout the 10,000 generations. This
is thus an "unresolvable evolutionary chase," i.e., there is
no ESS.

In Table 2, the most frequently "occupied" strategies in
the chase are marked with a + and as before, strategies that
are eliminated are marked with -. Note that there is no
dependence on starting frequency. The apparent stability of
the simulation with K = L = .1 is trivial. Because there is
no possibility of negative payoffs, both opponents show drive
towards the high cost end of the distribution. Males win this
race, because selection intensity is higher on males. Once
$p_5 = 1$, then there is no further selection on the female,
since Q_0 is as good as Q_5 against P_5. The males stay at P_5
because some females play Q_0.

It seems likely that unresolvable evolutionary chases of
this type will be commonest for asymmetric games in which one
opponent can play a strategy giving a positive payoff which
would force the opponent to play a negatively yielding strategy in order to win. The conventional ESS is impossible
because, if the losing opponent then "settles" for zero, selection forces the winner into the zone where the loser can
again achieve a positive payoff by playing a higher cost

strategy. Whether there is a mixed ESS solution to this game
is unclear, but seems unlikely; certainly the simulations
suggest that noncontinuous distributions of strategies will
give unresolvable chases.

The significance of these games as applied to sexual conflicts over mating decision can be summarized as follows:
Sexual "wars of attrition" should resolve into conventional
ESSs in which the "winning" sex is prepared to play more than
the value of the resource, and the "losing" sex plays zero.
The outcome depends on the selection intensity on the two
sexes (payoff asymmetry), on the starting conditions, and on
the asymmetries in cost functions. The "opponent-independent
costs" game, at least when there is not an infinite variation
of possible strategies, can result in unresolvable evolutionary chases to which there are no ESSs.

It is extremely difficult to know whether such cyclical
chases exist in nature. They would be restricted in amplitude to the zone of positive payoffs of the sex (or other
opponent) with the higher cost function, i.e., the sex which
incurs the higher cost to achieve an equal chance of win
against a unitary increase in the opponent's costs. This
zone could be a relatively small one. For sexual conflict
concerning mating decision, perhaps some evidence for chases
would be provided if the probability of rape showed marked
differences in separated local races, assuming there are no
other obvious reasons for the difference. Certainly strains
of *Drosphila* have long been known to show differences in the
levels of male courtship persistence and the probability of
remating of females, though this is open to a number of alternative explanations. The amplitude of these chases could
be very small if the disparity in relative cost functions is
very high.

Some Other Forms of Sexual Conflict

Finally, some other examples of sexual conflict will be
reviewed very briefly. So far the conflicts examined have
depended on mating (or gamete fusion) "decisions" in which
selection favors males "wanting" to mate and females "wanting"
to reject. As discussed, there are ways in which each sex
can "win," and the outcome depends on what the other sex can
do by way of retaliation, i.e., on the dynamics of the evolutionary chase and whether or not this leads to an ESS. Some
sexual conflicts are simpler and preclude complex evolutionary
chases for the simple reason that there is virtually nothing
that one sex can do to counter a conflict adaptation in the
other sex.

1. Parental Investment

Clearly, where male PI is less than female PI, the female parent could potentially always benefit from an increase in male PI, though this may not concur with male interests. This sort of conflict has attracted recent discussion (Trivers, 1972; Dawkins and Carlisle, 1976; Maynard Smith, 1977). In a characteristically stimulating paper, Maynard Smith (1977) has analyzed the ESS solutions to the problem of which sex (if any) might be expected to show extended parental care, which are based on the assumption that there is nothing (at least directly) an individual can do to prevent desertion by its mate. This seems to be an entirely reasonable assumption; it is difficult to see how a mate can be forced into giving PI if selection favored desertion. It is also difficult (but not always impossible, see Trivers, 1972) to see how a mate can be "tested" or "assessed" as to its future investment probability. Thus an ESS for *both* sexes to invest will depend on this "decision" being advantageous to both sexes, i.e., there is no conflict. There is likely to be conflict when the ESS is for only one sex to invest. Maynard Smith argues that in species with a discrete breeding season and when the male's chance of finding a second mate decreases with time, there is a female strategy which makes it more likely that a male will stay and invest. This is when females delay mating until the male has been paired long enough for his strategy of searching for a second mate (desertion) to have a much lower value than that of investing parental care. Thus the example appears to resolve into one of mating decision; males should want to mate immediately. But even if females "lost" and allowed early matings, there is no gain to the male if the female witholds reproduction until later; the mating is merely superfluous. Whether it is in the female's interests to delay rather than to breed earlier in the season will depend on the cost: benefits of early versus late breeding and male invest-ment versus zero male investment, etc.

Where there is conflict, then normally one sex will "de-sert" and the other invest, though the ESS can be for both to desert (no parental care). It is possible to make very extensive generalizations as to which sex will invest and which will desert, based on major biological differences such as internal versus external fertilization. Maynard Smith's approach certainly represents a major development in the un-derstanding of mating systems.

2. Infanticide

Males (e.g., langurs: Sugiyama, 1967; Hrdy, 1974; and lions: Bertram, 1976) sometimes slaughter young offspring

soon after they take over a social group from a previous
dominant male. This has been seen (Trivers, 1972) as a
sexually selected feature which increases male reproductive
success by bringing females more quickly into estrus. Similarly, in various pinnipeds harem-guarding bulls not uncom-
monly trample and kill conspecific infants which get in their
way during intramale disputes for supremacy of the harem
(Le Boeuf, 1972). Though there is no male benefit here from
the infanticide, there is little if any loss since the tram-
pled offspring would have been fathered the previous year,
in all probability by a different male. To avoid the offspring during disputes may mean a considerable reduction in
harem-guarding success. Similarly, the slaughtered lion cubs
are unlikely to be related to their assassin. Both these
forms of infanticide seem to represent sexual conflict, the
male gains and the female loses. However, it is not obvious
that females are completely at a loss to retaliate via
counter-selection. If there is nothing direct the female can
do to guard the infant, it seems surprising that more subtle
adaptations have not occurred. For instance, if male lions
will always kill young offspring after taking over a pride,
then it would seem best for the female to eat them, thus
recouping some of her losses.

This sort of selection may be significant (see Trivers,
1972; Dawkins, 1976) in the "Bruce effect" in mice. If exposed to the smell of a strange male, female mice sometimes
spontaneously abort during the first four days of pregnancy
(Bruce, 1960; Sadleir, 1967). It is not uncommon for female
mammals, after some form of environmental disturbance (which
may signify that future survival prospects of the offspring
will be low), to (1) resorb embryos, or (2) to abort and eat
more advanced foeti, or (3) to kill and eat neonates.

3. Mate Feeding and Mate Cannibalism

In a few insects the male feeds the female during courtship, as a preliminary to mating. This has been seen for some
predatory species as a possible appeasement mechanism relating
to avoidance of cannibalism of the male by the female (e.g.,
Manning, 1966). It is perhaps more likely to be a mechanism
of male PI, assuming that the progeny which will benefit are
his own (Downes, 1970). Certain male insects allow the female
to feed from the male's saliva (e.g., *Panorpa*: see Manning,
1966) or from the metanotal glands in *Oecanthus* (Orthoptera)
and some blattids (see Chapman, 1969). Donation of food by
male insects is not different evolutionarily from the donation
of time and effort as male PI. Insects can show all the
possible parental investment ESSs discussed by Maynard Smith
(1977). Though zero parental care in either sex is most

common, males may guard eggs (e.g., *Rhinocoris albopilosus*: Odhiambo, 1959). Much more frequently the female alone guards, or both sexes may guard and provision (e.g., *Canthon imitator*: W. Marshall, unpublished manuscript).

A few insects (notably mantids) and spiders may show female cannibalism of the male after or during mating. It is possible that if females mate only once per lifetime (so that the male's chances of finding another female are poor), then selection could favor males which donate their soma to their offspring in this way. Higher female mortality (giving a male-biased sex ratio) would help here. For there to be no conflict over the cannibalism merely requires that the increased fitness of the offspring exceed the value of the male's searching alternative. Where this inequality is reversed, mate cannibalism would constitute sexual conflict and the interests of the two sexes would be opposed. Male mantids are smaller than females, and hence the odds may be weighted against the male.

In dung flies, the female is generally smaller than the male, and hence it is usually feasible only for males to cannibalize females. Normally male dung flies mate immediately with gravid females. If numbers of each sex are confined together in the laboratory, the males will at first mate repeatedly with females, even if the females have laid their eggs in the dung provided. However, after a day or so in warm conditions, the males begin to cannibalize the (now non-gravid) females. The value to a male of a mating with a non-gravid female is only about 3 eggs, relative to 35 eggs for a mating with a gravid female (Parker, 1970a). It is tempting to speculate that as physiological deficits increase, the male can do better by cannibalism than by mating, i.e., the female is worth more as a food resource to increase future mating prospects than as a mate yielding only an expected payoff of 3 eggs.

4. Multiple Mating

When a female has been mated and contains enough sperm to effect full fertilization, there seems to be little evolutionary advantage to the female in remating. The male does gain by mating, however. For insects, this problem has been discussed in detail elsewhere (Pease, 1968; Parker, 1970d; Boorman and Parker, 1976; see also Labine, 1967; Taylor, 1967). Briefly, a male always benefits by displacing the sperm of another male from the female's sperm stores and introducing his own (for population genetics, see Prout and Bundgaard, 1977). The female may lose only to the extent of the time wasted in supernumerary copulations, though this need not be a weak selective force. (Some authors have seen

advantages to multiple mating in terms of maintenance of
genetic diversity, though such arguments usually rely mainly
on group selection.) There thus may commonly be mating-
decision conflicts between a courting male and a mated female.
Sometimes males appear to win this conflict (e.g., *Scatophaga*:
Parker, 1970c); sometimes females seem generally to win
(e.g., *Musca*: Zingrone et al., 1959).

SUMMARY

   The present paper attempts to analyze circumstances in
which there is a conflict of evolutionary interests between
the two sexes. A common sexual conflict concerns mating
decision; in a given encounter males are often under selection
to mate, and simultaneously females are under selection to
refuse mating. A model is analyzed in which a sex-limited
gene gives a competitive mating advantage to males, but the
male behavior associated with the gene inflicts some cost
upon the female (e.g., direct damage) which may be felt by
the progeny. Because the female may benefit via sons from
a mating with a male having the mating advantage, then selection on the female does not necessarily oppose selection on
the male, though for there to be a benefit (via sons) to the
female demands a relatively high mating advantage or a
relatively low cost. Thus there would only *sometimes* be
conflict at the start of spread of a dominant sex-limited
gene conferring a male mating advantage which results in
female cost, or at fixation of a similar recessive gene.
There will *always* be conflict, however, concerning the spread
of a recessive gene, or at fixation of a dominant gene.
Observable behavior in nature suggests that sexual conflict
may be common.
   The primordial sexual conflict concerned the establishment
of anisogamy itself. Ovum-producers would fare better without
males to "parasitize" the investment in each ovum. Males are
likely to have won this earliest conflict if sexual outcrossing is better than parthenogenesis, and if anisogamy first
established under random fusion before genes for assortative
fusion of ova arose.
   Sexual conflict concerning mating decision will be common
in encounters between individuals of different species, races,
or ecotypes in which the progeny would be less fit than
normal. The probability of conflict increases with increasing
disparity in relative parental investment (PI) of the sexes,
and there is a greater likelihood that selection will be more
intense on males to persist than on females to reject. Similar conflicts will occur when individuals can make "assess-

ments" of the goodness of a potential mate's genes for the
fitness of the offspring. As PI disparity increases, so does
the probability that indiscriminateness is the male's best
strategy, and that an "optimal selectivity" is favored for the
female. When both sexes show an "optimal selectivity," the
sex with the higher PI should be most discriminate. Both
these conclusions imply sexual conflict. Incest may also
result in a conflict depending on the extent of inbreeding
depression and again on relative PI. Many of these conclusions seem intuitively obvious, but there has been a tendency
to regard selection for discriminateness as simply weaker in
the lower investing sex, rather than in terms of opposition
of evolutionary interests in the two sexes.

Models are examined to ascertain the outcome of sexual
conflict over mating decision. It is assumed that either sex
could potentially win against a given level of adaptation in
the other sex, by increasing its expenditure on winning (its
costs). However, the selection intensity will vary (payoff
asymmetry) for the two "opponents," and so will the cost
functions, i.e., the cost of achieving an equal chance of a
win against a unitary increase in the opponent's costs. Cost
functions will also be asymmetrical; i.e., it may cost a female far less to prevent a male mating than it would cost the
male to ensure that he could manage to mate. The other important determinant of the outcome of such games is the starting
condition, i.e., the initial state of ability of each opponent
to win the dispute. Such games often result in rather complex
"evolutionary chases" to their eventual ESS. This happens
when the game is a sexual "war of attrition," i.e., where the
opponent which wins is the one which persists or rejects longest. The ESS is here of the conventional type, i.e., where
one opponent plays zero and the other is prepared to play a
cost greater than the resource value. This solution was
already known (Maynard Smith, 1974; Maynard Smith and Parker,
1976).

However, other games can result in "unresolvable evolutionary chases" to which there is (apparently) no ESS. This
happens where the costs (unlike the "war of attrition") are
independent of the opponent, as they might be if size or some
other morphological specialization determines the outcome.
Here the "play" of each opponent fluctuates cyclically within
the smallest zone of positive payoffs (set by the opponent
with the higher cost function). It is difficult to assess
the importance of unresolvable evolutionary chases in natural
populations; their amplitude may be very small if the disparity in relative cost function is high.

Other instances of sexual conflict are reviewed; sometimes
outcomes are easier to predict because there is little one
sex can do to counter a conflict adaptation in the other sex.

ACKNOWLEDGEMENTS

I am deeply indebted to Murray Blum for extending the
invitation (on behalf of the appropriate committee) for me
to attend the International Congress of Entomology in Washington, and for so graciously accomodating to the difficulties
I may have caused by being (eventually) unable to attend. I
must also thank Dan Otte for encouragement and for his extreme
patience in awaiting the manuscript of this paper, which has
become much more speculative than the one I would have
presented at the Congress. It is a pleasure to thank John
Maynard Smith, Richard Dawkins, Bob Trivers, Mark Macnair,
and Peter Smith for showing me in press manuscripts, and/or
for discussions and/or for recent influences which have
affected my thinking on the subject. Susan Watts did some
earlier work for her M.Sc. project on sexual conflict concerning interspecific mating decisions. Not least, I am
most grateful to Miss Anita Callaghan for working overtime
to get the manuscript typed as quickly as possible.

REFERENCES

Bateman, A.J. 1948. Intra-sexual selection in *Drosophila*.
    Heredity 2:349-368.
Bertram, B.C.R. 1976. Kin selection in lions and in evolution.
    In Bateson, P.P.G. and R.A. Hinde (eds.), *Growing Points
    in Ethology*. Cambridge Univ. Press, Cambridge.
Boorman, E., and G.A. Parker. 1976. Sperm (ejaculate) compe-
    tition in *Drosophila melanogaster,* and the reproductive
    value of females to males in relation to female age and
    mating status. *Ecol. Ent.* 1:145-155.
Bruce, H. 1960. A block to pregnancy in the mouse caused by
    the proximity of strange males. *J. Reprod. Fert.* 1:96-103.
Chapman, R.F. 1969. *The Insects: Structure and Function*.
    English Universities Press, London.
Charlesworth, D., and B. Charlesworth. 1975. Sexual selection
    and polymorphism. *Amer. Nat.* 109:465-469.
Charnov, E.L. 1973. Optimal foraging; some theoretical
    explorations. Ph.D. Thesis, Univ. of Washington.
Charnov, E.L., J. Maynard Smith, and J.J. Bull. 1976. Why
    be an hermaphrodite? *Nature* 263:125-126.
Darwin, C.R. 1871. *Sexual Selection and the Descent of Man*.
    John Murray, London.
Dawkins, R. 1976. *The Selfish Gene*. Oxford Univ. Press,
    Oxford.
Dawkins, R., and T.R. Carlisle. 1976. Parental investment,

mate desertion and a fallacy. *Nature* 262:131-132.

Downes, J.A. 1970. The feeding and mating behaviour of the specialized Empidinae(Diptera).; observations on four species of *Rhamphomyia* in the high arctic and a general discussion. *Can. Ent.* 102:769-791.

Felsenstein, J. 1974. The evolutionary advantage of recombination. *Genetics* 78:737-756.

Fisher, R.A. 1930. *The Genetical Theory of Natural Selection*. Clarendon Press, Oxford.

Gadgil, M., and C.E. Taylor. 1975. Plausible models of sexual selection and polymorphism. *Amer. Nat.* 109:470-471.

Greenwood, P.J., and P.H. Harvey. 1976. The adaptive significance of breeding area fidelity of the blackbird (*Turdus merula* L.). *J. Anim. Ecol.* 45:887-898.

Hammer, O. 1941. Biological and ecological investigations on flies associated with pasturing cattle and their excrement. *Vidensk. Meddel. Dansk Naturhist. Foren. Kjob.* 105:1-257.

Hrdy, S.B. 1974. Male-male competition and infanticide among the langurs (*Presbytis entellus*) of Abu, Rajasthan. *Folia Primatol.* 22:19-58.

Huxley, J.S. 1938. The present standing of the theory of sexual selection. *In* DeBeer, G. (ed.), *Evolution*. Oxford Univ. Press, New York.

Kalmus, H. 1932. Über den Erhaltungswert den phänotypischen (morphologischen) Anisogamie und die Entstehung der ersten Geschlectsunterschiede. *Biol. Zentral.* 52:716-726.

Kalmus, H., and C.A.B. Smith. 1960. Evolutionary origin of sexual differentiation and the sex ratio. *Nature* 186:1004-1006.

Knowlton, N. 1974. A note on the evolution of gamete dimorphism. *J. Theor. Biol.* 46:283-285.

Labine, P.A. 1967. Population biology of the butterfly, *Euphydryas editha*. IV. Sperm precedence--a preliminary report. *Evolution* 20:580-586.

Le Boeuf, B. 1972. Sexual behaviour in the northern elephant seal *Mirounga angustirostris*. *Behaviour* 41:1-26.

Manning, A. 1966. Sexual behaviour. *In* Haskell, P.T. (ed.), *Insect Behaviour. Symp. Roy. Ent. Soc. London* 3:59-68.

Manning, J.T. 1976. Gamete dimorphism and the cost of sexual reproduction: are they separate phenomena? *J. Theor. Biol.* 55:393-395.

Maynard Smith, J. 1956. Fertility, mating behaviour and sexual selection in *Drosophila subobscura*. *J. Genet.* 54:261-279.

Maynard Smith, J. 1971. What use is sex? *J. Theor. Biol.* 30:319-335.

Maynard Smith, J. 1974. The theory of games and the evolution of animal conflicts. *J. Theor. Biol.* 47:209-221.

Maynard Smith, J. 1976. A short term advantage for sex and recombination through sib-competition. *J. Theor. Biol.*

63:245-258.
Maynard Smith, J. 1977. Parental investment--a prospective
    analysis. *Anim. Behav.* 25:1-9.
Maynard Smith, J., and G.A. Parker. 1976. The logic of
    asymmetric contests. *Anim. Behav.* 24:159-175.
Odhiambo, T.R. 1959. An account of parental care in *Rhinocoris
    albopilosus* Signoret (Hemiptera-Heteroptera: Reduviidae),
    with notes on its life history. *Proc. Roy. Ent. Soc. London
    A.* 34:175-185.
O'Donald, P. 1962. The theory of sexual selection. *Heredity*
    17:541-552.
O'Donald, P. 1974. Polymorphisms maintained by sexual selec-
    tion in monogamous species of birds. *Heredity* 32:1-10.
Orians, G.H. 1969. On the evolution of mating systems in birds
    and mammals. *Amer. Nat.* 103:589-604.
Parker, G.A. 1970a. Sperm competition and its evolutionary
    effect on copula duration in the fly *Scatophaga stercor-
    aria. J. Insect Physiol.* 16:1301-1328.
Parker, G.A. 1970b. The reproductive behaviour and the nature
    of sexual selection in *Scatophaga stercoraria* L. IV. Epi-
    gamic recognition and competition between males for the
    possession of females. *Behaviour* 37:113-139.
Parker, G.A. 1970c. The reproductive behaviour and the nature
    of sexual selection in *Scatophaga stercoraria* L. V. The
    female's behaviour at the oviposition site. *Behaviour*
    37:140-168.
Parker, G.A. 1970d. Sperm competition and its evolutionary
    consequences in the insects. *Biol. Rev.* 45:525-568.
Parker, G.A. 1974. Courtship persistence and female guarding
    as male time investment strategies. *Behaviour* 48:157-184.
Parker, G.A. 1978. Selection on non-random fusion of gametes
    during the evolution of anisogamy. *J. Theor. Biol.* (in press).
Parker, G.A., R.R. Baker, and V.G.F. Smith. 1972. The origin
    and evolution of gamete dimorphism and the male-female
    phenomenon. *J. Theor. Biol.* 36:529-553.
Parker, G.A., and R.A. Stuart. 1976. Animal behavior as a
    strategy optimizer: the evolution of resource assessment
    strategies and optimal emigration thresholds. *Amer. Nat.*
    110:1055-1076.
Pease, R.W. 1968. The evolutionary and biological significance
    of multiple pairing in the Lepidoptera. *J. Lepidop. Soc.*
    22:197-209.
Prout, T., and J. Bundgaard. 1978. The population genetics of
    sperm displacement. *Adv. Genet.* (in press).
Sadleir, R. 1967. *The Ecology of Reproduction in Wild and
    Domestic Mammals*. Methuen, London.
Scudo, F.M. 1967. The adaptive value of sexual dimorphism:
    I. Anisogamy. *Evolution* 21:285-291.
Smith, C.C., and S.D. Fretwell. 1974. The optimal balance

between size and number of offspring. *Amer. Nat.*
108:499-506.
Sugiyama, U. 1967. Social organization of Hanuman langurs.
In Altman, S. (ed.), *Social Communication Among Primates*.
Univ. Chicago Press, Chicago.
Taylor, O.R. 1967. Relationship of multiple mating to fertil-
ity in *Atteva punctella* (Lepidoptera: Yponomeutidae). *Ann.
Ent. Soc. Amer.* 60:583-590.
Trivers, R.L. 1972. Parental investment and sexual selection.
In Campbell, B. (ed.), *Sexual Selection and the Descent
of Man, 1871-1971*. Aldine, Chicago.
Trivers, R.L. 1974. Parent-offspring conflict. *Amer. Zool.*
14:249-264.
Trivers, R.L. 1976. Sexual selection and resource-accruing
abilities in *Anolis garmani*. *Evolution* 30:253-269.
Williams, G.C. 1975. *Sex and Evolution*. Princeton Univ.
Press, Princeton.
Williamson, D.I. 1951. On the mating and breeding of some
semi-terrestrial amphipods. *Rep. Dovemar. Lab.* 3:49-62.
Zahavi, A. 1975. Mate selection--a selection for a handicap.
J. Theor. Biol. 53:205-214.
Zingrone, L.D., W.D. Bruce, and G.L. Decker. 1959. A mating
study of the female housefly. *J. Econ. Ent.* 52:236.

WINGLESS AND FIGHTING MALES IN

FIG WASPS AND OTHER INSECTS

W. D. Hamilton

The University of Michigan

INTRODUCTION

From June 1975 to February 1976, my wife and I gathered
life-history and behavioral data on the fig wasps of two
species of wild fig trees *(Ficus)* that were common around
Ribeirão Prêto, Brazil. This account firstly summarizes these
data and outlines the mating and breeding systems that they
imply.

The 18 or so species of fig wasps covered by our survey
showed (1) many possessing *wingless males,* (2) *lethal combat*
among several types of these wingless males, and (3) several
cases of profound *male dimorphism,* that is, a normally winged
male occurring as alternative to a wingless male. Literature
suggests that our findings may be fairly representative
throughout the world distribution of *Ficus:* yet only (1) is
well known (Grandi, 1961). In insects as a whole (1), (2),
and (3) are rare. The second object of this paper is to
consider why three rare phenomena should be common in fig
wasps, which they are to the extent of occurring not just
separately within the aggregate of species that we observed,
but in some cases within single species. Other relevant
instances of male winglessness, fighting, and dimorphism in
insects--which sometimes also concur, although usually no more
than two at a time--will be reviewed.

THE FIGS AND FIG WASPS

The species we called *Ficus* 1 provided the largest trees
in local natural woodlands and had a few large trees on the
campus of Faculdade de Medicina de Ribeirão Prêto. Their figs
were apt to be inaccessible for collection and fruitings were
infrequent, perhaps not more than once a year. *Ficus* 2 trees
were small (not more than about 8 m) and common on terrace
walls and in waste places. They fruited at least twice a

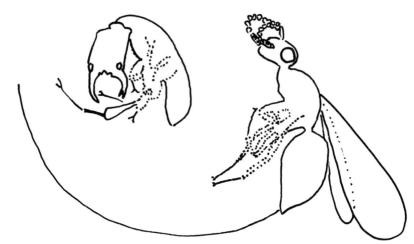

Fig. 1. Sexual dimorphism in Idarnes F2: *large male (left) and large female (right)*.

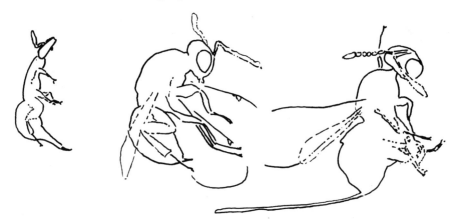

Fig. 2. Sexual and male dimorphism in parasite species F: *micropterous male (left), normal male, female (right)*.

year. Hence we gathered much more data for this species.
Both species of *Ficus* belong to the section *Americana* of sub-
genus *Urostigma* (Corner, 1958).

A summary of data obtained by rearing fig wasps from
ripening figs is presented in Table 1. Our makeshift taxonomy
of the wasps, which assigns letters for species, is further
explained below. Figs. 1, 2, 3, and 4 give a rough impression of selected species and their morphs. In all the species
females were always winged (only three individual exceptions
to this were noted and these were obviously runts). Table 1
shows that the males in some species were always winged; in
some, always wingless; and in some, dimorphic for wings. For

each species absence of any wingless male in a fig is made
the basis of classifying the fig's females separately from
those occurring in figs with wingless males: the significance
of such division will appear later.

Due to the diversity and the often extreme differences
between males and females, the task of sorting adult wasps
into species was difficult and some uncertainties remain.
The genus *Idarnes* was the most problematic. Females easily
separated into types (by size, length of ovipositor, and
antennae: two types in *Ficus* 1 and four in *Ficus* 2), but males
gave a fairly continuous range of variation, and some instances of mating suggested that perhaps any type of male
could mate any type of female. Since previously only one
Idarnes species has been reported for each *Ficus,* it seems
possible that our cases also concern only single species which
have a very marked polymorphism in the females and more continuous but wide-ranging variation, similar to that described
by Grandi (1930) and others (e.g., Wiebes, 1966) for males of
Philotrypesis and other Old World genera, in the males. Polymorphism in ovipositor length could well be concerned with
drilling to hit female flowers layered at different depths
in the young fig (see Richards, 1961, and Brues, 1922, for
possible parallels in other Parasitica), but equally striking
and correlated variation in the antennae favors separate
species. A similar problem with suspicion of conspecificity
regarding three or four fig wasps currently put in distinct
genera has been raised by Wiebes (1968). Since males could
not be ascribed with certainty, the one-species view has been
taken, rightly or wrongly, in Table 1 and subsequent analyses.

There was no evidence that any one species was breeding on
both fig species. Nevertheless most species had an obvious
"sister" in the wasp series of the other *Ficus,* and our use
of capital and small letters as species symbols attempts to
reflect this. Some similarity groupings among the parasites
of each *Ficus* were also apparent. The following arrangement
of the symbols illustrates our tentative groupings within and
between the two series:

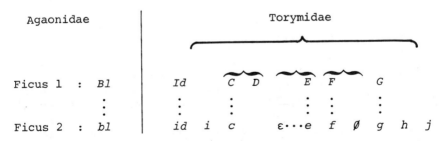

Dotted lines indicate the most obvious correspondences.

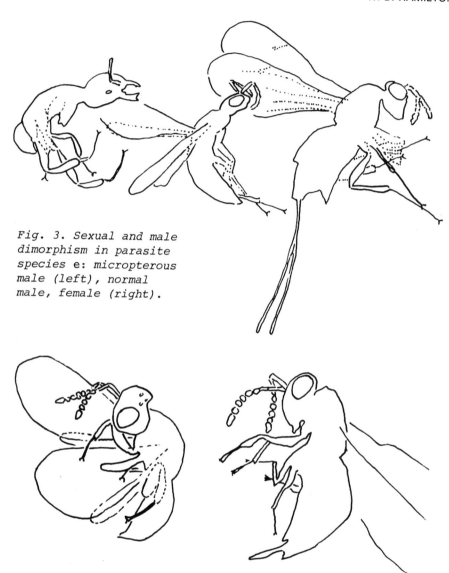

Fig. 3. Sexual and male
dimorphism in parasite
species e: micropterous
male (left), normal
male, female (right).

Fig. 4. Parasite species c: male (left) and female (right).

Lists of Hymenoptera do not, of course, exhaust the
sycophilous insects found in the figs. Larvae of a beetle,
a moth, and a cecidomyid fly, for example, were fairly common.
A tarsonemoid mite was even more common and a nematode was
abundant (transmission of these was phoretic and parasitic,
respectively). Even with these added, our observed diversi-
ty--even for *Ficus* 2--certainly does not exceed that recorded

TABLE 1

Polymorphism in fig wasps. Wasps of two Ficus of southern Brazil: brood data classified for sex & wings

Species (S)	Frequency of figs with S in random sample	No. of figs with S in total sample	MALES Alate	MALES Flight-less	FEMALES Flight-less males absent	FEMALES Flight-less males present	TOTAL	Sex Ratio (males ÷ total)	Wing ratio in males (winged males ÷ all males)	Numbers of S in figs having any Mean	Numbers of S in figs having any Standard deviation
Blastophaga F 1	12/12	11	0	89	0	1177	1266	.070	0	115.1	33.0
Blastophaga F 2	39/39	55	0	303	72	2956	3331	.090	0	60.6	68.1
Idarnes F 1 (Id)	12/12	12	0	169	0	433	602	.281	0	50.2	33.5
Idarnes F 2 (id)	38/39	57	0	1045	0	1900	2945	.355	0	51.7	27.4
C	5/12	5	12	0	12	0	24	.500	1	4.8	6.5
c	6/39	15	15	0	11	0	40	.725	1	2.7	1.8
E	4/12	3	1	2	2	3	8	.375	.333	2.7	2.1
e	17/39	36	36	26.6	37	44	143.6	.436	.574	4.0	3.8
	1/39	7	7	2.4	17	4	30.4	.309	.745	4.3	4.2
F	5/12	5	1	7	1	34	43	.186	.125	8.6	6.1
f	16/39	24	40	14	29	16	99[a]	.529	.907	4.1	4.2
Ø	15/39	26	11	102	6	17.7	296	.382	.097	11.4	13.1
G	2/12	2	0	0	2	0	2	0	1	1.0	0
g	7/39	9	11	0	1	0	12	.762[b]	1	1.3	0.5
h	2/39	2	0	0	2	0	2	.250[b]	1	1.0	0
i	4/39	17	72	0	137	0	209	.383[c]	1	12.3[c]	12.1

[a] Record omits three very small brachypterous females.

[b] Sex ratio includes specimens additional to main data.

[c] Common only in one crop of one tree.

for at least one Old World *Ficus* (Hill, 1967). Likewise the
strange sight when one of our figs at the right stage is
opened--the winged wasps in varied shapes and colors that,
by the hundreds, run out and fly, and the grotesque, brownish,
wingless forms that remain behind, roaming the fig cavity--is
also fairly well-paralleled by a description for an Old World
Ficus (Baker, 1913; see also Fig. 9b).

FIGHTING IN FIG WASPS

   The family Agaonidae includes all the pollinator fig wasps.
For the most part, its species are in one-to-one correspon-
dence with species of *Ficus*. The family Torymidae includes
most of the other chalcidoid wasps that breed in figs. The
torymid fig wasps have various *parasitic* relationships (details usually unknown) with agaonids or with the *Ficus*. The
great majority of male fig wasps are wingless, and this
applies whether we count overall numbers bred (which gives
great weight to the always wingless males of the agaonids) or
survey taxonomic lists (which tends to emphasize the torymids). Winglessness and precocious mating of male agaonids
is classic knowledge. The parallel wingless states that occur
in male torymids, however, although often even stranger than
those of agaonids, have records and comment confined to
specialist journals, and even there the information is eso-
teric even to most entomologists. This is because the process
of pollen transfer and fruiting in *Ficus* is unique, so that
the animals dependent on this process form a community which
has no close parallel.
   Even in specialist literature there has been little attempt
to interpret the adaptive functions of the strange modifications of torymid males (Grandi, 1959), although these are
often quite different from those of agaonid males. Only one
author has reported fighting in Torymidae (*Philotrypesis*:
Joseph, 1958), and this report did not relate fighting to
morphology nor attempt to generalize. Our own information
strongly suggests that some of the recurrent modifications of
torymid males, notably large head and mandibles, are always
concerned with fighting.
   We watched mortal fights between wingless males of *Id, id,*
E, e, and *Ø* and on grounds of morphology strongly suspect its
occurrence in ε and *D*. Fighting males were always conspecific.[1]

---

[1] Except for occasional mistakes, interspecies fighting would
be surprising. Milder fighting is known, however, in rather
similar circumstances, for two scelionid parasitoids of bug
egg masses (Eberhard, 1975). Its function is unexplained.

Apart from large head and mandibles and perhaps shield-like formations of head and pronotum in the neck region, other modifications of wingless male fig wasps are probably attributable to selection not connected with fighting. For example, the common tendency for the head to be most darkened and sclerotized compared to the rest of the body, and for the abdomen to be least sclerotized, can be attributed to the way all wingless male parasites have to actively look for females in galls and to the help (far from altruistic) which they give in opening the hole which lets her out. Some other modifications are probably connected with the exact site of mating, e.g., flattened, flexible body (*Id, id, Ø*; Fig. 1) or small size (*F, f*; Fig. 2) for those which enter the gall with the female, or elongated abdomen and enlarged forelegs and hind legs (with reduced mid legs) for those which cling to the gall and insert only the genitalia (*Blastophaga*). (For reasons not yet clear, the wing-reduced *F* and *f* males, although entering to mate, show an approach to the same modifications.) As the wingless males of *E, e,* and *ε* (Fig. 3) lack any of these further specializations, predictably they merely mate each female outside the gall after helping to make her exit hole. Perhaps in consequence of this--being mobile fighters and little else--they present a striking, superficial resemblance to soldier ants and may have sometimes been mistaken for ants. The male of *D* was rather similar, but so rare that we saw nothing of its habits.

Most of our observations on fighting concern *Idarnes;* wasps of this genus were present in almost every fig.

Male behavior must be at least slightly upset when a fig is cut open. Light alone affects the behavior to an unknown degree, and manipulation of males even with hairs of a fine brush tends to intimidate them (giving the impression, perhaps, that they are being pushed or lifted by a very powerful adversary). Even so, it was easy to provoke fights by adding a gall with a female about to emerge to a half fig containing two or more live large males. A male's fighting movements could be summarized thus: touch, freeze, approach slowly, strike, and recoil. Their fighting looks at once vicious and cautious--cowardly would be the word except that, on reflection, this seems unfair in a situation that can only be likened in human terms to a darkened room full of jostling people among whom, or else lurking in cupboards and recesses which open on all sides, are a dozen or so maniacal homicides armed with knives. One bite is easily lethal. One large *Idarnes* male is capable of biting another in half, but usually a lethal bite is quite a small puncture in the body. Paralysis follows a small injury so regularly and quickly as to suggest use of venom. The males certainly have mandibular glands and appear not to have any mouth (Gordh, 1975). The glands are present in the male forms of other genera which parallel *Idarnes* (see Wiebes, 1966, 1967). But females have the glands, too.

Once wounded in the body, an *Idarnes* or ∅ male stops fighting and moves more and more spastically until he dies. Although he does not attempt to hide, he is ignored by the victor. (On the other hand, an e male was once seen to remain beside a damaged rival and bite at him repeatedly, eventually severing his body.) If no serious injury results from the first or second reciprocal attempts to bite, one of the males, injured perhaps by loss of a tarsus or in some way sensing himself outmatched, retreats and tries to hide. Usually he finds an empty gall into which he plunges, turns, and comes to rest with mandibles agape at the gall's opening. From this position he can bite at the legs of the victor or another passing male with much less danger. Such an inactive male only ventures out again when long undisturbed and then very cautiously. In some figs the males' sharp reaction to contact with other males is muted and they brush past each other un- concernedly. This seems more likely to happen when females are in rapid flush of emergence from their galls (c.f. Browne, 1922, for a like observation on *Melittobia* males). Perhaps with matings freely available, the gains from fighting come to be less than worth the risk.

Similar lack of reaction holds generally for small *Idarnes* males. These also sometimes fight mortally but seem on the whole less aggressive and do not try to monopolize a fig cavi- ty as large males do. Instead they spend much time forcing their way between the fig flowers and mating females in hidden galls that are not easily reached by large males. I never succeeded in getting them to attack large males, whereas I did sometimes see them killed by large males, which, however, seemed less sensitive to their presence than they are to others of their own size.

For one fig of *Ficus* 2, Table 2 lists the *Idarnes* comple- ment emerged from galls but still inside the fig. The extent of injury shown is unusual: it probably follows from the untypically large number of males and small number of females in this fig. Nevertheless, on the basis of a low estimate of 10 males dying in mortal combat per fig, one fruiting of a large tree of *Ficus* 1 (a tree larger than those for which Hill (1967) gives a crop of 100,000 figs) probably involves several million deaths due to combat.

The strategy of small *Idarnes* males--of being first to reach hidden galls--is also that adopted by wingless males of *F*. These are small compared both to their females and to conspecific winged males (Fig. 2) and, compared to wingless males of other species, have their heads reduced instead of their gasters. I never saw them fight, whereas I did once

TABLE 2

Live and dead Idarnes *in one fig, 31 December 1975*

LIVE:

FEMALES:
15 of which 5 emerged at once and approximately 10 were in
galls ready to emerge.

MALES:
1 : LARGE, in cell with female, missing part of one tarsus.
1 : LARGE, wandering, missing parts of two tarsi.
1 : MEDIUM, in empty cell, missing one tarsus.
2 : SMALL, both perfect.

MORIBUND:

MALES:
1 : SMALL, missing parts of fore- and mid leg on one side,
        viscera extruding.
1 : SMALL, seems perfect.

DEAD:

LARGE MALES:
1 : seems perfect.
1 : one front leg missing from base of tibia (and almost
        severed at base of coxa); hind leg on same side
        missing from base of femur.

MEDIUM MALES:
4 : seem perfect (one thorax lop-sided congenitally).
4 : seem perfect but dark areas in thorax suggest wounds.
1 : one tibia and one tarsus missing.
1 : one tarsus missing and darkened mid thorax.
1 : with head missing.
1 : body almost severed in two places; one rear corner of
        head and three legs missing.
1 : almost severed in thorax; one tarsus missing.
1 : rear corner of head perforated and darkened; dark spot
        on thorax.
1 : twisted and blackened neck; part of one tarsus missing.
1 : mid coxa with black band (cut across?).
1 : one hind leg missing.
1 : one front tarsus and one antenna missing.
1 : one front leg from base of femur and one part of a tarsus
        missing.
1 : one antenna missing.
1 : abdomen eviscerated, one mid tarsus missing.

TABLE 2 (continued)

---

1 : dark spots at back of pronotum, one mid tarsus missing.
1 : dark spot at neck, antennae missing, one mid tarsus
        almost severed.
1 : mid leg severed at base of femur and dark wounds on
        thorax nearby.
1 : blackened at neck; part of one tarsus missing.

   SMALL MALES:
7 : seem perfect.
7 : seem perfect but with dark areas on thorax.
2 : hind tarsus missing.
1 : three tarsi missing on one side.
1 : body severed between hind and mid legs.
1 : hind leg missing from base of tibia.
1 : seems perfect but dark mark at base of abdomen.

SUMMARY:

TOTAL NUMBER OF MALES
    (a)   APPARENTLY PERFECT: 12⎱
    (b)   OBVIOUSLY OR PROBABLY INJURED: 42⎰ 54

TOTAL NUMBER OF FEMALES   15

---

find two jammed fast, back-to-back, halfway into a gall containing an F female. This suggests that they compete for
matings by energetic but peaceable means. Small wingless
males of f were probably similar in habits but were too rare
for much observation, and as a morph were so variable that
they could be considered runts if their modifications were
not so similar to those shown more markedly by the clearly
defined wingless morph of F.

The explanation of the peaceful competition in these species may lie in an evolutionary difficulty of associating a
trend to smallness with a trend to pugnacity. It is very
generally true for small taxonomic units throughout the animal
kingdom that where pugnacity varies, it is the largest animals
of a group that fight most. The present case may illustrate
a general reason: the male who is most successful through
smallness in reaching hidden females in galls is the male
least likely to win a fight, so that the supergene (or
switched set of genes) controlling size and morph cannot
easily come to include elements promoting aggressiveness.

A more important problem is to explain why the wingless
males of Blastophaga, which are not particularly small, do not
fight. To judge from morphology (small head and mandibles,

neck region unshielded), this puzzle may apply to all the pollinating agaonids: the only agaonid males which look much like fighters *(Alfonsiella)* are probably nonpollinator parasites (Wiebes, 1972). Yet due to the lower sex ratio, a successfully pugnacious *Blastophaga* male among nonpugnacious rivals could expect to monopolize a much larger harem than could a dominant *Idarnes* male.

At the same time, the low sex ratio may show a path to the answer since it reflects breeding structure (Hamilton, 1967) and hence also the level of relatedness inside the fig. It is tempting to suggest that, since fighting involves both energy loss and danger for both rivals and since a lone surviving *Blastophaga* male might well be unable to fertilize all of 100 or so females (whereas an *Idarnes* male would have less difficulty with the 50 or so *Idarnes* females), *a difference in mean relatedness between rivals* accounts for the different male behaviors (Hamilton, 1964). That is, to anthropomorphize and oversimplify, *Blastophaga* males may be restrained because (1) many of the rival males are brothers, and a male doesn't care so much whether he or a brother does the mating; (2) many of the females are his sisters, and he doesn't wish to risk that some sisters remain unmated; and (3) for those that are his sisters, a male may actually prefer to have them mated by an unrelated male because of the opportunities this will give for useful recombination in the next generation.

A reasonable case for higher relatedness among *Blastophaga* males can be made straight away from the behavior of their mothers. Once a foundress *Blastophaga* female has struggled through the osteole into a fig, losing her wings and often her antennae, she is committed to laying her whole brood there: she never escapes. *Idarnes* females on the other hand lay a few eggs at most each time they drill with a long ovipositor from the outside. They are free to fly from one fig to another between acts of drilling and normally do so. Other parasites with shorter ovipositors were observed to be even more restless, and these almost certainly lay only one or two eggs per act of drilling. With *Ficus* 2 figs at the right stages, it was common to see several *Idarnes, e,* or *f* females drilling at once on single figs. While drilling, females are often chased off or caught by ants. The dense, dark speckling which *Ficus* 2 figs acquire at this stage is a further index to this erratic activity. The speckles are due to pricking by fig wasp ovipositors. Even though most pricks are only trials, a number lead on to deep drilling and, presumably, to egg laying.

The evidence from sex ratios assessed in the light of recent theory (Hamilton, 1967, 1972) reinforces these impressions of vagility: it rather strongly indicates that the *Idarnes* are more panmictic than the *Blastophaga* and that the

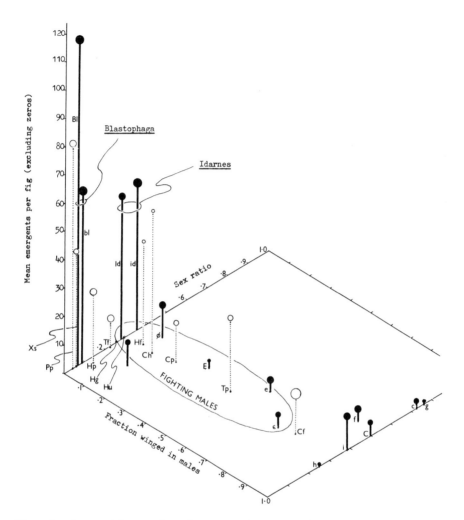

Fig. 5. Sex ratio, male wings, and group size in some fig wasps and other male haploid insects. For Ficus 1, *species are indexed as follows: Bl* = Blastophaga 1, *Id* = Idarnes "AB", *C, E, F (genera unknown). For* Ficus 2: *bl* = Blastophaga 2, *id* = Idarnes "aαbβ", *c, e, f, g, h, i, ε, Ø (genera unknown). The remaining species (nonfig wasps) are: Cf* = Cephalonomia formiciformis, *Cp* = C. perpusilla, *Ch* = Chilalictus sp., *Hf* = Hoplothrips fungi, *Hg* = H. sp., *Hp* = H. pedicularius, *Hu* = H. ulmi, *Pp* = Pygmephorus sp., *Tf* = Theocolax formiciformis, *Tp* = Telenomus polymorphus, *Xs* = Xyleborus saxeseni.

Heights of columns for fig wasps show mean numbers of adults emerging per fig when figs with zero counts are excluded. For other insects column height is mean number per brood (Cf, Pp, Tp) or per site of (continued on facing page)

other parasites, taken together, are more panmictic still.
Fig. 5 shows how the sex ratios of the species are distributed and shows that other wingless fighting males have sex
ratios similar to *Idarnes* (although this sex ratio alone, as
wholly winged species show, is not necessarily connected with
fighting). Plots from data (Table 4) of various other nonfig wasp species are also included in Fig. 5: the relevance
of these will be made clear later.

With *Blastophaga*, the data on which Fig. 5 is based offered
the possibility of a check on the sex ratio theory, since the
remains of dead foundresses could be counted even when the
Blastophaga progeny were eclosing. Fig. 6 shows how foundress number correlated with sex ratio in total progeny in the
mature figs that were analyzed, and Table 3 shows some independent counts of foundresses in young figs. The mean foundress numbers in the two sets of figs were 1.86 and 3.21. On
the straightforward theory, these figures demand a much higher
level of sex ratio than was observed (.195 and .315 compared
with the observed mean sex ratio .090). So according to this
test, either the facts are misleading or the theory needs to
be modified. However, the trend for sex ratio to rise with
increasing foundress number, although slight, is of the right
kind.

Two excuses easily suggest themselves for the generally
poor success of the test just mentioned.[2] Unfortunately both
are beyond the bounds of data that could check them. The
most promising excuse is that earliness of entering or aggression between females (Ramirez, 1970)[3] creates markedly unequal

---

[2] Other less obvious excuses are suggested in Hartl's (1971)
discussion of low sex ratios in single foundress situations.
On the whole, however, the factors discussed by Hartl are as
germane to raising evolutionarily stable sex ratios as to
depressing them.

[3] Female aggression is itself a problem for kinship theory.
Taking other cases, there may be a negative correlation with
fighting in the males. Thus ovipositing females of *Melittobia*
and of two scelionids (Eberhard, 1975) are unaggressive but
produce males that fight.

Figure 5 continued:

*collection (Ch, Cp, Hf, Hg, Hp, Hu, Xs). Sizes of "balls" at
column heads (black for fig wasps, white for others) denote
roughly the total number of individuals classified. The four
sizes from smallest to largest indicate numbers in the
following intervals: 1-10-100-1000-3000.*

TABLE 3

Counts of *Blastophaga* females in young figs of individual trees

Date	Foundresses per fig:																												Excluding zeros:		
	0	1	2	3	4	5	6	7	8	9	10	11	12	13	14	15	16	17	18	19	20	21	22	23	26	27	28	31	Total	n̄	s.d.
	Observed distribution for each tree:																														
July '75	3	18	12	4	3	1		2		2																			42	2.45	2.11
August '75	0	14	3	2																									19	1.37	.68
23/9/75	2	55	3																										58	1.05	.22
25/9/75	103	193	8	1				1																					204	1.11	.69
4/10/75	7	77	32	3	2	2			1																				117	1.50	.93
21/10/75	1	13	5	13	4	14	9	11	8	9	5	9	14	7	4	3	2	2	3	1	2	3	3					1	148	9.03	5.96
26/11/75	11	9	5	7	8	4	4	2	1	1			1		1		1		1										45	4.76	4.46
27/11/75	0	6	6	1	4	3	2																			1			23	4.00	5.50
27/11/75	0	7	8	5	7	4	3																						34	3.06	1.61
1/1/76	25	23	1	1																									25	1.12	.44
1/1/76	8	31	8	3																									42	1.33	.61
1/1/76	5	3	1		1																								5	1.80	1.30
21/1/76	11	39	8	4	1	1																							53	1.43	.86
22/1/76	3	9	8	8	9	8	3	1	2	2																			50	4.20	3.33
3/2/76	4	7	9	7	8	3	2	2	1	2	1	2	1	1	1										1				50	5.46	5.08
5/2/76	0	6	4	3	5	6	3	3	1	7	1	2	1	1	1	1	1	1	1										50	7.76	6.16
TOTALS	183	510	121	62	52	46	24	24	13	17	14	13	16	11	6	5	4	3	3	5	1	2	5	4	1	1	1	1	965	3.484	4.456

Unweighted mean of means: 3.21

With zeros included: 2.9286   4.280

TABLE 4

Polymorphism in haplodiploid arthropods: brood data showing classification for sex and "wings"

	Number of "broods" included	TOTALS IN BROODS					Sex ratio	Wing ratio in males	Mean	s.d.
		MALES		FEMALES						
		Alate	Flightless	Alate	Flightless	Total				
Pygmephorus priscus	11	0	36	650.5[e]	182.5	869	.041	0	79.0	42.4
Hoplothrips pedicularius	20	4	52	93	354	503	.111	.071	25.2	24.0
Hoplothrips fungi	9	13	89	90	136	328	.311	.128	36.2	33.8
Hoplothrips ulmi	2	0	38	8	83	129	.295	0	64.5	10.6
Hoplothrips sp. g	2	0	137	6	384	527	.260	0	263.5	289.2
Cephalonomia formiciformis	96	362	85	229	698	1374	.325	.810	14.3	13.0
Cephalonomia perpusilla [a]	18	18	62	42	127	249	.321	.225	13.8	19.1
Theocolax formiciformis [b]		4	158	11	623	796	.204	.025	10	
Telenomus polymorphus [c]	19	78	84	328	0	490	.331	.481	25.8	22.6
Chilalictus [d]	1	2	13	35	0	50	.300	.133	50	
Xyleborus saxeseni	13	0	35	492	0	527	.260	0	40.5	23.5

[a] Evans (1963)
[b] Becker and Weber (1952), Taylor (1964)
[c] Lima (1944)
[d] Houston (1970)
[e] Phoretomorphs

181

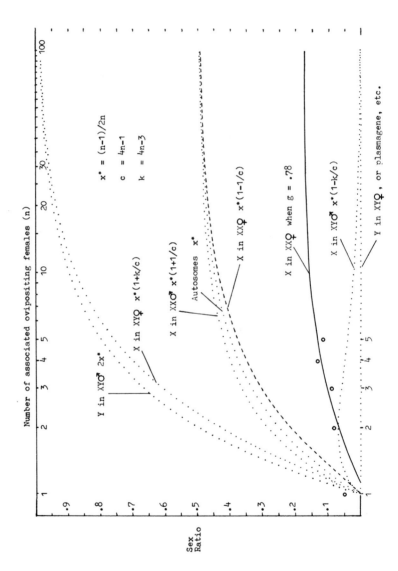

Figure 6

broods so that relatedness is higher in the assemblage of progeny than the equal-brood assumption of the model suggests it should be. Another excuse assumes that the erratic selection pressures on fig wasps give a large extra incentive to having progeny capable of effective recombination. If g is the disadvantage which a chromosome will have through being unable to recombine effectively with genes at other loci, then it always has this disadvantage in the haploid males (fitness factor $1-g$), but in the females only has it in proportion to the extent that loci have allele pairs that are identical by descent (so that the fitness factor is $1-Fg$). Combining these factors with consideration of relatedness (Hamilton, 1972), we obtain the following genetic fitness valuations of a son and daughter by a mother:

$$\beta_u = \tfrac{1}{2}(1+F)(1-g) \quad \text{and} \quad \beta_v = \tfrac{1}{2}(1+3F)(1-Fg).$$

Assuming the model conditions of Hamilton (1967), we have the evolutionarily stable sex ratio ("unbeatable sex ratio" in sense of Hamilton, 1967; "ESS" sex ratio in sense of Maynard Smith and Price, 1973):

$$x^* = \frac{\beta_u}{\beta_u + \beta_v} \cdot \frac{V_{WG}}{V_T}$$

Fig. 6. (facing page) Sex ratios of Blastophaga *in figs according to number of foundresses and theoretical curves bearing on the struggle for the sex ratio in sperm-storing species with early local mating. Actual mean sex ratios in* Ficus *2 synconia are shown as open circles and, from left to right, are based on counts in 21, 7, 4, 3, and 2 figs.*

In formulas given $x^* = (n-1)/2n$, $c = 4n-1$, and $k = 4n-3$. *Dashed line shows evolutionarily stable sex ratio appropriate for male haploids if the recombinational disadvantage of being inbred is not important. Solid line shows the modified curve appropriate if the disadvantage to genes on chromosomes unable to undergo effective crossing over is given by a fitness factor .22 (argument and calculation explained in the text).*

Dotted lines show evolutionarily stable sex ratios for other components of genome and plasmon under other systems of sex control including female heterogamety. The two lowest dotted curves (corresponding to male-control of sex ratio and control by a plasmagene or symbiont with ovarial transmission) are those most likely to have bearing on the Blastophaga *sex ratios shown.*

where V_{WG} and V_T are within group and total genic variances, respectively. The differently arranged and more general result appearing in this formula compared to that of my 1967 account results from (1) the relatedness-weighted fitnesses of offspring now used and (2) reworking of the argument using Price's hierarchical analysis of natural selection (for outline, see Hamilton, 1975). The most reasonable and simple assumption to fix the ratio of the variances is that females settle in groups at random. If the mean size of these groups is n, standard procedures of statistics and of population genetics enable us to find $V_{WG}/V_T = (n-1)/n$ and $F = 1/(4n-3)$, respectively, and with these formulas we are in a position to evaluate the unbeatable sex ratio for any given values of n and g. By trial and error it was found that at $g = .78$ the model fits the *Blastophaga* data quite well (Fig. 6). But due to the uncertainty of the assumptions, little weight can be placed on this fact. In particular, such a high value of g implies that in the hindsight of a distant future generation, the outbred individuals will appear to have been about 40% more fit than their sib-mated sisters. This implies that *Blastophaga* would evolve more outbreeding via winged males or more shared laying in figs if *Ficus* would let it. Perhaps so, but at present this line of thought only evaporates in speculation. It is, of course, very possible that both of our excuses present part of the truth, and with this in mind the theory has no serious difficulty as yet: on present evidence it is reasonable to accept that sex ratios in *Blastophaga* and the other species reflect levels of outbreeding, and fighting adaptations only arise when the average rival has a chance somewhat less than one-third of being a brother.

WINGED MALES AND MALE DIMORPHISM

No less extraordinary than the bizarre forms and pugnacity of some of the males is the fact that these males were sometimes associated with conspecific males, quite possibly their brothers, which had totally different form and behavior. These other forms were winged and very like the females. When a fig was opened, they were always among the first to run out and attempt to fly. Wingless males, in contrast, hardly ever even wandered onto the outside of their halved fig--if they did so it was usually as fugitives, i.e., in prolonged rapid ambulation following aggression by another male. We never found the winged males mating or even showing interest in the females inside the figs, but after they had been allowed to run or fly outside for a few minutes, they would readily mount females and apparently mate them when put together in a jar. Whether they had to fly before they would do this was

not obvious, but it seems probable that normally they are
programmed to mate only after a dispersal flight. Obviously
they then compete--in a quite different mating arena from the
wingless males--for those females which have escaped mating
by wingless males in their fig of origin. Possibly they may
also compete to remate nonvirgin females, but we saw no
evidence of this. The only males actually seen at fig trees
where females were ovipositing were rare examples of *c*, a
wholly winged species: females of *e*, *ε*, *f*, and *∅* which were
searching for sites and drilling were not visited by males.

In addition to the species with male dimorphism *(E, e, ε,
F, f, ∅)*, there were an equal number of species *(C, c, G, g,
h, i)* which in all probability are wholly winged in the male
(Fig. 4 shows *c*). These males were similar in degree of
resemblance to their females and in behavior to the winged
males of the other species; they included both the brightest
patterned *(c)* and the most sombre concolorous *(h)* males. In
no winged males of any kind did we see any fighting.

With the exception of species *i*, the sex ratios of the
wholly winged species tend to confirm the outbreeding which
their wings and habits imply. In fact, apart from *i*, it was
excesses of *males* that were hard to explain, but again, apart
from *i* in one fig crop of one tree, numbers of these parasites
were everywhere very low.

Male dimorphisms and switches from "homeomorphic" to
"heteromorphic" males within a genus have been noted in Old
World fig wasps (Grandi, 1961; Joseph, 1964; Wiebes, 1967),
but the startling extent of the divergence in some cases does
not seem to have had the emphasis it deserves. So far as I
know these are the most extreme dimorphisms of the male sex
that are known in the animal kingdom. (Soldier-alate divergences in termites are of similar degree but apply to both
sexes.) They must reflect long continued selection of a
peculiar, disruptive kind.

Comparing the heights of the columns in Fig. 5, the abundance of progeny in figs colonized by a species seems to be
important: common parasites tend to have wingless males and
rare ones, winged males. This is easily understandable on
the grounds that in a common parasite a male is fairly certain
to find plenty of females to mate in his fig, and the females
are fairly certain to have a male mate them before they fly
out. In a rare parasite on the other hand, both sons and
daughters would often die without mating if all males were
wingless. The wing reduction is probably partly in the interest of redirection of growth into greater sperm production
and (sometimes) into fighting adaptations, and partly simply
because wings are an encumbrance for the males' activities
inside the fig. They are lost here for the same reasons as
they are in so many other insects which spend their adult

lives in soil or rotting wood and disperse themselves ade-
quately by other means (including flight prior to wing loss
in those which shed their wings).

Dimorphisms might be expected to show levels of abundance
between those of the species groups with wholly winged and
wholly wingless males. Except for species E and i, the levels
of abundance in occupied figs (not true means for abundance
in all figs because zeros are excluded) are roughly as expected. F and $\emptyset$ are both common in their figs and have high
fractions of wingless males, and e, ε, and f are less common
(while more common than the wholly winged species except C
and i) and have higher fractions of winged males. Variability
of numbers per fig suggests itself as another factor which
might be favorable to polymorphism. It can be seen from the
standard deviations of the truncated frequency distributions
given in Table 1 that the high populations of the *Blastophaga*
and the *Idarnes* showed less variation relative to mean level
than the rest, but among the rest there was no tendency for
the dimorphic-male species to be more variable. Overall the
truncated distributions tended to show standard deviations
about equal to the means. Thus the variability is indeed
great, but this does not seem to be the important factor.

Without necessity to expect greater variability in the
dimorphic cases, provided there is some randomness in the way
wasps are apportioned to figs, a simple basis for stable
dimorphism is easily found. The crucial requirement for this
is a reasonable frequency of male-less figs, i.e., figs
producing females which have no male capable of mating them
prior to their escape. Then, rather on lines that Gadgil
(1972) has argued for other male dimorphisms, we can see the
advantages of wings and winglessness to be frequency-dependent
in a way that promotes stability. For a very simple model,
the argument can be shown as follows:

Assume females lay one egg per fig and move on; that if
male, an egg develops as a wingless male with probability s
(this parameter being supposed a genetic trait either of the
egg itself or of the mother who lays it); and that a winged
male is unable to mate females inside the fig--to do so
conflicts too sharply with his adaptations as a flier. Random
laying of eggs and random determination of type will give
numbers of winged and wingless males (and of females and
totals, although this fact will not be needed) in Poisson
distributions. If M is the mean of all males reared per fig,
then the mean for wingless males is sM. The fraction of all
figs having no wingless male is e^{-sM}. Consequently, this is
also the fraction of females not mated in the figs and therefore available to the winged males outside. Hence the reproductive values are proportional to $v' = e^{-sM}/(1 - s)$ for winged
males and to $v = (1 - e^{-sM})/s$ for wingless males. As $s \to 0$,

$v' \to 1$ and $v \to M$, so a gene for producing a wingless morph can start to spread if $M > 1$, otherwise not.[4] The stable equilibria for dimorphism in this model, possible for all $M > 1$, are shown in Fig. 7. The curve is rapidly asymptotic to $s = 1$; already at $M = 5$ less than 1% of males are expected to be winged. Thus although the model shows an advantage to winged males at $s = 1$ for all values of $M(v' \to \infty, v \to 1 - e^{-M})$, the simplicity of the model plus the practical difficulty of maintaining genetic program and switch gear for a complex adaptation that is hardly ever produced make it not at all surprising that the winged morph is completely absent in the more common fig wasps.

Also in Fig. 7 are plotted the mean numbers of males per fig (zeros included) for the various species. The graph gives true means (zeros excluded) for the model: unfortunately we cannot easily adjust either the points (downward) or the graph (upward) to remove this discrepancy owing to the involvement of females (and therefore sex ratio) in the truncation implied in the data. Actually any adjustment on these lines would be slight compared to the spread of the points, and this, combined with the known crudity of the model, does not encourage an attempt: accepting that the comparison would not be much affected by a slight upward adjustment of the curve towards the right, we may conclude that the fit is far from impressive but perhaps good enough to suggest that the model is of the right general kind.

In the way it has the fraction of wingless males so rapidly asymptotic to zero as population per fig is raised, this model effectively narrows the band of abundances within which dimorphism can occur. To explain the very deep divergence of morphs, we would hope for less rapid convergence and a broader band: this would imply that both morphs could persist over varying fortunes of the species (i.e., varying abundances) and so find time to reach a high degree of adaptive improvement. But the asymptotic curve obtained depends on use of the Poisson distribution, and not only is this not observed in any case, but in some has its underlying assumptions denied by the observed behavior, e.g., the egg-laying behavior of *Blastophaga* and *Idarnes*. Various possibilities, including fighting, may help to keep up the fraction of male-less figs in the more common species. Actually the present data do not suggest much in detail about how this "band of stability" might be broadened. However, the data can provide a comparison which

---

[4] If there is a selective advantage, c, to matings by flying males because more certain to be outbred, this condition becomes $M > 1/(1 + c)$.

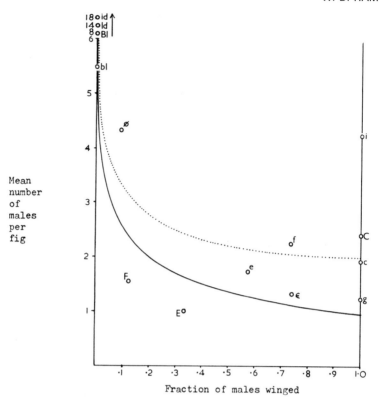

Fig. 7. Data for fig wasp male dimorphisms compared to the
stable states expected in a model which assumes (a) that egg
laying and sex and morph determination are at random, and
(b) that winged males only mate outside figs and only mate
those females which have not been exposed to mating by wingless males inside figs. Solid curve shows evolutionarily
stable states if a female has no fitness disadvantage from
being mated by a wingless male (i.e., from being more likely
to produce inbred offspring); dotted curve shows the stable
states when a wingless-male mating yields half the fitness of
a winged-male mating.

tests the main principle of the model more directly, and so
avoids the uncertainties underlying the comparison in Fig. 7:
we can test for equality of reproductive values of winged and
wingless males without assuming random egg laying. The
principle of the model was that reproductive values will be
equal if the fraction of winged males is the same as the
fraction of females that they can expect to mate with, i.e.,
those not mated by wingless males in the figs. Fig. 8
compares these fractions for all the species other than those
wholly winged. (For wholly winged species the equality of the

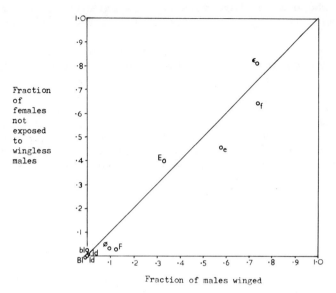

Fig. 8. The correlation of fraction of males that are winged with the fraction of females expected to leave figs while still unmated. Equality of these fractions, implying equality of reproductive values of winged and wingless males, tends to support the basis for evolutionary stability explained in the text. Since for wholly winged species the equality of the fractions is trivial (both fractions unity), these species are omitted.

fractions is trivial.) It can be seen that the correlation of the fractions is such that all points lie reasonably close to the 45[0] line.

OTHER WING-REDUCED, FIGHTING, AND HAPLOID MALES

   In a 1967 publication, I briefly reviewed situations with flightless males in inbreeding situations. Many more cases could be added now. The correlation with probable incest remains very strong, but some exceptions and evidence--not least the evidence on foundress numbers in *Blastophaga* (Grandi, 1929; Galil and Eisikovitch, 1968; and this study) and on sex ratio in *Idarnes*--suggest that male winglessness is connected less with incestuous situations *per se* than with having, besides female ability to store sperm, what might be called a "seraglio" situation, that is, a predictable abundance of females who are more or less confined at the site where the males mature. Fig. 5 has various points for

species whose males have more or less seraglio situations of
this kind. The data from which these points derive are set
out in Table 4.

Rotting logs are a habitat in which inbreeding and male
wing reduction are common. Whole logs provide sites for
intrademic inbreeding and their smaller inhabited cavities
set up potential seraglios that might encourage incest at the
family level. To take a case at the extreme, I have observed
a species of *Pygmephorus* mite (close to *P. priscus*) whose
females suck hyphae of *Stereum* and become extremely physogas-
tric. (Fig. 17 in Cross and Moser, 1971, illustrates exactly
this state of a *Pygmephorus* female.) Their broods, with two
to four males among 16 to 160 females, develop and mate inside
the mother; but since the mother usually bursts before all her
eggs have hatched and since two mothers are sometimes pressed
together (e.g., in crevices of contracting rotted wood), outbreeding can certainly occur. Do these wingless mites really
qualify for discussion under the present heading? The females
wander away as soon as the mother bursts, but the males are
extremely reluctant to do so and continue to patrol the pile
of remaining eggs. The females, moreover, are of two forms:
with and without strongly developed chelae on the forelimbs.
The chelate females are "phoretomorphs" (Moser and Cross,
1975), adapted for dispersion by clinging to the hairs of
larger arthropods. In this sense they are analogous to the
flying morphs of various wing-polymorphic insects of the
habitat[5] and so emphasize the sedentary "wingless" character
of the males. It is of particular interest here to note that
the males do not fight at all, and being virtually headless
and with all eight legs unmodified and alike, it is difficult
to visualize that they could. The scene of peaceably scrambling and mating males amidst the numerous lethargic females
(as seen through the transparent balloon-like hysterosoma of
the mother) is very reminiscent of the peaceful mating activity of *Blastophaga* inside a freshly opened fig at a corresponding stage.

At levels of inbreeding which are less extreme, we can find
mites with fighting males which correspond in the same rough
way to *Idarnes* (*Tetranychus*: Lee, 1969; Potter et al., 1976;
Caloglyphus: Woodring, 1969; *Rhinoseius*: Colwell, 1973). In

[5] Variability of morph ratios in various mothers showed that
female dimorphism in the *Pygmephorus* is not simply genetic:
the same is usually found with wing dimorphism in multivoltine
or continuously breeding insects. But two genetic cases are
claimed (see footnote 6).

Caloglyphus one of two male morphs is a fighter,[6] and in
rotting wood the mite *Pyemotes dimorphus* has a male dimorphism
that may be parallel, although there is again a definite dimorphism (phoretic) in females as well (Cross and Moser, 1975).

Prominences and enlargement of the forelimbs in male tub-
uliferan thrips of the same habitat (Ananthakrishnan, 1969) at
least suggest fighting adaptations. Usually there is a grada-
tion from large "armed" males to smaller ones resembling
females, but the changes are complex and not purely allometric
(Ananthakrishnan, 1968), and some females may be better armed
than some males. Fig. 5 includes four points for *Hoplothrips* from field-collected samples. The species with the
most pronounced oedymery of forelegs in its males *(H. fungi)*
lies well within the region of other fighting males, while a
species with much less oedymery *(H. pedicularius)* has fewer
males and lies near to *Blastophaga*. Another unknown species
is intermediate in oedymery and in sex ratio. Less satisfactory, a sample of *H. ulmi* had almost as high a sex ratio as *H.
fungi* yet shows very little oedymery; but this sample was
small and from only two collections.

Under bark in Southeast Asia, a larviform male beetle exists
which looks like a fighter (Hamilton, 1972; Fig. 9a). It is
so strange that two very widely separated families have been
proposed for it. Present considerations together with the
known forms of parthenogenesis and of male modification in
other bark beetles favor its placement in Scolytidae rather
than in Histeridae as suggested by Crowson (1974). In other
words, I believe the male much more likely to be that of *Ozopemon brownei* as originally suggested by Browne (1959, 1961).
Browne's brief description of the communal galleries of
Ozopemon under bark outlines a seraglio situation that would
make precocity, winglessness, and fighting advantageous in
a male; and the fig wasps show how profoundly males can
diverge from their females when such conditions hold (Figs. 1,
3, and 9b).

Whether or not *Ozopemon* is a parallel to *Idarnes,* another
scolytid genus, *Xyleborus,* probably parallels *Blastophaga*

---

[6] In *Caloglyphus* induction of this morph is pheromonal, but in
the related *Rhizoglyphus echinopus,* common in rotting wood but
better known as a pest of bulbs, the induction of a similar
male morph may require a gene difference (Foa, 1919; cf. wing
dimorphism in male *Cephalonomia gallicola,* Kearns, 1934). Both
Rhizoglyphus and *Caloglyphus* can also produce, in both sexes
and in response to some environmental switch, a hypopal stage
adapted for dispersal by phoresy. Neither *R. echinopus* nor
Caloglyphus has haploid males. (J.H. Oliver. 1977. *Ann. Rev.
Ent.* 22:407-429)

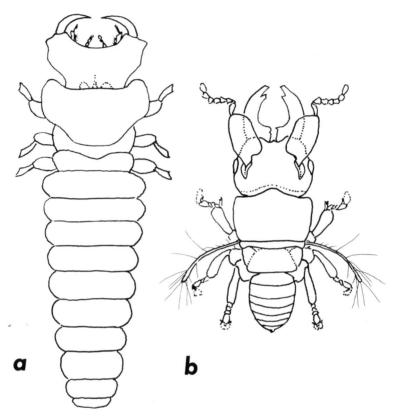

*Fig. 9. Adult male insects predicted to be fighters: (a)
presumed male of* Ozopemon brownei, Scolytidae *(from Browne);
(b) male of* Philosycus monstruosus, Torymidae *(from Grandi).*

fairly well. Adults mature in crowded ambrosia galleries
in live or freshly dead trunks, branches, stalks, etc. Each
gallery usually derives from a lone-founding female. Although
galleries sometimes coalesce and although cases of associative
nest founding *(X. saxeseni* and *X. dispar)* are not rare (Hopkins, 1898; pers. obs.), the mean degree of relatedness seems
to be too high for males to fight. No record that I know
suggests that the haploid, flightless, small, brown, half-
blind, and harmless-looking males ever do fight. Fighting
between larvae or killing of pupae by adults (see Matthews,
1975; also Hopkins, 1898) is perhaps a more possible mode of
aggression, if any occurs. A difference from *Blastophaga*
affecting breeding structure lies in the site's capacity to
support more than one generation.
    In contrast, in the generally more outbred ambrosia beetles

of the Platypodidae, severe fighting has been recorded
(Hubbard, 1897). But since these males are, as far as I
know, winged and diploid (and also horned on the elytra), this
case is considered later.

In the tropics rotting logs are a characteristic habitat
for ants of the genus *Hypoponera* (Kempf, 1962; pers. obs.).
This genus has species with wingless males. I have verified
that the ergatoid males of *H. punctatissima* (in a colony from
soil in a London hospital) fight each other for occupancy
of the chamber where queens are being reared. Fights look
rather slow and ineffective; nevertheless males often lose
legs and antennae and death soon follows. The squared-off
heads of the males (illustration in Wheeler, 1937) are larger
than those of workers[7] and are reminiscent of *Idarnes* and of
our wingless *e*-type males. The winner mates the queens in the
nuptial chamber soon after they eclose. If the males are
brothers and the females their sisters, why--contrary to the
cases of *Blastophaga, Pygmephorus,* and others--should the
males fight? Nothing is known of the normal mode of colony
foundation; if it could turn out to be associative as in
various other ants, this difficulty would be resolved. If
association leads on to permanent polygyny (which admittedly
would be unusual: Hamilton, 1972; West Eberhard, 1975), a
crop of sexuals may not be a sibling group. Transferences
which I tried between colonies suggested no strong hostility
to strangers, so adventive queens might be accepted by a
colony. Since males are wingless either such acceptance, or
associative founding, or fusion of colonies, would be needed
to secure any useful outbreeding. Similar speculations have
to be applied to the similarly unexpected pugnacity of *Melittobia* (see Dahms, 1973; Hamilton, 1972). In *Melittobia* it is
known that males do sometimes fight with actual brothers

---

[7] In the ant genus *Cardiocondyla,* the wingless males have two
types of head form (Smith, 1944), one of which is suggestive
of fighting. This may accentuate a puzzle as to why two free-
living genera should have fighting males, while a whole host
of parasitic species (Buschinger, 1974; Hamilton, 1972) have
wingless males that look relatively unpugnacious and are not
known to fight.

(Alston, 1920), but perhaps in nature multiple colonization of a host is more common than we know.[8]

Panmixia of females combined with associative founding could be the normal background to all the cases of lethal fighting discussed so far. Although mites can't fly, tetranychid females can balloon on silk threads, and *Caloglyphus* is a genus that is commonly phoretic (Hughes, 1948; Théodorides, 1955).[9]

In a different superfamily (Proctotrupoidea) in the Hymenoptera, a complex polymorphism, which sounds rather similar to those in the chalcidoid fig wasps, has been described. It concerns a situation that is surprisingly "open air" for a wingless male (egg masses of a bug, apparently attached to leaves and twigs), but one not wholly without parallel (e.g., *Trichogramma semblidis* on *Sialis* egg masses). The bug is the reduviid *Heza insignis* and the parasite is *Telenomus polymorphus* (Lima, 1944). The females are all winged and the males are polymorphic in melanization, wing reduction, and head size. Wingless males are always yellow rather than brown and may or may not have specially enlarged heads. Lima (1944) gives neither statistics for large-headedness in his rearings nor any behavioral notes that might reveal fighting, but the position his data take on Fig. 1 suggests that his large-headed male is a fighter like the wingless e-type males that it most resembles. It is very possible that the winged males also fight in this species, although probably less fiercely. Such likelihood arises from the known pugnacity of other male scelionids on bug egg masses (see Hamilton, 1967). Recently Eberhard (1975) described the circumstances of fighting for two species that attack the eggs of a pentatomid. Fighting

----

[8] In a recent report on fighting in two species of *Melittobia*, Matthews (1975) mentioned another possible factor, that a male may need to feed on rivals before he becomes equal to his task of mating a hundred or so females. The same report raises the suspicion that the sex ratio of *Melittobia* may be underestimated because the first one or two males to mature may destroy others as pupae. For these reasons the genus is not included in Fig. 5 (where, on known data, it would come close to the *Pygmephorus*).

[9] I know of no information about phoretic tendency for either of the two morphs in *Caloglyphus*, but already it seems that the unarmed males are probably more nearly analogous to the small males of *Idarnes* than to the winged males of fig wasps *E*, *F*, etc.

was never fatal, but occasionally a leg or antenna was lost.
The eggs, and consequently the females at stake in the fighting, were in much smaller batches than those of *Heza*. Eberhard's data do not quite match with kinship expectations since
male behavior seemed slightly *less* fierce and exclusive in the
species where associative parasitism seemed *more* likely to
occur. On the other hand, the sex ratio in this species did
deviate from the other slightly in the direction expected
(mean broods, male:female, were 3.1:13.3 as against 1.5:4.8).

A large-headed, short-winged male bee which looks like a
fighter, coexisting with a normal winged male, has been
described in the genus *Chilalictus* (Houston, 1970).[10] Data
from the one described colony are included in Fig. 1. It
falls among the fighting fig wasps, but since this is only
one instance and there is uncertainty about presences and
absences in the nest, this carries little weight. Similar
male head variations reported in *Evylaeus ohei* seem not to be
associated with wing reduction and not to show bimodality.
Similar head enlargements are known in various female bees
(Sakagami, 1974). Wherever they occur, I suspect that, like
the similar head modifications in the cuckoo aculeates in
Sulcopolistes and *Psithyrus,* they are for threatened or actual
fighting.

Sakagami's list of cases includes several of bees that are
communal or semi-social and none that are known to be solitary. In the recently studied *Centris pallida* (Alcock et
al., 1977), nests are merely aggregated. The males show
a wide range of size in which enlargement of the head appears
to be no more than isometric, but perhaps they are, nevertheless, on the road to the more extreme kind of polymorphism
known in at least one other *Centris* (Moure, 1963). In *C.
pallida* the large males, accompanied by some small males, tend
to specialize in patrolling the ground surface and in digging
for females that are about to emerge from the soil, while
small males specialize in high aerial mating with females
that have somehow escaped the attentions of the ground males.
On the ground, males fight to usurp excavations and to defend
them, and large males almost always win. Gregarious mating,
the markedly different mating strategies, and this fighting

---

[10] A very similar situation exists in a species of *Perdita*
(Andrenidae) in Arizona (J. G. Rozen, pers. comm.). For this
species as for Houston's *Chilalictus,* there is reason to
suspect communal nest founding. In British andrenids no
short-winged males are known, but large-headedness is marked
in exactly those two species which have communal nests (Yarrow
and Guichard, 1941).

combine to suggest a distant but most interesting parallel
to the dimorphic fig wasps. Other observations (Orlove, 1973)
suggest that a divided arena of mating--near to the nests and
also some place distant from them--is quite widespread in
bees. It may well occur in sphecids and eumenids as well.

In males of the eumenid wasp *Synagris cornuta,* we find
another grotesquely enlarged and modified head. Here the size
and showiness of the male wasp, with his unreduced wings and
hypertrophied horned mandibles, seem a link from *Chilalictus*
to showy and grotesquely horned beetles (see below). In the
present context it is noteworthy (a) that a larger-headed male
has been observed driving off others with lesser heads from a
clay nest on a leaf where a female was emerging (Poulton,
1913), and (b) that although this nest was solitary with only
four cells, large aggregations of nests occur (see photograph
in Wheeler, 1928), giving the male a situation which may be
rather similar to situations in *Chilalictus* and *E. ohei.* In
Synagris low relatedness of fighting males would tend to be
assured by the nature of the aggregation (which is obviously
"communal" in the sense of Michener, 1969) and the free flight
of both sexes, whereas in the two bee species (probably in the
former, more certainly in the latter), it is assured by nest
sharing by several independent free-flying females, and, in
E. ohei, potential flight by the fighting males.

In sperm-storing species, wing reduction in females obviously has quite different implications for the breeding system
from wing reduction in males.

If females are totally wingless, this usually means that
either they or the young stages have alternative means of
dispersion (generally wind or phoresy, the latter including
transport as a parasite [as in stylops] and by their own
winged males [as in thynnids, some mutillids, phorids of
Chonocephalus, etc.]). Although in some ectoparasitic cases
the males are wingless too, such species are outside the
present purview: constantly hitchhiking around on their large
hosts the parasitic species, for example, have a mobility
almost as if both sexes were winged. Winglessness in phoretic
and parasitic insects gives little guidance as to relatedness
and inbreeding, although naturally species do exist among them
with incestuous habits and sex ratios biased accordingly (most
are mites, e.g., *Dichrocheles, Syringophilus, Demodex,
Pyemotes, Iponemus,* but there is also one possible case in a
flea [Radovsky, 1972]).

If merely some females are wingless, the situation is
quite different. It suggests that a habitat, when found, can
support a colony for at least a few generations before exhaus-
tion of food, discovery by enemies, or other terminating events
prevail. The wingless female is adapted to increase the colony

while the going is good; the winged female, to be prepared to seek a new habitat when conditions worsen--or when reliable signs show that they are about to. Aphids provide the most studied example. We would generally expect that in the growth phase the colony would be largely isolated: the sex ratio would therefore be low and, if this phase is sexual at all, the few males worked hard to accomplish all the matings available to them. However, if colony founding is commonly associative, we would expect ideally that the first generation sex ratio would be high (about $(n-1)/2n)$) and that its males would fight, while in subsequent generations the frequency and pugnacity of males would fall off, perhaps rising again whenever colonies coalesce.

It seems possible that such an outline could apply to the underbark thrips already mentioned and account for the graded variability of their males. But published data on another hymenopteran parasitoid in dead wood (*Theocolax formicformis*: see Fig. 5) show sex and wing ratios similar to those of the *Hoplothrips*, and yet no unusual variation or behavior in the male is reported (Becker and Weber, 1952; Taylor, 1964). This ant-like parasitoid searches for larvae of wood-boring beetles.[11] This is a claustral habitat very like that of *Hoplothrips* or *Melittobia*. However, only small broods are possible in particular larvae (not more than nine), and this can create only a rather unattractive seraglio compared to that encountered by *Melittobia* or even *Idarnes*: to mate many females the *Theocolax* male probably needs to be adapted for tunneling and searching rather than for fighting.[12] The same applies to the wingless males of other ant-like dead-wood parasitoids in the Bethylidae. In Fig. 1, data for *Cephalonomia perpusilla* (Evans, 1963) give a point in the midst of the fighting fig wasps, but my own data for *C. formiciformis*--in which the winged forms were much more common, especially in the males-- give a point outside. In many parasitoids wingless varieties seem to have the status of occasional underfed runts (Salt, 1952: This probably applies to the wingless females we found in fig wasp *f* and perhaps to some extent to the uncommon wingless males of this species). In *Cephalonomia* wingless males

---

[11] Taylor mentions that *females* sometimes fight for larvae.

[12] In discussing fighting generally, Ghiselin (1974, p. 145) rightly emphasizes the factor of high density (to evolve fighting for females the males must at least frequently meet). On the other hand, defendability of resource is hardly mentioned in his discussion and the factor of relatedness is ignored.

are indeed smaller and nutrition may be a factor, but at the
same time they show clear morphological differences that
parallel those in the wingless females, which are quite as
large as their winged sisters and clearly not produced by
underfeeding. In *Cephalonomia gallicola* evidence has been
recorded that the wing polymorphism in males is simply genetic
(Kearns, 1934); but in *Sclerodermus domesticum* the occasional
wingless males are described definitely as runts (Kühne and
Becker, 1974), although the species seems to have much the
same conditions of life as *Theocolax*. Wing development and
dispersal in Bethylidae need further study to resolve these
contrasts.

WINGLESS DIPLOID MALES

All the cases of polymorphism, male winglessness, and male
fighting discussed so far are in groups for which male haploidy is either known or can be suspected. Others where males
are more wingless, or more often wingless than their females,
occur scattered in various groups which are unlikely to be,
or known not to be, male haploid. Not all these have mating
situations especially favorable to incest and not all have
female-biased sex ratios, although I know of no exception to
the rule that a marked bias exists if the male is always
wingless and the female usually winged. Even in male haploid
groups, always-wingless males can occur in nonincestuous
situations. For example, while wingless male thrips in galls
(Mound, 1971) and in the similarly flask-like flowers of
Erica (Hagerup and Hagerup, 1953) extend the range of cases
of ready-made seraglios, some other wingless male thrips seem
to be fairly normally phytophagous although still tending to
specialized diets and to secluded windless environments
(Morison, 1971, 1973). To these external phytophages can be
added others that have come to notice in halticid flea
beetles (Champion, 1910; Gentner, 1928). Presumably in these
cases there is less brother-sister incest, but the "perennial-
ity" and patchy distribution of the plant hosts are such that
there may be fairly intense intrademe inbreeding. The same
applies to wingless male Psocoptera feeding on lichens under
dense webs on bark and sometimes on leaves and twigs (New,
1973a, b; pers. obs.) and to the flightless male Plecoptera
that mate their females among stones by the mountain streams
where they breed. But just why some species and not others
should become inbreeders with female-biased sex ratios and
reduced wings in the male is not clear. For example, another
psocid making webs on bark, *Reuterella helvimacula,* has the
female wingless and the male winged.

Mention may also be made in passing of some other phytophagous insects, including more flea beetles (e.g., *Longitarsus rubiginosus*: pers. obs.) and sundry leaf hoppers, which show wing reduction in most specimens but have an uncommon macropterous form. In such species the macroptera are more common among females than among males, although sex ratios are fairly normal.

Under dead bark a situation similar to this is shown by the minute beetle *Ptinella aptera* (Taylor, 1975) and the psocid *Psoquilla marginepunctata* (Broadhead, 1961). In the latter, at least, the fraction of winged individuals can increase very markedly in some circumstances, winged females remaining more common. In *Ptinella* normality of the sex ratio probably reflects the females' inability to store many of the relatively enormous sperm, which are as long as the animals (Taylor, 1975). Zoraptera present a similar case, but in some species the winged morph is much more rare in the male (e.g., *Zorotypus hubbardi*: Riegel, 1963). Also under bark, Hemiptera (Anthocoridae, e.g., *Xylocoris cursitans*: pers. obs.) and Psocoptera (Broadhead, 1961) show parallel features, although *Embidopsocus*, with males always precocious and wingless, can have the sex ratio under one-third (pers. obs.). In *Ectopsocus richardsi* in the related habitat of human-stored products, males are always brachypterous and the only sex ratio recorded was one-sixth (Pearman, 1942). Similar cases in rotting wood are known in sciarids and there is one case (sex ratio not recorded) in Cecidomyiidae (Mohrig and Mamaev, 1970).

The absence of male structural modifications which could be for fighting (and absence of records of fighting) in all these nonmale haploid cases is in striking contrast to their frequent presence in the haploid males already discussed. Perhaps this difference will prove less real than it seems. For example, the excuse given for the *nonfighting* F-type wingless males of the fig wasps can serve as well for *Embidopsocus* males, which are small through being sexualized one instar earlier than the females (Broadhead, 1947, and thus "protothetelic" in the sense of Southwood, 1961). And on the other side, it is conceivable that the enlarged and sometimes spined hind femora of *Zorotypus* males are used for fighting. Further, in *Xylocoris*, males do show a kind of sexual assault on other males and may succeed in certain species in making them effective vehicles of their sperm (Carayon, 1974). However, on the whole such points are weak when set against the proven pugnacity of so many haploid males. In so far as it is real, this contrast is not easy to explain.

When inbreeding occurs, but is less than total, males are expected to be less related to male rivals in their colony than diploid males would be. But the slight difference seems

unlikely to be important. It is maximal when the fixation
index is 1/2, that is, when the relatednesses of brothers are
3/4 and 5/6, respectively. With sex ratio under the control
of mothers and strong selection incentives for mothers to
gamble with the sexes of progeny in a sex ratio game (Hamilton, 1967), the haplodiploid species are much more apt to
create situations where a nonsibling male can greatly increase
his inclusive fitness, through size of his expected harem, if
he is a fighter. Nonhaplodiploid species have more difficulty
in changing the sex ratio, and when they find a means (as
Embidopsocus, Ectopsocus, Xylocoris have apparently found
one), the female bias they achieve is steady, moderate, and
probably closely connected to the mean male relatedness. It
follows that where harems are potentially largest, a male
would have to be fighting closely related rivals in order to
win them.

FIGHTING DIPLOID MALES; FIGHTING IN GENERAL

   Examples of fighting in normally diploid males are also
found in rotting wood. Hubbard (1897) recorded lethal fighting in polygynous males of a *Platypus*. These males have small
horns on the elytra. Platypodids are ambrosia feeders like
Xyleborus but usually have a very different breeding system,
with mating *after* flight to the new host tree, and a normal sex
ratio. The situation is not known for certain for Hubbard's
species, but it is likely that the males are much less related
than are *Xyleborus* males in one gallery. I have observed
fighting in *Gnatocerus cornutus* (see also Morison, 1925) and
have seen signs of it in *Siagonium quadricorne*. Unfortunately
the latter is too photophobic to be observed easily. It is
found under bark in groups usually consisting of one male and
several females (and often larvae as well). Both *S. quadricorne* and *G. cornutus* have striking horns on their mandibles.
Gnatocerus too probably comes originally from dead phloem
(Sokoloff, 1972; Brendell, 1975), and for horned beetles in
general, rotting wood is the most favored habitat. In a
related habitat, mining in tough bracket fungi, the horned
males of *Cis bilamellatus* fight at entrances of burrows where
females are feeding (C. T. David, pers. comm.). Almost all
these horned beetles, including those just mentioned, are
winged in both sexes, but apart from the implication of similar dispersive abilities this may not be very important.
Wingless primitive crickets with huge-jawed males (Stenopel-
matidae) live in and under dead trunks (e.g., Coquerel, 1848),
and one is recorded in polygynous situations (Hudson, 1920)
like that mentioned for *Siagonium*.
   Similar habitat and habits are probable for cockroaches of

the genus *Gromphadorhina* (Chopard, 1950). In captivity males
of this genus are seen to fight by butting. They possess
(most conspicuously in the large males of *G. portentosa*)
short, forward-directed horns bordering a scooped declivity
of the pronotum. *Cryptocercus* males have a faint trace of a
similar armature and these, although apparently monogamous,
fight over females in burrows (Ritter, 1964). Stick insects
normally evoke a greener, more open world than that of rotting
wood; but in its last oceanic refuge (an islet off Lord Howe
Island), a large primitive wingless phasmid, *Dryocelus
australe,* with grotesquely enlarged nipper-like hind legs in
the male, lives in large colonies in beetle holes in dead
wood (Lea, 1916). And a few other related eurycanthine
phasmids that are similarly sexually dimorphic may also hide
away in rotting wood, emerging at night (like *Dryocelus*) to
feed (Gurney, 1947).

It seems open to conjecture whether the enlarged, spined
hind femora of these primitive phasmids (which in *Eurycanthus
horridus* are so strong that they are used as fish hooks) are
functionally convergent with similar developments of the hind
femora of males in certain coreid bugs and in certain gonyleptids in the Arachnida. For the last two groups, it is at
least recorded that the structures can give a sharp nip to a
human finger (Bristowe, 1924).

So far as I am aware, the swollen-legged coreids are unex-
ceptional plant feeders and are all winged. Yet the occurrence of a "high-low" range of variation in the legs of males,
in for example, *Acanthocephala femorata* (Gibson and Holdridge,
1918), so like the variation of stag beetle mandibles, strongly suggests that males fight. If they do, it would be of
interest to know what special circumstances make it worthwhile. Gonyleptids live in cavities; and in general, outside
of rotting wood, the most characteristic habitats for horned
beetles are burrows around dung and carrion (Arrow, 1951).
Thus horned beetles along with various pugnacious crickets
(Alexander and Otte, 1967), the bees already mentioned,
stomatopods (Caldwell and Dingle, 1976), and other marine
Crustacea and worms (Brown and Orians, 1970; Evans, 1973)
suggest an important common factor: defense of burrows.

Fighting is expected to evolve when an object valuable for
fitness is not obtainable (or retainable) by other means and
when not too much inclusive fitness is lost through any damage
a fighter has to inflict (i.e., the antagonist is not too
closely related: Hamilton, 1964; see also Eberhard, 1975;
Alexander, 1974). Any object that has been laboriously made
(for mating, egg protection, larval feeding, etc.) is worth
the risks and the energy costs of violence to usurp or
defend. A burrow, a dung ball (Matthews, 1963; Marshall,
1976), for example, can be such an object. Its value, of

course, lies in what can be done with it and is in no way sen-
timental. Similarly any compact resource which can simply be
found and then counted on to yield richly in fitness--what
Wilson (1971) called a "bonanza" situation--is also worth
fighting for. Here might be cited a carrion (Pukowski, 1933;
Milne and Milne, 1976), a nest aggregation with emerging
females (Alcock, 1975), and a position near or in special
flowers or food sources where mateable females come, as in
some bees, some Hawaiian *Drosophila* (Spieth, 1974), some
lucanid beetles, and perhaps some nitidulids (see Arrow, 1951).
Since, obviously it is best to avoid the risks of an outright
fight if there are strong signs that the opponent will win,
we would expect the amount of overt fighting, but not of
weaponry, to be reduced according to how well an individual
is able to form a true appreciation of the fighting ability
of rivals and also according to the probability that alternative opportunities can be found elsewhere if a fight is
declined. Probably part of the reason that fighting in the
fig is so damaging (as also between parasitoid larvae: Hamilton, 1964) is that there is no possibility of going off to
another fig. Nevertheless, as already pointed out, the males
in the fig do seem to assess the strength of rivals and if
weaker, often employ a "waiting" strategy which occasionally,
no doubt, brings mating opportunities later.[13]

When an owner of an object has an initial positional
advantage, the assessment that an intending usurper has to
make is perhaps more difficult and a trial of strength correspondingly more likely. The fighting which W. G. Eberhard
has observed in the dynastine beetle *Podischnus agenor* rather
suggests this. Here it seems probable that chances of mating
with more than one female are at stake in the fighting; in
other words, that the ownership of the object of fighting--a
feeding gallery--sometimes enables a male to attract and mate
several females (Eberhard, pers. comm., and this volume).

When I watched a scolytid *Pityogenes bidentatus* with a
situation apparently similar to that hypothesized for the
dynastine just mentioned (except that the polygyny is simultaneous and continued), I did not see fighting or usurping,
but I did see males blocking entrances to their nuptial
chambers against other males but admitting females (these
observations were very brief). Among scolytids it is particularly the males of polygynous species like *P. bidentatus* that
often have small horns on the ends of the elytra (Richards,

---

[13] Such waiting by defeated males is also observed in a scelionid, *Phanuropsis semiflaviventris* (Eberhard, 1975, and pers.
comm.).

1927). In *P. bidentatus,* males are on the average slightly
larger than females and use the flattened and horned elytral
declivity to block their entrances. Table 5 shows a census
of polygamy in gallery systems very soon after their establishment and some counts made a little later. Obviously some
males are getting many more females than others. Yet the
distributions seem to end up almost as if females had arrived
at random ($\mu \simeq \sigma^2$), which seems to imply little favoritism
for particular males. Although as in other outbreeding
polygamous scolytids (Hamilton, 1967), there is an unaccounted
deficiency of males (since the sex ratio at the pupal stage is
about 1:1), and although the change in distribution from "May"
to "June" shows that some females are leaving the most over-
crowded systems, the superficially random distribution that
results suggests that sexual selection of males either through
combat or female preference is not very strong.

A case of fighting in tunnels by a polygynous male with
small horns on the elytra has already been mentioned. This
was in Platypodidae. Yet another family, Bostrychidae, has
examples converging strongly to the morphological facies, at
least, of the polygynous scolytids and platypodids,[14] but here
there is sometimes a complication in the existence of a sharply defined class of variant males (Lesne, 1898). In *Bos-
trychopsis uncinata,* variant males have sharp points around
the elytral declivity exactly like ordinary males, but completely lack a pair of barbed prongs at the front of the
pronotum. As with most bostrychids, the gallery system is in
wood (not phloem) and is not ambrosial. Based on a few observations which I made in Brazil, the gallery system is not
unlike that of *Pityogenes* or *Ips.* Its shape is somewhat glove-
like with an entrance near the base of the "palm." Close
inside a male is normally waiting with head inwards. Some
"fingers" of the glove are close below the surface of the
wood and admitting to these is sometimes another window or
entrance. The barbed prongs appear designed to give a purchase in the wood when a male is initiating a burrow. Slight
as they are, my data suggest that an initiating male is usually, or perhaps always, pronged; and that prongless males may
enter galleries later.

In three systems in October 1975, I found one such prongless male alone with six females, two together with one

---

[14] Some marine wood-boring Crustacea converge to the same
facies (Kühne, 1965), but social organization and behavior
are hardly known. Hole dwelling rather than wood boring,
however, is probably the important factor for the convergence
of male adaptations (see Plate VIII of Barrett and Yonge,
1958).

pronged male and two females, and one pronged male alone with
three females. A month earlier I had found in the same log
just one pronged male together with eleven females. If, even
using prongs, initiating a system is a difficult and dangerous
task, and if, through sexual dissatisfaction of females or
simply their clumsy mining, a fraction of the systems acquire
windows through which prongless males can enter, we see a
possible basis for the stable dimorphism akin to that suggested for the fig wasp dimorphism.

Other equally sharp and even more impressive dimorphisms are
known in horned beetles (Arrow, 1944; the contrasting morphs
in *Enema pan* are well shown in a photograph in Smith, 1971).
This is quite distinct from the usually graded series from
"low" to "high" males which is often found in the same species, but is connected with it in the sense that only one
morph shows the more graded "high-low" variation, while the
other occurs only among large ("high") males. The function
of this variation is unknown, but one might suggest that if,
as in *Idarnes*, large males do more real fighting, an uncommon
variant may get an advantage similar to that of a left-handed
boxer, while perhaps being slightly disadvantaged in other
respects because the genes for his armament are not so well
coadapted with the rest of the genome or with the environment
(as may also be the case with left handedness). The rare
occurrence, noted by Arrow (1951), of bilateral mosaics for
the two male forms in the beetles, slightly suggests that
besides adequate feeding (to give large size), a different
genotype is needed for the variant to appear.

Although male horns seem to be most extravagant in the
species that are known to be polygamous (or reasonably supposed to be so), many of the apparently monogamous hole-dwelling
males have horns (e.g., *Lethrus apterus, Typhoeus typhoeus*),
and even where lacking (as with *Cryptocercus punctatulus*,
Ritter, 1964; *Dendroctonus ponderosae*, McGhehey, 1968), the
male may fight to defend the burrow. Paralleling male adversity to other males, we would expect females in these monogamous situations to resent the presence of other females if
they ever got in. Within-sex resentment is actually illustrated in beetles of *Necrophorus* where, after the phase of
cooperation during burial of a carcass, fighting begins and
continues until only one male-female pair remains. Similar
intrasexual conflict over dung balls by both males and females
is known in a ball-rolling scarab (Marshall, 1976). In some
scarabaeines, however, there are hints that pairs may fly as
pairs from one site to another (Halffter and Matthews, 1966),
and if they can, they might be expected to fight for their
burrow or food object as a bonded pair too. This might help
to explain the very occasional but almost equal horn development in the two sexes (e.g., *Megaphanaeus*). In rotting wood,

TABLE 5

Distribution of polyggyny in Pityogenes bidentatus

Date	Number of females per system: 0	1	2	3	4	5	6	7	8	9	10	11	Total	$\bar{n}$	s^2
Systems with 0 males present:															
May '67		5	1	2	2								10	2.10	1.66
June '67	4	16	1										21	.86	.23
Systems with 1 male present:															
May '67	13	4	9	6	5	7	5	5	5	4	1	1	65	3.95	9.73
June '67	6	8	13	11	13	8	5	3					67	3.13	3.57
Systems with 2 males present:															
May '67	1												1	0	
June '67	1		1										2	1	
Systems in 1970 (all one-male)[a]															
June '70	4	6	16	50	79	87	51	18	14	5	1		331	4.65	2.82
All one-male systems surveyed in June															
	10	14	29	61	92	95	56	21	14	5	1		398	4.39	3.26
***P. hopkinsi* (mature systems, Blackman, 1915)[b]**															
	6	17	22	12	2	1							60	2.83	1.16

[a] Data gathered by R. Kowalski. [b] Blackman, N.W. 1915. *N.Y. Coll. Forest. Tech. Publ. No.* 2:11–66.

again, there are some strange cases of horns developed equally
in both sexes. Of the habits in these also almost nothing is
known, even though one such genus (*Priochirus,* Staphylinidae)
has been the subject of a phylogenetic study based on morphology and biogeography (Greenslade, 1972a, b). That horns of
some bisexually armed tenebrionids are used in fighting is
shown by Eberhard in this volume.

Since Darwin, appreciation of fighting in the selection of
epigamic characters has a rather checkered history. Such
appreciation has been overdaring and vitalistic (Hingston,
1933), or overcautious (Lameere, 1904; Huxley, 1938), or even
almost denied (Arrow, 1951). In view of the frequent difficulty of demonstrating fighting in horned beetles and the
apparent ineffectiveness of fighting when seen, varied alternative hypotheses have been tried. The most reasonable of
these, due to Darwin, emphasizes selection through female
preference. The bright colors which some of the most grotesque males have in addition to their horns suggest that this
factor does play a part. But various objections have been
urged against the factor of female preference. One of the
most weighty is that the female seems to accept any male.
Nevertheless it is generally not excluded on present evidence
that she may have some means to control sperm precedence in
favor of the male she likes best.

Another point deemphasizing female preference is that
biologists seem to have too hastily assumed that large horns
cannot be efficient weapons of combat. This point is strongly
made by Eberhard (this volume). The huge mandibles of
Chiasognathus granti obviously have a poor mechanical advantage: Darwin in his *Voyage of the Beagle* commented that he
found them "not strong enough to pinch my finger so as to
cause actual pain." I observed these beetles in Chile in
March 1975. With regard to a finger, I found much the same
as Darwin, but I was not sure about lack of strength: I
thought they were not biting as hard or holding as tenaciously
as they do when fighting each other and suspect that they
restrain their strength in deterrent biting of a large animal
to lessen the risk of a lethal reaction. In any case, the
literature shows that in nature fighting males do at times
pierce each other and even tear each other apart (Claude-
Joseph, 1928; Ureta, 1934). Fights are not normally sanguin-
ary but are hardly less decisive: one male secures a grip
that enables him to lift his opponent until all legs are free
(the long mandibles and long legs play their part here, although, of course, the lifted beetle can use his for hanging
on) and then drops him. Fighting and mating usually occur
on tree trunks around sap flows (Claude-Joseph, 1928; infor-
mants in Chile) or flowers of a tree vine so that dropping
disposes of the loser, at least for a while. Probably he does

not normally return, for I found a loser reluctant to engage
the victor again, and if he did so at my prompting, the
result was always the same. A dropped male walks hurriedly
away, climbing if possible, and tries to fly. Males with
small mandibles fought each other much more readily than they
fought large males, and they always lost to large males if
they did fight them. I have found the same with *Lucanus
cervus* in Britain, and Mathieu (1969) the same for other
lucanids in the U.S.; Mathieu also found that large males (in
Lucanus and *Platycerus*) sometimes pierced and killed small
males. Very similar methods of male fighting on tree trunks
have recently been recorded for a grotesquely elongate
brenthid, *Lasiorhynchus barbicornis*, which also showed (1) the
use of a long appendage (the rostrum) for holding out and
dropping an opponent and (2) reluctance of small males to
engage large ones (Meads, 1976).

I suspect that horned-beetle fights have too often been
staged in the bottoms of boxes, and that here the lifting-and-
dropping theme looks unduly like a fight to rules, resembling
human wrestling (Beebe, 1944, 1947). Had the fights been
watched on the more natural elevated surfaces (like the
branches of the fallen tree where Beebe [1944] found his
Megasoma males), the effectiveness of the methods would have
been obvious. I suspect that similar methods will be found
for many male insects that are clumsy fliers and fight on
elevated objects. This may be suggested, for example, for
the strange horned males of plataspids (Heteroptera) in those
cases where the females live on tree trunks, as some do, and
perhaps for some membracid males as well.

COMMUNICATION IN SEXUAL SELECTION

It is possible to imagine selection processes by which
horns can evolve, at least in some variants, beyond the point
of their maximum effectiveness in fighting, or can evolve
when not used in fighting at all. These possible processes
ascribe a more subtle function than pinching or throwing an
opponent: they require that, perhaps prior even to contact,
the horns can be used to communicate something (see Fisher,
1930, various papers by O'Donald, 1963 to 1973). What
they can communicate is either "true" information--regarding
principally, (a) *ability to fight* (to males) or (b) *desirability as a mate* (to females)--or else, as their owner may at
least hope, "false" information--such as (c) *bluff*, mainly
about (a) (to males), but also about (b) as implied by (a)
(to females). Perhaps because of the intriguing suggestion
of a positive evolutionary feedback (Fisher, 1930; O'Donald,
1967), it is, as already mentioned, desirability as a mate (b)

that has received most attention from the time of Darwin.
The other factors cannot cause such feedback, but it is
questionable how often data really call for it or show sexual
preference to be effective. Ability to fight (a) has the
recommendation of simplicity and seems unduly neglected. On
behalf of desirability as a mate (b), the positive allometry
so often observed in the features in question is just what is
needed to make characters so conspicuous that they will impress even half-blind females--as females of the horned species are sometimes claimed to be in the course of a somewhat
illogical objection to the role of female preference (Arrow,
1951). But the same allometric exaggeration of certain parts
will make them conspicuous and sensitized advertisements of
size, with which goes, in most cases, real superiority in
fighting.[15] Thus again, whether eyesight is good or bad, the
allometry could usefully impress other males as well.

Horns that communicate fighting ability to other males
would be expected to be, in most cases, the actual weapons
used in any fighting that occurred, but they would not have to
be. Aspects of size and large-headedness in *Scatophaga*, as
discussed by Borgia in this volume, may be relevant here as
nonweapon characters that communicate strength. McAlpine
(1975, and this volume) discusses this matter for the eight
or so dipteran families in which strikingly megacephalic and
"stalk-eyed" males are known and indicates a connection with
head-to-head fighting. Bristowe (1924) described the modestly
"stalk-eyed" males of the drosophilid *Zygothricha dispar* as
fighting by butting amid a crowd of females on a fungus. He
likened them to fighting male Bovidae, but it is unlikely
that the points of the "horns" are used to jab opponents since
these bear the compound eyes.[16] Among the uniquely numerous
and diverse *Drosophila* of Hawaii are species whose males form

---

[15] Regarding insects with no special weapons, the advantage
of size in fighting is mentioned by Alexander (1961) for
crickets and documented statistically by Alcock et al. (1977)
for the bee *Centris pallida,* and, even more thoroughly, by
Marshall (1976) for the ball-rolling scarab *Canthon imitator*.
Some other cases of small *horned* males being reluctant to
engage large ones, and of real fighting advantages to the
latter, have already been mentioned.

[16] Horns of rather similar aspect occur on the thorax in some
male pentatomids: I suspect these males fight and that the
horns display size.

"leks" on surfaces close to sites where females come to
feed and oviposit. These species include the largest known
Drosophila and also the most sexually dimorphic. Among other
differences, the males are larger than their females. In
some cases males wrestle head-to-head and, in a preliminary
display, the elongate forelegs are used in a special upright
posture. This, combined with bobbing movements, shows off
both the legs and size generally. Small males retreat from
obviously larger males after such display. However the long
legs and the head (also especially enlarged) are used in the
fighting if this ensues (Spieth, 1974; Hardy, 1965). In one
case, that of *Drosophila heteroneura,* the male head has a
distinct stalk-eyed tendency. Taking advantage of interfer-
tility with another species, an ingenious genetic analysis
has already strongly implicated the X-chromosome as the site
for the switch gene for this male-limited character (Val,
1977; Templeton, 1977).

Acanthocinus aedilis, a cerambycid beetle whose larvae
feed in dead phloem of conifers, has males which have long
been known to fight (Rye, 1866), although of how and for what
they fight there seems to be no detailed description. Even
for this "long horn" family (and compared to their own females), males of *A. aedilis* have extremely long antennae.
Since it is very difficult to imagine they can be weapons,
their most probable function is perhaps long-range detection-
assessment of rivals and females. But parallel to our hypothesized function of eyestalks in flies, these antennae could
also be serving as advertisements of size and strength.

Such advertisement might be expected to accrete an element
of bluff. Returning to beetle horns used as weapons, my own
scanty observations tend to favor a largely honest communicative function towards other males, but as regards a resid-
uum--a small margin of excess that may not correlate with real
fighting ability--they tend to favor bluff[17] rather than
Darwin-Fisher exaggeration through female preference. In
three "tournaments" that I have been able to arrange (two of
Lucanus cervus and one of *Chiasognathus*), I found that the
winner was the second largest male. In *Chiasognathus* the
males fought vigorously although no female was present. In
Lucanus the presence of a receptive female was necessary to
stimulate more than brief posturing by the males (see also
Mathieu, 1969), but the female herself showed no interest and

---

[17] The subject of animal "deceit" is beginning to attract
attention (e.g., Wallace, 1972; Otte, 1975), but as regards
bluffed displays fixed by genotype, I know of no theory beyond
brief comments by Fisher (1930).

passively allowed mounting by any male. However, her coopera-
tion--by slight raising of the elytra--may have been needed
before intromission could take place. Sometimes a mounted
male bit quite hard at a female's head so that an element of
bullying to gain cooperation also seems possible.

In leaving little necessity to invoke restraint or ritual,
the view which these observations (and points of theory) tend
to support departs rather widely from a long-held general
interpretation of animal fighting (e.g., Arrow, 1951; Harrison
Matthews, 1964; and critique in Ghiselin, 1974). Yet it
accords well with various scattered eyewitness accounts and,
as regards horned animals generally, is by no means original
(Geist, 1966, 1974).

Most combinations of the selection processes able to affect
horns are not mutually exclusive. Female preference, however,
will hardly work for horns if the interactions of males are
effectively eliminating all basis for choice. But even in
this aspect, if females are freely mobile, the fighting of
males will only affect choice within one mating site: it is
open to mobile females to go off and be available at another.
For example, *Chiasognathus* females could go off to another
sap flow, perhaps to that with the most "splendid" male in
charge. The changing distribution of females in *Pityogenes*
single-male systems (Table 5) has given a hint of movements
of this kind, although in that case the way the females were
opting did not seem strongly selective and, correspondingly,
the special structures of their males are modest. But, as
also with *Chiasognathus* and all the other cases we have discussed, the work of apportioning functions to these struc-
tures--tools, weapons, or ornaments, lies or truth--is hardly
begun.

CONCLUSIONS

The coincidence of winglessness, fighting, and dimorphism
in male fig wasps is not accidental. Correlations of the
same kind are widely present in other insects.

Aggregation of females is evidently a factor underlying
all three phenomena, and it seems essential for the extremes
of male fighting.

The evolution of *fighting* requires the distribution of a
resource in masses compact enough to be guarded and valuable
enough to be worth risks to obtain--as reckoned by inclusive
fitness. In fig wasps, moderate aggregation of colonizing
mothers often leads to this situation through the intense
aggregation of their daughters and the formation of groups of
males that are not too closely related.

To judge from cases surveyed, structures that look like

weapons in males often are weapons. Theory remains open, however, to the existence of positively allometric structures
which, while not used as weapons, serve as valid (or slightly
bluffed) signals of fighting strength for direction at weaker
(and slightly stronger) males. Contrary to Darwin, appreciation by the females appears less important than such male-male
display and fighting for most weapon-like and size-related
characters.

Male fighting correlates with size both within and between
species: small size and pugnacity do not easily coevolve.
Enlargements of the head and of mandibles are particularly
indicative of fighting; but alternative massive enlargements
elsewhere, e.g., particular legs, thoracic horns, are frequent.

Provided (a) that males are with females initially,
and (b) that the females can carry stored sperm, *male
winglessness* tends to evolve in situations similar to those
favorable to male fighting (as in parasite fig wasps). But
situations with relatedness too high for fighting can still
easily be favorable to winglessness (as with pollinator fig
wasps). The economy of winglessness provides for virility
and sometimes for the adaptations for fighting. Wings have
no value inside figs and are probably an encumbrance there,
as suggested by their convergent tendency to disappear in
such similarly claustral habitats as soil and rotting wood.
Outside of figs, wings have value at least sometimes. Total
male aptery is expected only if the average value of having
wings is very low, which tends to be the case if average fig
populations are high. If populations are low, wholly winged
males are expected; and, given that a substantial proportion
of females are maturing in male-less figs, intermediate average densities in figs are expected to lead to *male dimorphism*.
These expectations are reasonably fulfilled. It is not clear
yet whether the kind of frequency dependence here postulated
is especially likely to maintain both morphs over long periods
and varying abundance of the species. Disruptive selection
that is either long continued or very intense seems needed to
explain the wide divergence of male morphs in some fig wasps.

ACKNOWLEDGEMENTS

My visit to Brazil was arranged by the Royal Society of
London and financed by awards from the Leverhulme Trust and
the Conselho Nacional de Pesquisas of Brazil. I thank R.
Zucchi and L. A. de O. Campos for showing me the fig wasps,
and R. Zucchi, F. A. M. Duarte, I. Ferrari, L. S. Goncalves,
and W. E. Kerr for the facilities kindly provided at various

stages during my stay at the two Faculdades of Ribeirão Prêto.
Opportunity to observe *Chiasognathus* arose during an expedition assisted by the Royal Society, the Forestry Commission,
the Manchester University Museum, and the Corporacion Nacional
Forestal of Chile. Wing-polymorphic insects of rotting wood
in Britain were studied with assistance of a grant (GR3/1383)
from the Natural Environment Research Council. Work of J.
Auckland, R. Wilkinson, and J. Fethney contributed much to my
knowledge of these insects. R. Edwards and J. Newton helped
me to obtain colonies of *Hypoponera punctatissima*. For
various facts, ideas, and bibliographic items, I also thank
R. W. Barth, A. Camonsseign, W. G. Eberhard, G. Gordh, R.
Kowalski, P. Levin, D. K. McAlpine, D. Otte, T. J. Palmer, V.
A. Taylor, and J. T. Wiebes.

REFERENCES

Alcock, J. 1975. Territorial behaviour by males of *Philanthus
    multimaculatus* (Hymenoptera: Sphecidae) with a review of
    territoriality in male sphecids. *Anim. Behav.* 23:889-895.
Alcock, J., E. Jones, and S.L. Buchmann. 1977. Male mating
    strategies in the bee *Centris pallida* Fox (Anthophoridae:
    Hymenoptera). *Amer. Nat.* 111:145-155.
Alexander, R.D. 1961. Aggressiveness, territoriality, and
    sexual behavior in field crickets (Orthoptera: Gryllidae).
    Behaviour 17:130-223.
Alexander, R.D. 1974. The evolution of social behavior. *Ann.
    Rev. Ecol. Syst.* 5:325-383.
Alexander, R.D., and D. Otte. 1967. The evolution of genitalia
    and mating behavior in crickets (Gryllidae) and other
    Orthoptera. *Misc. Publ. Mus. Zool. Univ. Michigan* 133:1-62.
Alston, A.M. 1920. The life-histories and habits of two
    parasites of blowflies. *Proc. Zool. Soc. London* 1920:
    195-243.
Ananthakrishnan, T.N. 1968. Patterns of structural diversity
    in the males of some phlocophilous Tubulifera (Thysanop-
    tera). *Ann. Soc. Ent. France (N.S.)* 4:413-418.
Ananthakrishnan, T.N. 1969. *Indian Thysanoptera.* C.S.I.R.
    Zoological Monographs 1. New Delhi.
Arrow, G.J. 1944. Polymorphism in giant beetles. *Proc. Zool.
    Soc. London* 113:113-116.
Arrow, G.J. 1951. *Horned Beetles.* Dr. W. Junk, The Hague.
Baker, C.F. 1913. A study of caprification in *Ficus nota.
    Phillipine J. Sci. (D)* 8:63-83.
Barrett, J.H., and C.M. Yonge. 1958. *Collins Pocket Guide to
    the Sea Shore.* Collins, London.
Becker, G., and W. Weber. 1952. *Theocolax formiciformis*

Westwood (Hymenoptera: Chalcididae) ein Anobien-parasit. *Z. Parasit.* 15:339-356.

Beebe, W. 1944. The function of secondary sexual characters in two species of Dynastidae (Coleoptera). *Zoologica* 29:53-58.

Beebe, W. 1947. Notes on the hercules beetle, *Dynastes hercules* (Linn.) at Rancho Grande, Venezuela, with special reference to combat behavior. *Zoologica* 32:109-116.

Brendell, M.J.D. 1975. *Coleoptera; Tenebrionidae*. Handbooks for the Identification of British Insects, Volume V, part 10. Royal Entomological Society of London.

Bristowe, W.S. 1924. Notes on the habits of insects and spiders in Brazil. *Trans. Ent. Soc. London* 1924:475-504.

Broadhead, E. 1947. The life-history of *Embidopsocus enderleini* (Ribaga) (Corrodenta, Liposcelidae). *Ent. Monthly Mag.* 83:200-203.

Broadhead, E. 1961. The biology of *Psoquilla marginepunctata* (Hagen) (Corodentia, Trogiidae). *Trans. Soc. British Ent.* 14:223-236.

Brown, J.L., and G.H. Orians. 1970. Spacing patterns in mobile animals. *Ann. Rev. Ecol. Syst.* 1:239-262.

Browne, F.B. 1922. On the life-history of *Melittobia acasta*, Walker; a chalcid parasite of bees and wasps. *Parasitology* 14:349-370.

Browne, F.G. 1959. Notes on two Malayan scolytid bark beetles. *Malayan Forester* 22:292-300.

Browne, F.G. 1961. The biology of Malayan Scolytidae and Platypodidae. *Malayan Forest Records* 22:1-255.

Brues, C.T. 1922. Some Hymenopterous parasites of lignicolous Itonididae. *Proc. Amer. Acad. Arts Sci.* 57:263-288.

Buschinger, A. 1974. Polymorphismus und Polyethismus sozialparasitischer Hymenopteren. *In* Schmidt, G.H. (ed.), *Sozialpolymorphismus bei Insekten,* Wissenschaftliche Verlagsgesellschaft MBH, Stuttgart.

Caldwell, R.L., and H. Dingle. 1976. Stomatopods. *Scientific Amer.* 234:80-89.

Carayon, J. 1974. Insémination traumatique hétérosexuelle et homosexuelle chez *Xylocoris maculipennis* (Hemiptera: Anthocoridae). *C. R. Acad. Sci.* 278:2803-2806.

Champion, G.C. 1910. Note on the sexual characters of *Longitarsus agilis* Rye. *Ent. Monthly Mag.* 46:261.

Chopard, L. 1950. Sur l'anatomie et le développement d'une blatte vivipare. *Proc. Eighth Int. Cong. Ent. Stockholm,* pp. 218-222.

Claude-Joseph, F. 1928. El *Chiasognathus grantii* Steph. *Revista Universitaria, Santiago* 13:529-535.

Colwell, R.K. 1973. Competition and coexistence in a simple tropical community. *Amer. Nat.* 107:737-760.

Coquerel, C. 1848. Observations entomologiques sur divers

insectes recueillis a Madagascar (2° partie). *Ann. Soc. Ent. France* 1848:275-284.

Corner, E.J.H. 1958. An introduction to the distribution of *Ficus. Reinwardtia* 4:15-45.

Cross, E.A., and J.C. Moser. 1971. Taxonomy and biology of some Pyemotidae (Acarina: Tarsonemoidea) inhabiting bark beetle galleries in North American conifers. *Acarologia* 13:47-64.

Cross, E.A., and J.C. Moser. 1975. A new dimorphic species of *Pyemotes* and a key to previously described forms. (Acarina: Tarsonemoidea). *Ann. Ent. Soc. Amer.* 68:723-732.

Crowson, R.A. 1974. Observations on Histeroidea with descriptions of an apterous larviform male and of the internal anatomy of *Sphaerites. J. Ent. (B)* 42:133-140.

Dahms, E. 1973. The courtship behaviour of *Melittobia australica* Girault 1912 (Hymenoptera: Eulophidae). *Memoirs Queensland Mus.* 16:411-414.

Eberhard, W.G. 1975. The ecology and behavior of a subsocial pentatomid bug and two scelionid wasps. *Smithsonian Contrib. Zool.* 205:1-39.

Evans, H.E. 1963. A new species of *Cephalonomia* exhibiting an unusually complex polymorphism (Hymenoptera, Bethylidae). *Psyche* 70:151-163.

Evans, S.M. 1973. A study of fighting reactions of some nereid polychaetes. *Anim. Behav.* 21:138-146.

Fisher, R.A. 1930. *The Genetical Theory of Natural Selection.* Clarendon Press, Oxford.

Foa, A. 1919. Studio sul polimorfismo unisessuale del *Rhizoglyphus echinopus* (Fum. and Rob.) Murray corredato da osservazioni biologiche, anatomiche e citologiche. *Memorie Accad. Pontificia Nuovi Lincei. Roma. Ser. V.* 12:3-109.

Gadgil, M. 1972. Male dimorphism as a consequence of sexual selection. *Amer. Nat.* 106:574-580.

Galil, J., and D. Eisikovitch. 1968. On the pollination biology of *Ficus sycamorus* in East Africa. *Ecology* 49:259-269.

Geist, V. 1966. The evolution of horn-like organs. *Behaviour* 27:175-213.

Geist, V. 1974. On fighting strategies in animal combat. *Nature* 250:354.

Gentner, L.G. 1928. The systematic status of the mint flea beetle (Chrysomelidae, Coleoptera), with additional notes. *Can. Ent.* 60:264-266.

Ghiselin, M.T. 1974. *The Economy of Nature and the Evolution of Sex.* Univ. California Press, Berkeley.

Gibson, E.H., and A. Holdridge. 1918. Notes on the North and Central American species of *Acanthocephala* Lap. *Can. Ent.* 50:237-240.

Gordh, G. 1975. The comparative external morphology and
    systematics of the neotropical parasitic fig wasp genus
    Idarnes (Hymenoptera: Torymidae). *Univ. Kansas Sci. Bull.*
    50:389-455.
Grandi, G. 1929. Studio morphologico e biologico della *Blasto-
    phaga psenes* (L.). *Boll. Lab. Ent. R. Istituto Superiore
    Agrario Bologna* 2:1-147.
Grandi, G. 1930. Monografia del genero *Philotrypesis* Forst.
    Boll. Lab. Ent. R. Istituto Superiore Agrario Bologna
    3:1-181.
Grandi, G. 1959. The problems of 'morphological adaptation'
    in insects. *Smithsonian Misc. Collections* 137:203-230.
Grandi, G. 1961. The hymenopterous insects of the super family
    Chalcidoidea developing within the receptacles of figs.
    Their life-history, symbioses and morphological adaptations.
    Boll. Istituto Ent. Univ. Studi Bologna 26:i-xiii.
Greenslade, P.J.M. 1972a. Distribution patterns of *Priochirus*
    species (Coleoptera: Staphylinidae) in the Solomon Islands.
    Evolution 26:130-142.
Greenslade, P.J.M. 1972b. Evolution in the Staphylinid genus
    Priochirus (Coleoptera). *Evolution* 26:203-220.
Gurney, A.B. 1947. Notes on some remarkable Australasian
    walking sticks, including a synopsis of the genus *Extato-
    soma* (Orthoptera: Phasmatidae). *Ann. Ent. Soc. Amer.*
    40:373-396.
Hagerup, E., and O. Hagerup. 1953. Thrips pollination of *Erica
    tetralix*. *New Phytologist* 52:1-7.
Halffter, G., and E.G. Matthews. 1966. The natural history of
    dung beetles of the subfamily Scarabaeinae (Coleoptera:
    Scarabaeidae). *Folia Ent. Mexicana* 12-14:1-312.
Hamilton, W.D. 1964. The genetical evolution of social behav-
    iour. II. *J. Theor. Biol.* 7:17-52.
Hamilton, W.D. 1967. Extraordinary sex ratios. *Science*
    156:477-488.
Hamilton, W.D. 1972. Altruism and related phenomena, mainly
    in social insects. *Ann. Rev. Ecol. Syst.* 3:193-232.
Hamilton, W.D. 1975. Innate social aptitudes of man: an
    approach from evolutionary genetics. *In* Fox, R. (ed.),
    Biosocial Anthropology. Malaby Press, London.
Hardy, D.E. 1965. *Insects of Hawaii, Vol. 12*. Univ. Hawaii
    Press, Honolulu.
Hartl, D.L. 1971. Some aspects of natural selection in
    arrhenotokous populations. *Amer. Zool.* 11:309-325.
Harrison Matthews, L. 1964. Overt fighting in mammals. *In*
    Carthy, J.D., and F.J. Ebling (eds.), *The Natural History
    of Aggression*. Academic Press, London.
Hill, D.S. 1967. *Figs (Ficus spp) of Hong Kong*. Hong Kong
    Univ. Press, Hong Kong.
Hingston, R.W.G. 1933. *The Meaning of Animal Colour and*

Adornment. Arnold, London.

Hopkins, A.D. 1898. On the life history and habits of the "wood-engraver" ambrosia beetle--*Xyleborus xylographus* (Say.), *saxeseni* (Ratz.). *Can. Ent.* 30:21-29.

Houston, T.F. 1970. Discovery of an apparent male soldier caste in a nest of a halictine bee (Hymenoptera: Halictidae) with notes on the nest. *Aust. J. Zool.* 18:345-351.

Hubbard, H.G. 1897. The ambrosia beetles of the United States. *U.S. Dept. Agric., Div. Ent., Bull., New Series* 7:9-30.

Hudson, G.H. 1920. On some examples of New Zealand insects illustrating the Darwinian principle of sexual selection. *Trans. New Zealand Inst.* 52:431-438.

Hughes, A.M. 1948. *The Mites Associated with Stored Food Products*. His Majesty's Stationary Office, London.

Huxley, J.S. 1938. Darwin's theory of sexual selection and the data subsumed by it, in the light of recent research. *Amer. Nat.* 72:416-437.

Joseph, K.J. 1958. Recherches sur les chalcidiens *Blastophaga psenes* (L.) et *Philotrypesis caricae* (L.) du figuier *Ficus carica* (L.). *Ann. Sci. Nat.* 20:197-260.

Joseph, K.J. 1964. A proposed revision of the classification of the fig insects of the families Agaonidae and Torymidae (Hymenoptera). *Proc. Roy. Ent. Soc. London (B)* 33:63-66.

Kearns, C.W. 1934. Method of wing inheritance in *Cephalonomia gallicola,* Ashmead (Bethylidae). *Ann. Ent. Soc. Amer.* 27:533-541.

Kempf, W.W. 1962. Miscellaneous studies on Neotropical ants. II. *Studia Ent.* 5:1-38.

Kühne, H. 1965. Über Beziehungen zwischen *Teredo, Limnoria* und *Chelura*. *In* Becker, G., and W. Liese (eds.), *Holz und Organismen*. Duncker und Humblot, Berlin.

Kühne, H., and G. Becker. 1974. Zur Biologie und Ökologie von *Scleroderma domesticum* Latreille (Bethylidae, Hymenoptera), einem Parasiten holzzerstorender Insektenlarven. *Z. Ang. Ent.* 76:278-303.

Lameere, A. 1904. L'évolution des ornements sexuels. *Bull. Classe Sci. Acad. Royale Belgique* 1904:1327-1364.

Lea, A.N. 1916. Notes on the Lord Howe Island phasma and an associated longicorn beetle. *Trans. Proc. Royal Soc. South Australia* 40:145-147.

Lee, B. 1969. Cannibalism and predation by adult males of the two spotted mite *Tetranychus urticae* (Koch) (Acarina: Tetranychidae). *J. Aust. Ent. Soc.* 8:210.

Lesne, P. 1898. Revision des coléoptères de la famille des Bostrychides. 3e Memoire. Bostrychinae. *Ann. Soc. Ent. France* 67:438-621.

Lima, A. da Costa. 1944. Quarta contribuicao ao conhecimento da biologia do *Telenomus polymorphus* n. sp. (Hymenoptera: Scelionidae). *Anais Acad. Brasileira Ciencias* 15:211-227.

Marshall, W.E. 1976. Optimization of parental investment: pre-oviposition care of brood balls in the dung beetle *Canthon imitator*. M.A. Thesis. Univ. Texas, Austin.

Mathieu, J. 1969. Mating behaviour of five species of Lucanidae (Coleoptera: Insecta). *Can. Ent.* 101:1054-1062.

Matthews, E.G. 1963. Observations on the ball-rolling behavior of *Canthon pilularis* (L.). *Psyche* 70:75-93.

Matthews, R.M. 1975. Courtship in parasitic wasps. *In* Price, P.W. (ed.), *Evolutionary Strategies of Parasitic Insects and Mites*. Plenum Press, New York.

Maynard Smith, J., and G.R. Price. 1973. The logic of animal conflict. *Nature* 246:15-18.

McAlpine, D.K. 1975. Combat between males of *Pogornortalis doclea* (Diptera, Platystomatidae) and its relation to structural modification. *Aust. Ent. Mag.* 2:104-107.

McGhehey, J.H. 1968. Territorial behaviour of bark-beetle males. *Can. Ent.* 100:1153.

Meads, M.J. 1976. Some observations on *Lasiorhynchus barbicornis* (Brenthidae: Coleoptera). *New Zealand Ent.* 6:171-176.

Michener, C.D. 1969. Comparative social behavior of bees. *Ann. Rev. Ent.* 14:299-342.

Milne, L.J., and M. Milne. 1976. The social behavior of burying beetles. *Scientific Amer.* 235:84-89.

Mohrig, W., and B.M. Mamaev. 1970. Neue flügelreduzierte Dipteren der Familien Sciaridae und Cecidomyiidae. *Deutsche Ent. Z.* 7:315-336.

Morison, G.D. 1925. Notes on the broad-horned flour beetle *Gnathocerus cornutus* Fab. *Proc. Royal Physical Soc. Edinburgh* 21:14-18.

Morison, G.D. 1971. Observations and records for British Thysanoptera. XV. Thripidae, *Thrips discolor* Haliday. *The Entomologist* 104:276-281.

Morison, G.D. 1973. Observations and records for British Thysanoptera. XVII. Thripidae, *Baliothrips dispar* (Haliday). *The Entomologist* 106:157-164.

Moser, J.C., and E.A. Cross. 1975. Phoretomorph: a new phoretic phase unique to the Pyemotidae (Acarina: Tarsonemoidea). *Ann. Ent. Soc. Amer.* 68:820-822.

Mound, L.A. 1971. Gall-forming thrips and allied species (Thysanoptera: Phlaeothripinae) from *Acacia* trees in Australia. *Bull. Brit. Mus. (Nat. History) B. (Entomology)* 25:387-466.

Moure, J.S. 1943. Sôbre origin do Meloponinae parasitas (Hymenoptera: Apoidea). *Ciência Cultura, S.P.* 15:183-184.

New, T.R. 1973a. South American species of *Nepiomorpha* Pearman and *Notiopsocus* Banks (Psocoptera). *The Entomologist* 106:121-132.

New, T.R. 1973b. The Archipsocidae of South America (Psocoptera). *Trans. Royal Ent. Soc. London* 125:57-105.

O'Donald, P. 1963. Sexual selection and territorial behaviour. *Heredity* 18:361-364.

O'Donald, P. 1967. A general model of sexual and natural selection. *Heredity* 22:499-518.

O'Donald, P. 1973. Models of sexual and natural selection in polygamous species. *Heredity* 31:145-156.

Orlove, M.J. 1973. *A contribution to the biology of the great carpenter bee* Xylocopa virginica: *geographical variation in courtship, mimicry and rearing methods.* Thesis (1087) for Diploma of Imperial College (part).

Otte, D. 1975. On the role of intraspecific deception. *Amer. Nat.* 109:239-242.

Pearman, J.V. 1942. Third note on Psocoptera from warehouses. *Ent. Monthly Mag.* 78:289-292.

Potter, D.A., D.L. Wrensch, and D.E. Johnston. 1976. Aggression and mating success in male spider mites. *Science* 193:160-161.

Poulton, E.B. 1913. Mr. Lambourn's observations on marriage by capture in a West African wasp. *Report of the British Assoc. Advancement Sci.* 1913:511.

Pukowski, E. 1933. Ökologische Untersuchungen an *Necrophorus* F. *Z. Morph. Ökol. Tiere* 27:518-586.

Radovsky, F.J. 1972. Fixed parasitism in the Siphonaptera. *J. Med. Ent.* 9:487-494.

Ramirez, B.W. 1970. Taxonomic and biological studies of neotropical fig wasps (Hymenoptera: Agaonidae). *Univ. Kansas Sci. Bull.* 49:1-44.

Richards, O.W. 1927. Sexual selection and allied problems in the insects. *Biol. Rev.* 2:298-364.

Richards, O.W. 1961. An introduction to the study of polymorphism in insects. *In* Kennedy, J.S. (ed.), *Insect Polymorphism.* Symposia of the Royal Ent. Soc. London 1.

Riegel, G.T. 1963. The distribution of *Zorotypus hubbardi.* *Ann. Ent. Soc. Amer.* 56:744-747.

Ritter, H., Jr. 1964. Defense of mate and mating chamber in a wood roach. *Science* 143:1459-1460.

Rye, E.C. 1866. *British Beetles.* Reeve, London.

Sakagami, S.K. 1974. Sozialstruktur und Polymorphismus bei Furchen- oder Schalbienen (Halictinae). *In* Schmidt, G.H. (ed.), *Sozialpolymorphismus bei Insekten.* Wissenschaftliche Verlagsgesellschaft MBH, Stuttgart.

Salt, G. 1952. Trimorphism in the ichneumonid parasite *Gelis corruptor.* *Quart. J. Microscop. Sci.* 93:453-474.

Smith, A. 1971. *Mato Grosso.* Michael Joseph, London.

Smith, M.R. 1944. Ants of the genus *Cardiocondyla* Emery in the United States. *Proc. Ent. Soc. Wash.* 46:30-41.

Sokoloff, A. 1972. *The Biology of Tribolium with Special Emphasis on Genetic Aspects. Vol. 2.* Clarendon Press, Oxford.

Southwood, T.R.E. 1961. A hormonal theory of the mechanism of wing polymorphism in Heteroptera. *Proc. Royal Ent. Soc. London (A)* ·36:49-88.

Spieth, H.T. 1974. Mating behaviour and evolution of the Hawaiian *Drosophila. In* White, M.J.D. (ed.), *Genetic Mechanisms of Speciation in Insects*. Reidel: Dordrecht, Holland and Boston, U.S.A.

Taylor, J.M. 1964. Studies on *Theocolax formiciformis* Westw. (Hymenoptera, Pteromalidae), a parasite of *Anobium punctatum* (Deg.) (Coleoptera, Anobiidae). *Bull. Ent. Res.* 54:797-803.

Taylor, V.A. 1975. *The biology of feather-winged beetles of the genus* Ptinella *with particular reference to coexistence and parthenogenesis*. Thesis for degree of Ph.D., Univ. of London.

Templeton, A.R. 1977. Analysis of head shape differences between two interfertile species of Hawaiian *Drosophila. Evolution* 31:630-641.

Théodorides, J. 1955. Contribution à l'étude des parasites et phoretiques de coléoptères terrestres. *Actualités Scientifiques Industrielles* 1217:1-310.

Ureta, R.E. 1934. Sobre algunas costumbres del *Chiasognathus grantii*, Steph. *Rev. Chilena Historia Natural* 38:287-292.

Val, F.C. 1977. Genetic analysis of the morphological differences between two interfertile species of Hawaiian *Drosophila. Evolution* 31:611-629.

Wallace, B. 1972. Misinformation, fitness, and selection. *Amer. Nat.* 107:1-7.

West Eberhard, M.J. 1975. The evolution of social behaviour by kin selection. *Quart. Rev. Biol.* 50:1-34.

Wheeler, W.M. 1928. *The Social Insects*. Kegan Paul, London.

Wheeler, W.M. 1937. *Mosaics and other anomalies among ants*. Harvard Univ. Press, Cambridge.

Wiebes, J.T. 1966. Bornean fig wasps from *Ficus stupenda* Miquel (Hymenoptera, Chalcidoidea). *Tijds. Ent.* 109: 163-192.

Wiebes, J.T. 1967. Redescription of Sycophaginae from Ceylon and India, with a description of betotypes, and a world catalogue of Otitesellini (Hymenoptera, Chalcidoidea, Torymidae). *Tijds. Ent.* 110:399-442.

Wiebes, J.T. 1968. Fig wasps from Israeli *Ficus sycomorus* and related East African species (Hymenoptera, Chalcidoidea). 2. Agaonidae (concluded) and Sycophagini. *Zool. Medelingen* 42:307-320.

Wiebes, J.T. 1972. The genus *Alfonsiella* Waterston (Hymenoptera, Chalcidoidea, Agaonidae). *Zool. Medelingen* 47:321-330.

Wilson, E.O. 1971. *The Insect Societies*. Belknap, Harvard Univ. Press, Cambridge.

Woodring, J.P. 1969. Environmental regulation of andropoly-
    morphism in tyroglyphids (Acari). *Proc. Int. Cong.
    Acarology* 2:433-440.
Yarrow, I.H., and W.M. Guichard. 1941. Some rare Hymenoptera
    Aculeata, with two species new to Britain. *Ent. Monthly
    Mag.* 77:2-13.

ADDENDUM

    After this manuscript had been completed, I found that the
existence of "trimorphisms" (i.e., dimorphisms of males) in
fig wasps of southern Brazil had been previously noted by
Fritz Müller in 1886 (*Trans. Ent. Soc. London* 1886:x-xii;
Kosmos (Leipzig) 18:55-62; 19:54-56. Müller found the
phenomenon, then known through only one previous example in
the Old World, in three or perhaps four of the fig wasp
genera of his area and pointed out that correspondingly
several genera previously erected to contain the wingless
types must be dropped. Some of my species are almost certainly congeneric with his. He seems to have said little of the
wingless males' known or possible biology beyond remarking
that it was unreasonable to suppose that wingless males would
consistently be collected from figs where their females--
treated till then as wholly unknown--did not occur. These
observations further attest to the breadth of interest of a
great naturalist. Müller, an esteemed correspondent of
Charles Darwin, is perhaps best known for his concept of
"Müllerian mimicry."

AGONISTIC BEHAVIOR IN *ACHIAS AUSTRALIS*

(DIPTERA, PLATYSTOMATIDAE) AND THE SIGNIFICANCE

OF EYESTALKS

David K. McAlpine

The Australian Museum, Sydney

INTRODUCTION

Flies in which the head capsule is laterally extended to form peduncles supporting the eyes at their extremities are known in at least eight families of Diptera, viz., Diopsidae, Drosophilidae, Micropezidae, Otitidae, Periscelididae, Platystomatidae, Richardiidae, Tephritidae. In each of these families the stalk-eyed condition has evolved independently, and in Platystomatidae it has evolved more than once. In Diopsidae the condition occurs in most representatives of the family, but in the other families it is of restricted occurrence and may be limited to the males. In the platystomatid genus *Achias* F. (about 70 species in New Guinea and Queensland), the stalk-eyed condition is restricted to males of certain species. *Achias australis* Malloch, 1939, and *A. kurandanus* Hennig, 1940 (= *A. brachyophthalmus* of Malloch, not Walker), are species which occur sympatrically in northern Queensland from the Tully River to the Daintree River. The range of the former species also extends southwards to the vicinity of Paluma on the Seaview Range. In *A. australis* the eyes of the male are stalked, though occasionally the stalks are very short. In *A. kurandanus* the male has the eyes on lateral cephalic tubercles of variable size, or in a few large individuals the tubercles are sufficiently elongate to be termed stalks.

In view of what has been observed or surmised to be the function of head modifications in males of some other Diptera (see McAlpine, 1975), an attempt has been made to observe agonistic behavior among males of these two species in the hope of obtaining data on the function of eyestalks. Useful results were achieved only for *A. australis*.

221

MATERIAL AND METHODS

Adults of *Achias australis* and *A. kurandanus* were observed
and collected at intervals over a long period commencing in
December 1958 in a small area of riverine forest between the
Gillies Highway and the Mulgrave River, approximately 6 km
west of Gordonvale. These species were also observed occasionally at other localities within their range.

In late December 1966 and early January 1967, G.A. Holloway
and the author attempted to collect a series of males of *A.
australis* at the above-mentioned locality without bias to size
or development of eyestalks. This was done by scanning tree
trunks for flies and always attempting to capture the first
individual seen if more than one was in view at the same time.
The main limitation on the randomness of this sample is that
individuals resting elsewhere than on tree trunks were not
collected. The resulting sample of males has been used as the
basis of measurements discussed below. This sample has also
been reported on by Shillito (1971), who was unable to distinguish smaller males from females and who, through misunderstanding a conversation with the author, gave a misleading
evaluation of the randomness of the sample.

In January 1976 the author made field observations on this
population. Attempts to observe agonistic behavior of males
were unsuccessful for the following reasons: the population
level appeared lower than in previous years; it was difficult
standing in mud to maintain the necessary stillness to observe
individuals for long periods without disturbing them; mosqui-
toes were very numerous. A number of flies were then captured
(9 ♂♂ of *A. australis*, 12 ♂♂ and 2 ♀♀ of *A. kurandanus*) and
placed in a nylon cage. These were given water and a mixture
of sucrose and milk, though black molasses and milk would
probably have been more satisfactory. The cage was suspended
from a curtain rod at the window of a hotel room. Though the
specimens of *A. kurandanus* died within about 24 hr., most
of those of *A. australis* survived for several days, enabling
numerous observations of agonistic behavior.

OUTLINE OF ADULT HABITS

Adult males of *Achias australis* occur on trunks of various
tree species in closed-canopy riverine forest and are most
numerous in this situation during early afternoon. Though
sometimes more than one male can be seen on a tree trunk at
the same time, they are not gregarious. These habits differ
from those of *A. kurandanus* in the same forest in that the
latter species shows a marked preference for resting on trunks
of *Ficus* sp. and may sometimes occur in aggregations of up to

about 50 individuals, which tend to disperse when approached. Adults (principally ♂♂ observed) of *A. australis* are somewhat wary and difficult to approach, but those of *A. kurandanus* are much more so.

Both *A. australis* and *A. kurandanus* consistently rest in the shade, often in quite deep shade. When movement of the canopy foliage or of the sun causes shafts of sunlight to rest on them, they become agitated and move about until again attaining a shaded position. Very few females of these species are seen on tree trunks. Copulating pairs of *A. australis* are sometimes seen on the trunks. Females of *A. australis* and *A. kurandanus* can sometimes be found on the lower surfaces of leaves of young trees, a situation in which detection is relatively difficult. It is surmised that males, when not on the trunks, also rest on foliage.

A possible explanation for this distribution of the sexes follows: Copulation (at least in *A. australis*) takes place on tree trunks during the afternoon, and during this time males wait on the trunks for receptive females. The females only visit the trunks when ready to copulate. As males can presumably copulate effectively at frequent intervals, their numbers on the trunks will be much greater than those of females, which need copulate only occasionally (perhaps, as in some other Diptera, only once in a lifetime) for maximum reproductive activity.

As in several other platystomatid genera, adults of *Achias australis* and *A. kurandanus* are sometimes attracted to human feces for feeding.

Courtship and mating of *Achias* were not observed in detail in the field, as the flies became disturbed by the proximity of the observer. Oviposition has not been observed, and the early stages of *Achias* are unknown.

AGONISTIC BEHAVIOR OF CAGED ADULTS

Frequently, when one male of *Achias australis* encounters or is approached by another, it beats at the nearest part of the other with its front legs. Attacks are often accompanied by a little forward lunge of less than 1 cm. The front legs are the principal and almost sole weapons of combat (as in some *Euprosopia* spp.). The ventral spines on the fore femur subserve this function as explained below.

Face-to-face encounters between ♂♂ proceed generally as follows: The combatants approach, making initial contact with sparring movements of the forelegs. The wings are spread widely and facial regions of heads and the proboscides make mutual contact, while the anterior parts of the body are raised a little from the substrate. The eyes and eyestalks

do not make contact, but the eyes come exceedingly close
together (as in Fig. 3), especially if the heads of the combatants are of nearly equal width. The movements of the
forelegs now change to grabbing movements at the opponent's
forelegs, which, if successful, enable one fly to grip a
foreleg of the other between the spinose femur and firmly
flexed tibia. It is not clear what pressure or torque is
applied to the opponent when thus gripped, but it generally
struggles loose and retreats immediately. The whole battle
generally lasts no longer than 5 or 6 sec.

At any stage during the above proceedings, one fly may
retreat by walking or flying out of range. Sometimes both
combatants may simply stop fighting at the initial sparring
stage. Sometimes both retreat at any stage of the combat.

As most of the flies observed were of somewhat similar
head width, it was difficult to determine through the nylon
mesh if the wider-headed individual tended to win, but on a
few occasions this appeared to be so. The one individual
that was markedly smaller, with markedly narrower head, was
not seen in combat, apparently avoiding the larger individuals
as much as possible.

While under observation in the cage, one large male took
up a position at the summit of a fold of fabric which it
defended from all comers for ca 45 min., striking with the
front legs at the nearest part of intruders of its own species
or *A. kurandanus*. This is the only observation made which
indicates that the agonistic behavior involves defense of a
territory. However, it may be taken as confirming suspicions
arising from knowledge of similar behavior in other Diptera
and of the habits of this species that fighting is directed
towards gaining and holding courtship territory.

VARIATION IN DIMENSIONS

Adults of *Achias australis* show great variation in size.
Measurements for length of thorax (a significant index to
overall size for dried flies) give a range of 3.8-6.4 mm. In
view of the fact that the smaller individuals are apparently
more slender than large ones, this means that the former have
less than 21% the bulk of the latter. Size variation of a
similar order has been observed in other platystomatid flies,
particularly in species of *Brea, Duomyia, Euprosopia, Lampro-
gaster, Loxoneuroides,* and *Peltacanthina.*

Study of size distribution in *A. australis* (see Fig. 1)
shows that there are a greater number of individuals near the
maximum size for the sample than near the minimum. In fact,
the smallest size categories include very few individuals and
form a "tail" in the histogram.

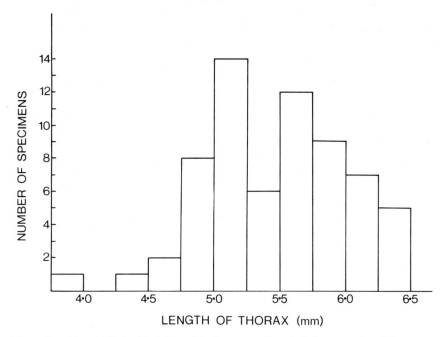

Fig. 1. Size distribution histogram for Achias australis *based on length of thorax.*

These facts seem to indicate that a normally compact size range is extended in its lower limit by highly variable factors which operate only on a part of the populations and produce more extreme effects on only a small percentage of insects. I suggest that these factors, which reduce the size of some individuals, are the nature and availability of larval food. Larval nutrition is known to affect adult size in some species of *Musca* (see, for example, Hughes et al., 1972) and of *Scatophaga* (Borgia, this volume).

Head width in male *Achias australis* (and apparently in numerous other species of *Achias*) provides an example of male heterogony, for, though largely a function of size of the rest of the insect in a variable series of specimens, it is not in simple proportion to size. (See Huxley [1932] for other examples and discussion.) In such cases, the power (k) to which the size of the insect (x) must be raised in order to make it proportional to the size of the heterogonic organ (y) is greater than unity. Head width has been chosen here as a convenient dimension to demonstrate heterogony as it is readily defined and measured. However this dimension is the sum of several elements (dimensions of eyes, head capsule, eyestalks), only one of which is markedly heterogonic, viz., the length of the eyestalk. This dimension has proved too

indefinite for accurate measurement but clearly is the component most responsible for the heterogonic measurements of
head width. The largest male of the series studied has a
head 3.4 times as wide as that of the smallest, but the
eyestalk is approximately 13 times as long.

     Head width, when compared with length of thorax, gives a
fairly constant value for growth-partition coefficient of
k = 2.4, as shown by the slope of the curve in Fig. 2. The
value of k does not noticeably diminish for individuals in the
largest size categories as it does for heterogonic organs in
certain male Coleoptera (Huxley, 1932). Perhaps the reason
for this is indicated in the size-distribution histogram
(Fig. 1), which shows a fairly definite upper size limit.
The absence of a "tail" at this limit for the sample could
indicate that no individuals extend into the size category
where limitations of "raw material" for eyestalks in the pupa
have reduced the value of k.

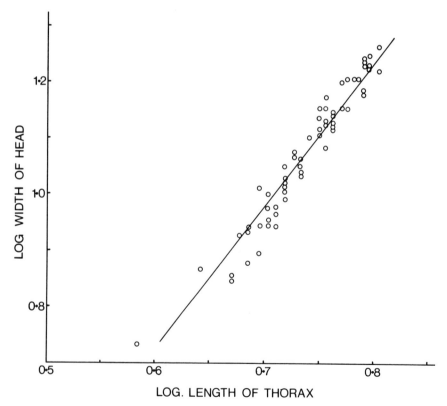

Fig. 2. Logarithmic graph, head width against length
of thorax, for Achias australis. Growth-partition
coefficient given by slope of curve, k = 2.4.

FUNCTIONAL SIGNIFICANCE OF EYESTALKS

Despite reservations expressed by several authors (e.g., Robson and Richards, 1936; Arrow, 1951), the writer considers it reasonable to expect that secondary sexual structures of animals have a positive functional value and have been produced and maintained by some form of natural selection. Natural selection as a general causative factor in evolution is now a matter of mathematical certainty even though, like some definite integrals, it is hard to express quantitatively. One therefore no longer recognizes "apparently useless characters," but rather characters or structural modifications *of unknown function*. Investigation of function of these modifications is a valid pursuit and is one of the aims of the present study. I have previously recorded or suggested the function of some secondary sexual structures in acalyptrate flies (McAlpine, 1973, 1975, 1976).

Arrow (1951) offers explanations of the development of male secondary sexual adornments (in particular of enlarged mandibles and horns in Coleoptera) which are in large part outside of natural selection. He argues, from allometry in the development of horns among individuals of a species and among species of a genus, that "a gradual increase of body-size has automatically entailed a less gradual increase in the horns." He regards the horns themselves as very often functionless and considers that "not use but disuse appears to have determined the first inception of such structures..." He further suggests that "because a process [of evolution] is long continued it is not easily discontinued." Arrow's explanations are unacceptable not only because there is no known mechanism for how such factors could act, but because there are positive reasons why gross structural adornments which serve no function must be selected against, as fitness depends on the economical use of available resources.

Arrow has raised as an objection to the functional importance of male secondary sexual adornments the great degree of (heterogonic) variation in their development. However, if it is assumed that for males of *Achias australis* greater head width confers some advantage in mating frequency on its possessor, the advantages of the heterogonic variation descriscribed above are explicable as follows: When a larval food supply becomes exhausted or unsatisfactory, underfed larvae may either perish or survive to become small adults. Survival may depend on economic use of larval materials needed to form the adult body. Selection favors individuals which can make most economic use of available materials when starved, e.g., by reduction of such luxury items as eyestalks. Clearly survival of the genotype is better ensured by production of adult males with some disadvantage in mating ability than by failure of males to survive at all because of inability to make the best use of resources. Hence it is only a selective advantage for males to have long eyestalks when there are adequate food resources. A similar argument could perhaps be applied to heterogonic mandibles and horns in Coleoptera.

A further cause of heterogony may occur in those male insects in which the heterogonous organ is physically used in fighting other males, e.g., certain Coleoptera and the platystomatid *Pogonortalis doclea* Walker (McAlpine, 1975), but not in *Achias australis* if my interpretation, given below, is correct. As strength is a function of size, the smaller individuals have a disadvantage in fighting and can less often (very rarely in the smallest individuals) make effective use of agonistic structures. Hence selection has operated for ability to reduce size of these structures when overall size is small (from whatever cause).

Arrow has pointed out (to support his argument that size in itself is the cause of heterogonic outgrowths) that the larger species within the one genus are often those with the best developed male modifications. This also seems to be the case in the genus *Achias,* although not every species can be placed accurately in a size sequence from eyestalk development. The largest species, *A. rothschildi* Austen, has the greatest relative development of the eyestalks, with a head width of up to 34 mm. Contrary to Arrow's view, it may be more logical to look for a common cause for both great overall size in an insect species and heterogonic enlargement of a male structure rather than to regard one phenomenon as the cause of the other. If male agonistic behavior is of great importance in a species, larger (and consequently stronger) individuals could have an advantage over smaller ones, and evolutionary pressures could increase average size for the whole species. Heterogonic structures concerned in fighting in the species could also become enlarged simultaneously from the agonistic advantages which this enlargement confers on individuals. In *Achias kurandanus* (a smaller species than *A. australis* with little development of eyestalks), it might be inferred that agonistic behavior is less important from the fact that males are at least on some occasions gregarious. A further Australian *Achias* species (near, but distinct from *A. thoracalis* Hendel) has eyestalks which may be as long as those of *A. australis* and is of solitary habits so far as known.

It has been inferred above that greater length of eyestalk confers some advantage in mating upon male *Achias*. Such inference seems reasonable in view of the known function of other secondary sexual modifications of platystomatids and other flies. The full mating sequence of *Achias* has not yet been observed, but in brief observations of pairs in copula no evidence as to the function of eyestalks was found.

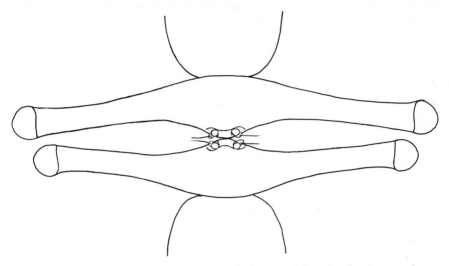

Fig. 3. Diagram of relative positions of heads in two males of Achias australis *fighting with facial regions in contact.*

Furthermore, the agonistic behavior of *Achias australis* involves no direct contact of eyestalks or eyes between the combatants. A feature of agonistic behavior does suggest a function of eyestalks. When a pair of males fight with heads pressed together, the opportunity for each to gauge visually the head width of its opponent with remarkable accuracy is presented. As the heads are placed with facial regions together, the median lines of the head coincide, and the relative position of the eyes then indicates whether the one fly has a wider or narrower head than the other (Fig. 3). As the eyestalks lie extremely close to those of the other individual of the opposed pair, each fly can presumably see readily whether the eyes of its opponent lie mesad, laterad, or exactly opposite to its own eyes. As head width is a function of overall size, and thus of strength, the ability of an individual to react to differences in head width would be advantageous as it could determine the probable outcome of the struggle without risk of physical injury. Under these circumstances superiority in head width could itself confer the advantage to its possessor of a higher probability of victory prior to engaging in a possibly injurious struggle.

The following hypothesis is advanced to explain evolution of stalked eyes in male *Achias*: Broadened heads evolved in males of several platystomatid lineages as a simple adaptation to fighting with the facial regions appressed. In these evolving populations there was variation in male head width and larger, stronger flies tended to have the broadest heads.

The ability of a fly to compare its own head width with that of an opponent, being a selective advantage, became an attribute of the population. Thus, superiority in head width conferred not only a physical advantage but also a psychological advantage in fighting. In an early form of the *Achias* lineage, selection on the basis of psychological agonistic advantage favored lateral extension of the head capsule beyond the requirements of physical fighting, resulting in the stalk-eyed condition.

ACKNOWLEDGEMENTS

I am indebted to Miss M.A. Schneider for assistance during the preparation of this chapter and to Mr. G.A. Holloway for assistance in the field. This work has been aided by a grant from the Australian Research Grants Committee.

REFERENCES

Arrow, G.J. 1951. *Horned Beetles, a Study of the Fantastic in Nature*. Dr. W. Junk, The Hague.

Hennig, W. 1940. Aussereuropäische Psiliden und Platystomiden im Deutschen Entomologischen Institut (Diptera). *Arb. Morph. Taxon. Ent.* 7:304-318.

Hughes, R.D., P.M. Greenham, M. Tyndale-Biscoe, and J.M. Walker. 1972. A synopsis of observations on the biology of the Australian Bushfly (*Musca vetustissima* Walker). *J. Aust. Ent. Soc.* 11:311-331.

Huxley, J.S. 1932. *Problems of Relative Growth*. Methuen, London.

Malloch, J.R. 1939. The Diptera of the Territory of New Guinea. VII. Family Otitidae (Ortalidae). *Proc. Linn. Soc. N.S.W.* 64:97-154.

McAlpine, D.K. 1973. Observations on sexual behaviour in some Australian Platystomatidae (Diptera, Schizophora). *Rec. Aust. Mus.* 29:1-10.

McAlpine, D.K. 1975. Combat between males of *Pogonortalis doclea* (Diptera, Platystomatidae) and its relation to structural modification. *Aust. Ent. Mag.* 2:104-107.

McAlpine, D.K. 1976. Spiral vibrissae in some clusiid flies (Diptera, Schizophora). *Aust. Ent. Mag.* 3:75-78.

Robson, G.C., and O.W. Richards. 1936. *The Variation of Animals in Nature*. Longmans Green, London.

Shillito, J.F. 1971. Dimorphism in flies with stalked eyes. *Zool. J. Linn. Soc. London* 50:296-305.

THE FUNCTION OF HORNS IN *PODISCHNUS AGENOR* (DYNASTINAE)

AND OTHER BEETLES

William G. Eberhard

*Universidad del Valle and
Smithsonian Tropical Research Institute*

If we could imagine a male *Chalcosoma* . . . , with its
polished bronzed coat of mail, and its vast complex horns,
magnified to the size of a horse, or even of a dog, it
would be one of the most imposing animals in the world
(Darwin, 1871).

The bizarre, beautiful, and astonishingly varied shapes of
beetle horns have long intrigued zoologists. The horns,
usually restricted to males, are found in a number of unrelated families (e.g., Arrow, 1951). Perhaps because many of
the horned species are tropical, surprisingly few studies of
the beetles have been made in their natural habitats. Consequently, most of the discussions of horn function have been
speculations based on the study of dead specimens.
The most prominent hypotheses are these:

1. horns serve as male adornments used by females to choose
between potential mates (classical sexual selection:
Darwin, 1871);

2. horns function to protect the beetles against predators
(Wallace in Arrow, 1951);

3. horns, while originally developed to carry refuse from
burrows, have subsequently become adapted for fighting
(Lameere, 1904, in Arrow, 1951; Beebe, 1944, 1947);

4. horns serve to dig, perforate, or lacerate plants,
permitting the beetle to feed on the plant or its sap
(e.g., Smyth, 1920, for *Strategus barbigerus*; Walcott,
1948, for *S. quadrifoveatus*; and Doane, 1913, for *Oryctes
rhinoceros*);

5. horns are in general functionless, selectively neutral
characters; since their increased development is linked
with increased body size, they are an incidental result
of selection for larger size (Arrow, 1951).

Some of these hypotheses seem untenable on logical grounds.
Females are unlikely to be able to sense males' adornment in
many natural situations where there is no light (Arrow, 1951);
females would seem to need predator defense as well as males
(Arrow, 1951); and the dedication of such relatively large
amounts of body material to horns seems unlikely to be a
selectively neutral character. But they cannot be definitive-
ly rejected or accepted without observations of the behavior
of live beetles. This chapter describes such observations
made on eight different species in and near Cali, Colombia.
In at least seven of the eight, it appears that the horns
function as weapons in battles with conspecifics.

The objective of the observations was to see if the beetles
behaved in ways which suggested specific functions for their
horns. The criteria used to decide on a particular function
were these:

1. the behavior which involved use of the horns was performed in more or less natural conditions;

2. the behavior was relatively stereotyped and was seen
repeatedly;

3. the successful execution of the behavior was biological-
ly important;

4. the horns' form matched the hypothesized function, so
that their mechanical properties were particularly suitable
for the effective realization of the function.

If other behaviors observed in the same context were consistent with the apparent purpose of the horns, this was taken
as a confirmation of the biological significance of the horn
function.

The descriptions below are summaries of more extensive
observations which will be presented elsewhere. In several
species, small individuals have reduced horns, and unless
otherwise noted, all descriptions refer to the behavior of
large individuals with well-developed horns.

Podischnus agenor (Oliv.) (Dynastinae)

Large males of this species have a long, thin, slightly
curved head horn which projects dorsally and a thick prothoracic horn with a crescent-shaped tip projecting anteriorly
(Fig. 1). Small males have reduced horns and females do not
have horns. This species ranges through Central America and
northern South America (Blackwelder, 1944), where it is
locally common in sugar cane and corn fields (Ritcher, 1958;
Guagliumi, 1962; T. Jaramillo and D. Rizo, pers. comm.).

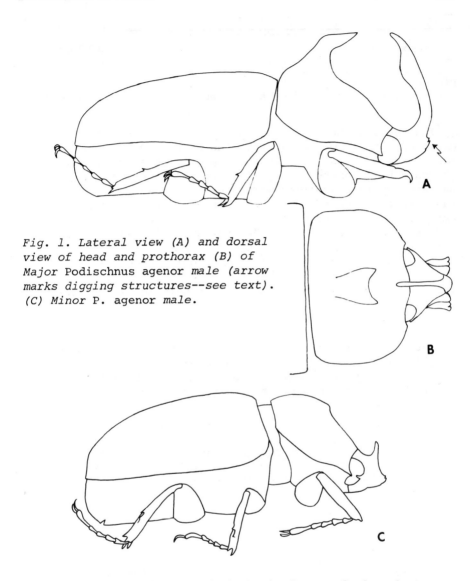

Fig. 1. Lateral view (A) and dorsal view of head and prothorax (B) of Major Podischnus agenor male (arrow marks digging structures--see text). (C) Minor P. agenor male.

Eggs are laid in the ground where the larvae feed on humus and develop to maturity. The adults are relatively seasonal, emerging in the Cauca Valley near Cali principally during the rainy season. The adults dig burrows in sugar cane stalks (Fig. 2), the tunnel being just wide enough to permit the passage of the beetle's body. Solitary individuals of both sexes as well as pairs (almost always a male and a female) occur in the tunnels. When with a male, the female is almost always facing upward and is above the male, farthest from the mouth of the burrow.

Fig. 2. *Typical form of* P. agenor *burrow in a sugar cane stalk.*

The beetles' burrowing technique in sugar cane was closely observed, and it was clear that the horns did not function in this process. Instead, the small prominences on the head near the mandibles (arrow in Fig. 1A) and the anterior and lateral surfaces of the mandibles were used (as shown in Fig. 3) to rasp small pieces of cane free. The prominences and the anterior part of the closed mandibles engaged the cane first, and then both the head and the prothorax were flexed upward while the entire body was thrust forward. As the head moved upward, the mandibles were opened, and the cane was thus simultaneously cut and shredded. A small piece of cane came loose with a snap, and the beetle jerked slightly forward as his head and prothorax snapped upward. He then lowered his head again to repeat the process. Females dug in an identical manner.

Both sexes also burrowed readily in the ground, and their digging technique was observed in cages formed by glass plates with earth between. Again the horns played no part. Most of the work was performed by the front legs. Using the tibiae,

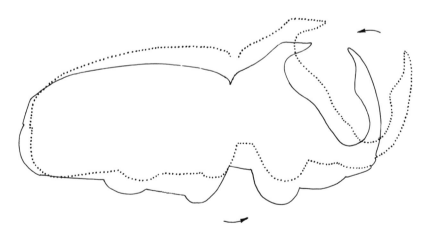

Fig. 3. *Digging movement of* P. agenor *in sugar cane stalk.*
The beetle first lowers his head and arches at his prothoracic-mesothoracic junction (dotted lines), then faces the head up and the prothorax down (solid lines and arrows). The slight forward movement imparted by the legs and the straightening of the body are not shown.

several scoops of earth from just in front and below the
animal were scraped back under the prothoracic-mesothoracic
joint, and then the accumulated loose earth was passed back
by the middle and hind legs to be deposited behind the beetle.
The beetle then moved forward, flexed its head and prothorax
dorsally so they pressed tightly against the roof of the
cavity, and began scooping earth again with the front legs.
There was no difference in the behavior of males and females.

Males brought into captivity in their burrows often emerged
partway from the entrance at night and produced a pungent odor
similar to that of musty apples (Fig. 4). On the basis of
studies of the movements of marked beetles to and from burrows
in the field, the sequence of activities in Fig. 5 seems typical for the species. The male initiates the burrow and then
probably uses his odor to attract a female. She sometimes
mates upon arrival, and sometimes she is later allowed to enter
the burrow to feed at the upper end. On numerous occasions,
a male which had been found and marked in a given burrow had
been replaced by another male when the burrow was revisited,
suggesting that males may also be attracted to and fight for
the possession of burrows.

The possibility of fighting was tested by placing pairs of
males in burrows carved in cane stalks and covered with

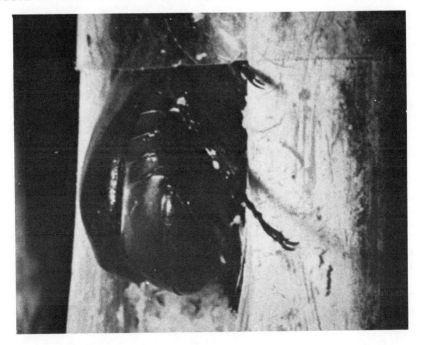

Fig. 4. Male P. agenor *releasing odor at the entrance to an
artificial burrow.*

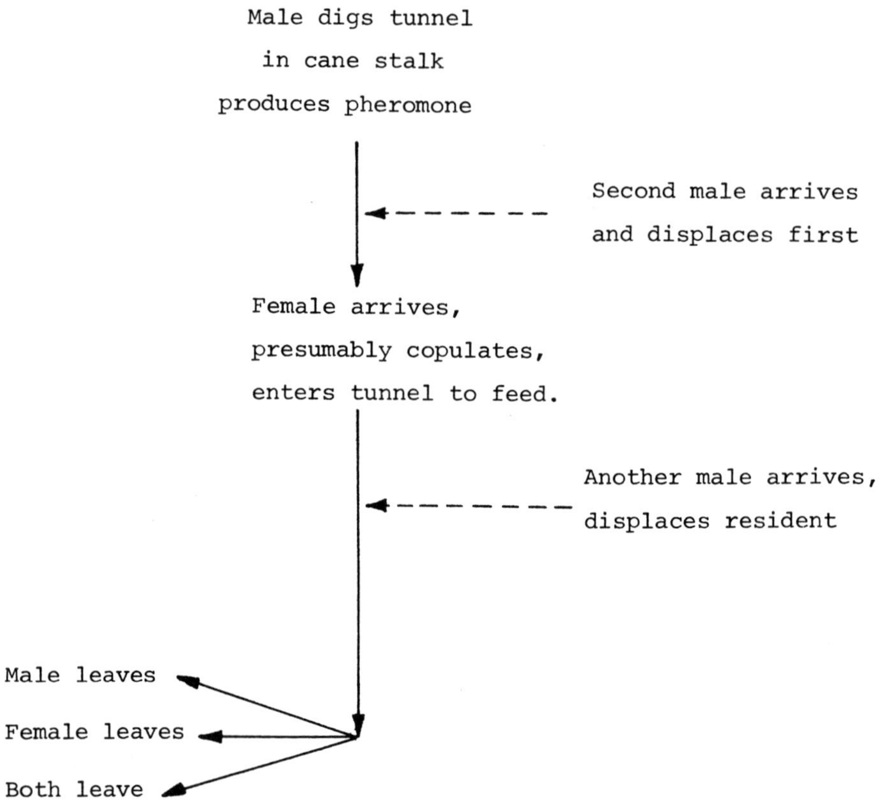

Male digs tunnel

in cane stalk

produces pheromone

Second male arrives

and displaces first

Female arrives,

presumably copulates,

enters tunnel to feed.

Another male arrives,

displaces resident

Male leaves

Female leaves

Both leave

Fig. 5. Common sequence of activities associated with burrows in sugar cane by P. agenor.

clear plastic to permit observation of activities inside (Fig. 6). One male (the resident) was allowed to stay at least 12 hr. undisturbed in the burrow, where he usually fed at the upper end, or, at night, emitted an odor at the entrance. Then the other male (the invader), which had been kept alone in a small jar with a piece of sugar cane to feed on, was placed at the entrance. As expected, the beetles did fight, using complex and somewhat stereotyped behavior in attempts to dislodge each other from the cane stalk. Fighting sequences were variable, but two basic patterns were apparent.

Head-to-Head Combat

My introduction of the intruder into the entrance usually caused the resident to climb part way up the tunnel, and the

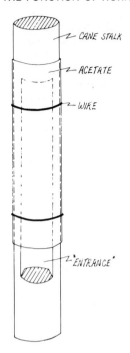

*Fig. 6. (left)
Artificial burrow
used to observe
fights of* P. agenor.

*Fig. 7. (right)
Males of* P. agenor
*pushing each other
inside an artificial
burrow (drawn from
a photograph). The
upper beetle (resident)
braces his body across
the tunnel to block it;
the invader lowers his
head, but not enough
to get the horn under
the resident's abdomen.*

intruder moved on into the tunnel until he was completely
inside. When the beetles came into contact, they both began
to push each other and/or to brace themselves tightly against
the tunnel wall. The head horn and often the prothoracic
horn of the intruder were against the rear of the resident
(Fig. 7). This pushing stage lasted from 2 to more than 15
min., with the beetles moving up and down inside the tunnel
and periodically resting. The position of the invader with
respect to the resident was variable, and both his head and
thoracic horns made contact and failed to make contact with
the elytra and abdomen of the resident in a variety of ways.
Since conditions #2 and #4 for establishing an evolved
function were not fulfilled (#2 there was no stereotyped use
of the horns during pushing, and #4 their forms did not appear
especially effective), it was concluded that they are not
adaptations for fighting inside burrows.

When the beetles were of about equal size, it appeared
that the intruder consistently pushed harder than the resident. This difference is probably due to the beetles being
built to develop more power moving forward than backward, as
is clear, for example, from the positioning of their legs and
spines (Fig. 1A).

After a variable length of time, the beetles finally moved

down the tunnel to the entrance. Usually I could not tell whether the resident forced the invader downward or whether it was the invader who allowed the resident to descend, but, in a few cases in which the resident was old and sluggish, it was evident that it was the invader who initiated the final descent. By the time they arrived at the mouth of the burrow, the beetles had almost always assumed standard positions--the resident with his ventral surface toward the open side of the burrow entrance and the invader with his dorsum toward the same side (Fig. 8A). The only exceptions occurred when the resident was much smaller than the intruder and, probably as a result of having sensed the latter's superior strength during the pushing inside the tunnel, simply left without attempting to defend the burrow.

When they reached the entrance, the invader backed part way out of the burrow, allowing the resident to swing his abdomen upward and turn himself part way around (Fig. 8B). While in this position, the resident male kept his head flexed

Fig. 8. Behavior associated with the resident's turn in the entrance. (A) Positions of the males as they back down the tunnel just prior to the turn by the resident. (B) Resident male (above) halfway through his turn. At this stage the invader can repeatedly "punish" the resident.

ventrally so that the horn blocked the tunnel, but he had
very little purchase on the walls of the burrow with his legs.
The invader, meanwhile, remained firmly ensconced in the
entrance, and he frequently "punished" the resident by repeatedly driving upward into the tunnel. The curved tip of
his prothoracic horn fit snugly against the resident's dorsal
surface and often caught in the prothoracic-mesothoracic
joint as he pushed upward, forcing the resident's anterior
end part way back into the tunnel.

Gradually, after. administering a variable amount of punishment, the intruder backed farther and farther out of the
entrance, allowing the resident to complete his turn, assume
a downward-facing stance, and begin the final fight. This
was a critical time since the invader had to retreat enough
to allow the resident to turn. The footing outside the
entrance was much more difficult, and to retreat too far meant
having poor purchase in the test of strength which was to
follow.

The definitive fight, which was usually much shorter than
the preliminaries, began when the resident had completed his
turn (Fig. 9). Each beetle attempted to "clamp" the other by
getting his head horn under the other's head and prothorax

*Fig. 9. A head-to-head fight in cutaway view. The resident
beetle (above) has clamped the invader and is beginning to
lift him. The invader clutches at the shredded cane to avoid
being dropped free.*

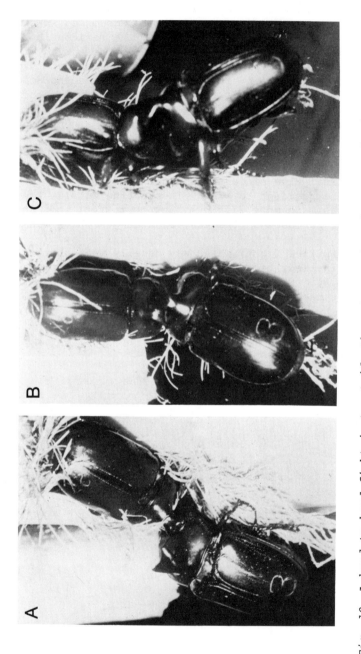

Fig. 10. A head-to-head fight just outside the entrance to a burrow. The invader (#3) shifts from side to side (A and B), attempting to get his head horn under the resident's lowered prothorax, but fails and is clamped and lifted (C). Shortly after photograph C was taken, the resident dropped the invader.

and then, by flexing his head dorsally, to clamp his opponent
with his head and prothoracic horns. Sometimes the beetles
engaged each other tentatively several times before achieving
a clamp hold. Often both succeeded in clamping simultaneously,
but soon one predominated (perhaps by squeezing harder or
having better footing on the cane) and the other released his
hold (Figs. 9 and 10). The beetle with the clamp hold then
lifted his opponent away from the cane stalk by extending his
legs (Fig. 10C), and, after holding him there for a moment,
released his hold. Usually the result of the lifting was that
the losing beetle lost his foothold, and he thus fell to the
ground when released. Typically the winner then stridulated
vigorously by scraping the tips of his elytra with the dorsal
surface of his abdomen. On a few occasions the lifted beetle
kept his foothold and did not fall free when released, but
returned to do battle with his opponent (and occasionally won
the rematch). In fights observed in natural burrows, which
had accumulations of frayed cane around the burrow entrance
(Fig. 9), beetles which had been lifted and dropped were more
often able to retain a foothold and avoid falling. Another
less common variant was for the intruder to back down below
the entrance after the resident made his turn, and when the
resident followed him down to attempt a clamp, to try to
scramble around the resident and into the vacated entrance.

Neither residents nor invaders were consistent winners,
and the results were variable even in rematches between the
same individuals in the same situation. The only clear tendency was for beetles substantially larger than their opponents to win.

Blocking the Entrance

Sometimes the resident did not move up into the tunnel
when the intruder was introduced but, instead, remained in
the entrance facing upward and blocking the hole with his
dorsum. The invader's response to this was to attempt to
insert his head horn at the resident's side, get it under
him, clamp him and lift him from the hole (the resident seemed
to be able to offer little resistance), and drop him to the
ground. When the invader could not get his horn in under one
side of the resident, he sometimes moved across the resident's
back to attempt to insert it under the other side. The
resident had two responses to these attacks. As the invader
climbed across his back, the resident extended his legs and
held his body away from the cane, a movement which more or
less broke the invader's contact with the cane stalk and
which in several cases caused him to fall. When the invader
did attempt to introduce his horn at the side, the resident
leaned toward that side, reducing the space between his body

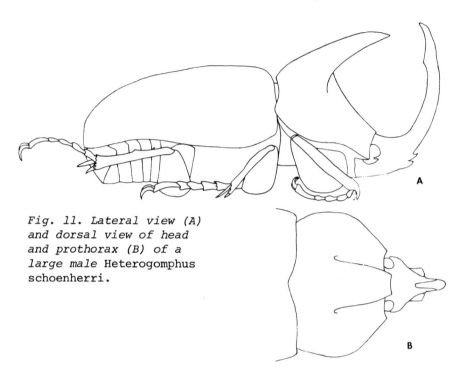

Fig. 11. Lateral view (A)
and dorsal view of head
and prothorax (B) of a
large male Heterogomphus
schoenherri.

and the side of the tunnel. He also tilted his body so that
his dorsum was toward the intruder.

Heterogomphus schoenherri Burm. (Dynastinae)

   Fighting between large males of *H. schoenherri* (Fig. 11)
placed in grooves carved in sugar cane stalks (the natural
habitat of this species is unknown) was similar to that of *P.
agenor* males. If the males were not head to head, they
turned, leaving the head in the groove and swinging the abdomen out and around 180° so as to face each other. Then they
clamped, lifted, and dropped one another just as described
for *P. agenor* (Fig. 12). They also used their head horns to
pry opponents (especially their posterior ends) out of the
groove. They used their heads and mandibles to dig in the
cane with a rasping action similar to that of *P. agenor*. The
major difference between the two species is that *H. schoenherri* has longer horns which can be strongly clamped together
and inflict real mechanical damage. A male *Golofa porteri*
(a species with much weaker elytra), after being kept in the
same container with several *H. schoenherri* males, had damaged
areas which were exactly the same size and shape as the *H.*

Fig. 12. A head-to-head fight between large males of Heterogomphus schoen-herri *in a groove cut in a sugar cane stalk. The upper male has his head horn under the other's prothorax and front leg, and is clamping him and lifting him out of the groove.*

schoenherri prothoracic horns. A similarly shaped hole, this time an apparently mortal wound to the ventral surface of another *H. schoenherri* male, was inflicted by a male which had pinned his victim at the end of a tunnel in a sugar cane stalk.

Ceracis cucullatus (Mellie) (Ciidae)

This species, like the three other ciids that follow, is very small (1 mm long or less) and lives in complex galleries in sporophores of bracket fungi. All species were observed by placing the beetles on small pieces of sporophore in cages formed between two plates of glass and then placing the plates under a microscope. The beetles could thus be observed under relatively natural conditions. Beetles were also observed in narrow tunnels formed by cutting tiny grooves in strips of polypore which were then covered with microscope slides. Both sexes of all four species dug--using only their mandibles--in the polypore and sporophore.

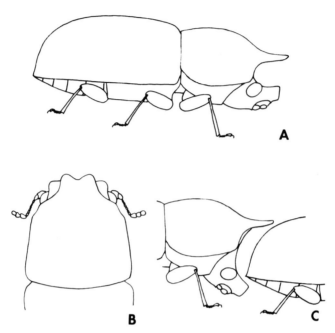

Fig. 13. Lateral view (A) and dorsal view of head and
prothorax (B) of a large male of Ceracis cucullatus (Ciidae)
(C) Curved head and prothoracic plates of a male being used
to push against a conspecific male's abdomen.

Males of *C. cucullatus* have a plate-like forward extension
of the prothorax (Fig. 13A) and plate-like lateral extensions
of the anterior surface of the head (Fig. 13B). When males
interacted aggressively, they usually lowered their heads,
and the combination of the head and prothoracic plates plus
the curved front of the head formed a smooth surface closely
approximating the shape of a conspecific's body (Fig. 13C).
Fights generally involved one animal lowering his head and
pushing the other, engaging his opponent's abdomen more or
less as shown in the drawing. In some cases the head was not
lowered this far and only the upper and lower plates made
contact with the opponent. Head-to-head interactions were
variable, rare, and of low intensity; sometimes the head was
lowered, and sometimes it was kept up so that the two plates
were close together. The pushes were usually "jerky" rather
than steady, and sometimes a male flexed his head upward
briskly several times during a push. Winning individuals
sometimes pinned their adversaries against a tunnel wall for
hours at a time.

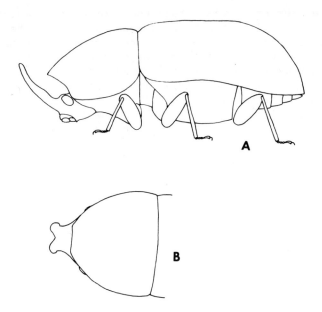

Fig. 14. Lateral view (A) and dorsal view of head and
prothorax (B) of a large male Ceracis sp. near furcifer
(Ciidae).

Ceracis sp. near furcifer (Ciidae)

Males of this species have a single bifurcated head horn
(Fig. 14A) but no projections from the prothorax (Fig. 14B).
Again in this species, a male's first reaction to the presence
of a beetle in front of him was generally to lower his head
so that the horn was directed more or less forward. The
fights which developed differed from those of C. cucullatus
in that there was little sustained pushing, but rather, repeated series of short, quick thrusts or jabs. Both front
and back surfaces of the horn as well as the tip and sometimes
the mandibles made contact with opponents. Victors sometimes
pursued retreating foes for short distances, prodding them
repeatedly under the abdomen with their head horns. During
attacks on the side or rear of another beetle, the horn was
sometimes inserted under the opponent, and in this case the
front edge of the prothorax sometimes made contact during
brief pushes, but otherwise most contact with opponents was
with the head horn.
Head-to-head encounters occasionally resulted in relatively
intense fighting. The males moved back and forth along the

sporophore, thrusting with their head horns like fencers,
pausing occasionally in mutual attempts to insert their horns
under each other. The majority of the contacts seemed to be
with the tips and anterior surfaces of the horns, but the
beetles' movements were very quick and difficult to follow.
On two occasions I saw a male, which seemed to be getting the
worst of an exchange, lean slightly to one side and then flex
his head dorsally so that the fork in the tip of his head
horn engaged the horn of his opponent and pushed it to the
side.

Cis sp. near *tricornis* (Ciidae)

Males of this species have one long head horn projecting
dorsally (Fig. 15A) and a pair of forward-directed thoracic
horns (Fig. 15B). Males attacking other beetles from the
side or rear usually lowered their heads, often inserting
their head horns below their opponents' bodies and moving
forward to bring their thoracic horns into contact. Usually
they performed a series of short thrusts and shoves without
shifting their feet, in contrast to the sustained pushes of
Ceracis cucullatus. In at least some cases, it was possible
to see that the thrusts had an upward component produced by
moving the entire anterior portion of the body upward (rather
than by flexing the head upward as in the dynastines). At
other times they did not lower their heads and used the front
surface of the head horn to push, rub, and hit opponents.

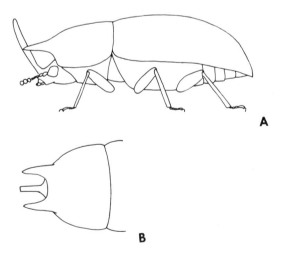

A

B

*Fig. 15. Lateral view (A) and dorsal view of head and
prothorax (B) of a large male* Cis *sp. near* tricornis *(Ciidae).*

   Head-to-head battles between aggressive males resembled
those of *Ceracis* sp. near *furcifer,* with rapid forward and
backward lunges combined with side-to-side movements.   At
times both males thrust repeatedly, their heads lowered and
their prothoracic horns engaging each other's prothoraces.

Cis sp. near *taurus* (Ciidae)

   Males of this species have a pair of large, forward-directed head horns, but lack prothoracic projections (Fig. 16).
The most common type of aggressive movement was for a male
to lower his head, insert his horns under the body of another,
and give a series of quick lifting thrusts.   The beetles did
not engage in sustained pushing and seldom shifted their
footing as they fought, simply rocking forward and back in
one spot.   Both head-to-head and head-to-abdomen interactions
involved similar lifting thrusts.   Only very seldom did I
observe contact between an attacking male's prothorax and his
adversary.

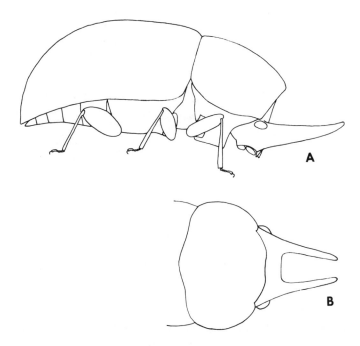

*Fig. 16. Lateral view (A) and dorsal view of head and pro-
thorax (B) of a large male* Cis *sp. near* taurus *(Ciidae).*

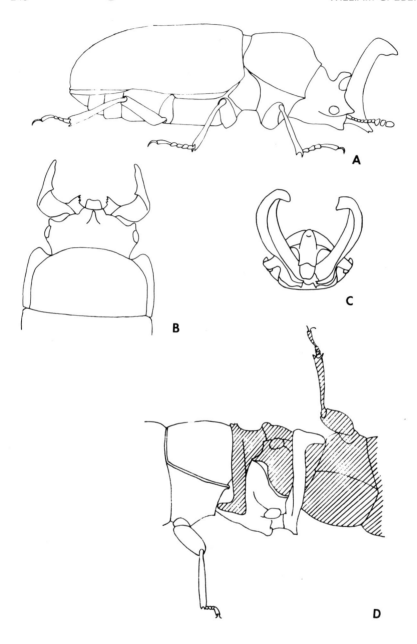

Fig. 17. Lateral view (A), dorsal view of head and prothorax (B), and frontal view of head horns (C) of a Molion sp. near muelleri (Tenebrionidae). (D) Pair of males mutually locked during an aggressive encounter.

Molion sp. near *muelleri* Kirsch (Tenebrionidae)

   This species, found in rotting logs at high altitudes, was
observed in cages made by carving horizontal grooves in a
flat piece of wood and covering them with a glass plate. The
beetles dug the partially rotten wood of their cages by biting
free small pieces with the lower, toothed portion of their
mandibles. There was no suggestion of the horns being used
for this task.
   Both males and females have identical horns, consisting
of long dorsal extensions of the mandibles (Fig. 17B), and
in one population, a short, forward curving horn on the head
(Fig. 17C). The sexes could not be differentiated by visual
inspection. Subsequent dissections suggested that nearly
all the beetles were relatively young and that they had
probably grown up as larvae in the logs in which they were
collected.
   Pairs of beetles were placed in short tunnels facing each
other but separated by a cardboard partition until the
observations began. Aggressive encounters began when one
of the pair of beetles contacted the other. The one being
contacted usually lowered its head to the substrate, while
the other, if aggressive, slowly spun 180° on its longitudinal
axis so that its dorsal surface was against the dorsal surface
of its opponent (Fig. 17D). It then moved forward with its
mandibles open, pushing when its horns came into contact with
the other. As it did so, it opened and closed its mandibles
repeatedly. When pushing forward, its head horn sometimes
made contact with the opponent, hooking its prothoracic-
mesothoracic joint, which apparently aided in the push. In
several cases, one beetle grabbed the other with its mandible
horns, and one drew blood from a pierced intersegmental
membrane. One pair of males collected in nature (by L.
Gonzalez) was mutually locked (Fig. 17D).

Peneta sp. near *muchicornis* Gebien (Tenebrionidae)

   Both males and females of this species have a plate
extending posteriorly from the head to cover the anterior
part of the prothorax (Fig. 18). Again in this species
I could not distinguish males from females without dissecting
them. The beetles were collected in rotting logs and
observed in the same type of cage as *Molion*. They showed
only low levels of aggression, although they did push or nudge
at almost every encounter. They swung their abdomens to place
them in the paths of passing beetles, and leaned so as to
present their dorsal surfaces to beetles which touched them
(both behavior patterns were also seen in *M. muelleri*). They

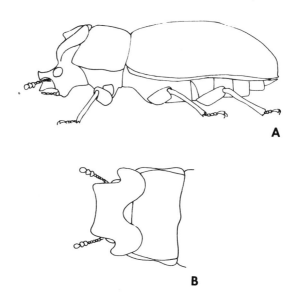

A

B

Fig. 18. Lateral view (A) and dorsal view of head and prothorax (B) of a Peneta *sp. near* muchicornis *(Tenebrionidae).*

also frequently wedged their anterior ends between other beetles and the sides of the tunnels, and then "pried" dorsally, lifting by raising the entire anterior portion of the body and usually keeping the head more or less immobile. In a few cases the head flexed dorsally somewhat during a pry, but in general it had very little mobility.

DISCUSSION

Table 1 summarizes the evidence with regard to the functions of male horns in *P. agenor,* showing that the criteria of functionality are met with respect to there being more than one function for both head and prothoracic horns. The multiplicity of functions is perhaps not surprising, since once a structure has evolved in one selective context, behavior may evolve to make use of it in additional contexts. The functions are all associated with aggression, thus supporting the "weapon" hypothesis (#3) presented in the Introduction. The existence of these functions invalidates the selective neutrality hypothesis (#5). It was also clear that the horns did not function in digging behavior (#4). No observations were made relative to the predator defense hypothesis (#2), but as noted in the Introduction, it seems unlikely on other grounds. The sexual selection hypothesis

TABLE 1

Functions of the horns of P. agenor *which fulfill the
conditions for functionality (see text)*

Structure	Function	Comments
Prothoracic horn	Push resident during his turn at burrow entrance (Fig. 10).	Crescent tip fits curve of resident's dorsum.
	Form one side of clamp used in head-to-head fights to hold opponent while lifting and dropping him (Figs. 11-13).	Crescent tip results in usually two points of prothoracic horn rather than one holding opponent, making for a more secure grip.
Head horn	Block tunnel against invader as resident executes turn at entrance (Fig. 10).	The slight curve and thinness of horn do not seem particularly de-signed for this use.
	Form one side of clamp used in head-to-head fights to hold opponent while lifting and dropping him (Figs. 11-13).	The curve could help hold the opponent in the clamp, and the thinness could ease insertion of the horn under the opponent.
	Pry under a resident which blocks the entrance with his body in order to raise him so he can be clamped, lifted, and dropped.	(same)

(#1) was not tested, although females arriving at males'
burrows in the field showed no obvious signs of attempting
to judge the size of the resident male's horn before entering,
and readily entered burrows inhabited by minor males. On
balance, it seems likely that horns have evolved in this
species for use in intraspecific combat.

The present environment of *P. agenor,* with huge fields of
host plants like sugar cane and corn, is certainly different

from the environment in which the species evolved. Although
relatives of both corn and sugar cane are native to the
neotropics, suitable host plants (presumably thick-stemmed
monocots) must have been less common. The resource over
which the males fight--a burrow in a suitable host--may
thus have been less common formerly, and it is possible that
the competition over burrows in the present day is a non-
adaptive "anachronism" remaining from previous evolutionary
history.

It may seem puzzling that in fights in burrows invading
males do not simply try to lift out resident males instead
of allowing them to make their 180° turns and thus bring
their potentially dangerous horns into play, and also that the
residents consent to come down to the entrance to do battle
at all when they are in an essentially impregnable position
inside the tunnel. The answers are probably these: If the
resident were to stay inside the tunnel, he would continue to
have access to the feeding end of the tunnel, but would be
vulnerable to punishment from the intruder and would not have
access to arriving females. The fact that he invariably
chooses to come down emphasizes the sexual rather than feeding
importance of the burrow for the males. As for the invader's
allowing the resident to turn, he has no other alternative if
he is to remove the resident (apparently important), since he
can only clamp and lift him clear and drop him when the
resident is exposed at the entrance. In backing out enough
to allow the resident to become exposed, the invader necessarily leaves enough room for him to execute his turn. The
readiness of most residents to turn confirms that they usually
fight more effectively when facing their opponents, although
the size relations of the opponents, the position of the
invader (clinging to the shredded cane below the entrance,
or firmly ensconced on top of it after backing out of the
entrance), and the details of the burrow entrance (footing
just outside, size of entrance hole) may also influence the
results.

The behavior of the other seven species, although studied
in less detail, also suggests that their horns function as
weapons in intraspecific combat. The only exception is
Peneta sp., in which this is possible but was not established,
perhaps due to the generally low intensity of the interactions
observed. One might object that the observations of *Heterogomphus schoenherri* were made in unnatural situations, but,
as will be argued elsewhere, their natural habitat may well
be similar to grooves in sugar cane.

It is interesting that six of the eight species used their
head horns and/or heads to lift their opponents away from the
substrate in one way or another. The reason why this should
be common (and thus a reason why forward-projecting head horns

could often be favored) seems simple. If two otherwise equal
individuals are pushing each other, the one which can position
his center of gravity lower (closer to the substrate) than
that of his opponent will have an advantage, since he will be
better able to brace his thrust against the substrate.

Several other observations of beetle horns being used as
weapons in natural situations can be added to those reported
here. Detailed studies of *Chiasognathus grantii* (Lucanidae)
(Joseph, 1928; Ureta, 1934; Hamilton, in this volume), *Diloboderus abderus* (Dynastinae) (Daguerre, 1931), and *Dynastes
hercules* (Dynastinae) (Beebe, 1947) in natural or nearly natural conditions, show that the male horns of all three function
as weapons in male-male combat. Although the *Dynastes* battles
were artificially staged, it is likely that they occur
naturally in similar open situations (see below). (Probably
the most unnatural aspect of the encounters was their
being carried out on a flat surface rather than on something
like tree branches where the victor's dropping his opponent
would be an effective way of ending the interaction.) Other
less complete studies of horned species also suggest that
horns serve as weapons. Beebe (1944) observed male *Megasoma
elephas* and *Strategus alaeus* (both Dynastinae) using their
anterior horns (but not their lateral horns) to turn conspecific males on their backs in battles staged in the open.
Smyth's observations (1920) of *Strategus titanus* and *S.
quadrifoveatus* in the wild indicate that these species live
in burrows rather than in the open; Smyth also notes in passing that *S. titanus* males fight, using their horns "to best
advantage" to send their adversaries rolling. Pace (1967 and
pers. comm.) saw males of *Bolitotherus cornutus* (Tenebrionidae) fight in nature, using their horns to pry rival males
off the backs of females (Fig. 19). Several observers
(Davis, 1833; Kirby and Spence, 1818; Westwood, 1840--all
cited in Darwin, 1871) have seen *Lucanus cervus* (Lucanidae)
males fight using their enlarged mandibles. Ohaus (1900)

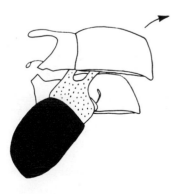

*Fig. 19. Fighting behavior
of* Bolitotherus cornutus
*(Tenebrionidae) drawn from
the notes of Ann E. Pace.
One male, mounted on the
back of a female, is pried
off by a second male.*

observed that in captivity the dynastines *Enema pan*, *Hetero-gomphus achilles*, and *Megasoma typhon* all flexed their heads dorsally so that their head horns tightly pinched offending objects such as fingers or pencils. Howden and Campbell (1974) saw males of *Golofa porteri* in nature using their elongated front legs and their head horns to dislodge con-specific males from apparent feeding sites (but they did not note any use of the long prothoracic horns). Wallace (1869, in Darwin, 1871) saw two males of *Leptorhynchus angustatus* pushing at each other with their elongated rostra near a female, and M. Cooper (pers. comm.) also saw unidentified brenthids hit each other with their heads. E. Sleeper (pers. comm.) observed what appeared to be an aggressive interaction between two male brenthids which had pairs of long horn-like structures projecting posteriorly from their elytra. The males approached each other backward along a tree trunk, and as they closed on one another, made rapid tentative "probing" motions backwards. One then succeeded in using his horns to flip the other off the tree with a quick twist.

Thus, although there are few observations and some are only fragmentary or are from unnatural situations, it is striking that all of the reasonably careful studies of living beetles suggest that horns are used as weapons rather than anything else. In sum, the data suggest that usually beetle horns function in fighting.

Continuing this line of thought, it seems permissible to make one general statement about the ways in which different horn types are probably used. There are two general kinds of situations in which fights may occur--in the open (on the ground, on tree trunks, etc.) or in restricted spaces such as burrows. Very long horns (e.g., *Chiasognathus grantii*, some *Golofa*, *Dynastes hercules*, some lucanids, some brenthids) are probably used in interactions which occur in the open, since long structures would be very difficult to maneuver in closed spaces. The observations in nature of *Chiasognathus*, *Golofa*, and the horned brenthid are in accord with this idea. Shorter horns do not necessarily indicate battles in closed spaces, however, since they are sometimes used in the open (e.g., *Diloboderus*, *Bolitotherus*) and sometimes in tunnels (e.g., the ciids and tenebrionids of this study).

An important problem for the weapon hypothesis, and one which troubled Darwin (1871), still remains. Beetle horns often vary widely between large and small individuals of the same species in both degree of development and shape, and two at least partially distinct morphs ("majors" and "minors") exist in some species (see Otte in this volume). How can one explain with a single function structures which vary so drastically within a single species? There are several possible answers: it is possible that the situation is more

complex, and that the structures are designed so that in
minor males they have one function and in majors another
(Darwin, 1871; Otte, in this volume); a structure may have
multiple functions in majors (as in *Podischnus*) and lose some
or all of these functions in minors (Gadgil, 1972, and
Hamilton, in this volume, discuss how selection could maintain such dimorphisms in a single species); or, as is apparently the case of the ciids of this study, smaller horns may
perform essentially the same functions as large ones, albeit
less effectively. In this last case, continuous gradations
rather than distinct dimorphisms in horn size might be more
likely to evolve. These are speculations, however, and detailed observations of the behavior of both major and minor
males are needed.

Further, as yet incomplete data for *P. agenor* suggest
that the essentially hornless minor males differ from majors
in more than just body and horn size. Small individuals
were relatively more common in some parts of the breeding
season than others, and were less often recaptured after
leaving the burrows where they were first observed. The
second difference suggests greater mobility in the "nonfighting" form, and accords with observations of other dimorphic
species discussed by Hamilton in this volume.

For some beetle species, the question of why they are so
highly evolved to fight is also not yet clearly resolved.
Podischnus, *Diloboderus*, *Bolitotherus*, *Chiasognathus*, *Golofa*,
and *Lucanus* apparently fight over highly localized resources
whose use is limited to one or a few individuals. *Lucanus
cervus* has been seen fighting near sap flows, just like *Chiasognathus* (M. Idar, pers. comm.), and would thus also be expected to evolve effective fighting mechanisms. But other
species, such as the ciids and tenebrionids of this study,
utilize resources which, although very localized, are so
large with respect to the beetles' size that it is difficult
to accept the idea that their use is limited to one or a
small number of individuals. It is possible that the burrows
rather than the substrate are for some reason particularly
valuable (attract females, difficult to dig, etc.), but I
could distinguish neither consistent associations between
males and females nor obviously delimited tunnels occupied by
given individuals in either the ciids or the tenebrionids. At
least in the densely populated substrates I inspected, the
tunnel systems were very complex and interconnected. Males
never showed sustained persecution of other males over long
distances such as would be required for monopolization of the
entire substrate. On the contrary, vanquished individuals
were pursued at most only a few body lengths. Another possibility is that the offspring of the first colonizers remain
in the substrate for several generations. This would increase

the substrate's value for the colonist. If the subsequent
generations maturing there tended to inbreed, the relatedness
of the eventual dispersers to the colonist would be increased,
raising the apparent value of the substrate to the colonist
even more. If one or both of these conditions obtain, small
differences in the reproductive contribution of the colonists
could be multiplied into large differences in their genetic
contribution to the next dispersing generation. There appear
to be no data on this point for either the ciids or the tenebrionids.

The reason for the presence of horns in both sexes of the
tenebrionids rather than just in the males is also unclear,
although Hamilton (this volume) has suggested a possible
cause. For all of these points, detailed studies of the
behavior and ecology of these beetles, especially during the
colonization of new substrates, are needed.

One final question arises with regard to the aggressive
function of horns in beetles. If horns are generally effective weapons, why are they so seldom found in other insects?
Selection in other groups should be equally strong in favoring
individuals able to defeat conspecifics in battles over
limited resources. Two factors suggest that in general
beetles are preadapted to develop horns:

1. Compared to many other insects, adult beetles tend to
live in relatively enclosed spaces. Physical contests in
such spaces are less likely to be decided by the contestants' speed or agility than by their brute strength in
pushing matches. In many other insects, agility is possible and has already evolved in other contexts (e.g.,
escape from predators, prey capture), and selection
favoring winners of intraspecific contests will often have
the effect of perfecting already existing systems that
increase agility. Even beetles such as coccinellids,
which do not live in enclosed spaces, but which conserve
the relative slowness and clumsiness of beetles, have been
observed to fight by pushing with their heads (M. Rodriguez,
pers. comm.: males of *Hypodamia convergens* fighting over a
female).

2. Many beetles dig in some sort of substrate, and morphological characteristics associated with digging--short
legs and a thick cuticle--make alternative ways of fighting
such as biting and kicking less effective. At the same
time, the mechanisms evolved for digging are in some cases
easily applied in intraspecific contests of force in which
horns are advantageous. This is well illustrated in the
cases of *Podischnus* and *Heterogomphus* where the forces
used to dig--forward thrust with the legs plus dorsal
flexion of head and prothorax--are the same as those

applied in battles. It is equally true, however, that
this idea does not apply in other cases such as the ciids
of this study, whose digging power, concentrated in the
mouthparts, is little employed in fights.

SUMMARY

The only function for beetle horns which has been confirmed
by detailed observations is that of weapons for use in intraspecific fights. Many horn designs remain to be studied, but
it seems likely that many of these will also be found to
function as weapons. More data are needed to answer outstanding questions about the significance of multiple horn designs
and the selective pressures favoring fighting in some species.
Several factors may have predisposed beetles to evolve horns
more readily than other insects.

ACKNOWLEDGEMENTS

I thank Dr. Mario Carpena of the Ingenio Meléndez for
facilitating work on *Podischnus*. Drs. H. Howden, J. Lawrence,
and T. Spilman kindly identified, respectively, the scarabs,
ciids, and tenebrionids. W. Hamilton called my attention to
ciids as subjects of study of horn function. A. Pace gener-
ously allowed me to use unpublished observations of *Bolitotherus*. W. Bell, M. Breed, M. Cooper, M.J.W. Eberhard, and
M. Litte read and criticized earlier drafts of the manuscript.
This work was supported financially by the Comité de Investi-
gaciones of the Universidad del Valle, and the División de
Ciencias of the Universidad del Valle made possible my
attendance at the International Congress of Entomology in
Washington, D.C.

REFERENCES

Arrow, G.J. 1951. *Horned Beetles*. Dr. W. Junk, The Hague.
Beebe, W. 1944. The function of secondary sexual characters
    in two species of Dynastinae (Coleoptera). *Zoologica*
    29:53-57.
Beebe, W. 1947. Notes on the Hercules Beetle, *Dynastes
    hercules* (Linn.), at Rancho Grande, Venezuela, with special
    reference to combat behavior. *Zoologica* 32:109-116.
Blackwelder, R.E. 1944. Checklist of the coleopterous insects
    of Mexico, Central America, the West Indies, and South

America. Part 2. *Smithson. Inst. U.S. Nat. Mus. Bull.*
185:189-341.

Daguerre, J.B. 1931. Costumbres nupciales del *Diloboderus abderus* Sturm. *Rev. Soc. Ent. Argentina* 3:253-256.

Darwin, C. 1871. The descent of man and selection in relation to sex, *in The origin of species and the descent of man and selection in relation to sex.* Random House, Modern Library, New York.

Doane, R.W. 1913. The rhinoceros beetle (*Oryctes rhinoceros* L.) in Samoa. *J. Econ. Ent.* 6:437-442.

Gadgil, M. 1972. Male dimorphism as a consequence of sexual selection. *Amer. Nat.* 106:574-580.

Guagliumi, P. 1962. Las plagas de la caña de azucar en Venezuela. *Centro Investig. Agron., Maracay Monog. No. 2.* Tomo I:1-482.

Howden, H.F., and J.M. Campbell 1974. Observations on some Scarabaeoidae in the Colombian Sierra Nevada de Santa Marta. *Coleop. Bull.* 28:109-114.

Joseph, C. 1928. El *Chiasognathus grantii* Steph. *Rev. Universitaria (U. Catolica) (Santiago, Chile)* 13:529-535.

Ohaus, F. 1900. Bericht über eine entomologische Reise nach Centralbrasilien. *Stettin Ent. Zeit.* 61:204-245.

Pace, A. 1967. Life history and behavior of a fungus beetle, *Bolitotherus cornutus* (Tenebrionidae). *Occ. Pap. Mus. Zool. Univ. Mich. No. 653:* 1-15.

Ritcher, P.O. 1958. Biology of Scarabaeidae. *Ann. Rev. Ent.* 3:311-334.

Smyth, E.G. 1920. The rhinoceros beetles. *J. Dept. Agr. Puerto Rico* 4:3-29.

Ureta, E. 1934. Sobre algunos costumbres del *Chiasognathus grantii*, Steph. *Rev. Chilena Hist. Nat.* 38:287-292.

Walcott, G.N. 1948 (1951). The insects of Puerto Rico. *J. Agric. Univ. P. R.* 32:1-975.

BEETLE HORNS:

SOME PATTERNS IN FUNCTIONAL MORPHOLOGY

Daniel Otte and Katharine Stayman

The Academy of Natural Sciences of Philadelphia

INTRODUCTION

Sexual selection, which implies the possession of considerable perceptive powers and of strong passions, seems to
have been more effective with the Lamellicorns than with
any other family of beetles. The horns . . . resemble those
of various quadrupeds, such as stags, rhinoceroses, etc.,
and are wonderful both from their size and diversified
shapes (Darwin, 1871, pp. 300, 306).

The importance of the perceptive powers in sexual selection
was later to be challenged (von Reichenau, 1881; Wallace,
1889; Arrow, 1951), but lest the reader doubt that beetles
have strong "passions," we include a short account of a fight
in *Megasoma elephas* which William Beebe (1944) was fortunate
enough to witness:

I introduced a major male on May 21, and after righting
himself he clambered awkwardly over the small male and
toward the female. His antennae played over *her* back for
a few seconds, and then the lesser male blundered past him.
Like a flash the major turned on the other beetle and the
fiercest fight we had seen thus far was on. Both of course
tried to get the curved horn under the other, both tried
to trip the other off balance. Three times Minor was
actually tossed into the air and landed on his back. He
levered himself upright and after the third even he seemed
to become thoroughly aroused and fought twice as hard as
before. His very smallness was a help in some way and the
locked horn gave the larger insect little advantage. Once
the giant was turned over and fell on the female and in-
stantly the Minor rushed over at both and while they were
tangled, butted and drove against them and rolled them
about. The larger finally got his opponent in a corner
and hooked and twisted violently, securing some strange,

secure lock and after a wrench we saw the right middle leg
of the smaller beetle break off near its base and lie
kicking by itself on the ground. Nor for a moment did the
injured beetle stop his efforts . . . . The same five-legged
Minor on the following day mated without trouble with two
freshly caught females (pp. 56-57).

The most impressive of the horned beetles are lamellicorns,
a diverse assemblage of insects which includes the scarabs

TABLE 1

Some major characteristics of the Lamellicorn beetle families
(summarized from Arrow, 1951)

Lucanidae (Stag beetles): Possess mandibular horns; larvae
    develop in rotting wood; at maturity beetles leave the logs,
    but females return to oviposit; hatched larvae are not
    tended by adults and may take several years to mature;
    adult life is short, lasting several weeks, and adults do
    not feed on solid foods; some small species are sexually
    monomorphic, and *Sinodendron* species (at least) are mono-
    gamous and display male parental care; most species are
    sexually dimorphic and probably polygynous-promiscuous;
    sexually dimorphic species generally display greater size
    variation in males than in females; most species show
    continuous variation in mandible size between large and
    small males, although future studies may demonstrate two
    frequency modes.

Passalidae: Usually hornless or with minute horns; sexually
    monomorphic; perhaps usually monogamous; male and female
    collaborate in rearing the young, which in the earliest
    stages must have food prepared for them by the parents;
    larval life is relatively short (compared to Lucanidae)
    and adults may live for several years; adult animals feed
    on solid foods.

Scarabeidae (Scarabs and chafers): Possess outgrowth horns,
    usually on the head and pronotum; most species of this
    exceptionally diverse group are not horned; there is much
    more variability in horn shape and number than Lucanidae;
    much variability in life history; both sexes in many spe-
    cies may prepare a nest and provision it with food; extreme
    sexual dimorphism, mainly in species in which males do not
    collaborate in rearing offspring; monogamous species show
    less sexual size dimorphism and both sexes may be horned,
    sometimes similarly and sometimes differently.

(Scarabeidae), the stag beetles (Lucanidae), and the Passalidae (Fig. 1). Some major biological characteristics of these
three groups are outlined in Table 1. Scarab horns are almost
always outgrowths of either the head or thorax, while stag
beetle horns are technically not horns at all, but enlargements of the mandibles. The horns of the mostly monogamous
passalids, in the few species which possess them, are un-
spectacular and frequently possessed by both sexes. In the
scarab species which bear them, usually only the males are
horned, but females of a few species have also quite spectacular horns. Only the males of stag beetles have enlarged
mandibles. The differences between the two sexes are so great
in some species that there is little morphological reason for
associating males and females of the same species. As we
shall see later, the presence of horns in the scarabs appears
to be connected to burrowing and nest construction.

THE ORIGINS OF HORNS

    Eberhard (this volume) has presented very plausible hypo-
theses on the conditions which may have favored horn development in Lamellicornia. On this question, Arrow (1951) noted
a connection between having horns and the feeding habits of
adults:

    In predaceous [beetles] mandibles are used chiefly for
    seizing prey and often project considerably, while in those
    that live upon vegetable *food,* they are generally equally
    important as biting organs. In neither case are they
    liable to develop into horns. There are many beetles,
    however, which during their brief adult life, take no solid
    food. The jaws of the females may be of importance to them
    for performing the operations necessary for the proper
    placing of their eggs, but those of the males are without
    that employment. It is amongst such beetles that mandible
    horns are often found and in some of them the jaws have
    developed to such an extent as to place them amongst the
    most fantastic of insects (p. 20).

    A problem posed by Fisher (1958) is one of how the develop-
ing horns attain "selective value." Once the horns are large
enough to damage a competitor, selection for improvements can
readily be appreciated. But if, as seems likely, horns increased by minute increments, it is difficult to see how
initial differences could have affected the beetles possessing
them. Hersh (1934) faced this problem in his discussion of
the evolution of horns in the extinct titanotheres. He
thought that the horns may initially have appeared as by-
products of selection for a greater bulk as "correlated

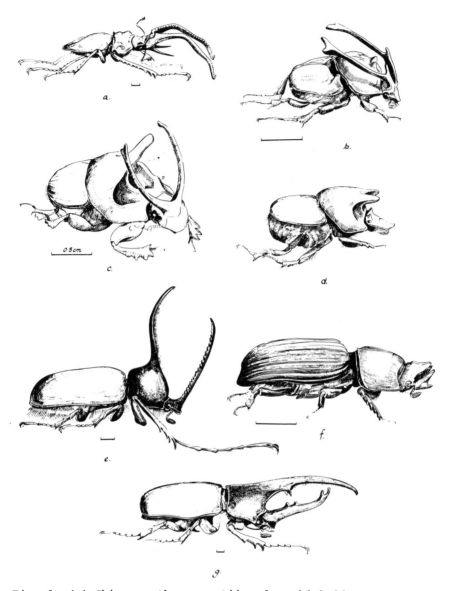

Fig. 1. (a) Chiasognathus grantii *male, which lives on tree*
trunks and feeds at sap flows in the forests of southern Chile
and Argentina. (b) Onthophagus rangifer *male, a dung beetle*
from Africa. (c) Onthophagus imperator *male from India show-*
ing the long prothoracic horn and deep depressions in the
pronotum. (d) Onthophagus seniculus *male.* (e) Golofa porteri
male from South America. (f) A passalid species, Ceratocupes
fronticornis, *showing an unusual development of horns.*
(g) Dynastes hercules *male from Venezuela.*

characters." And once established, they could be increased
in size by natural selection, provided that they were of use
in fighting. In scarabs a difficulty exists in accounting
for the development of prothoracic horns. Fisher states:

> The concept of attaining selective value, which is fairly
> common in biological literature, seems to cover two dis-
> tinct cases. In the first case we may imagine that, with
> increasing size, the utility of an organ shows no increase
> up to a certain point, but beyond this point increasing
> size is associated with increasing utility. In such a
> case . . . we are really only concerned with the question
> whether the variability in different members of the species
> concerned, does or does not reach as far as the critical
> point. If it does not do so the species will not be able
> to take the advantage offered . . . . [It] is sometimes
> assumed that, while at all sizes an increase of size may be
> advantageous, this advantage increases, not continuously,
> but in a step-like manner; or at least that increases below
> a certain limit produce an advantage which may be called
> "inappreciable," and therefore neglected. [But] survival
> value is measured by the frequency with which certain
> events, such as death and reproduction, occur, and . . . .
> psychophysical experiments make it perfectly clear that
> the selective advantages will increase or decrease con-
> tinuously, even for changes smaller than those appreciable
> to our own senses, or to those of the predator or other
> animal, which may enter into the biological situation
> concerned. If a change of 1 mm has selective value, a
> change of 0.1 mm will usually have a selection value
> approximately one-tenth as great, and the effect cannot be
> ignored because we deem the stimulus inappreciable. The
> rate at which a mutation responds to selection in favour
> of any increase or decrease of parts depends on the total
> heritable variance available, and not on whether this is
> supplied by large or small mutations. There is no *limen*
> of appreciable selection value to be considered (p. 15).[1]

Head horns, as well as mandibular horns, seem to present
lesser difficulties than thoracic horns. The mandibles, primitively used in feeding or burrowing, could easily have become
secondarily employed in contests and thereafter be improved
for combat. The head horns of scarabs could also have developed from projections or ridges used initially as shovels for
burrowing, especially if similar shoveling movements were
used in pushing and throwing matches between males.

HORN DEVELOPMENT AND PARENTAL CARE

Arrow noted that body size and horn development are more
nearly similar in the two sexes when males assist the females
in preparing burrows and rearing the young:

> A careful examination of many hundreds of examples belong-
> ing to about thirty different kinds of horned species led
> me to the conclusion that, when the two sexes do not great-
> ly differ or the horns of the male are of moderate size
> only, the forelegs of both generally show the effects of
> use in a similar degree, but where the male has an exag-
> gerated horn development, the evidence points to the labour
> performed only by the female. Either the existence of
> appendages of an embarrassing kind has served to prevent
> the male acquiring domestic accomplishments or the non-
> acquisition of the accomplishments has resulted in exagger-
> ated development of the appendages . . . . Where partici-
> pation by both sexes is found to occur there seems to be
> always a well-defined division of labour and the male's
> share is the rougher part, although it may be more stren-
> uous. The more delicate operations are always undertaken
> by the female, the usually hornless sex. Although certain
> adaptations of the horns of males for the better perfor-
> mance of their special duties have been noted, these are
> found only in cases where the horn development is of a
> very moderate kind. All the evidence seems to point to
> the conclusion that the lamellicorn beetles, both horned
> and hornless, while they include many of which males and
> females share the tasks of nidification, comprise a larger
> number with or without horns, of which in common with near-
> ly all other insects, the females alone perform all the
> tasks necessary for ensuring the well-being of their off-
> spring (pp. 54; 68-69).

In several stag beetle genera, male and female mandibles
do not differ. In some species for which this is the case,
the two sexes collaborate in preparing a burrow and provisioning it for the young. This is true for species of *Sinoden-
dron*. In these species the mandibles are not enlarged, but
there are small horns on the thorax and abdomen:

> While the female is occupied in extending her burrow and
> preparing brood-niches, the male travels backwards and for-
> wards, sweeping up and removing the accumulating debris
> with his rake-like legs and pushing it out with his scoop
> (p. 71). [In *S. cylindricum*, the burrow] was started some-
> times by a male and sometimes by a female but soon after-
> wards a pair were always found at work together, the female
> extending the burrow, while the male appeared to employ

himself chiefly in removing the excavated material (Arrow, 1951, pp. 34-35).

HORNS AS ORNAMENTS

Darwin believed that the more spectacular varieties of horns were probably used principally as ornaments for exciting females. He argued, for example, that it was improbable that horns developed for fighting, because:

> If the males had been habitual fighters, the size of their bodies would probably have been increased through sexual selection, so as to have exceeded that of the females; but Mr. Bates, after comparing the two sexes in about a hundred species of the Copridae, did not find any marked differences in this respect amongst well-developed individuals (Darwin, 1871).

Was it an oversight that he neglected to mention the considerable sexual dimorphism which he knew existed in many other groups? He was aware that males of many species fight, yet he did not believe that mandibles were used principally in fighting. For example, concerning *Lucanus cervus,* he said:

> . . . although the mandibles are probably used as efficient weapons for fighting, it is doubtful whether their great size can thus be accounted for. We have seen that they are used by the *Lucanus elephas* of North America for seizing the female. As they are so conspicuous and so elegantly branched and as owing to their great length they are not well adapted for pinching, the suspicion has crossed my mind that they serve as an ornament . . . (p. 306).

Darwin's judgment on the pinching powers of beetles was based, so far as we can tell, on his observations of *Chiasognathus grantii* (Fig. 1a) which he encountered in Chile:

> . . . this splendid beetle . . . has enormously developed mandibles; he is bold and pugnacious; when threatened he faces 'round, opens his great jaws, and at the same time stridulates loudly. But the mandibles were not strong enough to pinch my finger so as to cause actual pain (p. 306).

But *C. grantii* is an unusual stag beetle, possessing a very narrow head, as do members of the Australasian genus *Lamprima*. Had Darwin experimented with a broad-headed species, he might well have reached a different conclusion, and ornaments may have assumed a less important part in his theory of sexual selection, at least as it pertains to horned beetles. But other investigators also thought that horns were not used,

for the most part, to damage opponents. Beebe (1944), for
example, showed that males of *Megasoma elephas* and *Strategus
aloeus* throw one another, rarely causing damage. Arrow (1951)
writes:

> Contests between rival males of *Lucanus cervus* have often
> been seen. They push and struggle, open and close the
> mandibles and flourish them alarmingly but can cause no
> damage as might result from the smaller but much stronger
> jaws of the female. Not only are the elongated jaws of the
> male stag-beetle less powerful than the short jaws of the
> female, but the same shape of his body and elongation of
> the legs show plainly that he has not her digging power.
> Although the legs may be toothed, the teeth are feeble and
> far apart, unlike those of the other sex. This applies to
> all the large species in all parts of the world and it may
> be concluded that the manner of life does not greatly
> differ from that of *Lucanus cervus* (pp. 33-34).

The effectiveness of horns in male contests is becoming
much clearer as more species are observed (Mathieu, 1969;
Eberhard, this volume). Even the narrow-headed *Chiasognathus*
males may mortally wound one another, perhaps chiefly with
the sharp mandibular spine which could be used to pierce the
membranes of an opponent (Joseph, 1928; Ureta, 1934).
Hamilton (this volume) has observed how contests may produce
clear winners and losers even when no damage is done. Males
fighting on an elevated perch may win decisively if the losing
male, when thrown from the perch, has difficulty in quickly
returning to the same place. In the light of Hamilton's
discovery, the fights described by Beebe (1944) take on added
significance, especially if one imagines them taking place on
a vertical surface or up in a tree:

> Although the battle between each individual pair of male
> [*Megasoma elephas*] beetles is, to a certain extent, slight-
> ly different from every other, yet there are several
> fundamental phases which seem invariable. The opponents
> meet head-on and warily wait for the other to attack, or
> one may rush headlong and begin to encounter. Usually
> both spar at a little distance. The object first notice-
> able is an attempt with one or both fore tarsi and claws
> to trip and unbalance the opponent. There are quick
> forward lunges and reachings out with one or both legs,
> sometimes at the same moment by both insects. This may
> or may not succeed, but one will force the fighting and
> the result may be straight pushing and butting for a con-
> siderable period, exactly like two antlered deer. Now and
> then an effort will be noticed to lower the head and get
> the cephalic horn beneath the other insect. Again and

again this is tried, and both may attempt it at the same
moment. Then recur the rearing and tripping attempts.
Then, if at all, comes the final phase, the all-out attempt
to get the top of the bifurcated horn caught in the soft
skin of the ventral joint between the thorax and abdomen.
Once secured, we realized this is evidently the chief
object of the encounter. The successful one puts forth
all the strength of which he is capable and lifts again
and again with all his might. The higher the other is
lifted the more helpless he becomes as his feet, one after
the other, leave the ground, and with several superbeetle
flings, the victim of this grip is thrown over on to his
back. Not once, but again and again this was the end result.
Often the beetle simply rolled over and came back on his
feet again and the whole engagement recommenced (pp. 55,56).

Beebe (1944) observed both *Megasoma elephas* and *Stragegus
aloeus* crawling up on the trunks of jungle trees and two
elephas resting beneath an overhanging branch. It now seems
likely that battles occurring under such conditions would
usually have more decisive outcomes, since tossing an opponent
would effectively remove him from competition. Even the
initial tripping movements Beebe describes could easily cause
an opponent to lose his footing on a vertical surface and to
fall to the ground.

Mathieu's (1969) observations of American lucanids illustrate the advantages which larger males have in fights with
small males and the existence of initial testing bouts
perhaps, as Parker (1974) suggests, for assessing the strength
of an opponent. Such tests would be important to beetles
for gauging the probability of success (or of risk) should a
fight escalate. Mathieu writes:

Males of the same size did not injure themselves, although
they often had long fighting bouts, mainly when a female
was present. [Fights between] individuals of different
sizes often resulted in injury to the smaller individual.
In three cases in which very large individuals were allowed
to interact with very small ones, actual death of the
smaller one was caused by heavy mechanical mandibular
damage (p. 1060).

. . . recognition of a male odor triggers an aggressive
display. The initial aggressive display is followed by
active biting, grabbing, and head tossing which depends to
a greater or lesser extent on the situation and on the
species . . . . [Those individuals] with shorter mandibles
used these appendages in a more elaborate fashion during
courtship and copulation than those with larger and more
elaborate ones. The use of the mandibles to maintain a

position on the female has been reported for *Lucanus cervus*
(Weber in Arrow, 1951), although apparently this behavior
is not consistent (Brüll, 1952). These observations could
raise the question whether lucanids having strongly allometric mandibles originally used these appendages in a
courtship-copulation context and whether later they
developed into larger structures for performance in displays and somewhat ritualized ways of fighting (e.g.,
pushing, overturning, or dislodging) (pp. 1060, 1061).

. . . direct combat is minimized by means of ritualization
in fighting. Aggressive displays are common in stag-
beetles. A male upon feeling the proximity of another
male immediately faces the opponent, opening the mandibles
and exchanging short grabbing bouts before decamping. But
once a male is mounted on a female he becomes vulnerable
to side attacks by those males whose aggressive state is
high because of the presence of a female. It is only in
these short periods during copulation that a male could
be seriously wounded.

It is somewhat interesting to note that the two species
studied which have sharp pointed mandibles *(Lucanus placidus*
and *L. capreolus)* have very short matings and can disengage
copulation under extreme aggressive pressure from conspecifics. The European stag-beetle, *Lucanus cervus,* with
strongly allometric mandibles can mate four to eight times
in a short period of time (Tippmann, 1954), but Brüll
(1952) measured one mating lasting 11 minutes (p. 1061).

Arrow flatly disagrees with Darwin on the use of horns as
ornaments. On the matter of whether females can assess size
differences between males, he writes:

Indeed, it is not possible, so far as we can judge from
their eyes, for any horned beetle to form a clear picture,
as Darwin supposed, of another . . . . In India is found . . .
Aulocostethus archeri . . . possessing large horns in the
male, but with eyes reduced to such tiny vestiges that it
must be almost blind . . . . [Such] examples . . . serve to
illustrate the fact that the groups most conspicuous for
the number of horned beetles they include, are all far
inferior in visual power to those insects we can consider
as having fairly good sight. The great assemblage which
contains most of all the Scarbeinae, is perhaps the one in
which the faculty is at its worst . . . . [Had Darwin] become
aware of the facts . . . concerning the vision of horned
beetles, he would have recognized them as destructive to
his theory of Sexual Selection, so far at least as it
applies to those insects, for if, as he believed, certain
female insects were able to compare their various suitors

and select from among them those with the best physical attractions, such insects must surely be found among those with the best and not the worst quality of vision. Not only does all the evidence indicate indifference on the part of female insects, but we find, in the case of those under consideration that the differences so manifest to ourselves in the males cannot be perceived at all by the females (Arrow, 1951, p. 123).

Arrow was probably correct on the matter of ornaments and in his belief that females do not exercise much choice, but several points need emphasis. First, he cites no evidence supporting his belief that visual acuity in horned beetles is so poor that they would not see one another (indeed, Beebe believed they could). Second, it is possible that females assess the characteristics of males through touch. And third, he apparently did not fully understand that female choice is but one of several components of sexual selection. In fact, he cites a case of female choice noted by Fabre in which a female *Geotrupes typhaeus* "refused to start domestic life with a particular male provided her but at once accepted another."

The use of horns for carrying off the females has been observed in a number of species. Baron von Hügel, for example, noted that *Xylotrupes gideon* "immediately sought out the females and seizing them transversely, carried them about, held between the two horns, with evident satisfaction" (words of Bateson and Brindley, 1892). Female carrying has also been seen in *Lucanus elephas* (Darwin, 1871), *Dynastes hercules* (Beebe, 1944), and *Chalcosoma atlas* (Bateson and Brindley, 1892). But one may surmise that this behavior evolved secondarily after the horns had evolved in the context of combat. Here is Beebe's (1949) account of female carrying in *Dynastes hercules:*

One day after a Major had speedily defeated and transported a small Minor, and flung him down . . . the Major came up upon a female and with no hesitation picked her up and walked off as if she had been of the tribe of Sabines. On subsequent occasions . . . this performance was repeated and with such deliberation that we accepted it as a habit. The cause remained insoluble, and the certainty of occurrence could not be foretold. Time after time a male would approach a female, whether she was feeding or moving about, and mate at once. On other occasions he would touch her, playing over her back with the antennae, and soon pick her up and walk away. Twice females were carried as far as I dared let them go into the underbrush. Once only did I see a mating follow a short transportation. What significance this has in the sexual economy of *hercules,* when the event takes place perhaps at night in the jungle, I cannot even guess (pp. 317-318).

Figs. 1 and 2 show several interesting morphological
aspects of horned beetles. *Chiasognathus grantii* (Fig. 1a)
displays not only forceps-like mandibles, which can probably
not exert much pressure, but also a pair of ventral spines
which may be useful in injuring opponents in close battles.
Males also possess exceptionally long forelegs which are used
to raise the forepart of the body high above the substrate
so as to cause opponents, which are held clamped between the
mandibles, to lose their foothold (Hamilton, this volume).
Onthophagus rangifer (Fig. 1b), a rather small scarab, possesses long antlers which can be tucked back along the body,
presumably when it moves into burrows. It also possesses a
pair of upright horns on the wing covers which may be functionally connected to the long head horns. *Onthophagus
imperator* males (Fig. 1c) possess, in addition to the head
horns, a long, forward-projecting prothoracic horn which we
surmise must be used in conjunction with the head horns to

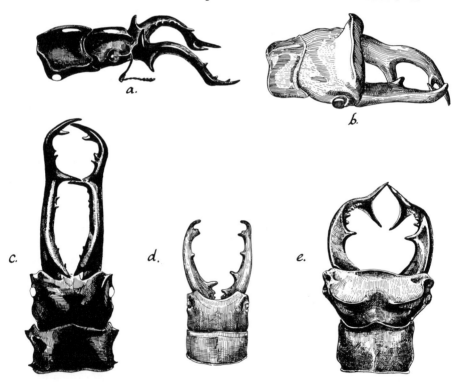

Fig. 2. A variety of mandible types in stag beetles. (a)
Hexarthrius fosteri, (b) Cyclommatus kaupi, (c) Cladognathus
giraffa, (d) Leptinopterus tibialis, (e) Lucanus elephas.

grasp or to crush opponents.   The deep depressions beneath the
prothoracic horns have no known function. *Golofa porteri*
males (Fig. 1e) possess extremely slender horns which are
probably used only for lifting and throwing of males (and possibly females). The hairs and serrations on the horns may
help to prevent opponents from slipping from their grasp, and
the exceptionally long forelegs are probably used for lifting
opponents high above the substrate.   In passalids, males and
females have either very small horns (as shown by *Ceratocupes
fronticornis:* Fig. 1f) or no horns at all. Passalids are
monogamous, display an extended period of parental care (Arrow,
1951), and the sexes are usually nearly identical in appearance.   *Dynastes hercules,* the species discussed by Beebe, also
possesses spines and hairs which would help to prevent an opponent from slipping from its grip.   In *Cyclommatus kaupi*
(Fig. 2b) the head is very broad and is strongly armored with
a dorsally projecting plate. *Cladognathus giraffa* (Fig. 2c)
displays long forceps-like mandibles which would appear to be
effective in keeping smaller males at bay.   At the base of the
mandibles, they have inward projecting spurs which could be
effective in close-in battles. *Leptinoperus tibialis* (Fig. 2d)
displays an unusual asymmetry between left and right mandibles. *Lucanus elephas* (Fig. 2e) has an exceedingly broad head

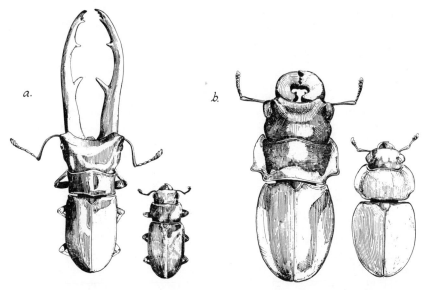

Fig. 3. (a) Male and female of Cyclommatus imperator, *with
the male displaying the "forceps" type of mandibles. (b) Male
and female of* Odontolabis lowei, *with the male displaying the
"pincher" type of mandibles.*

which is armored above with prominent plates; its mandibles
suggest the possibility of some danger to opponents.

Fig. 3 compares two basically different patterns of horn
development. *Cyclommatus imperator* males (Fig. 3a) possess
the forceps type of mandibles which are probably used for the
lifting and throwing of opponents, while *Odontolabis* males
possess very short and stout mandibles which would appear to
be more effective in severely injuring opponents.

SOME PATTERNS OF VARIATION AND HORN DIMORPHISM IN MALES,
MAINLY IN THE LUCANIDAE

In several species of insects in which the male bears
horns, Bateson and Brindley (1892) noted that horn sizes may
fall into two major size classes, which they called "high"
and "low." In several dynastine beetles in South America,
Beebe (1944) observed that some males were large, with dis-
proportionately sized horns, while others were considerably
smaller and had relatively much smaller horns. He called the
two kinds of males "Majors" and "Minors." Gadgil (1972)
discussed the theoretical significance of such dimorphisms
and attempted to explain how they might come about. Suppose,
he said, that fitness of males is determined principally by
two components: the survival probability of individual males
(S) and the number of females that a male can successfully
mate--his mating success (MS). Suppose, also, that there
exists some inverse correlation between S and MS so that as
reproductive effort increases, S tends to decrease and MS to
increase, and furthermore, that the overall reproductive
success (RS) is determined by the mating success multiplied
by the probability of survival. Now, if the S and MS curves
are properly adjusted, a bimodal RS curve may be obtained.
(Interested readers should see Fisher, 1958, and Trivers,
1972, for discussions of this topic.) Following the work of
Levins (1967), there has been a considerable amount of interest in the evolution of dimorphisms, especially when they
comprise different reproductive modes within a single species
or population (see Alcock's and Cade's discussions in this
volume).

Using the insect collections of the Philadelphia Academy
of Natural Sciences, it has been possible to measure horn
sizes in nearly 400 beetle species, mainly for the purpose of
seeing how horns vary in size in relation to changes in body
size and how prevalent horn dimorphisms are. We measured one
or more aspects of body and horn size in 399 stag beetle
species and numerous scarab species. In this paper we concentrate mainly on patterns of variation in stag beetles.

Our basic analysis involves measuring mandible length (M)

and plotting this length against the combined length of the
thorax and abdomen (or pronotum plus abdomen--P + A).   In
this analysis we have excluded head dimensions because the
head varies closely with the size of the mandibles, being
functionally linked to their operation. We will report on
the relationship between head dimensions and mandible length
in a later paper. The rest of the body is less tightly
coupled to horn function.

When M is plotted against P + A, using at first only the
largest males and females of each species, we see a large
amount of interspecific variation among the males, while the
females fall very tightly about a straight line (Fig. 4). We

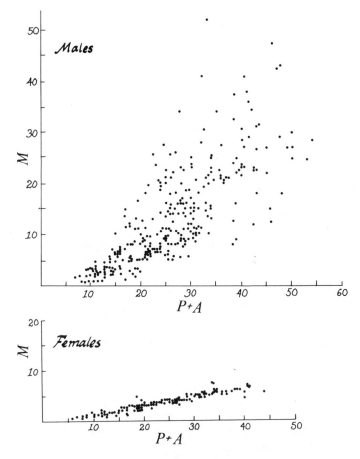

Fig. 4. Mandible length plotted against pronotum plus
abdomen length (i.e., body length minus the head and mandibles). Each dot represents the largest male or female from
a single species.

see reflected in this figure the highly variable effects of
sexual selection on the males, but no similar effect on
females. For females the relative length of mandibles increases very slightly as body size increases so that the
mandibles of larger species are, relatively, only slightly
larger than those of small species. Mandible size in females
would appear to be governed by other forces which operate
with equal force on the various species.

In Fig. 5 we have plotted the largest and smallest male
and the largest female from a number of species to show that
the mandible length increases at different rates relative to
body length in different genera, and that in genera in which
the animals are small, the difference between the sexes is
much less pronounced or the sexes are indistinguishable.

The regression of M on P + A differs appreciably from one
genus to another (Figs. 6, 7). The steepest intraspecific
slopes are seen in the genera which also display the greatest
degree of interspecific variation. The relationship between
M and P + A is also clearly linear, fitting very closely to
the linear regression equation, $y = a + bx$. The coefficient
of determination, r^2, which can be used to determine the
quality of fit achieved by the regression, was consistently
near 1.0 (the mean r^2 value for 46 stag beetle species was
0.90 with standard deviation 0.14).

In the species we measured, we have found no clear evidence
of dimorphisms, although some species would appear to be
more promising than others for ultimately revealing cases of
a bimodal distribution (Fig. 7). In the species for which we
have the largest sample sizes, dimorphisms are least evident.
Statements made by past investigators on the existence of
"high-low" dimorphisms (Gadgil, 1972; Ghiselin, 1974) must
therefore be taken with caution--at least when applied to
beetles. We have also failed to reveal clear dimorphisms in
the Scarabeidae. Most lucanid species we have measured are
admittedly represented by small sample sizes. Nevertheless,
persons who are convinced that dimorphisms should exist would
not be discouraged, on the whole, with the figures we have
presented. With few exceptions, a preliminary clustering
at the two ends of the size distribution can be imagined.
A major difficulty with museum collections is that not enough
specimens are collected from individual populations to allow
one to detect the presence of bimodal distributions. There
is also a potential difficulty that males coming from different locations may belong to different species.

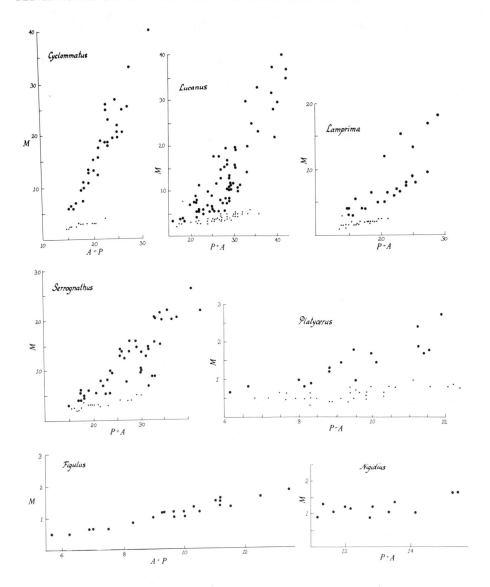

Fig. 5. In each lucanid genus shown, each species is represented by three dots, the largest and smallest males and the
largest female. In Nigidius and Figulus the sexes are alike.
Genera in which individuals are small display lesser degrees
of sexual dimorphism.

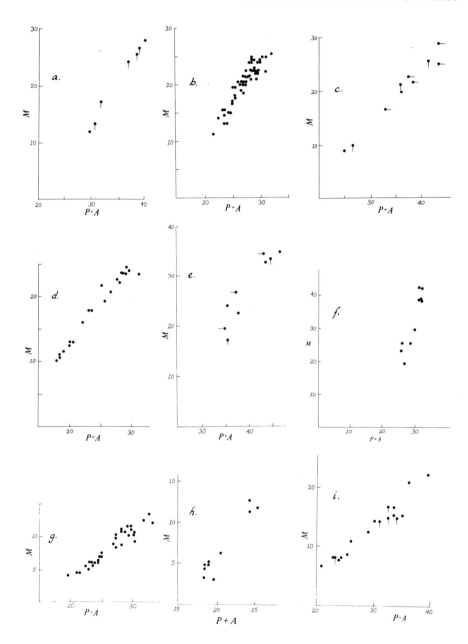

Fig. 6. (See caption on opposite page).

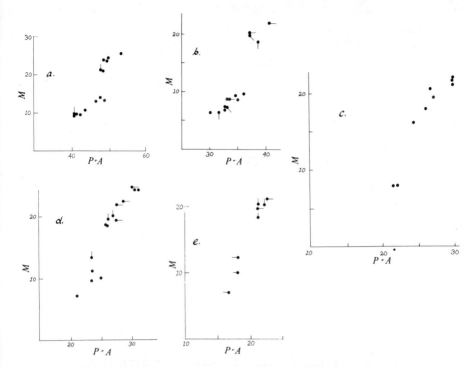

Fig. 7. Five species in which some clustering at the low and high ends seems evident (see also legend to Fig. 6). (a) Odontolabis siva, *(b)* Odontolabis cuvera, *(c)* Metopodontus savagei, *(d)* Psalidoremus inclinatus, *(e)* Cyclommatus freygesnerii.

Fig. 6. (opposite page) Mandible length plotted against pronotum plus abdomen length in nine stag beetle species (measurements in millimeters). Each dot represents one male. Dots with similar lines indicate that the specimens may have been taken at the same place (they bear the same locality labels). Dots without lines may represent the same or different localities but probably mostly the latter (we could not guess which). (a) Lucanus cervus, *(b)* Lucanus elephas, *(c)* Hexarthrius davisoni, *(d)* Lamprima alolphinae, *(e)* Cladognathus giraffa, *(f)* Chiasognathus grantii, *(g)* Prosopocoelus serricornis, *(h)* Serrognathus intermedius, *(i)* Serrognathus platymelus.*

TABLE 2

Relationship between body length and the rate at which
mandible length increases in relation to body length

Size class (P + A)	N	Mean slope $\bar{x}_b$	Standard deviation s
5 - 10 mm	11	0.40	0.20
10 - 15	12	0.91	0.53
15 - 20	16	0.69	0.36
20 - 25	33	1.04	0.55
25 - 30	20	0.97	0.68
30 - 35	13	1.16	0.42
35 - 40	10	1.02	0.43
40 - 45	8	1.27	0.79

NOTE: P + A, length of pronotum plus abdomen; b is the slope
        derived from the linear regression equation, $y = a + bx$;
        $\bar{x}_b$ is the mean value of b for an entire size class;
        size classes are based on the mode for each species.

   Fig. 8 compares the regression lines for different genera.
Each line represents the regression of a different stag
beetle species. Again, as in Fig. 5, we see a characteristic
pattern developing for each genus--not a surprising fact in
itself, but a situation that lends itself to an analysis of
different modes of fighting and allocation of effort. Fig.
8f shows a small portion of the regression around the mode of
the body size in numerous species. Here we can see clearly
the tendency for mandibles to increase relatively rapidly with
increasing body size as beetles become larger. These data are
further summarized in Table 2. It should be noted that some
of these regressions are based only on the smallest and
largest male available in a sample. Since the points are
usually scattered closely around the regressions (Figs. 6, 7),
such regressions probably approximate the actual regressions
quite closely.
   Fig. 9 shows how mandibles not only change in length but
may change in their overall structure. In some species, such
as *Serrognathus platymelus* and *Prosopocoelus serricornis*,
there is little change in the shape of the mandibles as they
become larger. But in others, such as *Prosopocoelus faber*,
Cladognathus giraffa, and Odontolabis siva, we see a marked
change in shape from a pincher-type to a forceps-type of
mandible. It seems likely that large and small males in these

latter species fight quite differently.

The shape of the mandibles of small males suggests that they could be used to damage opponents in close-in battles, while those of large beetles might be effective in keeping opponents at a distance where they could not inflict damage. In *Metopodontus bison* and *Cladognathus giraffa,* we see a most interesting feature--the largest males have forceps-type mandibles which retain pincher-type outgrowths at the base, as though the males of these species retain the option of close-in fighting should the opportunity arise.

THE BASIS OF HORN VARIATION

Although no evidence exists on the factors which cause horns or body size to vary in stag beetles, it is known that dietary condition is important in insects in general. It is also the most important factor in earwigs in which clear dimorphisms in the forceps' length have long been known (Bateson and Brindley, 1892; Diakonov, 1925). Diakonov showed that forceps' dimorphisms are common in the earwigs *Forficula auricularia* and *F. tomis,* and that this variation was not genetically based. He thought that although environmental factors were important in producing the variation, dimorphism in male *Forficula auricularia* occurred only in the size of the forceps whereas other body parts displayed continuous variation. The proportions of long and short forceps in his populations were variable, but in general varied with the mean body size. In populations which averaged larger, the proportion of large forceps individuals increased. He also discovered that individuals that were parasitized by fly larvae *(Digonichaeta setipennis)* in the juvenile stage were more likely to display short forceps as adults, presumably because of the inhibitory effect that such larvae have on growth. He wrote: "The only possible explanation . . . appears to be . . . that the parasite exhausts his host to such a degree that at its final moulting the formation of such considerable appendages as the forceps becomes impossible." Infected individuals were also smaller in body size than noninfected individuals.

Diakonov found both long and short forceps forms inhabiting precisely the same places under bark, and Bateson and Brindley (1892) found dimorphic individuals under the same stones. Diakonov also discovered that the long forceps forms were more frequent under bark of stumps than in the lignin. He felt that feeding conditions in the lignin were less favorable, so that the population averaged smaller. So far, then, all evidence seems to indicate that forceps size depends on body size, which in turn depends on diet. Diakonov failed to

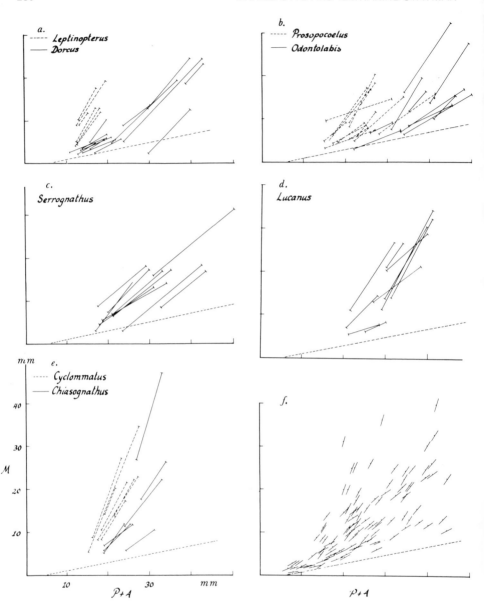

Fig. 8. (a-e) Regressions of mandible length against
pronotum plus abdomen length showing the tendency for the
species of a genus to display similar changes.   The dotted
line is the female regression (derived from Fig. 4). (f) A
small portion of the regression (around the midpoint of the
size range) in a large number of species to show the general
steepening of slopes in larger species.

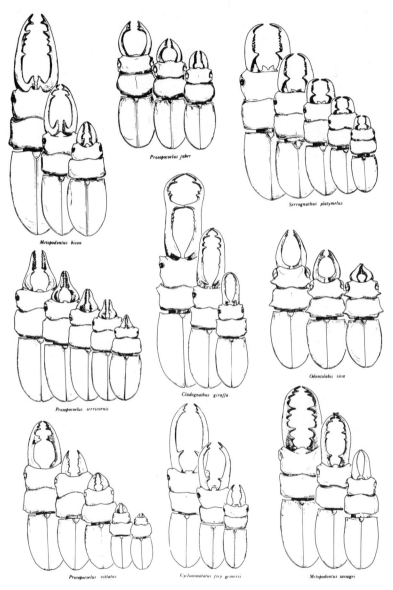

Fig. 9. Some changes in body and mandible size and shape in various stag beetle species. Note the much more rapid increase in mandible length in some species than in others and a much larger change in body size in Serrognathus platymelus *than, for instance,* Odontolabis siva *or* Metopodontus savagei, *which show a relatively much greater change in mandible size.*

discuss why forceps size is dimorphic while body size is continuously variable. This problem remains unsolved. Perhaps
we have something analogous to developmental switchpoints
seen in the production of social insect castes (Wilson, 1953).
The ultimate cause for the existence of switchpoints may be
that intermediate conditions of forceps or horn size are generally less advantageous than either the larger or smaller
types.

MODES OF COMPETITION: STRUCTURAL VS. BEHAVIORAL EXPENDITURES

   Great variation exists among beetle species in the relative
length of the horns and the width of the head. In such genera
as *Lamprima* and *Chiasognathus,* in which the head is narrow
and the mandibles very long, highly damaging fights are probably less frequent than in genera such as *Dorcus, Odontolabis,
Serrognathus,* and others in which the head is very wide in
relation to the length of the jaws (Figs. 2b, e). Although
we lack evidence, we predict that in species which remain
hidden in crevices, where throwing would tend to be a less
effective mode of combat, selection would favor males capable
of incapacitating competitors in some other fashion, either
by killing them or by severing limbs. Collections furnish
some evidence that broad-headed and short-mandibled males
engage in more dangerous fights. In such beetles as *Serrognathus titanus* and *S. alcides,* the tips of the mandibles are
sometimes broken, and some males bear teeth scars, especially
on the wing covers. Also, the heads of some species bearing
short mandibles are especially strongly armored (Fig. 2b),
thereby probably preventing damage to the head region. Arrow
(1951) wrote:

   [*Hexarthrius*] which have mandibles much stouter than usual,
   with teeth upon the open edges which appear quite capable
   of inflicting injury, [an] examination of numerous specimens . . . revealed various scratches and punctures upon
   the wing-cases, in all probability attributable to rival
   males (pp. 33-34).

   The fights described by Beebe and Mathieu (cited earlier)
and Hamilton (this volume) suggest several ways in which
beetles seem to fight:

   The coup. This is a contest which appears to be quick and
decisive, often producing clear winners and losers even in
closely matched males. Using focused strength, surprise,
good tactics, and perhaps a measure of deceit, a coup requires little expenditure of energy and, in fights on high
perches, would result in a very high gain to cost ratio for

the winner. It may involve little damage to either contestant, but the cost of battle to the loser is very high relative to that for the winner. The costs of a coup are measured mainly in terms of lost matings and lost time. And, finally, a lack of strength can be compensated for by quickness and good tactics.

Contests of strength and stamina. These contests differ from coups principally in that they may rely more on strength and stamina than on tactics. Battles between nearly equally matched males would tend to be more prolonged, although winning is probably more closely correlated with body size than in a coup. An important result of extended fights is that the costs of winning may be very high, even exceeding the benefits.

Even in species which engage in the second form of fighting, Beebe and Mathieu showed that contests proceed through several stages. They begin with some initial testing movements--probably to assess relative strength and the profitability of continuing the bout--and only in the case of closely matched contestants, moving to fights of strength and stamina. In animals which fight on tree trunks or on foliage, where a fall would terminate the battle, a coup would be highly effective and selection might favor an ability to throw, trip, or toss an opponent. It is in the foliage-inhabiting, biting cetoniine beetles that one encounters mostly the type of head horns which could not damage an opponent. The narrow-headed lucanids, *Chiasognathus* and *Lamprima,* live on elevated surfaces, either tree trunks or foliage. Their tong-like mandibles allow for effective lifting and throwing but would be relatively less effective for crushing and pinching. Among scarabs, *Golofa porteri* has very slender horns which appear to be designed for lifting opponents but not crushing them. The exceedingly long front legs of both *Golofa* and *Chiasognathus* doubtless allow the beetles to elevate the front end high above the substrate, thereby forcing their opponents to lose contact with the substrate (see also Eberhardt, this volume).

If *mating investment* is the energy that an adult must expend to maximize the number of matings, it may be useful to focus attention on two alternative modes of investment, at least as applied to competitive relations between males. A *structural investment* is energy allocated to the production of structures which give the animal strength and protect it from possible injury. Such an investment could augment the chances of winning fights or of successfully guarding resources. Horns, their supporting structures, muscles, and skeletal armaments would be examples.

Alternatively, a *behavioral investment* is a kinetic ex-

penditure of energy by individuals attempting to gain access
to mates. Here the emphasis is on encountering the maximum
number of females per unit of time rather than on fighting
for them. Conceivably the two forms of expenditure are
functionally incompatible so that, for example, a high structural investment precludes a high degree of dispersability
(see Pace, 1967). Most insects in which males are smaller
than females would appear to have adopted primarily a behavioral mode of gaining access to mates, while insects in which
the males are much larger than the females rely more on the
advantages of size and armament. It is at least an intriguing
possibility that the total energy expenditure might be quite
similar in species that have adopted quite different ways of
spending it.

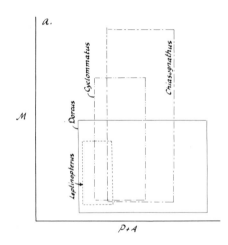

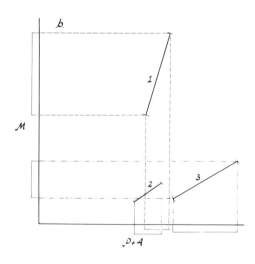

Fig. 10. Increments
in overall body size
may be allocated in
different groups. (a)
Squares enclose the
regressions of an
entire genus (from
Fig. 8). (b) Compar-
ison of different
allocations in three
stag beetle species.
1 and 2 are Chiaso-
gnathus species and 3
is a species of Odon-
tolabis. Species 1,
which displays huge
variation in mandible
length, probably re-
lies more on lifting
and throwing in
fights; while species
3 probably relies
more on strength and
an ability to wound
its opponents.

Fig. 10a illustrates the principle as it might be
operating in stag beetles. In some groups a greater portion
of the increments in size go into the size of the mandibles
(e.g., *Leptinopterus, Cyclommatus,* and *Chiasognathus*), while
in *Dorcus* a relatively greater portion of the increment is
diverted into body size. In Fig. 10b, lines 1, 2, and 3
represent changes in body and mandible length in three different species. In species 1 a relatively greater portion of the
size increment is taken up by the mandibles, while in species
3 the body length increases relatively much more, seemingly
at the expense of mandible length. Of course these figures
merely illustrate the possibility of a trade-off in energy
allocation and do not demonstrate it.

Beebe (1949) was interested in structural and behavioral
differences between large and small males. We include some
of his accounts (p. 304 et seq.) to show that the relationship
between structure and behavior may be much more complex than
we have indicated:

[A] Major and Minor [of *Dynastes hercules*] were put in
with three females. Both mated at once, but the Major soon
left his female and attacked the other mating pair. In
spite of his utmost efforts, he could not dislodge the
Minor although both he and his female were rolled over
and over. The unfortunate female bore much of the brunt
of the attack. The Major could not open his forceps
sufficiently to enclose and lift the mated pair. He soon
gave up and returned to his female.

A new-caught Minor showed more vitality and activity than
has any Major. Placed with five Majors and four females
the small male mated with all the females in turn, and
several times in succession with two of them, while the
much larger beetles took time off from feeding to mate with
only one or two. The matings of the Minor were as complete
and successful as those of the Majors . . . . In several
combats with two Majors, the Minor showed no lack of
courage and rushed his giant opponents, but always to no
purpose. He was invariably seized and carried off the
field high in the air . . . .

Day after day for more than a week I have matched two Majors against each other . . . . The equality was . . . almost
perfect, and the slight discrepancy neither conferred nor
denied any advantage . . . . In one conflict after another,
day after day, neither surfeit of food, sex, annoying combats or restful quiet altered . . . the respective method
of attack or changed the very distinct personalities shown
in contests between the two heavy-weight beetles. The
Black rushes the contest. Throughout, what we might call

rounds, he seizes the other, raises him on high and stum-
bles about with him, and finally bangs him down. During
all this, Olive is perfectly quiescent, putting up just
enough defense to show he is not actively trying to escape.
His very relaxation seems to preserve him from injury . . . .
When slammed down the fourth or fifth time, the lethargic
Olive is suddenly obsessed by what appears to be a most
unbeetle-like rage, and from now on the melee is full of
reciprocal action. The little bulging eyes must see more
than they appear to, for again and again Olive avoids the
scissors grip and snap of the dark opponent, and with what
I can call nothing but skill, suddenly smothers Black,
grips him, shifts his hold and rising so high that he seems
on the point of overbalancing backwards, hurls down the
bigger beetle, with his handicap of two grams, once or as
many as three times. Whereupon the victor turns and
scuttles off as fast as his six legs will carry him.

Always Olive was at first the underdog; invariably at the
end he was victor. But twice he fled as I have written
above; once he lifted his great citrine shards and un-
limbered the wide expanse of transparent, amber flight
wings. Only a quick grasp on my part kept him from heli-
coptering off the field of battle, over the jungle, into
the sky. Twice Olive watched his vanquished rival kick as
he swiveled around on his back, and both of these times
made his way to the nearest female and mated. And twice
his rage failed to cool and he continued the battle until
Black was reduced to complete immobility, although ultimately he recovered fully.

Do males know, prior to contact with other beetles, whether
they are large or small? That is, is there a predisposition
for small males to be less willing to fight? Beebe's observations suggest there is not:

The combats between a full-sized Major and a Minor were
always a foregone conclusion. The small one never refused
a tilt and would rush pellmell into the encounter, squeek-
ing as loudly as the giant. But it was of no use. His
instincts remained unchanged and his undersized dwarfed
weapons, which could not encompass even his own size, were
useless against the girth and weight of the Major. His
very lightness seemed to be an advantage in the end, for
only once did I see a Minor injured or stunned by the
slamming on the ground (Beebe, 1944, p. 310).

PARKER'S MODEL, BEETLE FIGHTS AND BEETLE HONESTY

Parker (1974) made a number of interesting postulates.
Let us consider several of these in the light of what we know
about beetle fighting:

1. ". . . there should be an escalation range of closely
matched combatants, and on either side of the range for a
given individual the higher ranking opponent should usually
be prepared to escalate and the lower one withdraw."
While in beetles this prediction seems generally to be
true, the great pugnacity of small hercules and rhinoceros
beetle males seems inconsistent. Also, size differentials
may, as we argued previously, be less important in a coup
than in battles of strength. But there is an explanation
for the competitiveness of small males, as we shall see.

2. "Antler and horn size appear to be judged directly in
many deer and sheep and fights occur only between closely
matched combatants . . . there seems little doubt from the
literature that assessment of RHP (resource holding power)
is occurring in most cases of animal combat." In beetles
the assessment evidently requires physical contact--there-
fore beetles are more likely to assess *real* prowess than
mammalian contestants who might make an assessment on the
basis of advertisement by looking one another over. The
propaganda of which Fisher (1958; see Otte, this volume)
spoke would seem more prevalent in species which advertise
their prowess through distance signaling than in species
which must prove it. At the same time, given a difficulty
in signaling one's RHP at a distance, there would tend to
be more fights between grossly mismatched males, which
should be reflected in the higher proportion of deaths in
species that must physically test one another. The very
quick grabbing and withdrawing movements described by both
Beebe and Mathieu would in general lower the dangers of
gross mismatches.

3. ". . . during a display, selection should mainly favour
presenting an opponent with a maximal impression of one's
RHP. Until a 'strategic decision' is reached, no information should be displayed to an opponent concerning withdrawal intentions, since there is the possibility that the
opponent may withdraw first." As just mentioned, displays
are probably important mainly in species with distance
signaling and especially in those that can signal how large
they are--that is, in visually signaling species. We see
little indication from the described cases of distance RHP
advertising in beetles, who are, perhaps on account of
their visual shortcomings, forced to lead less deceitful

lives. It may be useful here to distinguish between *RHP advertising* (which can lead easily to deceit) and *RHP proving* (which is less likely to lead to deceit since it leads to an accurate assessment of RHP).

4. "Prior conditioning and experience can also be very important in determining the outcome of aggressive disputes." So far there is little evidence bearing on this point from beetles. Beebe, we have noted above, discussed cases in which a given pair of beetles always fought in the same way, suggesting that experience is of lesser importance in lower organisms.

5. "Much RHP disparity must be environmental, due to experience, nutrition effects during development, accidental damage, etc. In insects adult size variation is very largely environmental in origin; if size is important in the combats, the main selective force acts on choice of oviposition site by the female." While experience may be less important in beetles, nutrition is almost certainly of great importance. But this point and the oviposition behavior of females is urgently in need of investigation.

A FURTHER NOTE ON SCALE EFFECTS

Why the larger individuals in a species (in beetles, deer, antelopes, rhinoceroses, ceratopsian dinosaurs, and others) possess relatively larger horns than smaller individuals is a major unsolved problem of functional morphology. For mammals it has been claimed that larger individuals gain some mechanical advantage by having relatively larger horns, i.e., that since large animals weigh more, their charges might produce more damage because of their greater momentum. Therefore, the benefits of larger horns should be greater in the larger forms (Ghiselin, 1974, and references). Huxley (1931) attributed the greater relative size of horns in larger species partly to an indirect consequence of increased body size. If growth were allometric, then larger animals would end up having relatively larger horns. But we are then left not knowing why the allometric pattern exists. Gould (1974) was not prepared to accept either the notion that enormous antlers "are a passive consequence of selection for larger bodies" or that "selection acted primarily upon the antlers and engendered large bodies as a consequence." He supposed instead that "larger bodies and relatively larger antlers were both favored by natural selection and that the physiological correlation reinforced a rapid attainment of both conditions."

Stonehouse (1968) thought that the antlers of deer,

especially in the velvet stage, could serve some thermoregulatory function, while Geist (1971) attributed to them
both a display and a combat function.

On the matter of the horns being deleterious, it has, of
course, long been claimed that the large antlers of Irish elk
were harmful. In one sense this view is not altogether
unreasonable, at least from the standpoint that the structures
entailed production and maintenance costs involving resources
which presumably could have been allocated to more vital
functions. But if by "deleterious" is meant that the costs
always exceeded the gains, then of course, the horns could
not have evolved. Gould, in general, seems to favor the
notion that large antlers, at least in Irish elk, served as
display organs directed to females and other males. While
this may be true, I think he might have underemphasized the
use of horns in fighting. Parker (1974) has, I think, perceived the true relationship between weapons and conventional
fighting. He suggested that animals engage in various
"ritualized" activities which allow them to gauge the strength
of opponents and to enter into battle only when each contestant believes that he is the stronger and when his opponent
fails to give way during the initial testing period. I do
not think that antlers could function purely as threat signals
and never be used in physical combat for, if they were so
used, they would soon come to be disregarded. On the other
hand, they might have functions analogous to the displays of
peacocks--whatever those may be.

We now present two models to explain the relatively greater
horn size in larger animals:

The overflow model. According to this model, we expect
those males which are relatively energy-starved to forego any
expenditures on horn development if a certain minimal horn or
body size must be attained for a significant reproductive
benefit to be realized. Relatively small males might, instead, opt for less risky lives and rely on high dispersability and increased longevity to augment their chances of
finding unowned females (see Pace, 1967). On the other hand,
males with access to abundant resources, and consequently
capable of easily attaining an optimal body size, might put
all available energy, after attaining the optimal size, into
horns and their supportive structures (Fig. 11). Viewed in
this way, horns are a luxury that only the males with access
to large quantities of resources can afford to possess.

This model would lead to the prediction that the range of
horn proportions should be similar in small and large species.
This does not appear to be the general case in Lucanidae
(Fig. 8). The model may be adequate to explain increasing
relative horn size within a population, but it does not

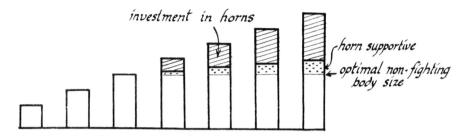

Fig. 11. Overflow model to explain scale differences in
mandible and body-size variation. Above a certain body size
necessary for the nonfighting functions, most raw materials
are diverted into increasing the structures used in fighting:
the mandibles themselves and various supportive structures,
such as the head.

explain why the largest horns of small species are proportionately smaller than the largest horns of larger species.

   Similitude models. According to elementary physics: "In
similar figures the surface increases as the square, and the
volume as the cube." This relation, which D'Arcy Thompson
(1917) called the Principle of Similitude, has important
implications to a host of behavioral and ecological problems.
Early natural historians marveled at the immense relative
strengths of ants and beetles, the great relative jumping
powers of fleas, the pronounced differences in the speed of
action between elephants and shrews, the greater variation in
size among aquatic vertebrates than among terrestrial vertebrates, the scarcity of small mammals and birds at high
latitudes, the different propensities of mammals varying in
size to hibernate, and the inability of the largest birds to
fly. In general, if one builds two animals geometrically
similar, the larger will be the weaker of the two. To counteract this tendency, the limbs of larger animals have to
become thicker and the whole skeleton bulkier and heavier.
While the strength of muscles and the resistance of bones
varies with their cross-section, the weight which muscles
must move and skeleton must support varies with the cube of
the linear dimensions.
   But are these factors operating in beetles? Are the horns
of larger beetles relatively larger than those of small males
to retain functional equivalency? If relatively small horns
on a large insect are less effective than similarly propor-
tioned horns on a small insect, natural selection may favor
a relatively greater allocation to horn development in larger
individuals. If the strength of a muscle increases as a
function of its cross-sectional area, then, other things being

equal, the muscles of a somewhat larger insect would be able to move a relatively larger set of mandibles than the muscles of a small insect. Two factors, however, are not equal: (1) the skeletal surface area available for muscle attachments becomes relatively smaller as body size increases and (2) the weight of the mandibles, and the muscles themselves, increases as a cube of their linear dimensions, while the strength of the muscles only increases as a square of theirs.

The general relationship seen in Fig. 8 might suggest that some underlying mechanical relationships having to do with the different ways that surface areas and volumes change with increasing body size are responsible for the greater horn sizes in larger beetles.

For the most part entomologists are still in the company of vertebrate biologists as to the reason larger males should have relatively larger horns than smaller males--both are in the dark. We may have made some progress since Beebe (1949) made the following statement, but not much.

It is hoped that naturalists will be on the watch for still other methods of combat, making use of the strange crook-headed pikes, harpoons, hammer-like and sword-like horns which are found in other species of tropical beetles. At present we are completely in the dark as to the why or wherefore of the great variation in this strange armory of nature (p. 317).

REFERENCES

Arrow, G.J. 1951. *Horned Beetles*. Dr. W. Junk, The Hague.

Bateson, W., and H.H. Brindley. 1892. On some cases of variation in secondary sexual characters, statistically examined. *Proc. Zool. Soc. London* 1892:585-594.

Beebe, W. 1944. The function of secondary sexual characters in two species of Dynastidae (Coleoptera). *Zoologica* 29:53-58.

Beebe, W. 1949. *High Jungle*. Duell, Sloane and Pierce, New York.

Brüll, H. 1952. Über die Bedeutung der Mundwerkzenge des männlichen und des weiblichen Hirschkäfers. *Natur. Volk.* 82:289-294.

Darwin, C. 1871. *The Descent of Man, and Selection in Relation to Sex*, 2nd ed. (1898). A.L. Burt Co., New York.

Diakonov, D.M. 1925. Experimental and biometrical investigations on dimorphic variability of *Forficula*. *J. Genetics* 15:201-232.

Fisher, R.A. 1958. *The Genetical Theory of Natural Selection*. Dover Publ., Inc., New York.

Gadgil, M. 1972. Male dimorphism as a consequence of sexual selection. *Amer. Nat.* 106:576-580.

Geist, V. 1971. *Mountain Sheep. A Study in Behavior and Evolution.* Univ. Chicago Press, Chicago.

Ghiselin, M.T. 1974. *The Economy of Nature and the Evolution of Sex.* Univ. California Press, Berkeley.

Gould, S.J. 1974. The origin and function of "Bizarre" structures: antler size and skull size in the "Irish Elk," *Megalocerus giganteus. Evolution* 28:191-220.

Hersh, A.H. 1934. Evolutionary relative growth in the Titanotheres. *Amer. Nat.* 58:537.

Huxley, J. 1931. The relative size of antlers in deer. *Proc. Zool. Soc. London* 1931:819-864.

Joseph, C. 1928. El *Chiasognathus grantii* Steph. *Revista Universitaria, Univ. Catolica, Santiago, Chile* 13:520-535.

Levins, R. 1967. *Evolution in Changing Environments.* Princeton Univ. Press, Princeton.

Mathieu, J.M. 1969. Mating behavior of five species of Lucanidae (Coleoptera: Insecta). *Can. Ent.* 101:1054-1062.

Pace, A. 1967. Life history and behavior of a fungus beetle, *Bolitotherus cornutus* (Tenebrionidae). *Occ. Papers Mus. Zool. Univ. Michigan* No. 653:1-15.

Parker, G.A. 1974. Assessment strategy and the evolution of fighting behaviour. *J. Theor. Biol.* 47:223-243.

Reichenau, W. von. 1881. Über den Ursprung des secundären männlichen Geschlectscharaktere, insbesondere bei den Blatthornkäfern. *Kosmos* 10:179-194.

Stonehouse, B. 1968. Thermoregulatory functions of growing antlers. *Nature* 218:870-872.

Thompson, D'Arcy. 1917. *Growth and Form.* Cambridge Univ. Press, Cambridge.

Tippmann, F.F. 1954. Neues aus dem Leben des Hirschkäfers. Ein Beitrag zur Bedeutung der Geweihahnlichen Mandibeln des Männchens. *Ent. Bl. Krefeld* 50:175-183.

Trivers, R.L. 1972. Parental investment and sexual selection. pp. 136-179. *In* B. Campbell (ed.), *Sexual Selection and the Descent of Man, 1871-1971.* Aldine, Chicago.

Ureta, E. 1934. Sobre algunas costumbres del *Chiasognathus grantii* Steph. *Revista Chilena Hist. Nat.* 38:287-292.

Wallace, A.R. 1889. *Darwinism: An Exposition of the Theory of Natural Selection with some of its Applications.* Macmillan, London.

Wilson, E.O. 1953. The origin and evolution of polymorphism in ants. *Quart. Rev. Biol.* 28:136-156.

SEXUAL SELECTION IN LUMINESCENT BEETLES

James E. Lloyd

University of Florida

Concealed talent brings no reputation (Erasmus).

You're nobody 'til somebody loves you (Dean Martin).

The revolution in biology that R.D. Alexander (1975) observed "literally pushed the study of social behavior almost into an entirely theoretical state, because most of the previous work was done with inadequate models" affects the study of the most primal of social interactions--mating behavior. For some time naturalists focused their attention on "species problems," such as mating signals and behavior, and reproductive isolation. Although in recent years (especially since Williams' 1966 classic), we did not explicitly champion or reason with or from species (population) adaptation, we expected animals to more or less behave in that fashion. With respect to sexual behavior, an animal was expected to get a mate of the same species (kind)--what else was there? In other words, until recently, much important behavior was dismissed as irrelevant, unimportant, and maybe pathological. Since becoming aware of some of the implications of sexual selection, I have seen fireflies do things I would not hitherto have expected of a beetle, while making lengthy observations of situations I would previously have considered fruitless.

This paper examines firefly mating behaviors and patterns which have actual, possible, or potential significance in sexual selection in luminescent beetles. Most of the species discussed are true fireflies (Lampyridae: some species are called glowworms), and a few are glowworm beetles (Phengodidae, close relatives of fireflies).[1]

---

[1] Luminescent click beetles or cucujos, family Elateridae, are not discussed because little is known of their behavior except that luminescence is used in conjunction with mating, and the click can be used by females to repel unwanted mounters and probably by males to repel competitors at a female (Lloyd, 1971 and unpublished).

There have been fireflies for millions of years--certainly
since the Cretaceous--a long time for change and divergence.
While a time-lapse replay of the luminescent behaviors of the
fireflies that have come, changed, and gone would be interesting, it would be more enlightening to know the specific forces
that have turned the kaleidoscope. These have included the
continued and transient actions of biological agents--para-
sites, predators, and competitors--as well as the adversity
of physical elements--wind, moonlight, glaciers, even tectonic
movements. Some forces have acted directly and strongly, and
others feebly and subtly. For example, the advertisement glow
of the female Knull's glowworm (*Lampyris knulli,* Florida),
which is unnecessarily bright or given at inappropriate times
for mate attraction, wastes ATP that could be put directly
into egg production: An exuberant glow is also more likely
to attract an attack by toads and spiders. Selective pressures oppose each other; a vigorous movement of the lantern
and locomotion during display increase chances of both mate
attraction and predation; the resultant compromise varies
with individual circumstances.

Among the most important factors that have affected firefly evolution are those included within the meaning of the
expression *sexual selection*. These phenomena are generally
divided into two categories--intra-and intersexual selection.
Sexual selection includes both obvious and subtle elements.
(This discussion assumes that the females of these beetles
make the greater investment in each offspring and will generally exercise greater mate selectivity and that competition
among males for females is typically rigorous (Trivers, 1972).)
Males competing for females shove, bite, and disable their
rivals. They race them upwind on pheromone plumes, thwart
their attempts to elicit answers from females by injecting
extra flashes into their coded patterns, mislead them with
flashes resembling female flashes or the flashes of "femme-
fatale" predators, and perhaps block or disable their sperm.
Females observe and select partners. There are overt, observable acts of this selection, although much of it remains
within the confines of the female sensory and data-processing
systems and is difficult to analyze (Fisher, 1958). Females
have neural templates of criteria for evaluating males (see
Otte, 1974) as well as programs for behavior that function in
filtering prospective mates.

MATING BEHAVIOR AND SEXUAL SELECTION

There is broad variation in the mating behavior of luminescent beetles. In some species, only lone, roving, glowing
males are seen. Males of other species search without glowing,

and unless taken in a trap of some sort, the only indication
of their existence is the occasional sighting of one of their
wingless luminescent females. At the other extreme, hundreds,
or hundreds of thousands, of males and females gather in trees
where the males flash in synchrony.

In examining these diverse mating protocols (a species' total mating scenario), it is useful to distinguish six phases:
decision as to where and how to search; search; decision to
begin (continue) pursuit; pursuit, including courtship; copulation; and postcopulation. (The first four of these are
analogized from MacArthur's predator-prey discussion [1972;
see Jackson, 1975].) The adult beetle, male or female, first
decides where and how to search. Alternative strategies may
exist in many species, with decisions depending upon population density, season, and age of the individual. Searching is
a major investment for males of most, but not all, species.
Search ends when an individual begins to track or orient to
a specific individual of the opposite sex. At this point the
decision of whether to approach (pursue) is made which may
later be reversed and signaling terminated. (The term *approach* will generally be substituted for pursuit.) Such a
moment in male behavior is most notable and noticeable when it
reverses an earlier decision, i.e., when after the approach
has been initiated, the male correctly rejects an aggressive-
mimic predator or incorrectly (?) rejects an answering conspecific female. Approach is sometimes begun at different

TABLE 1

*Mate filtering and selection in luminescent beetles, from the
female standpoint, in a promiscuous mating system*

PASSIVE FILTERING: males are not all capable of locating and
reaching females; many are out of the running during early
ontogeny, while others attain adulthood but get no further
(Fig. 1).
PASSIVE SELECTION: males are not all capable of besting rival,
conspecific males in searches, races, ploys, or combat directed toward gaining fertilizations (including intrasexual
selection).
ACTIVE FILTERING: before males reach female purview, female
behavior sometimes (optionally) contributes to the ease or
difficulty males experience in reaching them.
ACTIVE SELECTION: females monitor male performance, imposing
additional tests including the manipulation of male interactions, appraise male performance, and then make a selection
(intersexual selection).

---

moments by converging members of the signaling pair and ends
with the male mounting the female. Copulation ends with uncoupling. As this schedule proceeds, the major events for
both participants are mate location, identification, apprais-
al, and acceptance. (I present a broader spectrum of mating
activities than is strictly associated with sexual selection

Fig. 1. Photuris *firefly with "birth" defect. Hemocoelic
fluid under pressure during adult emergence leaked out of an
elytral vein causing the cuticle to inflate into a huge
bubble, which eventually hardened into a dry blister. This
seemingly trivial imperfection will prevent a male from
efficiently searching and competing for a mate: He may be
unable to fly at all.*

because of the likely interdependence of all the elements of
each protocol.)

The screening of males is both active and passive (from the
female's standpoint) (Table 1).

Passive filtering. When males must move to the female's
general location, some succeed and others fail (Fig. 1). The
intensity of such filtering varies, and chance plays some
role, i.e., some males may quickly and easily locate a female
because she matured and began advertising near their starting
point. Others, through misfortune, may spend their brief
adult lives searching for mates under unusually harsh environmental conditions--wind, low temperature, rain, or moonlight. The rigor of passive filtering depends upon the
various aspects of the species' biology. Its mean and variance, in many instances, may be important determinants of the
rigor and nature of events in later stages of approach, i.e.,
courtship.

Passive selection. During the search for and the approach
to a female, several males may simultaneously be in quest.
This aspect of screening involves not merely overcoming
physical and biological obstacles, but competing with conspecific males, and superiority over other individuals in
search and approach competence wins higher fitness. Competitive success depends on speed and efficiency in these behaviors: random or biased search patterns (where, when, and how
to search), signal detection/discrimination (what to approach), orientation and tracking, anticompetitor ploys as
well as their discrimination, and physical combat (how to
approach).

Passive filtering becomes passive selection when the upwind flight toward a female becomes a race, not merely a trip.
Classical intrasexual selection phenomena belong here.[2] The
continuum that exists between the two passive categories is
variable intraspecifically. How a male must perform depends
upon specific ecological circumstances prevailing at the time
and place, and upon the intensity of the competition. For
example, since no other male may be active in the area for
hours at very low densities, a solitary glowworm male has only
to get to the female and stamina and longevity will be rewarded. At high densities there may be a premium on speed, or
ability to drop to the ground accurately and mount quickly, or

---

[2] The term *intrasexual selection* has traditionally been used
for situations in which competitors are able to take direct
action against rivals, as in combat or manipulative ploys,
and not applied to contests in which the participants do not
interact, such as air races and search flights. This distinction seems artificial.

to fight. Various species may range characteristically about
one point or another along this density-competition gradient,
and this variation, when viewed and compared with intraspecific manifestations of it, has especial significance for understanding the evolution of the mating protocols.

Active filtering. The ease with which a male can approach a
female will depend to some extent upon her behavior, such as
her choice of perch or position during the period of mating
activity. Since mating activity entails some risk of predator
attack, female behavior is adjusted to both mating success
and predator avoidance. Greater risk taking occurs in females
as their chances of total reproductive failure increase. That
is, females of some species will adjust the intensity of male
filtering--making it easier for males to find and reach them--
depending upon their own circumstances of age (and presumably
egg condition) and their "projected" probabilities of getting
a mate. I believe it is reasonable to anticipate that facul-
tative manipulation of male filtering may also occur in a pure
sexual selection context; young females may be more selective
than old females, and by being so, obtain "better" mates. For
example, they may be able to adjust the rigor of filtering by
varying the duration or timing of signal (pheromone or luminescence) output.

Active selection. At some point during the approach of a
male, a female is finally able to directly observe or otherwise monitor, manipulate for observation, and evaluate the
nature of his flashing, flying, orientation, or fighting.
Depending upon circumstances and protocol, selection may be
made from among males present simultaneously or serially. In
Photinus collustrans (a Florida sp.) males are usually viewed
sequentially; in *Luciola obsoleta* (New Guinea) males are
usually viewed simultaneously; and in others both may occur.
It is also possible that after mating and accepting sperm, a
female of a seemingly sequential species may be able to manipulate the sperm--use, eject, digest, or store it--while she
makes decisions on that male's quality with respect to postcopulation observations on him and later (semicomparative)
observations on other males.

BEHAVIOR OF SOME LUMINESCENT BEETLES

Firefly Glowworms (Lampyridae)

Knull's glowworm. Lampyris knulli seems to be near one
end of the spectrum of mating protocols: females may never
have any mate choice, arriving males may have already been

highly filtered, and courtship may be virtually nonexistent.
Knulli is rare, and with two exceptions the 50 or so males in
collections were taken in black-light traps (various Florida
localities). I have found the eight known females at two
localities in Gainesville over a period of 13 years, yet have
visited these sites on hundreds of evenings, searched specifically for females, and investigated every likely glow at
dozens of sites within this glowworm's geographic range.

Females are flightless, with elytra (wing covers, modified
forewings) one-fifth the typical length and wings absent.
They emerge from underground burrows about 25 min. after
sunset, climb to low perches on grass 2.5-5 cm above the
ground, and glow for about 40 min. They then return to their
burrows (Lloyd, 1966a). Like many other glowworm females,
while glowing, they curl their bodies into C-shapes and aim
their lights generally skyward. Some (older ones ?) change
their position every few minutes and aim the light in different directions. Males have huge, contiguous eyes, reduced
mouthparts, small, simple antennae (see Fig. 2), and a small
luminous area on the ventral surface of the abdomen. I have
seen two males attracted to females during an aggregate total
of 7.8 hrs. of observation--the equivalent of 15.6 evening
glow-bouts--a rate of about one male per eight evenings of
advertisement.

Another observation demonstrates an additional problem and
dilemma. I placed a virgin female of a western United States
species (*Microphotus angustus,* Fig. 2a) in a *knulli* study site
to see if she would attract a *knulli* male. Her first evening
bout was twice as long and overlapped that of *knulli.* On the
second evening, 14 min. after beginning, she was seized
from her perch and eaten by a southern toad *(Bufo terrestris).*

European glowworm. The behavior of *Lampyris noctiluca,* similar to that of *knulli,* has been studied extensively. A major
difference is that males and females commonly appear in large
numbers during at least part of their season, although near
the end and in some localities only a few are active. Females
appear at dusk and may advertise for several hours. Upon
mating they stop glowing. Males glow very dimly or not at
all. From observations on 427 females over a period of 15
days (Dreisig, 1971), it seems that most females attract males
on their first evening of activity and in less than 2 hr.
Dreisig associated one noteworthy example of poor success: a
female glowed several hours on each of four evenings before
attracting a male--with a poor signaling station.

Schwalb (1961) made extensive observations on the behavior
of this glowworm. Searching males fly about 1 m above the
ground at less than 1 m/sec. Their eyes are specialized for
forward acuity and peripheral sensitivity. Upon sighting a

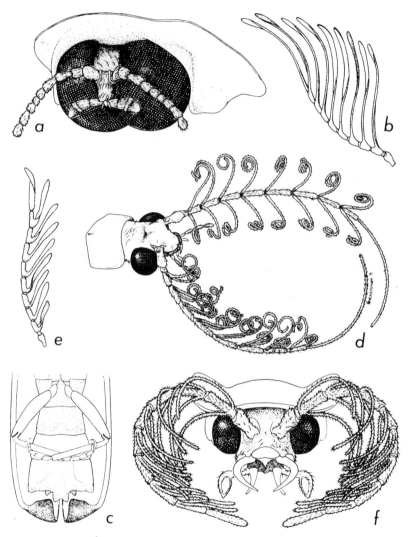

Fig. 2. *Morphological adaptations of luminescent beetles of significance in sexual selection and mate finding; all are lampyrids except d, a phengodid. (a) Male of* Microphotus angustus *(California) with large eyes, simple antennae, and small mandibles. The large structures below the antennae are palps. Males of Knull's glowworm are similar in appearance. (b) Antenna of* Ethra sp. *male (Brazil). (c) Ventral view of* Pteroptyx valida *(Malaysia) male abdomen, showing folded elytral apices. (continued on facing page)*

female, the male folds his wings and falls to the ground.
The accuracy of this drop is such that when Schwalb placed
females in cylinders with 3 cm openings, 65% of the males
attracted fell within; the remainder landed within 20 cm of
their targets. After an inaccurate fall, a male runs and
circles rapidly and then may climb, fly, and drop again.
Interestingly, after a second failure, males often leave.
Possibly they project--on the basis of time of evening, season, and other ecological factors--that the cost of finding
the female exceeds the average cost of reaching another, i.e.,
$P > \bar{S} + \bar{P}$ (MacArthur, 1972). Schwalb noted especially that
the behavior of males in the vicinity of females became very
quick. Upon reaching the female, they rapidly mounted,
oriented, and coupled. The reason for this haste is obvious--
male competition. Schwalb noted that when a female continued
to glow after copulation had begun, additional males gathered,
clustered about the female, and shoved against the copulating
pair with lowered prothorax. The female can therefore potentially manipulate male competition by varying the length of
her postcoupling glow. Dreisig (1971) noted that sometimes
this glow lasted as long as 30 min., although 15 min. was
usual.

Aging females of *noctiluca* gradually, over days, shine more
brightly, wander and circle their glowing stations, pulse and
scintillate their light, and wave and rotate their abdomens
(Newport, 1857; Schwalb, 1961; Dreisig, 1971), thus facilitating their discovery by males--and predators, too--as well as
using more energy. One would expect that as females age they
might spend more time advertising each evening, but this does
not seem to be the case in *noctiluca*. Dreisig (unpublished)
observed three individuals from the time they were discovered
until they died or had oviposited eggs (infertile), a period
of 12-13 days. They varied but did not gradually increase
the duration of their evening glow period.

One might also expect that females would not use energy or
expose themselves to predators at times when the chances of
attracting mates are poor. However, Dreisig found that at low
temperatures (12°C) and high winds (3.5 m/sec.) which resulted
in greatly reduced male activity, females were active.
Schwalb noted that mechanical stimulation caused females to

_The dark pigmentation of these supposed shades contrasts with
the pale condition of the remainder of the wing covers in
this and five other_ Pteroptyx _species. In ten other species
the elytra are dark. (d) Male of_ Phengodes _sp. (Colombia,
S.A.), which has a small ventral light organ. (e) Antenna of_
Lucidota _male (Colombia, S.A.). (f) Male of_ Psilocladus _sp.
(Colombia, S.A.) with large antennae and mandibles. (Drawing
by Stephen Sickerman)_

stop glowing for a time, and when strongly stimulated they
retreated to their "hideouts" for the duration of the evening.

In his work on circadian rhythms, Dreisig (in press) found
evidence for a change in a threshold or set (i.e., motivational state, tendency) in aging, unmated *noctiluca* females.
Younger females will usually not glow when kept in continuous
total darkness, but most older ones will.

Males of both *Lampyris* species are luminescent, but their
lights are not used during search and their function has not
been investigated. The light may convey significant information during courtship, e.g., that the male has functional
enzymatic systems for luminescence and hence the genes that
will be required by progeny that will use this chemistry
for success as larvae,[3] or as adult females for attracting
mates, or, of course, as adult males in intersexual selection.

Other glowworms. Females of the Indian Glowworm *(Lampri-
gera (=Lamprophorus) tenebrosus;* India, Ceylon) and *Dioptoma
adamsi* (India, Ceylon) advertise with tails lifted or arched
over their backs, thus exposing their light organs. When
their males arrive, they are not luminescing: "Males *(tenebrosus)* fly up with a loud buzzing sound, but without lights,
and drop close to her. They then become faintly luminous and
run around her" (Gravely, 1915). The approach of *adamsi* "was
not heralded by any display of fireworks on his part . . . I
was interested to observe that the male *Dioptoma* (hitherto
supposed to be nonluminous) displays--under sexual excite-
ment--a brilliant series of lights of emerald green colour"
(Green, 1912). With no information on the intensity of male
competition or on similar species active in the same area,
the message in the male luminescence remains unknown.

Males of other glowworm species emit bright luminescence
while searching for mates, e.g., the European *Lamprohiza
(=Phausis) splendidula* and *Phausis reticulata* of the eastern
United States. In the latter the glow will cause females
that are not already glowing to light their lanterns (Lloyd,
1965a). This increase of search effort is an evolutionary
manipulation of males; they are forced to search for females
with their lights on, perhaps exposing themselves to predators, and surely using energy that could otherwise be used
for searching for additional females. The restriction of

[3] The larvae of all lampyrid species, including species that
are nonluminescent as adults, so far as known, are luminescent. The larval lantern seems not to be, in most cases, the
ontogenetic precursor of the flashing adult organ. Its
function is unknown but the subject of rich speculation (see
Lloyd, 1971).

female glowing to a glow-response may have evolved in response
to predator pressure (Lloyd, 1966b) and represents an important stage in the evolution of firefly communication. This
manipulation may be used solely by young females; some females
(older ones ?) are commonly found glowing in nature without
recent male stimulation.

Among the luminescent beetles several species apparently
use long-range chemical signals, for they have fantastic
antennal specializations (Fig. 2). Regardless of their
sequential relationship in evolution with respect to the use
of luminescent signals, these evolved under conditions of
keen competition among males during search and approach.
Females of these species are specialized to emit chemicals
at higher levels than precursors that used contact chemicals

Fig. 3. Electron micrograph of Pleotomus *sp. male head:*
ventral view showing large, multifaceted eyes, large and
complex antennae, and small mouthparts. Inset shows portion
of antenna with sense organs that probably detect female
pheromone. Distance across eyes about 2 mm. (Micrograph by
T.C. Carlysle)

or perch markers. Whenever a pheromone evolved from such a
chemical, selection must have been favoring females with
greater and greater ability to help males by making their
searches and approaches faster and more certain--perhaps
because of new ecological circumstances resulting in reduced
population densities or increased patchiness of distribution.
Pheromone production in these cases may have first evolved
as an old female's option or crutch.

   Pleotomus sp. (USA) occur at low densities and have large
eyes and well-developed antennae (Fig. 3). Females are
brightly luminescent, and although males have at least weak
luminescence (King, 1880; Sleeper, 1969), they have not been
reported flying and glowing in nature. Males of *P. nigripen-
nis* glow brightly when "disturbed" (Sleeper, 1969), but there
have been no observations of courtship. Since males have
small mandibles, biting is probably not part of a male competition should more than one arrive at a female. Such may not
be the case with many South American species whose males have
light organs and large mandibles as well as large antennae
(Fig. 2).

Glowworm Beetles (Phengodidae)

   Members of the family Phengodidae are similar to some of
the glowworm fireflies in their mating behavior. Males have
large, plumose antennae, indicating the use of pheromones,
and lethal jaws (Figs. 2d and 4). The larviform females glow
brightly from a number of photophores, and, in some *Phrixothrix* spp., simultaneously in two different colors; males of
the various species are brightly, faintly, or not at all
luminescent (see Lloyd, 1971, for references). The eyes of
the males do not show obvious specializations like those of
fireflies, but their elytra are reduced to triangular
epaulettes. Most beetles elevate their elytra during flight,
and though this may increase stability, it greatly increases
drag. Under strong selection for speed and endurance, phen-
godids have lost the protection elytra would give them in
their deadly fights and against predators. Although there
have been no studies to determine the exact nature of the
protocols, males of *Phengodes* spp. of the eastern United
States apparently search for and approach females from long
range by using pheromones, and at close range, locate and
identify them by their luminescence. There is no evidence of
male luminescent displays during courtship, which is itself
apparently virtually nonexistent (Barber, 1906; Atkinson,
1887), although brilliant luminosity in some males has been
reported (Knab, 1905). Both males and females of a Brazilian
phengodid ("*Ptenophengus*" = *Cenophengus?* (Bristowe, 1924)) are

Fig. 4. Electron micrograph of Phengodes sp. male head:
frontal view showing portion of small eye, large complex
antennae (position not lifelike), and lethal mandibles.
Mandible length 2.2 mm. (Micrograph by T.C. Carlysle)

luminescent. Males and females of a Brazilian Phrixothrix,
a railroad worm with red and green lights, "stage a pyro-
technic display as they mate." Males of this species are
reported to mate only once, whereas females mate several times
(Tiemann, 1970).
    Zarhipis species (western United States), which use phero-
mones, are sexually active during the day in temperate seasons
and localities, but under conditions of low humidity probably
become crepuscular or nocturnal (Lloyd, 1971, 1977). When a
female begins signaling with pheromones, she may very quickly
get some action:

    Thinking a fresh supply of earth to be beneficial [to a
    presumed larva of Zarhipis riversi that would not eat],
    removed the jar into the garden and emptied the earth by
    the stump of a tree, and while in this act several speci-
    mens of Zarhipis pitched upon the discarded earth, and one

specimen dropped swiftly upon the until then supposed
larva, throwing the female into violent movements by the
suddenness of the attack.   The male soon attempted copulation . . . I captured 11 males (Rivers, 1886).

The simultaneous arrival of several males at a receptive
female sets the stage for push and bite.

Tiemann (1967) made a number of interesting observations

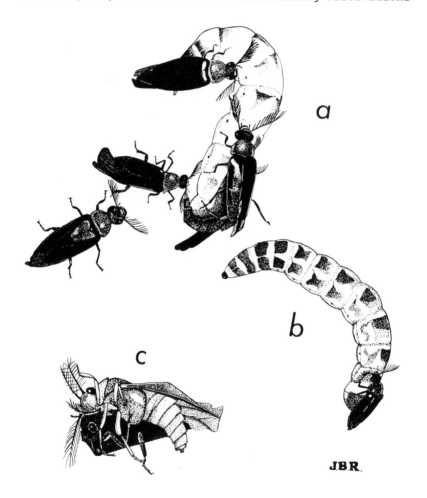

Fig. 5. The western banded glowworm, Zarhipis integripennis,
family Phengodidae, from photographs by D.L. Tiemann (1967).
(a) Several males attracted simultaneously to a female.
(b) Copulation.   (c) Males fighting, drawn in black and white
for clarity.   Note the extreme sexual dimorphism in morphology, which is a reflection of the behavioral dimorphism.
(Drawings by John B. Randall)

on the sexual behavior of the western banded glowworm beetle
(Zarhipis integripennis) in California. Signaling females
quickly attracted several males (Fig. 5): in three experiments
at different sites, captive females--or the containers and
soil they had been kept in--attracted nine males in 15 min.,
six males in 5 min., and five males in 15 min. Tiemann placed
four males in a container with a female.

Two males successfully mated with the female. Two of the
males approached the female, one mating with her almost
immediately. The other two immediately attacked each other
using their mandibles as weapons [see Fig. 5]. The fight
continued for quite some time, with the males twisting and
turning to make the most effective use of their mandibles,
sometimes grabbing each other, and sometimes lifting each
other in the air. Finally, one of them completely disabled
the other by puncturing its thorax.

Tiemann observed fighting among males of Z. *tiemanni:* he
placed seven in a container with a female of *integripennis*.
Fighting also occurs in *Phengodes laticollis*. After the 4
June 1908 meeting of the Washington Entomological Society,
"Mr. Barber exhibited living specimens, both males and females . . . members had . . . an opportunity to admire the luminosity of the larviform females . . . the mating of the sexes . . .
and the fierce combats of the males . . ." (Proc. Ent. Soc.
Wash. 10:119-120 [1908]).

Flashing Fireflies (Lampyridae)

The most common and abundant true fireflies, especially
in the New World and all but the northern Palearctic region,
are those that emit their luminescence in bright flashes or
flickers. Although study of these species has only just
begun, it is obvious that behavioral diversity is considerable.
Morphological sexual dimorphism is less than in glowworm fireflies. The most usual dimorphisms, other than in primary
sex-characters, are in the topography and size of the light
organs and the size (and presumably filtering and facet
angles) of the eyes, which in most cases are conspicuously
larger in males. In *Pteroptyx* spp., the color of light emitted differs in the sexes. The eyes of males in flashing
fireflies seldom or never reach the proportions of those found
in some glowworm males, although the eyes of some are phenom-
enal (Fig. 6). Of course, the most conspicuous and important
sexual dimorphism is in the mating behavior.

Luciola lusitanica. Floriano Papi's (1969) enviable study
of this firefly (range southern Europe and Eurasia) suggests

Fig. 6. Male of a Colombian Bicellonycha sp., related to
Photuris. The huge, unusually glossy eyes reflect the ring-
flash, making them appear smaller than they actually are.

considerable and subtle sexual selection. Males of lusitanica
begin flying and flashing soon after sunset, appearing in
greatest numbers during the first 2 hr., with activity
thereafter declining sharply. They fly ca 1 m above the
ground, lower in the wind, and orient to vegetational cues--
such as clumps of thick grass--that correlate with female
location. Females are far less conspicuous (numerous) than
males, and in areas where hundreds of males can be seen flash-

ing, only a few, or occasionally up to 30 females can be
found. (This situation has been found in nearly all flashing
species studied except lek-forming Luciolinae in Asia, as
discussed below.) Males of *lusitanica* emit short, sometimes
rapidly modulated flashes at ca 1 sec. intervals during
search flight. Females emit a similar, variable, somewhat
longer flash in response to each male emission (signal system
2: Lloyd, 1971), at a precise temperature-dependent time de-
lay--ca 250 ms at 20°C. Female success in attracting males
depends upon male density and the position of the female.
Free females attract males in minutes or within a half hour at
most. One female in thick grass was unsuccessful for one
hour, but attracted a male after she climbed up a grass stalk
where her flashes were more visible. Captive females placed
on the ground where many males were active were quickly approached by one or more males, often within a few seconds.
Females almost always can be choosy.

When a male perceives the answering flash of a female, he
flies straight toward it and pauses just above. A brief flash
dialogue (inspection-dialogue: Papi, 1969) ensues as he flies
irregular circles and spirals above the female. At this point,
males often emit continuous glows, up to 10 sec. in duration,
and flashing is suspended. Under natural conditions males
often fly off without landing, even after fairly long dialogues during which the interaction has apparently been normal. After a male lands, he often pauses 10 sec. or longer
before he resumes flashing and continues his approach. This
last leg of the approach may take from a few seconds to several minutes. Copulating females rarely respond to the flashes
of flying males.

Additional males are often attracted to the flashes of a
pair in dialogue. Females then respond to the flashes of
joining males, and some of these males land. Landing depends
upon whether their own flashes have been answered.

An active flash dialogue soon develops between a male and
a female placed on the ground in separate small glass containers. Other males soon arrive to inspect the pair and
about one-third to one-half of them actually lands. In
these conditions one pair was inspected during 25 min. by
12 males, five of which actually landed. If, however, the
male and the female are immobilized and the anterior end of
the female forced into an opaque tube so that she may only
see the flashing of her partner, the number of landing
males declines sharply. In one hour's time the experimental pair attracted 41 males but only four of them landed.
The result is significantly different from the previous
one (P < 0.05) and it is furthermore possible that the four
males may have been induced to land by some flash-responses

from the male in the glass container (Papi, 1969).

Papi observed and experimented with a number of responses and interactions that have considerable significance with respect to sexual selection:

> . . . males on the ground flash irregularly and sometimes deliver female-type responses to light stimuli. Such behavior is frequent in males which have engaged in a dialogue with a female not followed by copulation. With their flashing, these males induce other flying males to engage in inspection-dialogues with them and occasionally even to land.

Pseudo-female behavior may give a rejected male an opportunity to see and approach the female's flashed answers to another male, and thus another chance to mate with her (Lloyd, 1971; see Otte, 1974, for discussion and references on intraspecific deceit). Another remote possibility is that under certain circumstances females will not accept any male until he has performed in a contest situation, and so a male must procure others (see also Alexander, 1975). In consideration of lekking behavior found especially in other lucioline fireflies, including Asian congeners (see below), there may be considerably more to this behavior than first appears. Nevertheless, *lusitanica* has a complex protocol, and male deception is clearly part of it: (1) Males are attracted to male-female dialogue (in fireflies a recurring alternative strategy for mate location). (2) Rejected males give pseudo-female responses to other males. (3) In spite of intense competition for females and an absence of aggressive mimicry (see below), males often hover and make extensive dialogue-inspections before landing. This phase is not an essential component of courtship since it is sometimes omitted entirely. After a dialogue males sometimes fly off, even leaving responsive females. (4) Although the male flash is complex, variable, and 200-250 ms. in duration, females answer equally well to single, transient bursts of 1 ms. duration or long flashes that continue up to 4 sec., even when repeated after 300-400 ms. intervals. The female flash is similar though somewhat longer. The multiple modulations in male flashes may deceive approaching males and prevent them from determining which flash is actually of female origin and where she is perched. (5) After landing near a responsive female, a male ceases flashing for 10 or more seconds before continuing his approach, thus reducing the likelihood of another male detecting his approach to a female (a pattern found in other species, e.g., *Pyractomena dispersa* [Lloyd, 1964] and *P. angulata;* and *Photinus macdermotti,* see below).

Flash dialogues often occur between males that are confined

in glass cages or immobilized within sight of each other.
These males will "exchange flashes according to given rules"
(Papi, 1969) involving certain flash-answer relationships. It
seems unlikely that either male long mistakes his correspondent for a female. The significance of this behavior--to the
fireflies should it occur normally in nature or to investigators for analyzing the neural program as it relates to male-
female or male-pseudo-female behavior--remains unclear. It
may be relevant to subtle elements of competitor manipulation.

Blair (1915) made the following comments on the behavior
of another Italian firefly, identified by him as *Luciola
italica*. Its behavior, except for the flashing, appears to
be more like that of *Lampyris* than *lusitanica*.

> . . . In these insects . . . the initiative in seeking a mate
> appears to be with the female, as in the case of *Lampyris*.
> At times they will be quite dark, while sometimes they will
> glow with an almost steady, though not very bright, light.
> When "calling" for a mate, however, they flash with rather
> long, slow flashes, incompletely extinguished in the inter-
> vals . . . the light of the female was sometimes observed,
> or the insects found paired quite early in the flight
> period, yet they were much more conspicuous later, when the
> numbers of the males had considerably decreased; probably
> this was due to the females making more or less desperate
> efforts as the competition became keener [i.e., as their
> probabilities for remaining unmated increased].

Photinus spp. More than 50 of these species have been
studied, and in general they use a signal system similar to
that of *lusitanica*. Males fly about their habitat emitting a
species-typical flash pattern as they go. Male patterns vary
among the species from simple, single flashes to multiple
flashes and rapid and subtle modulations, while female responses are typically simple flashes. Habitats vary: grassland, open woodland, forests, stream margins, ponds and
marshes, and forest edges. Population sizes range from tens
to thousands, the latter being found in grassland. Usually
many more males are sexually active than females. This becomes obvious when an observer walks about the site of activity looking for dialogues or flashes a penlight in a manner
simulating the male pattern. Male fireflies make a sizable
investment in time and energy for each female found; perhaps
more fail than succeed as there are several hazards. Strong
selection has acted upon males in the competitive contexts of
search and approach, and the eyes, light organs, flash construction, postures and gestures during flashing, and other
characters (Lloyd, 1971), including male flash synchrony
(Otte and Smiley, 1977), show a number of features that promote competitive competence.

    Males of *Photinus collustrans,* a Florida grassland species,
emit a single ca 0.30 sec. flash each 2.2 sec. (22°C) as they
fly rapidly over the ground (altitude 0.5-1.5 m). During each
flash males usually make a lateral arc, an action that may
permit them to view more of the area just covered with the
flash (Lloyd, 1966b). The corridor that they search is asym-
metrically distributed along their actual flight path, depending upon the movements of their body (lantern and eyes)
during flight. Since the area actually searched depends upon
the range at which males can see female response flashes, the
nature of the grassy vegetation is an important factor.
    Recent investigations (Lloyd, work in progress) have begun
to quantify the investment that males make, as well as some
other of their problems, during the search phase of their
mating behavior. Individual *collustrans* males (n = 199) were
followed for periods as long as 10 min., for a total of 10.9
miles (17.5 km), and observed while they flashed 7,988 advertisements. They found two females and mated with them. The
evening activity period of this species is sharply limited:
at the beginning by high ambient light levels and at the end
by a sibling species *tanytoxus*. The average duration of male
activity is ca 15 min./period, and the chances of a male finding a female during a single activity period are 0.139. That
is, it will require 7.2 nights to find a female. Using only
data from the most extensively studied site, a pasture, the
chances of finding a female on a given evening are 0.201,
i.e., five evening periods are required to find a female.
Males arriving at females must usually be highly filtered.
    Two noteworthy problems encountered by searching males were
collisions with vegetation and specialized predators. Eleven
crashes occurred for 10.9 air miles, with time losses up to
15 sec./crash. Females of the genus *Photuris*, especially *P.
versicolor,* mimic the signals of *Photinus* females and attract
males and eat them (Lloyd, 1965b, 1973a, 1975). Two of these
predators, *P. versicolor and Photuris* sp. A (unnamed new
species), were active in the *collustrans* sites. None was
successful in capturing males, but of the 11 that answered
them, four attracted the males to land near them. One male
wasted 4 min. before he flew off (the departure times for
three males were not determined). When mimicking the sibling
species *P. tanytoxus,* these predators have a success rate of
0.2 (Lloyd, 1975). Combined data from three study sites give
a male the probability 0.139 of finding a mate, 0.764 for a
crash, 0.278 of being attracted, and 0.056 of being eaten by
a "femme fatale."[4]

---

[4] Probabilities based on data from 156 males observed during
the first 16 min. of search activity (see Fig. 8).

Previous observations on the success of *collustrans* females
attracting males were made with females that had been in captivity for at least 24 hr., and usually longer. It had been
observed that they were then more responsive and easier to
manipulate for electronic recording (Lloyd, 1966b). The females quickly attracted males to the outside of their glass
cages, and sometimes glowed continuously during the period of
male activity even before they had seen males. Recently, a
single free female was observed. She was found attracting a
male, which was removed. There were few males, their season
was virtually over. The following night no males passed
within 10 m of her, but she flashed spontaneously (n = 24) for
19.5 min. at intervals from 15 to 108 sec. Most of these
"flare" flashes were unlike the female response flash--they
were brighter and composed of two peaks, which appeared identical to the two flashes of a male and female in dialogue
(Fig. 7a, b). Females could use this strategy to attract
mates during times of low male density, utilizing a system
that will operate at distances greater than females can see
males. Since a single flare may be computed by a passing male
as "another male," unless it accidentally (probability = 0.07-
0.12) [5] occurred in correct relationship to his own flash, it
will be less successful in attracting males. A double flash
may be processed as "a male with an answering female--hurry!"
The following night, after flaring a few times, this female
was found and mated by a male that observed her answer to
another passing male. When males are scarce, females may age
considerably before attracting one, and then take whatever
they can get.

Variation was noted among *collustrans* males in their
flashing, speed, altitude, and duration of flight. A few
emitted poorly formed flashes with weak transients and low
intensity, and commonly their lanterns glowed quite brightly
between flashes. Such males probably had reduced chances of
stimulating a response from a female. Females might even be
selected to reject males that could not turn off their light,
even though they formed normal flashes, because: (1) energy
and chemicals are wasted, (2) predators will be a greater
hazard during copulation and for progeny, and (3) such glowing
may indicate that more serious mechanical problems in flashing
are likely, thus diminishing progeny mating success. With
respect to speed of flight, in a sample of 70 males (pasture
site, 23.5-24.5°C, 6.3 km) mean flight speed was 1.25 m/sec.,
with a standard deviation of 0.27 m. One individual that

[5] Calculated by dividing the range of variation of female
response delay-time with male flash interval, e.g., 0.27/3.15 =
0.085 (Lloyd, 1966b).

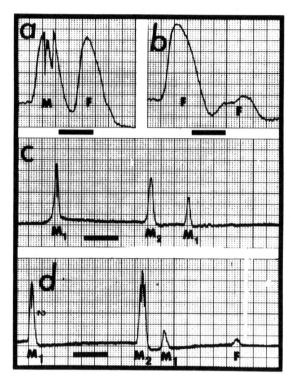

Fig. 7. Recordings of firefly flashes. Horizontal axis =
time, bars = 0.5 sec. Vertical axis = relative intensity.
(For recording technique, see Lloyd, 1969a, 1973c.)
    (a) Flash dialogue between collustrans male (m) and female
(f). Ragged peak on male flash is caused by overload alarm
resulting from intensely bright flash of male, timing not
affected.
    (b) Double-flash emitted by female in (a) a few minutes
before she attracted the male in (a). Possibly this flare
simulates a courtship dialogue and attracts males from greater
distances than the typical flash-answer system (see text; a
and b at 23°C). (c) P. macdermotti males competing for a
female. One male (m_1) emits normal pattern and the second
male (m_2) injects flash. Such an injection results in m_1
males terminating pattern, usually (?) or at least in most
situations observed to date. (d) Same as (c) except the
female answered m_1 (see text; c and d at 22.5°C; distorted
flashes from intensity overload, timing not affected).

searched at 2.13 m/sec., more than 3 s.d. above the mean,
probably had a poorer chance of seeing an answering female
than would males nearer the mean. Likewise, another male with

a speed of 0.48 m/sec. did not search effectively if this was sustained, though this speed might be more efficient if searching over taller grass. In fact, in a pine-savannah site where the grass was four to six times taller than that of the pasture, flight speed was significantly (p = 0.05) slower (mean = 1.04 m/sec., s.d. = 0.33 m, n = 26, 2.9 km, 23.5-24.5°C) and the 0.48 m/sec. male (from above) would be within 2 s.d. of the mean. One male in this site searched at 2.20 m/sec., more than 3.5 s.d. above the mean. The aberrations of these "too fast" and "too slow" males could be in their inability to discriminate and respond to the nature of the ground cover, rather than in mechanisms relating more directly to flying itself.

There is probably some optimum search altitude, depending upon conditions of ambient light intensity and vegetation height. During early evening most flight is below 1 m, and gradually more and more flashes are emitted above 1 m (Fig. 8). Two explanations seem reasonable. With failing light intensity and decreasing noise in the signal channel, conditions improve for photic signaling and flashes can be seen at greater distances. Higher altitudes will improve search efficiency. Also at lower light levels, the hazards of flight such as vegetation and spider webs are less easily seen and avoided. The male that emitted 0.68 of his flashes above 1 m (while the mean for this time of evening is 0.16 [s.d. = 0.21]), and was more than 2.4 s.d. from the mean, had reduced chances of seeing and being seen by a female. Later in the evening (10-11 min. after the start) when generally more than 0.66 of the flashes are given above 1 m, a male that emitted 0.98 of his flashes below 1 m had poorer vision and signaling range and was probably headed for a crash.

The duration of the evening search is important to male mating success. A male that searches after females have mated or ended their search (watch) wastes energy and exposes himself to predators longer than necessary, diminishing his chances for success on future nights. By flying after other males are through, he loses what may be important cues for remaining within an active site or for judging seasonal timing of fireflies (females) in the site (possibly important for emigration).[6] He may even mate with a *tanytoxus* female. If he quits too early, he restricts his chances of finding a mate that night, though to some degree he may increase his chances for subsequent evenings. Fig. 8 shows the time of flight termination for males. When males were being followed (n = 138) and they passed under or near a pine tree (scattered

[6] Local demes of many Florida species are commonly asynchronous to some extent.

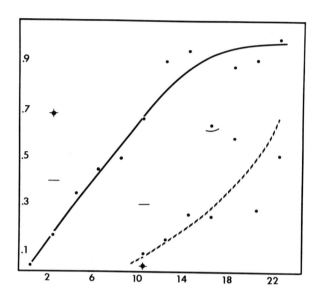

Fig. 8. Upper curve: proportion of flashes that collustrans
males emitted above 1 m altitude (as indication of their
flight, which is nearly horizontal) increases through their
twilight activity period (a time of rapidly decreasing ambient
light intensity). Horizontal axis = time in mins. after
activity begins (taken as when four males have begun flashing,
ca 20 min. after sunset; n = 71 males). Crossed dots indicate
extreme, presumably poorly adapted individuals (see text).
Straight, short bars indicate one standard deviation above or
below mean. Each male was observed for at least 20 and
usually 30 or more flashes; all observations were made at
pasture site. Few males continue after 20 min., rarely after
22.

Lower curve: proportion of males that flew up into pine
trees and stopped flashing, presumably ending search for the
evening (n = 24 males retired, of 138 observed). Early
quitters (before ≈ 16 min.) have reduced chances of finding
females. When males quit later than some optimal time, they
reduce their search chances and capacity for future nights
in return for poor chances of finding a female. Males average
ca 15 min. search time/night.

throughout the pasture), some (n = 24) flew up into the boughs
(5-10 m) and stopped flashing. The optimum time for quitting
is probably ca 16 min. after the start. The male that quit
ca 10 min. after the beginning of activity only used ≈ 0.63
the search time potentially available to him (though did not

necessarily reduce the probability of finding a female by ≈
0.37). The 18 males flying after 16 min. presumably were
unadaptively overtime, but 0.83 of these had landed by 22 min.
Male competitive success is obviously composed of many and
diverse parts, including the ability to adjust to varying conditions.

Photinus tanytoxus (Florida) males were also followed,
observed, and measured. This species is active immediately
following the retirement of collustrans. They emit a flash
pattern that is similar to, though somewhat longer than, that
of collustrans and fly 1.5-2.5 m above the ground. The male
activity period at the study site was about 30 min. in duration (60 min. or more at some other sites). Calculated on a
30 min. period, an average male travels slightly more than a
mile (6,700 ft. = 2,043.7 m) during the evening period, emits
755 flash patterns (a single flash ca 0.5 sec. in duration,
at 2.7 sec., $22^{0}C$), and has a 0.74 chance of seeing a female.
In this study both females that engaged males in a flash
dialogue were rejected (i.e., the males did not land). This
species is commonly preyed upon by aggressive mimics belonging
to three Photuris species, and although none answered males
during these observations, they were active in the area and
may account for the observed male "coyness."

Flaring occurs in tanytoxus females that have not seen male
flashes for a time. In this context the behavior of one particular male is interesting. He searched with low and slow
flight (0.5 m versus 2 m altitude; 1 m/flash versus 3.2 m/
flash; 0.41 m/sec. versus 1.14 m/sec.) within 3 m of a female.
When he flashed 1 m from her, she answered and his response
was immediate--he was above her at 20 cm in less than 2 sec.
I believe he had previously been attracted to her vicinity by
a flare.

More has been published on Photinus pyralis than any other
firefly in North America. Buck (1937) described the signaling
system and timing of the flash-dialogues, building on the
early work of McDermott (1910, 1911). At summer twilight across
most of the eastern United States, males fly above grassland
and emit a half-second flash each 6 sec.; females answer
with a similar flash from low perches, with a 2 sec. time delay. When females flash, they aim their light in the direction of the stimulus flash (Mast, 1912). Maurer (1968)
modeled the male-female interaction, and the following is
paraphrased from a portion of her description: The female
begins her response at the onset of the male flash. If the
flash is of the wrong duration, signal processing activity
subsides; if the duration is correct, impulses are fed into
the system at the right time to keep it going. Hence, the
first decision to answer or not occurs 200-500 msec. after the
male flash began. Extraneous flashes arriving before 800

msec. can enter the system without terminating the neural
response-function (a model for the female data, processing
system was developed for another species by Soucek and Carlson, 1975, see below). Flashes arriving later than that are
increasingly inhibitive. The first 800 msec. is the period
when the nearly synchronous flashes of males, if several are
present, occur. Flashes arriving during the inhibitory period
result in her not flashing. This mechanism may prevent a
female from answering males of other species whose flash patterns are composed of two flashes. The female then flashes,
ca 2 sec. having elapsed since the beginning of the male
flash, and may enter a refractory period. Maurer (1968) suggested that the significance of the refractory phase was that
it prevented females perched within sight of each other from
carrying out long dialogues, flashing back and forth, each
processing the other's flash as that of an approaching male.
These two imperatives--don't interact with two-flash species
or conspecific females--result in a framework within the data-
processing program within which there could evolve subtle male
competition.

One of the experiments Mast (1912) performed on *pyralis* to
determine the parameter of female flashes that males used for
recognition is of particular interest:

> Thirteen males were put into one glass liter jar and three
> females into another. These jars were then sealed and
> placed 25 cm apart on a sheet of paper spread out in an
> open place in the garden. Ten minutes later three free
> males had collected about the jar containing the females
> and none around the other jar . . . . One of the free males
> was captured and so oriented on the sheet of paper that he
> proceeded toward a point very nearly midway between the two
> jars . . . . One of the males in the jar [flashed] . . . . This
> did not appear to affect him in the least for he continued
> on his course without any apparent change until a female in
> the other jar answered . . . [ca 2 sec.], then he suddenly
> turned almost at once directly toward the female . . . this
> experiment was repeated several times with different individ-
> uals and essentially the same responses were obtained in
> all.

Maurer (1968) repeated Mast's experiment with a T-maze and
obtained similar results. Buck (1935) observed that in nature
males from more than 2 m will often converge on a male-female
dialogue, and by substituting a flashlight for the female, he
was able to attract 15-20 males simultaneously. He also observed that when the males gathered, they flashed in near-
synchrony with the flashes of the courting male. Maurer
(1968) suggested that the synchronous behavior was significant, i.e., adaptive, and it might prevent males from mistak-

ing the flashes of other males for those of females, or it
might avoid jamming females when they were surrounded by
several males. It was subsequently suggested that this behavior was involved in competition among males for females, and
perhaps permitted males to cut in on courting males and displace them (Lloyd, 1973b). Otte and Smiley (1977) discussed
additional aspects and possible functions of male synchrony
in fireflies with protocols similar to that of *pyralis*.

Maurer conducted a number of experiments whose results
lend themselves to speculation and interpretation about sexual
selection. When a cluster of males hovers and flashes near a
receptive female, the male toward which she aims her light
will gain some advantage. Since females time their responses
from the first flash received, when they are presented with
tandem flashes having various time separations up to 0.8 sec.
(Maurer, 1968), competing males should strive to be first in
flashing; but they must not flash during the female's refractory period. In experiments designed to elicit synchronous
flashing in males, Maurer found males tended to anticipate and
flash slightly earlier than appropriate for synchrony.

When Maurer stimulated males with trains of single flashes
at 10 sec. intervals, they responded with less delay than
anticipated. Instead of flashing at 5.5-6.5 sec., they flashed at 4.7 sec., and with lower variance than in other tests.
One explanation for this is that the males were interpreting
the artificial flashes as those of a female in dialogue with
a male that was hidden from sight, and they were flashing in
near synchrony with the "unseen" male. The delay of the males
in question, 4.7 sec., when added to the characteristic female delay at the same temperature, 1.8 sec., virtually equals
the 6.44 sec. delay of males to the "male" flash in an experiment in which males flashed after simulated male-female
dialogues presented at 10 sec. intervals (i.e., 4.7 + 1.8 ≃
6.44).

In another test, simulated male-female dialogues repeated
every 5.8 and 5.9 sec. elicited many responses 3.0 sec. after
the simulated male flash, i.e., 1 sec. after the simulated
female flash. These flashes occurred during the female refractory period, at a time when an interloping male could
perhaps inject a flash that would stop a female's next answer
to a competing male.

Maurer noted male jousting competition:

[Groups] of *pyralis* were frequently observed . . . they contained a copulating pair and 1 to 15 males all attempting
to copulate. One would be trying to insert himself between
the female and her male, another would be attempting to
copulate with the male, another with the head of the male.
Still another would be attempting to mate with one of the

males on the female's back (p. 109).

> The behavior . . . is difficult to understand. Unless the
> males can successfully dislodge the copulating male and
> take over, or unless the female is immediately ready to
> mate again, it seems a gross waste of time (p. 96). (See
> also Richards, 1927.)

G.O. Krizek (pers. comm.) observed the behavior of a late-
arriving *pyralis* male.

> . . . which attempted to copulate with the female already
> in copula, but did not attempt with his genitalia to join
> the female's genitalia. Instead, he repeatedly, for the
> next at least five minutes, attempted to copulate with her
> head, perhaps the oral parts. Because of this intense and
> repeated activity, it didn't look like a momentary disturb-
> ance or a mistake in orientation.

Unexpected or seldom seen male-male behaviors that occur in
the presence of females, or on substrates that have been im-
pregnated with female odor, are often viewed as either aber-
rancies, the failure of males to discriminate, or the release
of a behavior pattern in the improper situation. In many
cases these are misinterpretations. Although *pyralis,* like
many other firefly species, does not appear to be specialized
or adept in jousting competition, this could be due to a more
subtle strategy. Females may monitor the participants in the
scuffle and exercise some selectivity in terms of the next
mate; if another is taken, or possibly even in the male that
is currently mounted and ejaculating, sperm control could be
exercised on the basis of postcoupling observations. It
appears that late arriving males commonly direct their activities toward the female and not the male.

Photinus macdermotti (eastern United States) male flash
pattern is composed of two short flashes separated by about 2
sec., and the female response is a single flash at a 1 sec.
delay (ca $23^{\circ}C$) (Fig. 9a). During a 45 min. activity period,
an average *macdermotti* male in a xeric liveoak grove travels
795 m, flashes 364 patterns, has a 0.83 probability of seeing
a female, and has less than half that of mating with one.
Males are heavily preyed upon by the aggressive mimic *Photuris
versicolor,* which has a *macdermotti* capture rate of 0.09
(Lloyd, 1975).

Throughout most of its range, the flash pattern is given
at a period of 5-7 sec. The time intervals between consecutive flashes of searching males are ca 2-4-2-etc., depending
upon temperature. In eastern Maryland and New York, searching males flash 2-2-2- and during the approach to a female
switch to 2-4-2- (Lloyd, 1969a). The 2-2-2- pattern would
seem to be more efficient since potentially any pair of

Fig. 9. Details and models of macder- *motti male and female flashing biology. (a) Male flash pattern is composed of two flashes ca 2 sec. apart (23°C), female response is a single flash ca 1 sec. after second flash of male. (b) Soucek-Carlson response-function model. (The Soucek-Carlson model is actually more complicated and detailed than this, and involves time relationships in addition to those presented here.)*

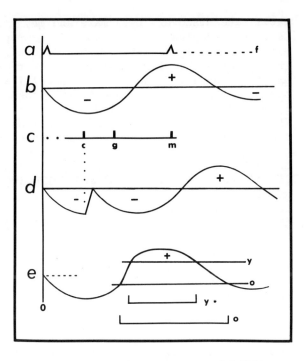

After seeing the first flash, the female enters an inhibitory phase, which is followed by an excitatory phase during which she is increasingly receptive to the second flash. When a female sees the pattern of sibling species males, e.g., consanguineus *or* greeni *with patterns indicated in (c), she resets her response-function as indicated in (d) as would happen when the female saw the second flash of* consanguineus. *This occurs about 0.5 sec. after his first flash. (e) The acceptance windows (indicated by brackets below) of* macdermot- *ti females change as the females adjust their reference levels (y and o; see Soucek and Carlson, 1975). It is here suggested that these reference levels may also be adjusted downward as females grow older without mating, and that the excitatory phase may be skewed as a result of strong selection in the context of reproductive isolation from* greeni *and the absence of a species in the next higher window (see text). Symbols: c =* consanguineus, *f = female response, g =* greeni, *m =* mac- *dermotti, o = older, y = younger.*

flashes in the sequence becomes the flash pattern. It may be that this pattern is advantageous only under specific ecological conditions, e.g., especially high male density and competition. Females sometimes respond to consecutive search flashes (Lloyd, 1969a; Soucek and Carlson, 1975). This would

facilitate discovery by a male and may occur only in older
females. Females often respond to improper patterns once or
a few times (Lloyd, 1969a, 1971; Soucek and Carlson, 1975).
This permits the pair to establish better signaling positions
and then to verify each other's species and condition. *Macdermotti* males also respond to the flashes of a pair in dialogue and to artificial flashes simulating a male and female
(Lloyd, unpublished). These simulations will attract males
from several meters, and they will often, with light glowing
brightly and continuously, dart in and land near the "female."
On one occasion, after several males had been attracted to the
ground near the simulation, and following a simulation, four
glowing males simultaneously rose 1 m from the ground within
20 cm of each other, then darted back to the ground and doused
their lights. Occasionally *macdermotti* males in the vicinity
of females emit pseudo-female flashes. This could cause a
competing male to reject the real female and approach the
male, or perhaps leave the area because of the common occurrence of pseudo-female answers by aggressive mimics. Some
observations suggest that aggressive mimics may launch aerial
attacks without waiting for duped males to land and walk to
them.

Male *macdermotti* sometimes flash synchronously with the
second flash of a pattern initiated by another flasher (this
behavior also occurs in *greeni,* a sibling species: Lloyd,
1969a). If an experimenter anticipates the pattern of a
searching male and flashes an instant before the male begins,
the firefly often skips the first flash of his own pattern and
emits the second, timed appropriately from the experimenter's
flash. At other times the male is delayed several seconds
and subsequently emits an entire pattern.

The description of the flash competition of *macdermotti* now
becomes more complex, and field and laboratory experimenta-
tion, neural model-building, and selection theory complement
each other. Soucek and Carlson (1975) stimulated *macdermotti*
(Long Island, NY) females with artificial flashes of various
interval characteristics. From responses obtained, they developed a female response-function model (Fig. 9b; also simulated with a computer: Carlson and Soucek, 1975). The neural
program that they have probed and begun to describe is important in male competition.

In the response-function of female *macdermotti,* as in that
of *pyralis,* there are periods of inhibition and excitation.
The first inhibition period, which is firmly anchored in an
ecological reality, provides the base for manipulation since
females will evolutionarily have difficulty escaping. At the
first received flash, the response-function begins with an
inhibition phase lasting about one-half the male interval. If
another flash is received during this period, the female is

reset (starts over: Fig. 9d). One significance of this phase
is that it prevents females from responding to the flash patterns of related, sympatric species (e.g., *consanguineus* = two
flashes at ca 0.5 sec.; *greeni* = two flashes at ca 1 sec.
[Fig. 9c, d]).

When a searching male observes a male-female dialogue, he
quickly approaches and competes for the female. Soucek and
Carlson noted that the -2- interval was shorter in the 2-4-2-
(approach) phrasing than in the 2-2-2- (search) phrasing. I
compared the timing of searching males with that of males that
were on the ground approaching females (on the same evening,
15.9°C) in Florida *macdermotti* (-2-4-2- in approach and
search). Search patterns of four males averaged 3.40 sec.
(n = 10, s.d. = 0.113; note that because of low temperature the
-2- interval was actually 3.4 sec.), whereas approach patterns
from two different groups of males with females averaged 2.87
sec. (n = 9, s.d. = 0.095, $\bar{x}$ = 2.85; n = 8, s.d. = 0.089, $\bar{x}$ = 2.80).
The differences are significant (1-tailed t-test) well beyond
the 0.005 level. (If the patterns of the flying males were
shorter, I presume we might have explained the difference on
the basis of physiology--inactive flight muscles upon landing
allowed body temperature to drop!) Males can perhaps sometimes foil the interloping strategy of nearby searching males
by such alteration in the timing of their flashes. In addition, if an approaching male does not shorten his interval,
another male could flash just before him and cause the female
to divert her aim toward the interloper. By accelerating his
second flash, an approaching male forces an interloper to
place an early flash into the female's late inhibitory phase,
with reduced chances for an answer. Females probably do not
restrict their opportunities to view additional males by
adjusting to the shortened male interval because when in dialogue with males, they lower their reference levels (Fig. 9e)
and actually accept broad variation (Soucek and Carlson,
1975). If a female sees a flash during the inhibitory phase
of her response-function, it begins again (Fig. 9d). Competing males near a female can potentially use the inhibitory
phase by inserting flashes that disrupt the timing of other
males or prevent females from answering them. *Macdermotti*
males do in fact inject flashes in response both to male-
female dialogues and to simulated ones. Recordings of such
flashes, made during two separate contests in which 2-3 males
were involved, reveal that most are injected at a time position 0.4-0.9 in the first male's flash interval (Fig. 10), and
perhaps are directed by two different tactics; some were given
during the mid to late inhibitory phase and others during the
early excitatory phase. Since a male can easily counter the
injected flash of his opponent, if he sees it, these flashes
may be aimed toward females, thus reducing the likelihood that

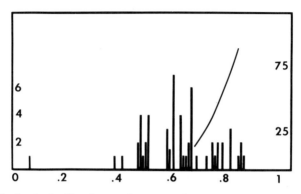

Fig. 10. Injected flashes of competing macdermotti males and
their relationship to female response tendencies. Horizontal
axis = time, in fraction of male flash-pattern elapsed. First
flash of first male (or artificial pattern) occurred at time
0, and his second flash would occur at 1 (ca 2 sec. at 23°C).
The competing males injected flashes as indicated by vertical
bars, number indicated on left vertical axis. Right vertical
axis is percent female response elicited when second flash of
male pattern is timed as indicated by curve--positioning approximate. Female response data from Soucek and Carlson
(1975). Exact details of timing and tactics of second male
are unknown, but flashes injected before 0.7 may terminate or
reset female response-function, while those injected later
may steal her response and aim (see text).

adversaries will be able to follow the ensuing dialogue.

On several occasions I have observed males on the ground
approaching females to inject flashes into the patterns of
flying males that had just received two to three answers from
the female. Because the injection of a flash into the pattern
of another male would be done only in the presence of a female, a searching male should respond to it. I injected single flashes at position 0.4 in several patterns of 10 flying
males. Males within 4 m flew closer, those beyond did not.
Males closer than 7 m usually omitted the second flash of
their pattern. Males can be attracted from much greater distances to artificial female responses, therefore distance
information is obviously being used in decision making; a male
near a female probably does not inject flashes into the patterns of searching males unless they are threats. Aggressive
mimicry may have been involved in the selective forces that
have shaped male responses in this context. Females of *Photuris versicolor* often answer *macdermotti* males by flashing 1
sec. after the first and the second male flash (Lloyd, 1965b,
1975). I have previously interpreted this as a mistake on the

part of the mimics because they usually omit the first after
a few responses, and because they use similarly timed answers
to attract males of other species. Actually since the "inept"
first flash falls in the 0.4-0.6 zone, a time of maximum male-
injected flashes, it should contribute to mimicry efficacy and
hence may be selected in such a context.

At times the best tactic is to stop flashing. On one occasion I observed a 5 min. blackout after two males had injected
flashes. Then, one male flashed without interference from the
others for two patterns; on the second he received an answer
from the female and moved several feet closer. A male then
began injecting flashes and another blackout followed.

Other "lab phenomena" observed by Soucek and Carlson (1975)
may eventually be found to function in natural situations.
For example, their so-called triple interval--flashes with
slightly longer than normal intervals--causes females to flash
after the third; this could be used by a male to prevent nearby males from detecting the dialogue.

If females change their discrimination as they age, it may
be possible to distinguish experimentally the effects of reproductive isolation in the relaxation of standards for mates.
Assuming that selection will have favored females that have
gradually widened their acceptance window for the second flash
(Fig. 9e), it cannot have favored females that have accepted
males of other species. It should therefore be possible to
distinguish between adaptive-permissive and unadaptive-patho-
logical widening of the window. The window-width changes
during the attraction of a male and the change is asymmetrical. In the graph given by Soucek and Carlson (1975: Fig.
1F) for the range of acceptable stimulus flash intervals,
with the frequency of response, the response probability on
the low side drops off more rapidly than that on the high
side (indicated here by skewing of the excitatory portion of
the response-function in Fig. 9e). The flash pattern of the
sympatric sibling *greeni* is composed of two flashes at ca
0.9 sec. That is, *greeni* operates in an adjacent and lower
window. Selection in the context of reproductive isolation
should have acted rigorously on *macdermotti* females that
ranged downward into *greeni's* range. Since there are no species operating in an adjacent higher window, selection
against females ranging upward would presumably have been
more forgiving. Old females may change the extent, rate, or
symmetry of the window alterations they make. This argument,
as well as other suggestions for other adaptive behavioral
changes in old females, depends upon the occurrence of male
variants outside the "normal" range in sufficient numbers to
bring about selection in the context of "a poor male is better
than no male at all."

Buck and Buck (1972) studied an interesting member of this

firefly group at Woods Hole, Mass. Their species is impossible to identify with certainty, as they noted. The timing
of the male pattern is similar to, though longer than, that of
greeni. The female acceptance range extends into the *macdermotti* male flashing range. The histogram of these responses
is more nearly symmetrical and spans more than 2X the coded
male flash interval for this population (1.2 sec.; versus
e.g., 0.6X in *macdermotti*). Perhaps this population is out of
the geographic range of *macdermotti,* i.e., released from
strong selection in the reproductive isolation context. If
so, it is one of the few (only?) known cases of character
displacement in insect-mating signals (Walker, 1974). It is
noteworthy that the female acceptance window, but not male
flash interval, ranges broadly. Males will be selected to
flash in the portion of the window common to most females.

    Photuris fireflies. Photuris species have achieved notor-
iety because of the difficulties taxonomists have had in
trying to sort out agreeable species. Many biologists have
given up on identification, and any *Photuris* is *pennsylvanica*
(e.g., Oertel et al., 1975). Barber's (1951) use of *Photuris*
flash patterns for recognizing species has been widely cited
as an example of the value of behavior in taxonomy. However,
Photuris flashing patterns are more complex than generally
realized, or as might be assumed from simplified charts used
to illustrate *Photuris* patterns (Lloyd, 1969c). They are
commonly not the simple or invariable patterns found in most
other fireflies. Many of the species, about one-fourth of the
40 or more I have studied, emit two or more flash patterns.
Photuris sp. A (Florida) emits long flashes (ca 0.4 sec.) and
short flashes (ca 0.15 sec.), as well as patterns consisting
of two to five short flashes. These variations seem in part
to be related to physical conditions of the habitat, such as
vegetation type and ambient light level. When answered,
multiple-flashing males switch to a single flash for the
approach. *Photuris fairchildi* (northern United States, Nova
Scotia) emits single flashes at some sites and predominantly
triple-flash patterns at others (Buschman, 1974). One Florida
species emits three patterns: a continuous glow, groups of
several rapid single flashes, and a short flicker. An unnamed
Missouri species emits a single flash and a long crescendo, as
does *Photuris lucicrescens* (Maryland). A small treetop
species of the southeastern United States emits flashes of two
lengths in variable groupings, commonly emitting single
flashes and a combination resembling the introductory "V"
rhythm of Beethoven's Fifth Symphony. *Photuris jamaicensis*
emits glows, single flashes, combinations of single flashes,
and slow and fast flickers: it presumably is the only *Photuris*
on the island of Jamaica (McDermott and Buck, 1959; Lloyd,

1969b; Farnworth, 1973, p. 115). Other species have a single, but complex pattern: one emits a crescendo flash with a 30-40 Hertz (depending upon temperature) flicker, and others have brief flashes with subtle, and to the human eye subliminal, modulations. Unquestionably these interesting and intricate modulations and combinations result in signals that are species-specific, important in reproductive isolation, and efficient under physical conditions peculiar to certain habitats. But for these purposes it would seem they could be much simpler than they are: why did this complexity evolve and what sort of selection maintains it in spite of pleiotropy and erosion and compromises in the genetic bases resulting from selection in other contexts? It would also seem that such complexity must occur in the face of severe limitations in the ability of the genome and nervous system to store information. Perhaps the answer is to be found in the various modes of sexual selection. The classical systematist's question--are signals more complex in areas where there are many species?-- probably reflects our misunderstanding of the significances of mating behavior. The dearth of evidence for character displacement in mating signals (Otte, 1974; Walker, 1974), in spite of the attention and significance being given it, is revealing (Alexander and Borgia, this volume). On the other hand, if sexual selection is a fundamental determinant of mating behavior and signals, animals that live in rich habitats producing high densities may be expected to have the more complex protocols. This will include many species from the northern latitudes or difficult, restrictive habitats where but a single or few species occur.

Buschman (1974) made a number of interesting observations on the Nova Scotian firefly *P. fairchildi*: Males emit single or multipulse patterns when they search. Upon receiving an answering flash (delay = 1.5 sec.) from a female, males approach and gradually increase the number of flashes in each pattern. Answering females gradually increase the number of flashes they emit. As they draw near, flashing increases until it is rapid and nearly continuous, and it is no longer possible to detect a specific timing relationship between the flashes of the two. Pair formation may even occur in the air, with the partners landing in order to copulate. Females on the ground move around and "escape" approaching males. Searching males are attracted to groups of flashing males on the ground, and will approach and sometimes land near random, repeated, and answering flashlight flashes, as well as the

Fig. 11. Copulating Photuris *SH from upstate New York. Per-haps in a defensive maneuver, they hang beneath the leaf and the male raises his middle legs. Males of several insects defend against other males during copulation by sweeping and striking with their legs.*

flashes of males and females.[7]

    Photuris SH (upstate New York) occurs by the thousands or millions in moist old fields. Males fly 20-40 cm above the tops of the dominating goldenrod, emitting a short bimodu-lated flash every 2 sec. They land frequently, and probably at any given time more males are perched than are in flight. Of 15 individuals followed, eight landed within 26 flashes ($\bar{x} = 12$), usually at a small group (two to seven individuals) of flashing, perched males. Perched males usually flashed in bouts of five to eight, then remained dark for up to 2 min. Females answered males with short flashes, delayed 0.5-1 sec.,

[7] A former student in the department, for aesthetic purposes, embedded numerous oscillators, batteries, and bulbs in a block of bioplastic (used for embedding biological specimens); the bulbs flashed independently and continuously for weeks. When he placed this thing in the field, it attracted *Photuris*.

and of a given bout would answer half or fewer. In three of
five observed approaches, the females moved away from approaching males; one secretively doubled back past the male
and avoided him, and two flew away before the males reached
them. (*Photuris* females are extremely active and agile, with
comparatively large eyes and light organs.) Although females
attract several males simultaneously, seemingly manipulating
them into forming transient little leks by intermittent answering, they also attract males in a more straight-forward,
prosaic fashion by simply answering them nearly continuously
until they meet. A photograph of a copulating pair (Fig. 11)
revealed an interesting defensive posture: The male had raised
his middle legs, perhaps leaving them free to use against the
attacks of interloping males as seen in other insects.

The females of many species of *Photuris* are specialized
predators of males of other species (Lloyd, 1965b, 1973a,
1975; Farnworth, 1973; Buschman, 1974). Prey species include
members of several genera including *Photuris*. These females,
as well as those of other predaceous insects and arachnids,
could use the success of a predation attempt on a male with
which they have just mated as a final test of his acceptabili-
ty. A (young)[8] male that is easily caught will produce sons
with a similar tendency, and hence have a reduced chance for
achieving further fertilizations. Sperm manipulation would
seem to be a reasonable expectation. With one exception
(Buschman, 1974) there is no direct evidence that female *Photuris* eat their own males, but there seems to be no reason why
they should not. It would not seem to reduce their fitness
because of risk of injury: Females are usually as large or
larger than conspecific males, and they sometimes attract and
eat related species of similar size. Capture rates for these
males may be low because they are more often successful in
their struggles to escape. However, it has been found that
after mating the females of *Photuris versicolor* gradually
become unresponsive to the flashes of conspecific males and
begin to answer the patterns of prey species (Nelson et al.,
1975).

Lekking Luciola. Many species of *Luciola* appear to behave
in the field much like *Photinus* and *Photuris*. Males fly about
their habitat, flashing as they go (Papi, 1969; Kaufman, 1965;
Lloyd, 1973c). The behavior of *L. obsoleta* of New Guinea
(Lloyd, 1972), and apparently that of the Gengi firefly, *Luciola cruciata*, of Japan (Kiichiro, 1961), is dramatically

---

[8] An old male, (or) one with little chance to find additional
females, may nuptially feed the female with his own body
(Thornhill, 1976; Richards, 1927).

different. Males and females gather in congregations and
obtain mating partners after lengthy and complex interactions.
     At dusk males and females of *obsoleta* begin broadcasting
from isolated stations on low vegetation (solitary signaling
phase). Most broadcasting males stand near or walk along the
edges of their leaf perches, with heads extended well out from
under their pronota and over the leaf edges. Occasionally
individuals change perches--males flickering as they fly,
females glowing continuously. Both sexes commonly land near
(decimeters) perched, luminescing conspecifics, and perched
males sometimes begin flashing when a firefly passes overhead.
Males hover and flicker above perched luminescing individuals,
darting toward and away from them, and sometimes landing near
them. Broadcasting patterns are usually sexually distinctive,
with males emitting various combinations of flashes and flickers and females emitting glows and modulated glows. Both
males and females flex their abdomens downward, and with the
tip nearly touching the substrate, their light is directed
forward and laterally, but not to the rear.
     When a female takes flight about 2 hr. after activity
begins, she is pursued by flickering males, usually one to
two, but up to four. Males spar during pursuit, darting and
striking at each other, and use similar tactics to force females to land. Within 9 m of takeoff the female and a male
land on a leaf, and after a walking-luminescing interaction or
dance, mating takes place. Copulating pairs sometimes remain
together throughout the night and next day, breaking up only
at dusk the following evening. This behavior continues inter-
mittently from dusk until dawn and seems to increase during
light rain.
     My original interpretation of this elaborate pair-forming
behavior was that a number of sympatric, sibling species,
which morphological evidence suggests occur (see also Ballantyne, 1968), make it necessary for reproductive isolation. It
seems obvious now that sexual selection is the context that
has produced it. In fact, the entire mating protocol appears
to be one, long, comprehensive examination during which males,
competing head-to-head in chases and aerial dogfights and
tail-to-tail with bioluminescent displays, are rejected in
several ways more often than they are accepted. Evolutionarily, females seem to have maximized their opportunity to monitor male behavior in order to exercise active selection.
     Table 2 gives details of chases and subsequent behaviors
following natural and experimentally induced (females released
near males) chases. There are no evident significant differences between natural and experimental chases. It is evident
that males must sometimes get females by joining chases in
progress, without displaying to them in the sedentary signaling phase, or they could not so easily be stimulated into

TABLE 2

Outcomes of 57 nuptial chases in Luciola obsoleta
(modified from Lloyd, 1972)

I. Unsuccessful Chases (n=28)
    A. One-male chases (7 unsuccessful)
        1. female turned off light (n=5)
            a. male landed with perched luminescing male (n=2)
            b. male fate undetermined (n=3)
        2. male "lost" female, dropped out of chase (n=2)
    B. Two-male chases (11 unsuccessful)
        1. other male landed with female (n=3, see below)
            a. male landed 45 cm from female and successful
            male (n=1)
            b. male sparred in flight with successful male, flew
            off (n=2)
        2. neither male landed with female (n=8)
            a. males sparred and flew off together (n=6)
            b. males dropped out of chase separately (n=2)
    C. Three-male chases (10 unsuccessful)
        1. none of the 3 landed with the female (n=6)
            a. female turned off her light (n=3)
            b. female eluded pursuers by other means (n=3)
        2. 2 of the 3 did not land with the female (n=4)
            a. males left chase and landed together (n=2)
            b. males left chase when female and 3rd male landed
            together (n=2), one flying on, other returning to
            original perch
II. Successful Chases (n=29)
    A. One-male chases (20 successful)
        1. female flew off immediately, male remaining (n=3)
        2. male mounted female immediately (n=3)
        3. male and female began walking-luminescing inter-
        action (n=8)
        4. outcome undetermined (n=6)
    B. Two-male chases (7 successful)
        1. male landed with female alone (n=3)
            a. female flew off immediately (n=1)
            b. male and female began walking-luminescing inter-
            action (n=2)
        2. male landed with female and other male (n=4, i.e. 2
        instances)
            a. male remained with female (n=2)
                i. female flew off immediately (n=1)
                ii. male mounted female immediately (n=1)
            b. male flew off, left other male with female (n=2)
    C. Three-male chases (2 successful)
        1. male landed with female alone (n=2)

TABLE 2 (continued)

---

a. male and female began walking-luminescing interaction (n=1)
b. female flew off immediately, male chases again,
landed with her, they began walking-luminescing
interaction (n=1)

---

chasing experimental females.

Of seven males that reached the mounting stage of a field
of 57 starters, none achieved insemination. It is interesting
that eight (of 28 total) unsuccessful chases occurred when the
female turned off her light. In one instructive chase that
was joined when a female ended copulation with one male and
flew off glowing, thus attracting a pursuer, the female ex-
tinguished her light and dropped to the ground. She then
turned on her light and flew upward, and the male resumed
pursuit. She landed, turned off her light, moved to the other
side of the leaf, and flew with her light off and without the
pursuing male.

Male-male interactions occurred in 12 unsuccessful pursuits. Sometimes males pursued males that glowed like females
and they sparred and flew off together. I originally assumed
these to be cases of "accidental" mistaken identity, but some
of these situations possibly involved male ploys of some unknown significance, or continued conflict between acquainted
individuals of adjacent advertising stations or territories.

In results of successful pursuits (i.e., when a male pursued a female and landed with her at the end of the chase),
continued female control is seen. In six instances the female
flew off immediately after landing, and in only one of these
did the male continue pursuit. In three, the female flew or
dropped from the landing site with her light off; in two, she
flew with her light on but the male did not follow.

Walking-luminescing interactions observed in their
entirety lasted 1-4 min. (n=8), although one interaction
observed only in part endured 40 min. These interactions
ended with males mounting the females (n=7), males flying away
(n = 3), or with females flying away (n = 2). Male exits are
enigmas. Do they indicate male adjudication of total,
irreconcilable failure--and a hastening to search for another
female--or is the act of abandoning the female itself the
failure? I believe the answer is usually the former.

Mounting was always (n = 11) accompanied by a series of
very bright flashes. Interestingly, this pattern resembles
the search flash patterns used by *obsoleta* relatives, and so

its signal (and other behavioral) antecedents in *obsoleta's*
protocol have seemingly been added to a simple flash-and-find
protocol. Males usually remained mounted 1.5-4 min., although
one lasted 25 and another 60 min. Some made probing motions
with their genitalia and none were successful. Females seemed
to initiate separation.

Males that are successful in fertilizing the eggs of discriminating females--females that make full employment of the
control they seem to have available to them at virtually every
stage of the game--have had to demonstrate considerable
physical endurance and competence both photically and mechan-
ically. Males that remain coupled for several hours may be
providing nutritional materials with the ejaculate, and/or
preventing other males from inseminating the female while she
is responsive, and/or because they are strongly odoriferous
(Lloyd, 1973a) and presumably distasteful, providing some
additional protection from predators (see Thornhill, 1976).

There is no obvious structuring of signal interactions in
sedentary-signaling. While long-term interactions between
individuals are not apparent, they undoubtedly are present
because luminescent display is prolonged with the animals in
almost continuous visual contact, and males and females adjust
their locomotory behavior on the basis of their mutual observations. The flickers and glows of both sexes during the
sedentary-signaling phase would seem to have been derived from
illumination emissions, such as those used by many species
during flight from perch to perch or through dense vegetation
and upon landing (Lloyd, 1968, 1973c; Papi, 1969). This would
suggest that mutual monitoring during their ancestral proto-
lek stages was of significance and is worthy of special attention as it now occurs in *lusitanica, macdermotti,* and other
species. With respect to the congregating behavior itself, I
believe that the availability of large numbers of males, often
the consequence of a "rich" habitat, and the physical ease
with which males can join such groups, resulting in great
variance in male quality (there has been little passive filtering before reaching the arena), has resulted in the elaboration of this lek protocol from such proto-lek beginnings
as described for *lusitanica, macdermotti,* and *Photuris* spp.
(see also Alexander, 1975).

The Gengi firefly apparently is similar in behavior to
obsoleta in some ways, but differs at least in the regular
occurrence of simultaneous flight.

There are certain hours that fireflies fly. My observations show that it occurs about three times a night; at
about 2100 hours, 2400 midnight and 0300 hours. More fireflies fly at 2100 hours. After showers or a night of heavy
rain they fly particularly briskly. In usual cases they

fly for a duration of two to three minutes, and then land
on bushes, but in rare cases they fly for five to six
minutes.

When fireflies fly all at once, the flight begins with one
firefly flickering light, and this followed by several
fireflies. This pattern spreads to others and most fireflies join in the flight . . . flickering sometimes takes
place all at once . . . . This is carried out in a way
similar to wholesale flight. Thus, when one firefly begins
to flicker, it spreads to others, and the fireflies in the
area join in regular flickering unison. It [generally]
lasts for 20 to 30 min., and then the fireflies retire to
the grass or trees, and everything becomes quiet thereafter . . . . Copulation begins this way: At first a male
firefly seeks the resting place of a female firefly or
chases after the latter. When the female rests on a leaf,
the male also stops there and attempts to fulfill his
purpose. However, the female seems to show a like or dis-
like of certain males. Thus, the female flees with its
tail hanging down from certain males . . . . The duration
of copulation is at the shortest three to four hours, and
at the longest 24 hours (Kiichiro, 1961).

Synchronizing leks, Pteroptyx spp. The folded-wing fireflies (*pter* = wing; *ptyx* = fold, Gr.) (Fig. 2) are at the opposite end of the protocol spectrum from Knull's glowworm.
The search expenditures of males and females may often be
minimal, whereas approaches can involve long periods of male
competition and salesmanship and female evaluation and
decision making. In fact, the latter may well be the synchronizing lek's primary or only *raison d'etre* (see also Alexander, 1975). In Thailand, trees in estuarian mangrove swamps
often hold thousands or millions of *Pteroptyx* fireflies
(Buck and Buck, 1966, and references). At the other extreme,
in a roadside swale in the highlands of New Guinea, only a
dozen or so males may be seen. Individuals in the congregations synchronize their flash patterns with those of their
neighbors by adjusting to previously observed flashes (Buck
and Buck, 1968). Mass synchrony is the result of local syn-
chronies that interconnect at high male density and unite an
entire chorus. There are no data or reasonable theoretical
models to support the older assumption that *mass* synchrony
itself is the context of selection that maintains it (Lloyd,
1973b, c; Alexander, 1975). A generalized behavior model for
Pteroptyx spp. that takes into account their many complexities
and variations, as presently understood, and one that is in
keeping with current evolutionary theory, has been proposed
(Lloyd, 1973b). Unless otherwise indicated, information used
in the following discussion is from Lloyd (1973b, c).

Lek mating is probably not obligatory in some or all
species. At low densities when individuals are away from or
unable to find a swarm tree, as would be the case with emi-
grants or colonizers, they may pair like nonlekking *Luciola*
spp. This is suggested by the observation that males away
from firefly trees can be attracted to a penlight simulation
of a female response. Two New Guinea species were found only
in this manner. Also, at a site in a rain forest with no
nearby swarms, I observed the attraction of a solitary passing
male to a lone perched female. But, presumably, the usual
situation in all *Pteroptyx*, i.e., the one that accounts for
most mating, is for males and females to join leks.

Within firefly trees males locate and approach females in
several different ways. Some take up flashing stations,
perhaps even territorial spaces or perches, walk about or
stand with their heads (eyes) extended, aim their lanterns,
and attract or fend off incoming fireflies. Buck and Buck
(1976) reported observations of mutual attraction and then
aggressive interaction in captive *Pteroptyx malaccae* males.
Pteroptyx males take flight and pursue females in a manner
like that of *obsoleta,* join chases that pass by (chases involving as many as nine males have been observed), and spar
with the males and bump the females. Males sometimes cruise
around the periphery of a swarm or tree. At high densities
they may be unable to find suitable flashing stations.
Cruising males may be executing alternative search strategies
and seeking isolated females or leks with females already
present. Interloping, the displacement of males in the late
stages of approach to a female by surreptitious or other
means (i.e., a satellite strategy), probably also occurs.

When females enter a firefly congregation, they may gain
an escort of chasers or select a landing site with male
candidates present. The selection of a site is probably made
on the basis of species-specific rhythm, modulations in the
flashing patterns, and perhaps the numbers and sexes of the
individuals present in the localized group--functional lek.
In geographic regions with several species present and sometimes even occupying the same tree (Lloyd, 1973c; Ballantyne
and McLean, 1970), species identification must be a primary,
and chronologically the first, context of mate selection.

The active selection of particular males by females,
apparently for further observation, occurs in several ways:
Females land near perched flashing males, sometimes moving
closer from more distant perches within visible range; flying
glowing females respond to response-flickers they elicit from
perched males, make low swoops over the males, and land near
them; and perched females emit luminescent patterns following
emissions of nearby perched or flying males, attracting them
to approach and land nearby. Lengthy interactions, similar

to those of *obsoleta* during the walking-luminescing interaction, occur between individual males and females. One female I observed seemed to view and reject two males and select
a third: she was flying along a hedge and received consecutive
flickering responses from three males that were perched along
the hedge about 2 m apart. After passing the third, she returned and landed 10 cm from him.

Flash emissions that were once used for enhancing vision
during landing and flying through foliage have apparently been
ritualized and become secondary flash patterns in some species
(Lloyd, 1968, 1977). These patterns are used in different
contexts and manners in three species I observed. It is
important here to note that this ritualization must have occurred because females were observing the approaches of individual males, and then selecting among males on the basis of
information these patterns contained. Recognition of sex or
species may have been important at first. Since mating errors
are more likely to occur between members of recently speciated
populations (with similar or identical mating behavior and
primary patterns), the secondary pattern may have been selected in the context of reproductive isolation. However,
divergence would ultimately be expected between the primary
patterns in such siblings, or the primary pattern in one species might be supplanted by the secondary pattern. I believe
that future study of these secondary patterns, in particular,
will provide many important clues to the specific nature and
extent of sexual selection in fireflies.

In most species the synchronized flash pattern is probably
the central element in sexual behavior and selection. Ability
to keep the identifying species-specific rhythm with conspecific males is critical to a male's success because it permits
him to enhance the attractiveness of his sublek in the swarm
as it competes with others for incoming females or females
that cruise around the swarm. All of an individual's characteristics that contribute to the general broadcasting success
of his local group are potentially monitored by females and
are of importance to her as she makes a subsequent selection
of a mate from among males in the local lek. Presumably,
lantern size, shape, brightness, and aiming; ability to produce sharp intensity-transients; and particularly a male's
ability to keep time could be important to him as an individual. A female might monitor his success with other
females (Alexander, 1975), his choice and defense of a signaling station, or his success in ploys or other forms of
competitor manipulation, e.g., in parasitizing the signaling
of other males at appropriate times. Females could monitor
male ability to sustain flashing for a long period--synchrony
making it possible to keep track of several simultaneously.
It would certainly seem that some of the speculations on this

list must exceed the level of behavioral complexity possible in these insects. Which ones?

Generally, though significant exceptions exist, the channel used for communication by an animal is the one that involves the senses that are of primary importance in "commerce with the nonsocial environment" (Bastian and Bermant, 1973). It would seem that in sexual selection the contexts and elements of primary importance in the evaluation of males by females will become significant in the competition between rivals (and they will also be lied about by the males). Since female *Pteroptyx* spp. must examine closely the ability of males to synchronize, and males competing in this activity are competing rigorously, it would be surprising if at times they did not attempt to make adversaries perform poorly by withholding or distorting information about their own flashing. The subtle modulations in the primary patterns of several species may have historically, if not presently, conveyed false information about flash phasing or timing. Males may hide their flashes from opponents at critical moments by selective aiming--they aim their light by twisting their abdomens (Polunin, 1971). If the enigmatic elytra of *Pteroptyx* males, the opaque folded-tips (Fig. 2c) that have puzzled all who have studied these animals, are found to be shades behind which males hide their light from opponents, it will be poetic justice.[9] To recognize *Pteroptyx* males as competitive egoists that might use such devices, and not altruists dissipating their energies in benevolent beacons, requires the selection models of Darwin, Fisher, and Williams.

CONCLUSIONS

Theoretically, it would seem that sexual selection should be inevitable, given the occurrence of sexual reproduction itself. But only recently have the implications that sexual selection theory has for the understanding of mating behavior in luminescent beetles become evident; not for a moment did we previously imagine that these stupid little animals, with brains the size of the comma in this sentence, could be scrutinizing and selecting among potential, conspecific mates, or that this could be very important to them. I personally reached a watershed between the *obsoleta* paper (1972) and the synchronizing-firefly model (1973b). After a number of years pursuing a taxonomic resolution of the genus *Photuris,* it is very exciting to discover a new angle on them with some very

[9] The trilobed and trisinuate terminal, abdominal sternites found in males of this genus may also relate to this function.

good and testable explanations for their inconvenient conduct.
Their behavior, as well as that of lekking *Pteroptyx* and
Luciola spp., seem now more a bonus than hindrance. A so-
called "Harvard Law" states that for every particular biological problem, there is some kind of animal well-suited for its
study. Emeritus Prof. T.H. Hubbell of the University of
Michigan once averred that with every animal you are stuck
with certain problems. Both maxims have merit, but my personal perspectives on the complexities of firefly behavior
have shifted emphatically, in some details, from the latter
to the former. I believe that lampyrids are especially
appropriate to investigations of sexual selection and can
become important in modeling and understanding mating behavior
of many other insects whose secretive and less luminous
natures prevent or restrict analysis in intimate detail.

ACKNOWLEDGMENTS

    I am indebted to several persons who have provided me with
helpful discussions, questions, criticisms, and ideas: R.D.
Alexander, J.B. Buck, L.L. Buschman, R.C. Paul, R. Thornhill,
and T.J. Walker; with unpublished manuscripts, data, and other
information: G. Borgia, L.L. Buschman, H. Dreisig, G.O.
Krizek, N.C. Leppla, D.B. Richman, D.L. Tiemann, and D.P.
Wojcik; to T.C. Carlysle for making the electron micrographs
in Figs. 3 and 4; to S. Sickerman for drawing Fig. 2; to J.B.
Randall for drawing Fig. 5; and to T.J. Walker for reading and
making helpful criticisms on the manuscript. In my studies
on Lampyridae the opportunity of singular importance, aside
from that of association with RDA and TJW, was to participate
in the 1969 Alpha Helix Expedition to New Guinea, sponsored
by NSF under grant GB8400 to the Scripps Institution of
Oceanography. Other important research support has been
derived from the National Science Foundation grant GB7407,
National Academy of Sciences, Sigma Xi RESA grants, and the
Center for Tropical Agriculture at the University of Florida.

REFERENCES

Alexander, R.D. 1975. Natural selection and specialized
    chorusing behavior in acoustical insects. *In* D. Pimentel
    (ed.), *Insects, Science and Society*. Academic Press, Inc.,
    New York.
Atkinson, G.F. 1887. Observations on the female form of
    Phengodes laticollis Horn. *Amer. Nat.* 21:853-856.

Ballantyne, L. 1968. Revisional studies of Australian and
    Indomalayan Luciolini (Coleoptera: Lampyridae: Luciolini).
    Univ. Queensland Papers 2:105-139.
Ballantyne, L.A., and M.R. McLean. 1970. Revisional studies
    on the firefly genus *Pteroptyx* Olivier (Coleoptera:
    Lampyridae: Luciolinae: Luciolini). *Trans. Amer. Ent. Soc.*
    96:223-305.
Barber, H.S. 1906. Note on *Phengodes* in the vicinity of
    Washington, D.C. *Proc. Ent. Soc. Wash.* 7:196-197.
Barber, H.S. 1951. North American fireflies of the genus
    Photuris. *Smithsonian Inst. Collections* 117:1-58.
Bastian, J., and G. Bermant. 1973. Animal communication: an
    overview and conceptual analysis. *In* G. Bermant (ed.),
    Perspectives on Animal Behavior: A First Course. Scott,
    Foresman and Co., Glenview, Ill.
Blair, K.G. 1915. Luminous insects. *Nature* 96:411-415.
Bristowe, W.S. 1924. Notes on the habits of insects and
    spiders in Brazil. *Trans. Ent. Soc. London* 72:475-504.
Buck, J.B. 1935. Synchronous flashing of fireflies experi-
    mentally induced. *Science* 81:339-340.
Buck, J.B. 1937. Studies on the firefly. II. The signal
    system and color vision in *Photinus pyralis*. *Physiol. Zool.*
    10:412-419.
Buck, J.B., and E. Buck. 1966. Biology of synchronous flashing
    of fireflies. *Nature* 211:562-564.
Buck, J.B., and E. Buck. 1968. Mechanisms of rhythmic synchro-
    nous flashing of fireflies. *Science* 159:1319-1327.
Buck, J.B., and E. Buck. 1972. Photic signaling in the firefly
    Photinus greeni. *Biol. Bull.* 142:195-205.
Buck, J.B., and E. Buck. 1976. Synchronous fireflies. *Sci.
    Amer.* 234:74-85.
Buschman, L.L. 1974. Flash behavior of a Nova Scotian firefly,
    Photuris fairchildi Barber, during courtship and aggressive
    mimicry (Coleoptera: Lampyridae). *Coleop. Bull.* 28:27-31.
Carlson, A.D., and B. Soucek. 1975. Computer simulation of
    firefly flash sequences. *J. Theor. Biol.* 55:353-370.
Dreisig, H. 1971. Control of the glowing of *Lampyris noctiluca*
    in the field (Coleoptera: Lampyridae). *J. Zool.*
    165:229-244.
Farnworth, E.G. 1973. Flashing behavior, ecology and system-
    atics of Jamaican lampyrid fireflies. Ph.D. Dissertation,
    Univ. of Fla., Gainesville, 278 pp.
Fisher, R.A. 1958. *The Genetical Theory of Natural Selection*.
    Dover, New York.
Gravely, F.H. 1915. Notes on the habits of Indian insects,
    myriapods, and arachnids. *Rec. Indian Mus.* 11:483-539.
Green, E.E. 1912. On some luminous Coleoptera from Ceylon.
    Trans. Royal. Ent. Soc. 4:717-719.
Jackson, R.R. 1975. The evolution of courtship and mating

tactics in a jumping spider *Phidippus johnsoni* (Aranae: Salticidae). Ph.D. Dissertation, Univ. of California, Berkeley, 271 pp.

Kaufmann, T. 1965. Ecological and biological studies on the West African firefly *Luciola discicollis* (Coleoptera: Lampyridae). *Ann. Ent. Soc. Amer.* 58:414-426.

Kiichiro, M. 1961. A study of fireflies. Published by the author, in Japanese. (U.S. Army translation no. 1-9415 (1966), I.D. no. 2204017766, 0371).

King, H.S. 1880. Life history of *Pleotomus pallens* Lec. *Psyche* 3:51-53.

Knab, F. 1905. Observations on Lampyridae. *Can. Ent.* 37:238-239.

Lloyd, J.E. 1964. Notes on flash communication in the firefly *Pyractomena dispersa* (Coleoptera: Lampyridae). *Ann. Ent. Soc. Amer.* 57:260-261.

Lloyd, J.E. 1965a. Observations on the biology of three luminescent beetles (Coleoptera: Lampyridae, Elateridae). *Ann. Ent. Soc. Amer.* 58:588-591.

Lloyd, J.E. 1965b. Aggressive mimicry in *Photuris:* firefly femmes fatales. *Science* 149:653-654.

Lloyd, J.E. 1966a. Signals and mating behavior in several fireflies (Coleoptera: Lampyridae). *Coleop. Bull.* 20:84-90.

Lloyd, J.E. 1966b. Studies on the flash communication system in *Photinus* fireflies. *Misc. Pubs. Mus. Zool. Univ. Mich.* 130:1-95.

Lloyd, J.E. 1968. Illumination, another function of firefly flashes. *Ent. News* 79:265-268.

Lloyd, J.E. 1969a. Flashes, behavior, and additional species of nearctic *Photinus* fireflies (Coleoptera: Lampyridae). *Coleop. Bull.* 23:29-40.

Lloyd, J.E. 1969b. Signals and systematics of Jamaican fireflies: notes on behavior and on undescribed species (Coleoptera: Lampyridae). *Ent. News* 80:169-176.

Lloyd, J.E. 1969c. Flashes of *Photuris* fireflies: their value and use in recognizing species. *Fla. Ent.* 52:29-35.

Lloyd, J.E. 1971. Bioluminescent communication in insects. *Ann. Rev. Ent.* 16:97-122.

Lloyd, J.E. 1972. Mating behavior of a New Guinea *Luciola* firefly: a new communicative protocol. *Coleop. Bull.* 26:155-163.

Lloyd, J.E. 1973a. Firefly parasites and predators. *Coleop. Bull.* 27:91-106.

Lloyd, J.E. 1973b. Model for the mating protocol of synchronously flashing fireflies. *Nature* 245:268-270.

Lloyd, J.E. 1973c. Fireflies of Melanesia: bioluminescence, mating behavior, and synchronous flashing. *Environ. Ent.* 2:991-1008.

Lloyd, J.E. 1975. Aggressive mimicry in *Photuris:* signal

repertoires by femmes fatales. *Science* 187:452-453.
Lloyd, J.E. 1977. Bioluminescence and communication. *In* T.
    Sebeok (ed.), *How Animals Communicate*. Indiana Univ. Press,
    Bloomington.
MacArthur, R.H. 1972. *Geographical Ecology: Patterns in the
    Distribution of Species*. Harper and Row, New York.
McDermott, F.A. 1910. A note on the light emission of some
    American Lampyridae. *Can. Ent.* 42:357-363.
McDermott, F.A. 1911. Some further observations on the light
    emission of American Lampyridae: the photogenic function
    as a mating adaptation in the Photinini. *Can. Ent.* 43:
    399-406.
McDermott, F.A., and J.B. Buck. 1959. The lampyrid fireflies
    of Jamaica. *Trans. Amer. Ent. Soc.* 85:1-112.
Mast, S.O. 1912. Behavior of fireflies *(Photinus pyralis)* with
    special reference to the problem of orientation. *J. Anim.
    Behav.* 2:256-272.
Maurer, U.M. 1968. Some parameters of photic signaling impor-
    tant to sexual and species recognition in the firefly
    Photinus pyralis. M.S. thesis, S.U.N.Y., Stony Brook, New
    York.
Nelson, S., A.D. Carlson, and J. Copeland. 1975. Mating
    induced behavioural switch in female fireflies. *Nature*
    255:628-629.
Newport, G. 1857. On the natural history of the glowworm
    (Lampyris noctiluca). J. Proc. Linn. Soc. London Zool. 1:
    40-71.
Oertel, D., K.A. Linberg, and J.F. Case. 1975. Ultrastructure
    of the larval firefly light organ as related to control of
    light emission. *Cell. Tiss. Res.* 164:27-44.
Otte, D. 1974. Effects and functions in the evolution of
    signaling systems. *Ann. Rev. Ecol. System* 5:385-417.
Otte, D., and J. Smiley. 1977. Synchrony in Texas fireflies
    with a consideration of male interaction models. *Biol. of
    Behav.* 2:143-158.
Papi, F. 1969. Light emission, sex attraction and male flash
    dialogues in a firefly, *Luciola lusitanica* (Charp.).
    Monitore Zool. Ital. (N.S.) 3:135-184.
Polunin, I. 1971. *In* P. Zahl, Nature's night lights. *Nat.
    Geog. Mag.* 140:45-69 (photograph of broadcasting
    Pteroptyx malaccae male).
Richards, O.W. 1927. Sexual selection and allied problems in
    the insects. *Biol. Rev.* 2:298-364.
Rivers, J.J. 1886. Description of the form of the female
    lampyrid *(Zarhipis riversi* Horn). *Amer. Nat.* 20:648-650.
Schwalb, H.H. 1961. Beitrage zur Biologie der einheimischen
    Lampyriden *Lampyris noctiluca* Geoff. und *Phausis splendid-
    ula* Lec. und experimentelle Analyse ihres Beutefang -und
    Sexualverhaltens. *Zool. Jahrb. Syst.* 88:399-550.

Sleeper, E.L. 1969. A note on luminescence in *Pleotomus*
    (Coleoptera: Lampyridae). *Ent. News* 80:251, 272.
Soucek, B., and A.D. Carlson. 1975. Flash pattern recognition
    in fireflies. *J. Theor. Biol.* 55:339-352.
Thornhill, R. 1976. Sexual selection and paternal investment
    in insects. *Amer. Nat.* 110:153-163.
Tiemann, D.L. 1967. Observations on the natural history of the
    western banded glowworm *Zarhipis integripennis* (Lec.)
    Proc. Cal. Acad. Sci. 35:235-264.
Tiemann, D.L. 1970. Nature's toy train, the railroad worm.
    Nat. Geog. Mag. 138:56-67.
Trivers, R.L. 1972. Parental investment and sexual selection.
    In B. Campbell (ed.), *Sexual Selection and the Descent of
    Man, 1871-1971.* Aldine, Chicago.
Walker, T.J. 1974. Character displacement and acoustic in-
    sects. *Amer. Zool.* 14:1137-1150.
Williams, G.C. 1966. *Adaptation and Natural Selection.*
    Princeton Univ. Press, Princeton.

THE EVOLUTION OF ALTERNATIVE MALE REPRODUCTIVE

STRATEGIES IN FIELD CRICKETS

William Cade

The University of Texas

INTRODUCTION

Competition for mates usually involves males contending
for a limited number of females (Darwin, 1871). This and
other sexual differences in behavior and morphology apparently
reflect discrepancies in male and female parental investments.
Parental investment, or the investment by parents in off-
spring--which results in an increased survival-probability of
offspring and a decreased ability to invest in other off-
spring--includes investment in zygotes, feeding or otherwise
caring for young, but excludes energy or time used in the
acquisition of mates. In most animal species, male parental
investment is negligible or less than the corresponding female
investment. It follows that in these species male reproductive success is limited by the number of successful matings,
whereas female reproductive success is limited mainly by the
resources needed to produce and rear offspring. Consequently,
in species characterized by low male parental investment, some
form of male-male competition for mates should predominate
(Trivers, 1972).

Mate competition occurs both before and after copulation
or sperm transfer, although precopulatory forms are usually
more obvious. Precopulatory mating competition is often
characterized by aggression, as in territoriality or dominance
behavior, by which males actively prevent other males from
mating. Also included is competition involving differential
male abilities in finding mates (Wilson, 1975).

Although the males of a species are sometimes thought to
exhibit a stereotyped form of precopulatory competition (for
example, see Johnson, 1964), in some reported cases, conspecific males in the same population adopt very different strategies in acquiring mates. Alternative male reproductive
strategies are known in a few species of acoustical Orthoptera.
In these and most other acoustical insects, male parental
investment is negligible, and the resulting mate competition

343

is expressed most apparently as acoustical signaling among
males. Several categories of acoustical signals are involved,
some of which affect the behavior of conspecific males and
also result in the attraction of sexually receptive females
(insect acoustical behavior is discussed more fully later).
Although acoustical communication is a principal mode of
competition for females, males may also acquire mates by
silently searching and waiting for females in the area of
acoustically signaling males. In this chapter, I examine the
evolution of alternative male reproductive modes in acoustical insects by discussing patterns of male-male competition
in the field cricket *Gryllus integer* (Orthoptera: Gryllidae).

EXAMPLES AND THEORY

     Species with males that vary greatly in sexual behavior
are known in very diverse groups. One striking example involves the Ruff, *Philomachus pugnax,* a member of the snipe
family (Aves: Charadriidae), which breeds in northern Europe
and Asia. In this species, Hogan-Warburg (1966) and van Rhijn
(1973) identified two principal groups of males occurring on
and near communal breeding arenas or leks. "Independent
resident" males are dark and usually occupy and defend territories. The nonterritorial "satellite males" are white and
often occur on or near the territories of resident males.
When females are present, satellites are often attacked by
residents, but at other times, both types of males peacefully
coexist. Mating success for both appears to depend on the
size of the aggregation, characteristics of individuals, and
the frequency of both types of males. Territorial males are
especially aggressive on large leks. Consequently, satellites
copulate infrequently, or not at all, in large aggregations.
However, on a relatively small lek, satellites represented
20% of the males present and accounted for 28% of the matings.
Whereas when satellites represented 39% of the males, they
performed only 10% of the matings (Hogan-Warburg, 1966).
Since transitions between the principal types of males do not
occur, Hogan-Warburg concluded that the persistence of alternative forms represented a stable polymorphism maintained by
opposing selective forces. However, Hogan-Warburg also proposed that the function of the polymorphism involved satellites insuring "species survival" by creating "the necessary
conditions on residences to enable resident males to attract
and stimulate females." Although van Rhijn's argument is
somewhat more complicated, he, too, proposed that satellites
and residents cooperate in that satellites attract and stimulate females. Accordingly, resident males must have satellites
present in order to mate, and satellites benefit by remaining

on a residence because females are sexually receptive there.
While such a cooperative relationship is possible, it seems
unlikely, since territorial males attack satellites more often
when females are nearby.

In the ruff, satellite males resemble females both in color
and behavior (van Rhijn, 1973), a "homosexual" condition
which occurs in many animals. In the ten-spined stickleback,
Pygosteus pungitius, Morris (1951, 1955) referred to male fish
that mimic females as "pseudofemales." In densely populated
aquaria, black stickleback males defend territories where they
build nests and court females. A sexually receptive female
pauses to release eggs while passing through a male's nest.
She is usually followed by the resident male who fertilizes
the eggs. Territorial males apparently can not distinguish
between pseudofemales and females, thereby permitting pseudofemales to intrude on territories without risking attacks
from residents. Pseudofemales are attracted to a nest by the
presence of females, and sometimes pass through the nest
immediately after a female has. Morris reasoned that pseudo-
female behavior and coloration resulted from males releasing
sexual energy that can not be released by typical male behavior at high densities. Morris recognized that fertilizations
by pseudofemales of eggs in another male's nest may occur,
but he believed this result to be accidental.

Morris (1951) also observed pseudofemales in *Gasterosteus
aculeatus,* the three-spined stickleback. Here, pseudofemales
do not as closely resemble females and are therefore attacked
by territorial males. Once, when a territorial male was
courting a female, a pseudofemale "stealthily" moved toward
the nest entrance but was repeatedly chased back by the resident. After the female entered the nest and oviposited, the
pseudofemale rushed to the nest and entered it by pushing the
resident aside. Van den Assem (1967) regularly observed
pseudofemale three-spined sticklebacks. He disagreed with
Morris and proposed that pseudofemale behavior functions in
"stealing" fertilizations from other males. Supporting this
hypothesis, van den Assem observed that territory holders
also behave as pseudofemales, that pseudofemale behavior
occurs in low density populations, and that pseudofemales
frequently enter nests after females and before the resident
males. Other workers (Barlow, 1967; Otte, 1974) also argued
that pseudofemale behavior and coloration permit stolen fertilizations.

While not involving "homosexuality," behaviors suggesting
alternative male reproductive strategies are known in some
anurans. For example, in the toad *Bufo compactilis,* large
males call to attract females, while small males do not call
but remain motionless near a calling male. Both callers and
noncallers try to clasp newly arrived females. Axtell (1958)

TABLE 1

*Species with alternative male reproductive strategies that
generally consist of territorial or
signaling behavior and nonterritoriality or nonsignaling*

Taxon	Source
Fish (Teleosts)[a]	
Pygosteus pungitius	Morris, 1951, 1955
Gasterosteus aculeatus	van den Assem, 1967
Polycentrus schomburgkii	Barlow, 1967
Amphibians and Reptiles	
Bufo compactilis	Axtell, 1958
Rana catesbeiana	Emlen, 1968
Anolis garmani[a]	Trivers, 1976
Birds[b]	
Philomachus pugnax[a]	Hogan-Warburg, 1966
	van Rhijn, 1973
Lyrurus tetrix	Kruijt et al., 1972
Insects	
Nauphoeta cinerea	Ewing, 1973
(Blattidae)	
Syrbula fuscovittata	Otte, 1972
S. admirabilis	
(Acrididae)	
Several species of	
Tettigoniidae	Spooner, 1968
(Phaneropterinae)	
Goniatron planum	Otte and Joern, 1975
(Acrididae)	
Pteroptyx spp.	Lloyd, 1973
Luciola spp.	
(Lympiridae)	
Several species of	
Sphecidae	Alcock, 1975
(Philanthinae)	

[a] Nonterritorial males resemble conspecific females in color
and behavior.

[b] Not included are many examples of nonterritorial males
that probably result from space competition (see Brown,
1969).

did not observe matings by noncallers, but he believed that
such matings may occur.

Alternative male mating strategies are known to occur in
several philanthine wasps (Hymenoptera: Sphecidae). In these
species, some males are territorial and defend perches on
desert shrubs. Territories are also frequented by "visitor"
males who probably steal newly arrived females. Mate theft
may be especially possible when residents are fighting other
visitors (Alcock, 1975, and this volume).

These examples (and others, see Table 1) indicate that
conspecific males acquire matings by different means. They
also raise the problem of explaining the maintenance of alternative forms in the same population. The occurrence of stable
polymorphisms, or genetically controlled discontinuous forms
within a species, results from an interaction of opposing
selective forces (Ford, 1945, 1971). The importance of
counter-selection in the evolution of reproductive strategies
is also well appreciated. It is generally argued (Cole, 1954;
Gadgil and Bossert, 1970; Williams, 1966) that the number of
offspring produced tends to increase with greater investments
of reproductive effort, but that the investor's (and in some
cases an offspring's) probability of survival decreases as
effort allocated for growth and maintenance is expended.
Also, greater predation may result from fighting, foraging, or
any reproductive behavior. The optimal reproductive strategy,
or the investment pattern resulting in the greatest number of
offspring reaching adulthood, represents a compromise between
fertility and mortality.

This trade-off is usually seen in comparisons between
species, but Gadgil (1972) applied the fertility-mortality
compromise in modeling the evolution of intraspecific
differences in male mating strategies. Citing examples of
nonallometric male differences in horn and mandible size in
various taxa, Gadgil assumed that these represented alternative reproductive strategies. He argued that investment in
a given strategy generally increases mating success and
decreases survival probability. Since male mating success is
relative to investments by other males, males who invest more
heavily than others mate more frequently, at least during the
period of investment. Males that do not invest heavily mate
infrequently, but live longer than more successful males. The
persistence of alternative male strategies should result from
different strategies giving, on the average, equal returns in
fitness. Large investors achieve many matings in a short
time, while males investing a small amount of effort mate an
equivalent number (considering sperm competition) of times
over a longer period.

Some data concerning the fertility-mortality compromise
are available when comparing reproductive strategies between

species, as in semelparity (one mass reproduction) versus
iteoparity (extended reproduction). However, most reports
involving intraspecific male differences in mortality and
fertility schedules are anecdotal. An exception is provided
by two separate studies on three-spined sticklebacks. In
some lakes in Canada, *Gasterosteus aculeatus* males show two
color patterns related to mating. Twelve to sixteen percent
of the sexually mature males have red throats, while the
remainder have dull-colored throats. Female sticklebacks
mate significantly more often with males having the red type
of coloration (Semler, 1971), but these males are more susceptible to trout predation (Moodie, 1972). The trade-off
between mating success and survivorship apparently results
in the persistence of both types of males in the same population.

ACOUSTICAL INSECTS

   Field crickets, the insects used in this study of mate
competition, are nocturnal and occur in most parts of the
world. In part because of their nocturnal behavior, cricket
communication primarily involves acoustical signaling. Males
stridulate by rubbing together the hardened forewings, each
stroke producing a single "pulse" of sound. Pulses delivered
in close sequences result in songs of different functional
types: the species-specific calling song, a rhythmic and loud
signal, attracts females; the aggressive song, a loud but
brief signal, functions in the context of fighting with other
males; and the courtship song, a quiet and rhythmic signal,
promotes copulation when a female is nearby. These and other
songs are characteristic, in varying degrees, of most crickets
(Alexander, 1962), although communication by acoustical signaling has been secondarily lost in many species (Otte, 1977;
Walker, 1974).
   Insect acoustical behavior was once interpreted without
considering its role in male-male competition. However,
Alexander (1975) and Otte (1977) have reconsidered previous
studies of acoustical insects and have identified several
types of behavior that probably represent strategies open to
competing males. Initially, males may spatially associate
with other males or they may migrate, the latter possibly
resulting in colonization of suitable areas and avoidance of
some competition. Both isolated and aggregated males acoustically signal for females, but some interesting variations
on this theme and nonacoustical behaviors occur in aggregations. A few examples illustrate these behaviors and provide
information on their functions.
   In field crickets (primarily *Gryllus veletis*), caged males

establish a dominance hierarchy through violent fighting and
intense acoustical signaling. Dominance is exhibited as a
form of territoriality that is characterized by the spacing
and attachment of calling males to certain sites. A male's
status may vary somewhat, with increased aggression being
evident after mating or when a male occupies a burrow.
Aggression ultimately functions in mating. Dominant males
almost always monopolize females, sometimes by searching out
and attacking signaling males (Alexander, 1961).

The regular spacing of signaling males occurs in some
conocephaline katydids (Orthoptera: Tettigoniidae). This
type of distribution results from agonistic signaling backed
by intense male fighting. Male-male spacing ultimately permits an individual male to monopolize nearby females (Morris,
1971).

In the acridids *Syrbula admirabilis* and *S. fuscovittata,*
males and females call while approaching one another. In *S.
admirabilis,* noncalling males rapidly approach a female
answering another male's call, perhaps leading to mate theft.
Stolen copulations by noncourting males may also occur in
both species as a result of these males assembling near a
courting pair. Mate stealing was observed in *S. fuscovittata*
when a noncalling male mounted a female who had just signaled
to a second male (Otte, 1972).

Finally, males of several species of phaneropterine
katydids (Orthoptera: Tettigoniidae) produce a complex calling
song. Conspecific receptive females respond with a faint
"tick" that attracts the calling male and also noncalling
males in the area. Matings by noncalling males were observed. In one species, a calling male reduces his song
intensity following the female sound, and in so doing may
lessen the likelihood of noncallers locating the female. In
some species, noncalling males are repelled by the conspecific calling song, thereby reducing the likelihood of mate
theft (Spooner, 1968).

Gryllus integer, the bivoltine field cricket used in this
study, occurs commonly in central Texas where it inhabits
lawns, old fields, or any grassy area. As is generally true
in grassland gryllids, both micropterous (short hind wings)
and macropterous (long hind wings) morphs occur (Alexander,
1968). During the late summer and early fall, population
densities sometimes reach very high levels. Such periods are
indicated most obviously by large numbers of macropterous
crickets flying to and landing near electric lights (Hunter,
1912). In 1973, during a period of moderately high population
density, I first observed both calling and noncalling *G.
integer* males in the same population. The research discussed
in this chapter was intended to investigate the evolution of
calling, noncalling, and additional male behaviors in terms

of their attached costs and benefits.

METHODS OF STUDY

   I conducted research on *Gryllus integer* biology in Travis
County in central Texas. Observations and experiments on
field populations were conducted at the Brackenridge Field
Laboratory of the University of Texas, on a large area of land
operated by the Texas System of Natural Laboratories, Inc.,
in city parks, and in residential areas. Crickets are, of
course, nocturnal and many observations were made using a
headlight. I believe cricket behavior was not affected greatly by the light. This was especially true if individuals were
already interacting (aggressive signaling, courting, mating,
etc.) when I began my observations.
   Some data on the behavior of individuals were obtained by
introducing numbered adult crickets (the pronotum was painted
with typewriter correction fluid and a number written with a
drawing pen) into an outdoor arena. The arena was enclosed by
cement walls (13.5 m x 13.5 m x 3.5 m) and open on top. After
much of the vegetation was removed from the arena, it was
divided into 25 quadrats (about 2.7 m x 2.7 m), each marked
with a flag. Fifty sawed-off ends of cinder blocks were
randomly placed in the arena and accompanying wood "roofs" (to
prevent overheating) were used as cricket shelters.
   Several procedures involved broadcasting tape-recorded
cricket song. In these procedures, Uher 4000 Report L tape
recorders, Uher condenser microphones, Ampex 651 magnetic
tape, and Realistic 40-1228 and 40-1224 high frequency speakers were used. Acoustical traps were sometimes attached to
loudspeakers (Fig. 1). Sound intensities were measured by

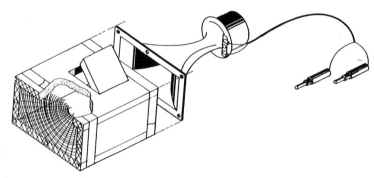

Fig. 1. Partially exploded view of an acoustical trap con-
sisting of a high frequency loudspeaker, a styrofoam box
(approximately 17 cm x 15 cm x 6 cm) with a panel for removing
animals, and an inwardly projecting aluminum screen funnel.

a General Radio model 1565-B Sound Level Meter held about 6 cm from either a loudspeaker or a calling male. Additional details on these and other methods follow.

RESULTS

   I present the results on the biology of *Gryllus integer* as follows: those obtained in naturally established populations, those obtained by broadcasting taped cricket song, and results on individual crickets. I also consider results on interactions between crickets and *Euphasiopteryx ochracea* (Diptera: Tachinidae), a parasitoid that acoustically orients to the mating songs of crickets (Cade, 1975).

Naturally Established Populations

   At times of low cricket population density, calling males were generally separated by long distances. In an extreme example, on July 12, 1974, an extensive search of one site revealed only two calling males separated by about 2.1 km (1.3 miles on a car odometer). At higher population densities, calling males usually occurred in groups of two or more. In a given field, I flagged the positions of simultaneously calling males and measured the distance between nearest neighbors. These measurements (Fig. 2) indicate the tendency of calling males to aggregate spatially, a result confirmed by nearest neighbor analyses (Clark and Evans, 1954) of individual populations (Cade, 1976). Although male-male distances vary considerably, there may be three classes of males with respect to nearest neighbor distances: males that are highly clumped (1.2-7.2 m), those that are moderately clumped (7.7-13.7 m), and those that are relatively isolated from other signaling males (15.7 + m). Nearest neighbor measurements also indicate that, although aggregated over a large area, simultaneously calling males were never closer together than 1 m.
   Calling males differed with respect to song intensities. Measurements for 24 males averaged 76.5 db and ranged from 46 to 92 db (S.D. = 11.14). Additional data regarding song intensities follow.
   Calling males also differed in the regularity of song production. Some males called constantly, while neighbors called infrequently. Also, males often began calling following the cessation of calling by a neighboring male (Fig. 3). For example, of 37 calling males that I intentionally disturbed and therefore silenced, 28 had previously silent neighbors that started calling within a 10 min. period

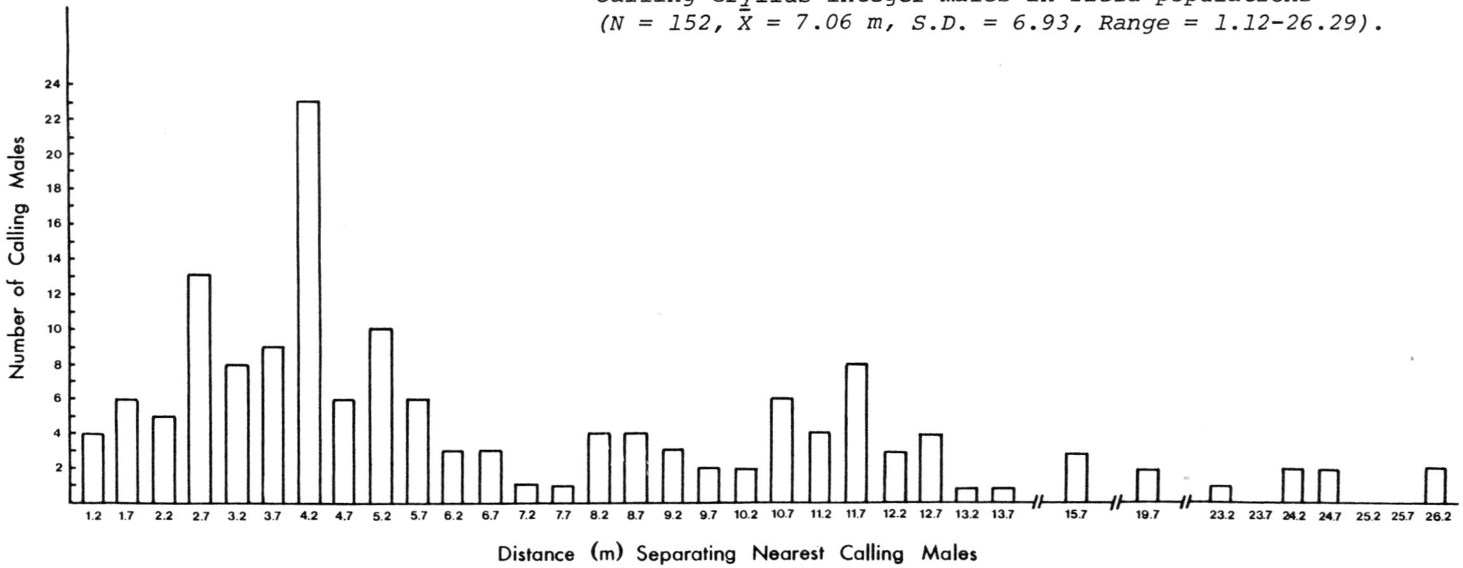

Fig. 2. Distances separating nearest simultaneously calling Gryllus integer males in field populations (N = 152, X̄ = 7.06 m, S.D. = 6.93, Range = 1.12−26.29).

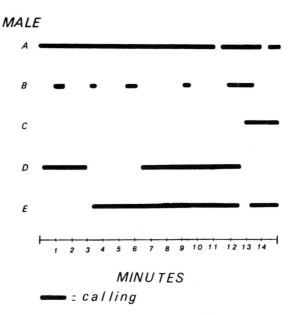

Fig. 3. Diagram illustrating the regularity and the super-
sedence of calling by Gryllus integer males at marked
positions over a 15 min. period.

$(x^2 = 9.8,\ p < .005)$.

   I observed 12 matings involving calling males. Each
time, the calling male started producing courtship song following contact with a female. Matings lasted only a few
seconds. Following mating, the males usually remained stationary, but did not resume calling (calling is dependent
on the presence of a spermatophore in crickets: Huber, 1962).
After mating, one previously calling male followed the female
out of the immediate area.

   Patterns of calling over a 12 hr. period were determined
by counting the number of calling males while I slowly
bicycled through a 30-block residential area. During a
period of high density, the number of calling males increased
from 8 to 10 hrs. after sunset (Kruskal-Wallis analysis of
variance, $p < .05$; see Siegel, 1956), or immediately before
and during sunrise (Fig. 4c). No comparable increase
occurred during a period of low cricket population density.

   No matings were observed at dawn. However, I collected
three females next to a softly calling male at 2 hrs. after
sunrise. All three females had fresh spermatophores attached,
indicating they had recently mated. A noncalling male was
also close to the calling male.

   Many birds become active at sunrise. On three mornings I

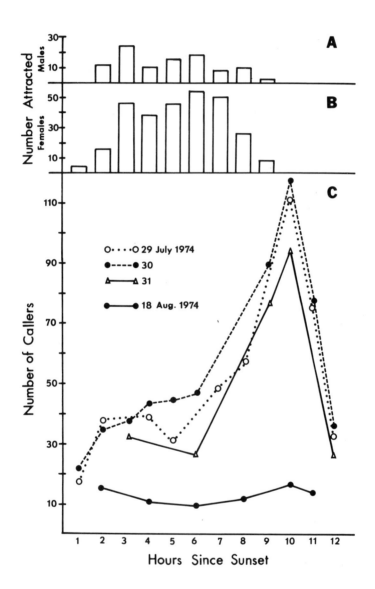

Fig. 4. Temporal patterns of Gryllus integer phonotaxis to
taped conspecific calling song (A and B) and calling behavior
(C). (July 29-31 was a period of high cricket population
density, and August 18 was during a period of low density.)

observed large groups of grackles, *Cassidix mexicanus* (Aves: Icteryidae), apparently feeding in an area that also contained many calling crickets. No information on the type of prey taken in this area is available, but I observed grackles catching *G. integer* on other occasions. My attempts to attract birds to artificially produced cricket song were unsuccessful.

In a single cricket aggregation, I assumed that flagged positions represented individual males, since these males were not otherwise marked. Calling behavior may thus be compared for different males during the night. This information (Table 2) indicates that in the early hours of the night, males at positions A and B called simultaneously and at the same sound intensity. At 7 hrs. after sunset, B still called, however, at a much lower intensity than three neighboring males who were all calling at the same intensity. Male B was still calling 8 hrs. after sunset, but at a much higher sound intensity than previously observed from that position. Nine hours after sunset, calling males were observed at many new positions. Although song intensities during the ninth hour are not significantly different (Mann-Whitney U Test) than those at other hours, some males called in the morning at relatively low intensities.

In addition to calling males, I often observed noncalling males walking in areas occupied by the callers. Near a calling male, I observed noncallers briefly courting females five

TABLE 2

Gryllus integer *calling song intensities measured at marked positions in the same area at different hours after sunset*

Hours since sunset	Song intensities (db) at marked positions															
	A	B	C	D	E	F	G	H	I	J	K	L	M	N	O	P
1	80	80														
2	80	80														
3	80	80														
7		80	87	87	87											
8		92		89			90	87								
9							83	86	75	70	87	63	63	47	63	65	52

NOTE: Only those measurements for regularly calling males are included; each position is assumed to represent an individual male.

separate times, although no matings resulted.

On one occasion I observed at least 12 noncalling males
within 0.5 m of a calling male. One noncalling male repeatedly attacked the caller. The attacked male stopped calling,
but produced short bursts of aggressive song. One male with-
drew, but his identity was unknown. In three additional
observations on calling males, I watched noncalling males
orient to the caller and attack him.

Broadcasting Taped Cricket Song

To observe the effects of conspecific song on a signaling
male, I broadcast previously recorded *G. integer* calling song
in the direction of a calling male at about the same sound
intensity as his own song. In 59 trials involving different
males, slow movement of the loudspeaker toward the test male
resulted in aggressive behavior 17 times (Fig. 5). These
males typically stopped calling, immediately and rapidly walked to the loudspeaker, remained motionless on the front of the
speaker for a few seconds, and then ran rapidly around the
immediate area of the speaker. Test males sometimes attacked
males tethered directly in front of the speaker by biting with
the mandibles and producing bursts of aggressive song. In 29
trials (Fig. 5), the males did not behave aggressively, but
stopped calling and usually remained stationary. Some of
these males walked, fed on vegetation, and called irregularly
in the area of the loudspeaker. Calling resumed in 14 of 18

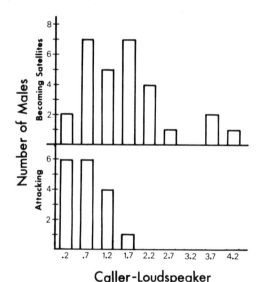

Fig. 5. Male-loudspeaker distances at which aggressive (attacking) and nonaggressive (satellite) behaviors resulted from broadcasting taped conspecific song to previously calling Gryllus integer *males.*

nonaggressive males after song broadcasting was stopped.
Males stopped calling and behaved nonaggressively at an
average distance of 1.65 m. In other males, aggressive behavior occurred at a mean distance of 0.68 m separating male and
loudspeaker. These two groups of males differed significantly
in regards to the male-loudspeaker distances which elicited
the respective behaviors (Mann-Whitney U Test, p = 0.0018).
In eight males tested by the playing of conspecific song, no
observable behavior resulted. Also, five males showed nonaggressive behavior initially and, following a reduction in
male-loudspeaker distance, behaved aggressively.

It was sometimes apparent that a male's song intensity
varied when song was broadcast in his direction. Sound
measurements in trials where changes occurred, and the resulting behavior (aggressive or nonaggressive), are summarized
in Table 3. If male 7 is ignored since he mated prior to
stopping stridulation, and male 6 is scored as behaving
aggressively and nonaggressively, then in five cases, males

TABLE 3

*Changes in song intensity and behavior resulting from
broadcasting taped conspecific calling
song to previously calling* Gryllus integer *males*

Male	Behavior in playback[a]	Sound levels (db)	Net change
1	A	85[b], 89	+
2	A	83, 72, 92, 87, 93	+
3	NA	75, 66	−
4	A	78, 82	+
5	NA	80, 40[c], 81[d]	−
6	NA & A	77, 70, 74, 81	+
7	e	78, 84	+
8	NA	77, 75	−
9	A	78, 85	+

[a] A = "attack" (aggressive) behavior; NA = nonaggressive
behavior.
[b] Sound levels are in sequence, the first measurement made
before the start of song broadcasting.
[c] An estimate, below the range of the meter.
[d] Measurement made 2 min. after song broadcasting was
discontinued.
[e] Male 7 mated and stopped calling.

that behaved aggressively first showed a net increase in song
intensity. No aggressive males showed a net decrease. In
three cases, males that behaved nonaggressively first showed
reductions in net song intensities, whereas an increase was
shown in one case. These proportions differ from those expected if there is no association between changes in song
intensity and aggressive and nonaggressive behaviors (Fisher
Test, p = 0.047; see Siegel, 1956). Two aggressive males and
three nonaggressive males did not show any changes in song
intensities before exhibiting the resulting behavior.

In one trial, a male calling at 71-73 db was located about
2 m from a loudspeaker producing much louder (90-92 db) song.
I released a highly receptive female at a point 3 m from both
male and loudspeaker. She immediately walked to the loudspeaker, but when song broadcasting was discontinued, she
walked toward the calling male. A resumption of song broadcasting immediately reattracted the female to the loudspeaker.
I then released this female 0.5 m from the male, but on the
side of the male opposite the loudspeaker. She walked in a
straight line toward the male and loudspeaker, collided with
the male, and mated.

In the Florida mole crickets, *Scapteriscus acletus* and
S. vicinus, Ulagaraj and Walker (1973) showed that flying
males and females are attracted to artificially broadcast
conspecific calling song. In *G. integer,* I studied sexual
behavior by broadcasting taped conspecific song to attract
individuals to areas suitable for, but not inhabited by, this
species. The number of crickets attracted was highly variable, but on some nights, many *G. integer* flew into the area.
Attracted females typically walked, oviposited, and fed on
vegetation in the general vicinity of the loudspeaker. Females also walked directly to the loudspeaker and entered
the attached trap. Hourly counts (Fig. 4b) indicate that
females oriented directly to the loudspeaker from 1 to 9 hrs.
after sunset. I observed a similar pattern, but not one
of such magnitude, on another occasion (Table 4). A total of
40 females were collected immediately before they entered an
acoustical trap. None of these females had attached spermatophores, but when examined later, 32 had spermatozoa in their
spermathecae.

Some of the males attracted to an area by taped song broadcasting started calling near the loudspeaker ($\bar{X}$ = 7.95 m,
N = 23, Range = 1.4-19.7, S.D. = 5.2). Ranking calling male-
loudspeaker distances with the nearest male-male distances
observed in a naturally established population ($\bar{X}$ = 7.65 m,
N = 14, Range = 2.7-14.8, S.D. = 4.7) shows no significant
difference (Mann-Whitney U test). Many attracted males did
not begin calling. Some noncalling males courted females in
the area of the loudspeaker. I observed such courtships 91

TABLE 4

Temporal patterns of Gryllus integer *and* Euphasiopteryx
ochracea *phonotaxis
to taped calling song in the field*

Number of	Hours since sunset (7:34 CDT)										sunrise	
	1	2	3	4	5	6	7	8	9	10	11	↓12
Crickets												
Males	1	0	1	1	0	0	0	1	0	0	0	0
Females	2	2	0	0	4	0	0	1	0	0	0	0
Flies	18	6	3	2	2	1	1	0	4	8	8	6

	Hours since sunrise (7:13 CDT)										sunset	
	1	2	3	4	5	6	7	8	9	10	11	12↓
Flies	5	1	1	1	0	0	0	0	0	1	1	19

NOTE: No crickets were attracted during the daylight hours.

times, but only five matings resulted. Courtship lasted from
a few seconds to several minutes, and some courting males
followed females walking in the area. Males also walked to
loudspeakers and entered acoustical traps. The male temporal
pattern of phonotaxis is similar to that for females (Fig.
4a; Table 4). When I tethered a male directly in front of the
loudspeaker, some of the attracted males violently attacked
the tethered male.

On some nights, I played the same song through two loudspeakers separated by 7 m. I amplified one signal to test
cricket phonotaxis at different song intensities. The total
number of crickets collected (Table 5) indicates that females
and males are attracted more often to a loud signal than to a
relatively less intense one. Ulagaraj and Walker (1975)
showed that the phonotactic response of mole crickets also
increases with increasing song intensity.

Behavior of Individuals

Despite the effort that went into preparation of the
arena, most introduced crickets disappeared in numerous attempts to establish populations. However, Table 6 contains

TABLE 5

Simultaneous phonotaxis of Gryllus integer *males and females and* Euphasiopteryx ochracea *to taped calling song broadcast at different sound intensities in the field*

Song intensities (db)	Number attracted		Flies
	Crickets		
	Males	Females	
87-90	16[a]	21[b]	18[c]
77-80	7	7	3
Control (no song)	0	0	0

[a] $\chi = 3.52$, P > .05
[b] $\chi^2 = 7$, P < .01
[c] $\chi^2 = 10.7$, P < .005

data on the acoustical behavior of one population of arena males that was observed for a relatively long time. (Female records appear elsewhere: Cade, 1976). In this population, noncalling males generally outnumbered calling males and acoustical behavior differed between individuals, as males 17, 27, and 39 were never observed calling, but male 3 regularly called. Other males called, but somewhat infrequently. I made observations in the arena within 3 hrs. after sunset each night, therefore acoustical records do not reflect behaviors occurring during the early and late morning.

The marked positions of individual crickets on maps of the arena were used to calculate the average distance moved from a previous observation for each individual. By this measure, females were significantly more mobile than males (Mann-Whitney U Test, $p = 0.01$), but no significant difference was found between males observed calling at least once and those never observed calling (Cade, 1976).

During the period the arena was under observation, the soil in the lower portion (the arena is on a slight incline) was damp due to a broken water faucet in the adjoining arena. In the lower 2/5 of the arena (quadrats 1-10), 34 observations of males and 78 observations of females were made. In the remaining 15 quadrats, males and females were observed 14 and 49 times, respectively (for males, $\chi^2 = 19$, $p < .001$; for females, $\chi^2 = 25.18$, $p < .001$).

To determine if all males are able to call, I collected a total of 33 males that had flown to electric street lights.

TABLE 6

Acoustical behavior of male Gryllus integer in the outdoor arena

Dates observed (1973)

Male	July														August			
	18	19	20	21	22	23	24	25	26	27	28	29	30	1	2	4	5	6
3	C	C	N	N[a]	N[a]	C	C	C	-	-								
17	N	N	N	-	N	N	N	N	D									
21	N	C	N	-	-													
27	N	-	N	N	N[b]	N	N	N	D									
29	N	N	-	N	N	N	N	N	N/C[c]	N	N	N	N	N	N	N	N	N[b]
39	N	N	N	D														
45	N	N	C	-	-													

NOTE: C = calling; N = not calling; D = dead.

[a] Wings raised as in stridulation.

[b] Courting stridulation.

[c] Second inspection.

These males were placed in individual cages and situated in separate parts of my house. Six died within a day of their collection. My somewhat casual observations indicated that all but 2 of the remaining 27 males called at least once.

Cricket-Fly Interactions

   During this study, it was discovered that larviparous female *Euphasiopteryx ochracea* (Diptera: Tachinidae) parasitize *Gryllus integer* by acoustically orienting to cricket calling song (Cade, 1975). To study fly behavior, I released individual flies into a box (0.8 m x 0.8 m x 1.2 m) lined with acoustical tile. Inside the box, a calling male was simulated by a dead cricket mounted to a loudspeaker broadcasting cricket song. Attracted flies deposited larvae around the male and on the surface of the loudspeaker. Tests conducted with only broadcast song (no cricket) indicated that calling song alone is generally sufficient to elicit fly larviposition. Deposited larvae are very sticky, as illustrated by their adherence to a cricket walking across a surface containing them. In one observation, when I placed a clay model of a cricket at the edge of a loudspeaker (5.5 cm removed from the aperture from which song emanated), an attracted fly walked to the aperture and remained there for about 17 sec. This fly then immediately walked to the model of the cricket and larviposited while walking on and around it.
   I determined the temporal pattern of fly phonotaxis to taped cricket song in the same manner as in the case of crickets. Flies are active during all hours when crickets sing, with much fly activity at sunset and about one hour thereafter (Table 4). During this period, crickets first start calling for the evening.
   Following the same pattern shown for crickets, high intensity cricket song attracts many more flies than one of a lower intensity (Table 5).
   To determine the incidence of *E. ochracea* parasitism in *G. integer,* I collected female crickets and calling and noncalling males in naturally established populations. I also collected crickets that had just flown to electric lights. All collected crickets were dissected in the laboratory and carefully examined for internally contained fly larvae. Also, the spermathecae of female crickets were smeared on slides and examined under the microscope for the presence of spermatozoa. Data collected in the above manner (Table 7) indicate that calling males were parasitized by flies significantly more often than noncallers, and that flying males and inseminated females were not parasitized by flies.
   Information regarding fly parasitism and cricket survivor-

TABLE 7

Incidence of Euphasiopteryx ochracea *parasitism in*
Gryllus integer *males and females*

Gryllus integer	Parasitized	Not parasitized
Males		
Calling[a]	11	3
Noncalling[a]	4	25
Flying[b]	0	15
Females		
(Inseminated)	0	21

NOTE: Collected August–October, 1975 and 1976.

[a] $\chi^2 = 19.78$, P < .001
[b] Collected at electric lights

ship was obtained by raising five male crickets collected as
late instars in the field. After molting into adults,
individual males were placed in separate cages which were
provisioned with food and water. I placed these cages in
separate rooms of my house and recorded each time I heard a
male call. On the night of October 15 and 16, 1976, males
were placed in individual cages which permit the entrance of
E. ochracea (cages consist of acoustical traps with the loudspeakers replaced with pieces of styrofoam). In the field, I
observed males 2, 3, and 5 calling at different times during
the night, but none of the five cages contained *E. ochracea*
when inspected during the night or the following morning.
However, female flies must have entered the cages of males 3
and 5 and then escaped, as these males died following the
emergence of fly larvae. At no other time than that described
above were these males exposed to fly predation. Data obtained
from the above procedure are summarized in Table 8.

I raised adult flies in the laboratory by placing larvae on
male and female *G. integer*. Larvae emerged from both sexes in
about a week ($\bar{X}$ = 7.57 days, N = 9, S.D. = 0.84). Parasitized
crickets always died before or just after larval emergence.

DISCUSSION

I observed calling and noncalling male crickets in the
arena, in naturally established populations, and in field

TABLE 8

Longevity and acoustical behavior of male Gryllus integer

Male	Date (Sept. 1976) eclosed	Age (days) First called	Died
1	4	7	a
2	9	3	103[b]
3	8	6	15[b]
4	9	35[c]	118[b]
5	7	5	14[b]

[a] Escaped, 9/16
[b] Death followed fly larva emergence
[c] Calling very softly

populations established by taped song broadcasting. As discussed previously, calling for females and silently searching
for them in the presence of calling males are alternative
mating strategies in some acoustical insects. In *G. integer,*
calling, noncalling, and variations on these male behaviors
apparently represent alternative modes of acquiring females.
This tentative conclusion and other functions of these behaviors are now discussed in terms of contributions to individual
male fitness.

Calling Strategies

Fretwell's (1972) definition of territoriality as any site-
dependent display resulting in conspicuousness and in avoidance by similarly behaving individuals is sufficiently flexible to apply to similar behaviors in many animals. By this
definition, calling male crickets are territorial since they
are conspicuous, always separated by a minimum distance, and
sedentary, at least while signaling. I observed few fights
involving previously calling neighbors, suggesting that male-
male spacing is usually maintained by acoustical signaling.
However, violent fighting is associated with field cricket
territoriality in the laboratory (Alexander, 1961). In *G.
integer,* the role of aggression in male spacing is best demonstrated by comparing the distances at which calling males
"attacked" when song was broadcast in their direction with
the distances separating neighboring calling males (Fig. 6).

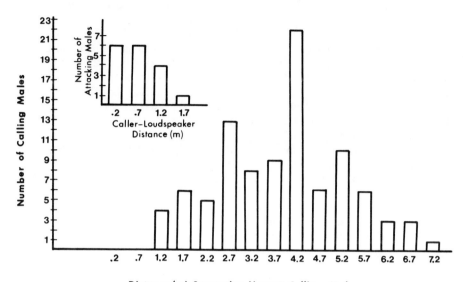

Fig. 6. Comparison of loudspeaker-male distances in trials where aggressive behavior resulted from broadcasting taped conspecific calling song to a previously calling Gryllus integer *male, and a portion of the distances separating nearest calling males in field populations.*

If song broadcasting to calling males simulates confrontations between territorial males, then most calling neighbors are separated by distances great enough to elicit few attacks. As discussed later, intense regular calling probably communicates a "threat" of physical aggression to neighboring males and is therefore usually sufficient to maintain spacing.

In *G. integer* and other acoustical insects, the major benefit attached to calling is clearly the attraction of conspecific females. This result is probably maximized in the immediate area by territorial interference with the ability of other males to attract females. Although calling permits males to increase their female quota, one possible cost associated with attracting females is parasitism by acoustically orienting Diptera. Biologists have long considered it possible that predators orient to the mating songs of their prey. However, Walker's (1964) report of domestic cats orienting to cricket song is, to the best of my knowledge, the only previous demonstration of this type of behavior by predators or parasites. In addition to the tachinid *E. ochracea* that parasitizes field crickets, *Colcondamyia auditrix* (Diptera:

Sarcophagidae) is known to orient to the mating song of its
host, *Okanagana rimosa* (Homoptera: Cicadidae) (Soper *et al.*,
1976).

The occurrence of parasitoid fly species that acoustically
orient to the mating songs of their hosts strongly suggests
that attracting such flies is a cost to males of attracting
females. However, it must be shown that a male's survival-
probability decreases as a function of calling if fly parasitism is to be considered such a cost. Although the evidence is
limited, a decreased survivorship does appear to result from
the attraction of parasitoid flies in *G. integer*. Of the
five males raised from nymphs in the laboratory, those parasitized as a result of calling during a single night in the
field survived a much shorter time than nonparasitized males
These five males were not again exposed to fly parasitism.
Given the high probability of a calling male in the field
attracting flies (indicated by the incidence of parasitism in
calling males and the attraction of flies to loudspeakers),
it is likely that in the laboratory group of five males, those
that first called early in life would, if continuously exposed
to flies, experience a decreased survivorship. However, one
male raised in the lab was not observed calling until a relatively old age. Also, in the arena population and in another
group of laboratory males, some individuals were never observed calling. Under field conditions, males that either
delay the onset of stridulation or those that never call
probably live longer than males calling at an early age.

If the presence of acoustically orienting parasitoids
represents a cost of attracting females, then the occupation
of burrows, commonly seen in ground-dwelling crickets, may
function in protection against flies or other parasites and
predators. In this respect, it is interesting that flies
larviposit both on and in the immediate area of a cricket,
and that sound alone is sufficient to elicit larviposition.
This type of larviposition behavior may permit the parasitism
of males occupying burrows.

Besides attracting female crickets and flies, calling in
crickets also attracts conspecific males. The behavior of
these males is discussed more fully later, but the possible
costs of calling that result from attracting males are of
present importance. As demonstrated by broadcasting taped
song in the field, attracted male crickets may start calling,
they may silently search for females, or they may orient to
the immediate source of conspecific song. If these behaviors
also result when a male calls, then each behavior may contribute additional costs to female attraction. These costs
include sharing females with attracted calling or searching
males and physical attacks from noncalling males. Noncalling aggressive males may injure calling males, displace

them from a signaling site, or in other ways (as discussed later) interfere with a male's stridulation. In any case, such attacks probably reduce a calling male's ability to attract females.

Much variation in calling behavior is seen in *G. integer*. One type involves previously silent males calling when a neighboring male stops calling. This observation suggests that conspecific song inhibits calling in some males, perhaps because of the threat of attack. But from the viewpoint of a second male that starts calling, song supersedure may result in matings with females attracted by another male. Matings of this type represent a form of mate theft in the sense that a male incurs costs in attracting females that mate with other males. However, the superseding male may also be susceptible to this form of mate stealing so that the benefits cancel out.

An especially obvious calling variation involves song intensities. Unless the immediate surroundings are involved, song intensity is a measure of the amount of energy a male puts into stridulation and hence competition for females. As indicated in the discussion on reproductive strategy theory, both costs and benefits should increase with greater allocations of reproductive effort. The phonotaxis of male and female crickets and parasitoid flies to cricket calling song broadcast at different sound intensities indicates such a relationship. Males calling at high song intensities probably attract not only more females, but also more noncalling males and flies than males calling at lower sound levels. Males calling at relatively low sound intensities should attract some females while avoiding many fly and male attacks. In addition, a softly calling male may intercept females that are orienting to the loud signal of a neighboring male. The observation of a female orienting repeatedly to high intensity taped song rather than a nearby softly singing male suggests that this type of mate interception occurs. When this female was released on a line with the male and the loudspeaker, she collided with the male and mated.

Parker (1974) reasoned that animal displays are a means by which competitors judge each other's ability to guard resources. This argument may be important in explaining changes in sound intensities that occurred when taped song was played to calling males. In trials where measurements are available, males that later showed aggressive behavior tended first to increase their sound levels. Some males that behaved in a nonaggressive manner, first decreased their song intensities before stopping stridulation entirely. In actual male–male confrontations, changes in song intensities may signal the aggressive tendencies of competing males and thereby enable males to avoid the expense of real fighting. Fighting in the context of territoriality is discussed later with respect to noncalling male strategies.

In high density populations, a sharp increase occurs in the number of calling males just before sunrise. But, judging by cricket phonotaxis to artificially produced calling song, females are not attracted to calling males during these hours. This result is somewhat surprising, since it might be expected that the greatest amount of calling would occur when females are most responsive. It is therefore necessary to explain why many males start calling just before dawn.

Parasitoid flies are most active at sunset when cricket males first start to call, but flies are still active at sunrise and for several hours thereafter. It does not therefore appear that the increase in calling behavior at dawn results from an absence of fly attacks in these hours. Furthermore, at sunrise, many birds become active. Although birds do not orient directly to cricket song, their presence in an area should be sufficient to select against long-range phonotaxis by male and female crickets.

Part of the explanation for this increase in calling behavior may be the fact that at dawn males no longer orient to calling song. If females are nearby and still sexually receptive, then the decreased probability of attracting noncalling aggressive males may result in increased calling. Judging from the marked positions occupied by calling males, most males calling at dawn did not call during the preceding hours when noncalling aggressive males orient to broadcast song. These "dawn-calling" males may remain silent at night because of the likelihood of attracting aggressive males. Furthermore, females are still sexually receptive (as opposed to being receptive to long-range phonotaxis) during the dawn hours, as collection of recently mated individuals near a calling male after sunrise indicates.

Males calling during the hours around sunrise tend to do so at relatively low sound intensities. Since at dawn, sexually receptive females are not attracted to conspecific song over long distances, high intensity song may be inefficient in terms of the number of females inseminated. Low intensity calling is probably sufficient to arouse nearby females sexually and may also result in a decreased vulnerability to fly attacks.

Noncalling Strategies

The term satellite, originally applied to nonterritorial male ruffs (Hogan-Warburg, 1966), appropriately describes noncalling male crickets that walk or remain motionless in areas occupied by calling males. Examples from other acoustical insects indicate that satellite behavior is a form of mate

theft in that satellites intercept females attracted by the
calling of other males. Mate stealing is apparently one
function of satellite behavior in *G. integer* as noncalling
males were observed courting females in naturally and artificially established populations, although such courtships
resulted infrequently in matings.

Satellites probably are assisted in locating females by
olfaction as *G. integer* males are able to recognize species-
specific odors (Otte and Cade, 1976). Also, olfaction is
important in the mating behavior of several nemobiine crickets
(Paul, 1976). In these species, it is most interesting that
when males are presented with the odor of conspecific females,
some males start calling, but others begin to search the
immediate area for females.

Intrusion on a territory is apparently possible because
satellite crickets don't call and consequently are not
attacked by the resident male. In at least some individuals,
satellite behavior probably results from the "threat" of
aggression by nearby calling males, as seen in the broadcasting of taped song to calling males. In this procedure, some
males stopped calling and behaved nonaggressively. The
behavior of nonaggressive males is very similar to that of
satellites in that they remained motionless or walked in the
area of the loudspeaker. Comparing male-loudspeaker distances
for "satellite-like" behavior with those for aggressively
behaving males (Fig. 5) indicates that the increased frequency
of satellite behavior is accompanied by an increase in the
likelihood of "attack" behavior. The possibility of attack
from what "sounds" like a competing male may result in
some males adopting nonaggressive and noncalling behavior.
Satellites of a loudspeaker often resumed calling after song
broadcasting was stopped, indicating that in the absence of
aggressive threats, males switch back to calling as a reproductive strategy. It therefore appears that some satellite
males benefit by avoiding attacks. This benefit, in addition
to the avoidance of acoustically orienting flies, should offset the infrequent matings that satellite males achieve.

When played taped song, most (63%) previously calling males
did not behave aggressively. The relative levels of aggression in male competition have long attracted the attention of
various workers. Wynne-Edwards (1962) and Lorenz (1966) argued
that the relative infrequency of real fighting (although it is
probably not as infrequent as they believed [Wilson, 1975]),
as opposed to signaling in agonistic conflicts, permits
species survival. However, this argument is not applicable
to most forms of animal behavior (Williams, 1971). Others
have explained the infrequency of fighting on the basis of the
potential for damage to an unrecognized relative (Wilson,
1971; see Hamilton, 1964). Maynard Smith and Price (1973)

argued that the relative absence of overt aggression results
from individual selection. In a computer simulation of the
effects of aggression on reproductive success, extremely aggressive individuals are selected against because retaliation
from conspecifics results in physical injury to the hyper-
aggressive individual.

In addition to satellite behavior, noncalling males
physically attack calling males. The threat of such attacks
may, as argued earlier, result in some males postponing
calling until dawn, a time when such attacks do not occur.
Fights with noncalling males clearly interfere with a male's
calling and, along with the prevention of calling in other
males until dawn, may result in more females remaining sexually receptive and therefore available to silently attacking
males. Attacking males may also displace a calling male and
then signal from the newly acquired site, but no information
is available on this possibility. However, in other *Gryllus,*
the possession of a suitable site greatly increases a male's
ability to win fights with other males (Alexander, 1961).

Whether there for purposes of attack or mate theft, silent
males close to a calling male may incur costs in the form of
living fly larvae deposited in the area. Larvae readily
adhere to a male walking on a surface containing them, as was
shown in the laboratory. Flies in the vicinity of a calling
male may also visually locate nearby noncalling males, as a
fly apparently did with a clay model of a cricket. In this
respect, it is interesting that some males collected while not
calling were parasitized, although the previous acoustical
behavior of these males was unknown.

Female Mate Choice

Judging from the relative infrequency of satellite matings,
female crickets apparently choose calling males as mates more
often than noncalling males. The choice of mates, usually by
females from an array of males, is a mode of sexual selection
in addition to mate competition (Darwin, 1871). In most
species in which mating preferences have been investigated,
female choice involves the selection of mates according to
whether they are conspecifics, the opposite sex, and with
respect to a potential mate's sexual maturity or competence.
However, much discussion has centered on the possibility that
females choose mates on the basis of some male character that
correlates with higher male fitness. Under this last form of
mate choice, females capable of making precise distinctions
between competing males experience greater reproductive success by combining their genes with those of the best males.
Male characters that function in mate competition are thought

to be the same employed by females in selecting mates. It is
therefore not surprising that in field crickets acoustical
signaling functions both in the interference with calling in
other males and in female mate choice, at least on some level.

Since only male crickets produce the species-specific
calling song, it is obvious that female choice of calling
males involves mate selection on the basis of right sex and
right species. Calling also indicates sexual maturity and
competence since possession of a spermatophore is a prerequisite for calling. However, no evidence exists to suggest that
female crickets pick mates on the basis of variations in male
fitness. If female crickets are able to choose mates on the
basis of differential male fitness, then such a preference
probably depends on individual variations in calling song. In
this study, variations in calling behavior having to do with
the regularity and intensity of calling song were obvious.
But Walker (1962) has shown that very fine differences in the
otherwise species-specific calling song occur in male crickets
occupying the same area. Such fine differences may be important in female mate selection.

Although matings involving calling males appear to occur
more frequently, some females may prefer to mate with noncalling males. Such a mating preference might arise if
acoustically orienting flies, or larvae from previous fly
visits, are likely to be present near a calling male. Satellite matings may then result because females avoid calling
males and thereby avoid being parasitized. Circumstantial
evidence for this type of female behavior involves not only
the occurrence of satellite matings, but also the complete
absence in field collections of inseminated and parasitized
females. Female avoidance of calling males should be more
obvious in young females who, because of their age and consequently high residual reproductive value, may behave in a
way to minimize risks. However, broadcasting of cricket song
in the field indicates phonotaxis by both inseminated and
uninseminated (presumably younger) females.

Resource Structure

The distribution of resources both in space and time is an
important variable influencing competition for these resources.
This principle applies equally when the limiting resource
is females in male-male competition and when other resources
are involved. Trivers (1972) considered the influence of
female distribution in time and space on the intensity and
form of male-male competition. With respect to temporal distribution, females are said to be dispersed if they become
sexually receptive over a predictable period. This is opposed

to all females becoming receptive simultaneously. Temporal
dispersal allows each male to ccmpete for newly receptive females, and competition for dispersed females should generally
be more intense than if females are clumped in time. In a
given night, sexual receptivity in female *G. integer* is tem-
porally dispersed, as shown by temporal patterns of female
phonotaxis to taped cricket song. As expected, male competition is especially keen during the hours when females are
attracted to taped song. This is evidenced by the simultaneous attraction of noncalling aggressive males and, in general,
by very intense song production relative to that at sunrise,
a time when females no longer orient over long distances
to taped song. An additional observation is that rapid
production of spermatophores, demonstrated by the ability of
G. integer males to resume calling following mating, should
result when females are dispersed in time. The same male may
acquire several newly available females over the course of a
night by an increased rate of sperm production.

Regarding distribution in space, both male and female
crickets generally occur in spatial aggregations at times of
high population density. In general, male conflicts over
females should be especially intense in aggregations, since
by increased competition a male may acquire multiple females.
Although intermediates occur, various species' aggregations
of breeding individuals are of two general types. In passive
aggregations, males associate together because females are
already clumped, or because there is a high probability of
females occurring in the area. In contrast, active aggregations are characterized by males associating together, not on
the basis of previously clumped resources, but for the purpose
of signaling and attracting females from outside of the group.
Active aggregations present an evolutionary problem in that
the advantages to males that join assemblies where competition
is intense need identifying. Some examples of active aggregations are known in insects and are represented in vertebrates
by the commonly witnessed leks of birds. In such cases,
signaling males may benefit by aggregating because clumped
individuals have a lower probability of predation or because
clumped males attract many more females than does an isolated
male, resulting in each male mating more often than if he were
isolated from conspecific males (Alexander, 1975; Brown and
Orians, 1970; Otte, 1977).

In mole crickets (Ulagaraj and Walker, 1973) and in *G.
integer,* flying females are clearly attracted to an area by
the signaling of males. Since attracted females feed, oviposit, and mate in the occupied area, it is likely that male
signaling indicates both the availability of suitable mates
and the presence of an otherwise suitable habitat. In the
sense that sexually receptive females are attracted from

outside of the group, mating assemblies in field and mole
crickets represent an active type of aggregation. Such assemblies are therefore likely places to locate females, and this
predictability probably accounts for the phonotaxis of conspecific males to the area. Mating assemblies in *G. integer*
are then also passive in that flying males join groups where
females are likely to be present. Additionally, the apparent
preference by male and female *G. integer* for a damp area of
the outdoor arena also suggests that mating assemblies in this
species may partially depend on the distribution of nonfemale
resources. While some elements of cricket aggregations are
active in nature, the advantages of such aggregations in terms
of predator avoidance or mating success are not identifiable
based on the available data. It is interesting to speculate
that the three groups of nearest-male measurements result
from *G. integer* males adopting alternative strategies with
respect to the costs and benefits involved in clumping.

Density, Frequency, and Individual Effects

Alexander (1961) demonstrated that with increasing population density calling behavior decreases in frequency. In
this study, very different patterns of calling behavior were
observed under different conditions of population density.
The commencement of calling by previously noncalling males
just before sunrise was characteristically observed at high
density, but was absent when crickets were less common. The
absence of this temporal shift in calling behavior suggests
that at times of low population density, satellite males do
not frequently occur. Alexander attributed the increase in
noncalling behavior with increasing population density to the
following factors: random collisions between males and females, and therefore matings not initiated by calling increase
with density; the effort required for territorial defense
increases with the number of competitors; and at times of
high population density, some males may be prevented from
calling because suitable territories are limited in availability. All three factors should result in increased costs of
calling, and in noncalling behavior, therefore, being more
successful reproductively than is the case at lower population
densities. The first two possibilities are reasonable assumptions, but in *G. integer* it does not appear that a lack of
suitable signaling sites forces males into satellite behavior.
One type of evidence that space limitation does not prevent
some males from territorial behavior is that, even when densities are very high, vast areas remain uninhabited. Although
the likelihood of an individual colonizing a new area depends
on the habitat and on characteristics of the individual,

the suitability of uninhabited areas is demonstrated by
establishment of populations in such areas by song broadcasting. In addition, in the arena population, many noncalling
males occupied shelters that were identical to and removed in
space from those occupied by calling males. And, as mentioned
before, males caged in the laboratory under identical conditions show different acoustical behaviors. Although suitable
areas are open to males at high densities, not calling and remaining in aggregations must, in at least some males, provide
greater returns in fitness than that possible from emigration,
colonization, and subsequent signaling in new areas.

In some instances, the operation of sexual selection is
dependent on the relative frequencies of different types of
males in the same population. This phenomenon is sometimes
referred to as the "rare male advantage" since the number of
matings is greatest for a particular type of male when that
type occurs at a relatively low frequency in the population
(Ehrman, 1970). This type of frequency dependence seems to
contradict Alexander's (1961) model concerning population
density and calling behavior. That is, as density increases,
the proportion of noncallers in the population increases as
do the benefits of noncalling. Nevertheless, although the
available data show no effect of relative frequencies on
mating success, such an effect may occur in individual aggregations of crickets.

In addition to population density and the relative frequencies of different types, a male's competitive ability should
depend on such individual variables as age, size or weight,
and previous experience or investment patterns. In competitive encounters a male should assess an opponent's fighting
ability relative to his own in terms of these variables.
Assessments provide a basis for the adjustment of an individual's strategy so that the greatest possible return in fitness
is realized (Parker, 1974). Assessment and selection of
competitive strategies may take place in ecological time, or
at the other extreme, an individual may be fixed in his optimal strategy. Some field cricket males adjust their strategies in present time, as seen by their switching from calling
to noncalling behavior in field populations and when calling
song was played in their direction. Alexander (1961) also
showed that aggressive behavior in male field crickets was
influenced by immediate environmental factors. On the other
hand, observations in the arena and in a laboratory, as well
as the occurrence of parasitized and nonparasitized males,
suggest that males are somewhat fixed in their acoustical
behavior. Bentley and Hoy (1972) demonstrated that the production of cricket song is dependent on multiple genes, some of
which are sex-linked. In female crickets, song reception
appears to result from the same genetic mechanism, or at least

one very similar to that underlying song production (Hoy and Paul, 1973; Hoy et al., 1977). Some of the work on cricket-song genetics involved *G. rubens,* a virtually identical sibling to *G. integer.* Given the multiple number of genes involved in cricket acoustical behavior, a large amount of individual variation is expected on the basis of genetic differences.

Alexander (1961) showed that aggressive behavior peaked at about 10-14 days of age in male field crickets. Although increased age, and hence decreased residual reproductive value (Williams, 1966), should tend to favor a male taking increased risks by calling, no such effect is seen in the data on *G. integer.* Alexander found that body size was not that important a factor in determining male aggressive behavior, and I observed no effect of male size on behavior in this study.

CONCLUSIONS

Male *Gryllus integer* behaviors that apparently represent mating strategies and their functions are summarized in Table

TABLE 9

Summary of male Gryllus integer *behaviors representing alternative reproductive strategies*

Behavior	Possible functions
I. Calling	
A. Regularly - high intensities (territoriality)	Female attraction Interference w/calling in other males
B. Irregularly - low intensities	Female attraction Avoidance of male attacks Mate theft Parasitoid avoidance
C. At sunrise	Avoidance of male attacks Stimulation of nearby females
II. Not calling	
A. Searching for females (satellite)	Mate theft Parasitoid avoidance Avoidance of male attacks
B. Attacking calling males	Interference w/calling in other males

9. Given the primarily nocturnal behavior of crickets, more
complete information on the contributions made to male fitness
by alternative behaviors is not available. Taking population
density and relative frequencies into account, calling probably results in a higher frequency of mating than does satellite behavior. This result is in agreement with data in
polygynous species where, in a fixed time, the most aggressive
males achieve a disproportionate share of the matings. However, if alternative forms are maintained in a population, the
effects of counter-selection must, on the average, balance
out. The evidence discussed in this chapter strongly suggests
a fertility-mortality trade-off in the maintenance of alternative reproductive strategies in male field crickets.

ACKNOWLEDGEMENTS

    I thank D. Otte, R. H. Barth, Jr., L. E. Gilbert, A.
Joern, D. Feener, J. Schall, and C. Jordan for reading and
making comments on an earlier version of the manuscript. I
thank Ms. Nevenna Tsanoff Travis, Secretary-Treasurer of the
Texas System of Natural Laboratories Inc., and Mr. and Mrs.
M.E. Hart, principal stockholders of Travis Ecology Inc., for
permission to use an area ideal for field research. I also
thank G. Esparza for illustrating the acoustical trap, E.
Cade for assistance in research and with the manuscript, and
Mrs. Frances Sanders for typing the manuscript and for making
helpful suggestions concerning its preparation.

REFERENCES

Alcock, J. 1975. Male mating strategies of some philanthine
    wasps (Hymenoptera: Sphecidae). *J. Kans. Ent. Soc.* 48:532-
    545.
Alexander, R.D. 1961. Aggressiveness, territoriality, and
    sexual behaviour in field crickets (Orthoptera: Gryllidae).
    Behaviour 17:130-223.
Alexander, R.D. 1962. Evolutionary change in cricket acousti-
    cal communication. *Evolution* 16:443-467.
Alexander, R.D. 1968. Life cycle origins, speciation, and
    related phenomena in crickets. *Quart. Rev. Biol.* 43:1-41.
Alexander, R.D. 1975. Natural selection and specialized
    chorusing behavior in acoustical insects. *In* Pimentel, D.
    (ed.), *Insects, Science and Society.* Academic Press, New
    York.
Axtell, R.W. 1958. Female reaction to the male call in two

anurans (Amphibia). *Southwest. Natur.* 3:70-76.

Barlow, G.W. 1967. Social behavior of a South American leaf fish, *Polycentrus schomburgkii,* with an account of recurring pseudofemale behavior. *Amer. Midl. Nat.* 78:215-234.

Bentley, D.R., and R.R. Hoy. 1972. Genetic control of the neuronal network generating cricket *(Teleogryllus Gryllus)* song patterns. *Anim. Behav.* 20:478-492.

Brown, J.L. 1969. Territorial behavior and population regulation in birds. *Wilson Bull.* 81:293-329.

Brown, J.L., and G.H. Orians. 1970. Spacing patterns in mobile animals. *Annu. Rev. Ecol. Syst.* 1:239-262.

Cade, W. 1975. Acoustically orienting parasitoids: fly phonotaxis to cricket song. *Science* 190:1312-1313.

Cade, W. 1976. Male reproductive competition and sexual selection in the field cricket *Gryllus integer.* Ph.D. Thesis, The University of Texas at Austin.

Clark, P.J., and F.C. Evans. 1954. Distance to nearest neighbour as a measure of spatial relationships in populations. *Ecology* 35:445-453.

Cole, L.C. 1954. The population consequences of life history phenomena. *Quart. Rev. Biol.* 29:103-137.

Darwin, C. 1871. *The Descent of Man, and Selection in Relation to Sex,* 2 vols. Appleton, New York.

Ehrman, L. 1970. The mating advantage of rare males in *Drosophila. Proc. Nat. Acad. Sci.* 65:345-348.

Emlen, S.T. 1968. Territoriality in the bullfrog, *Rana catesbeiana. Copeia* 1968:240-243.

Ewing, L.S. 1973. Territoriality and the influence of females on the spacing of males in the cockroach *Nauphoeta cinerea. Behaviour* 45:282-303.

Ford, E.B. 1945. Polymorphism. *Biol. Rev. (Camb.)* 20:73-88.

Ford, E.B. 1971. *Ecological Genetics.* Chapman and Holt Ltd., London.

Fretwell, S.D. 1972. *Populations in a Seasonal Environment.* Princeton Univ. Press, Princeton.

Gadgil, M. 1972. Male dimorphism as a consequence of sexual selection. *Amer. Natur.* 106:574-580.

Gadgil, M., and W.H. Bossert. 1970. Life history consequences of natural selection. *Amer. Natur.* 104:1-24.

Hamilton, W.D. 1964. The genetic evolution of social behaviour. I and II. *J. Theor. Biol.* 7:1-52.

Hogan-Warburg, A.J. 1966. Social behavior of the Ruff, *Philomachus pugnax* (L.). *Ardea* 54:109-129.

Hoy, R.R., J. Hahn, and R.C. Paul. 1977. Hybrid cricket auditory behavior: evidence for genetic coupling in animal communication. *Science* 195:82-84.

Hoy, R.R., and R. Paul. 1973. Genetic control of song specificity in crickets. *Science* 180:82-83.

Huber, F. 1962. Central nervous control of sound production in crickets and some speculation on its evolution. *Evolution* 16:429-442.

Hunter, W.D. 1912. Some notes on insect abundance in Texas in 1911. *Proc. Ent. Soc. Amer.* 14:62-66.

Johnson, C. 1964. The evolution of territoriality in the Odonata. *Evolution* 18:89-92.

Kruijt, J.P., G.J. de Vos, and I. Bossema. 1972. The arena system of black grouse *(Lyrurus tetrix)* (L.) *Proc. XV Int. Ornith. Congr.* 339-423.

Lloyd, J.E. 1973. Model for the mating protocol of synchronously flashing fireflies. *Nature* 245:268-270.

Lorenz, K. 1966. *On Aggression.* Bantam, New York.

Maynard Smith, J., and G.R. Price. 1973. The logic of animal conflict. *Nature* 246:15-18.

Moodie, G.E.E. 1972. Predation, natural selection and adaptation in an unusual three-spine stickleback. *Heredity* 28:155-167.

Morris, D. 1951. Homosexuality in the ten-spined stickleback *(Pygosteus pungitius)* (L.). *Behaviour* 4:233-261.

Morris, D. 1955. The causation of pseudofemale and pseudomale behavior: a further comment. *Behaviour* 8:46-56.

Morris, G.K. 1971. Aggression in male conocephaline grasshoppers (Tettigoniidae). *Anim. Behav.* 19:132-137.

Otte, D. 1972. Simple versus elaborate behaviour in grasshoppers: an analysis of communication in the genus *Syrbula*. *Behaviour* 42:291-322.

Otte, D. 1974. Effects and functions in the evolution of signaling systems. *Annu. Rev. Ecol. Syst.* 5:385-417.

Otte, D. 1977. Communication in Orthoptera. *In* Sebeok, T.A. (ed.), *How Animals Communicate.* Indiana Univ. Press, Bloomington.

Otte, D., and W. Cade. 1976. On the role of olfaction in sexual and interspecies recognition in crickets *(Acheta and Gryllus)*. *Anim. Behav.* 24:1-6.

Otte, D., and A. Joern. 1975. Insect territoriality and its evolution: population studies of desert grasshoppers on creosote bushes. *J. Anim. Ecol.* 44:29-54.

Parker, G.A. 1974. Assessment strategy and the evolution of fighting behaviour. *J. Theor. Biol.* 47:223-243.

Paul, R. 1976. Acoustic response to chemical stimulation in ground crickets. *Nature* 230:404-405.

Semler, D.E. 1971. Some aspects of adaptation in a polymorphism for breeding colours in the three-spine stickleback *(Gasterosteus aculeatus)* (L.). *J. Zool. London* 165:291-302.

Siegel, S. 1956. *Nonparametric Statistics.* McGraw-Hill, New York.

Soper, R.S., G.E. Shewell, and D. Tyrrell. 1976. *Colcondamyia auditrix* nov. sp. (Diptera: Sarcophagidae), a parasite which is attracted by the mating song of its host,

Okanagana rimosa (Homoptera: Cicadidae). *Can. Ent.* 108:61-68.

Spooner, J.D. 1968. Pair-forming acoustic systems of phaneropterine katydids (Orthoptera: Tettigoniidae). *Anim. Behav.* 16:197-212.

Trivers, R.L. 1972. Parental investment and sexual selection. *In* Campbell, B. (ed.), *Sexual Selection and the Descent of Man, 1871-1971.* Aldine, Chicago.

Trivers, R.L. 1976. Sexual selection and resource-accruing abilities in *Anolis garmani. Evolution* 30:253-269.

Ulagaraj, S.M., and T.J. Walker. 1973. Phonotaxis of crickets in flight: attraction of male and female crickets to male calling songs. *Science* 182:1278-1279.

Ulagaraj, S.M., and T.J. Walker. 1975. Responses of flying mole crickets to three parameters of synthetic songs broadcast outdoors. *Nature* 253:530-532.

van den Assem, J. 1967. Territory in the three-spined stickleback *Gasterosteus aculeatus* L. *Behav. Suppl.* 16:1-164.

van Rhijn, J.G. 1973. Behavioural dimorphism in male Ruffs, *Philomachus pugnax* (L.). *Behaviour* 47:153-227.

Walker, T.J. 1962. Factors responsible for intraspecific variation in the calling songs of crickets. *Evolution* 16:407-428.

Walker, T.J. 1964. Experimental demonstration of a cat locating orthopteran prey by the prey's calling song. *Fla. Ent.* 47:163-165.

Walker, T.J. 1974. *Gryllus ovisopis* n. sp.: A taciturn cricket with a life cycle suggesting allochronic speciation. *Fla. Ent.* 57:13-22.

Williams, G.C. 1966. Natural selection, the costs of reproduction, and a refinement of Lack's principle. *Amer. Nat.* 100:687-690.

Williams, G.C. 1971. Introduction. *In* Williams, G.C. (ed.), *Group Selection.* Aldine, Chicago.

Wilson, E.O. 1971. Competitive and aggressive behavior. *In* Eisenberg, J.F., and W. Dillon (eds.), *Man and Beast: Comparative Social Behavior.* Smithsonian Press, Washington.

Wilson, E.O. 1975. *Sociobiology, The New Synthesis.* Harvard Univ. Press, Cambridge.

Wynne-Edwards, V.C. 1962. *Animal Dispersion in Relation to Social Behaviour.* Oliver and Boyd, Edinburgh.

THE EVOLUTION OF INTRASPECIFIC DIVERSITY

IN MALE REPRODUCTIVE STRATEGIES

IN SOME BEES AND WASPS

John Alcock

Arizona State University

INTRODUCTION

In the past, intraspecific variation in behavior has not been greeted with much enthusiasm by students of animal behavior. The early ethologists, led by Konrad Lorenz and Niko Tinbergen, rightly emphasized the importance of identifying species-specific behavior patterns as an essential step in understanding the adaptive significance of behavior. Ethologists have been highly successful in finding clearly defined species-typical behavioral traits in an enormous variety of animal species. Yet this very success has had as a side effect the development of typological thinking in the field of ethology that has persisted until recent times. Students of behavior have tended to believe that there can be only one behavioral repertoire characteristic of a species. As a result, individuals that fail to exhibit the "typical" pattern have often been ignored or treated as aberrations, deviants that lack *the* adaptive pattern. At the very best, variants were sometimes said to be providing the raw material for evolutionary change, permitting the species to adapt to environmental changes should they occur in the future. But this view implies that these individuals sacrifice their fitness for the benefit of the group, a position held by few modern evolutionary biologists (Williams, 1966). At worst, individuals not behaving in a typical manner were assumed to be disadvantageous mutants whose genes were destined for early disappearance from the population. This view fails to consider the possibility that selection may result in an adaptive behavioral polymorphism within a species.

Studies of primate behavior over the past 15 years have played an important role in changing attitudes toward intraspecific variation in social behavior (see Wilson, 1975). The social organization of groups of the same primate species

living in different habitats can be markedly different, yet
adaptive, with each social system matching the ecological
demands peculiar to a particular environment. This research
and related work have led to the general conclusion among
vertebrate ethologists that behavioral flexibility may frequently occur in species that face highly variable ecological
conditions. Individuals may have the ability to adopt one of
several possible behavioral roles, each option being appropriate to a certain set of environmental conditions (Wilson,
1975). Thus intraspecific diversity in behavior may be fully
adaptive and may be maintained by natural selection.

Although vertebrate biologists have reevaluated their views
on intraspecific behavioral variation, relatively little
attention has been devoted to this phenomenon with respect
to insects and other invertebrates (although see Parker, 1970,
1974). This article will review information on intraspecific
diversity in the reproductive behavior of males of some bees
and wasps. My goal will be to show that there are different
classes of variation in male behavior within species and to
illustrate each category with examples taken from the literature and from my own studies. The paper will conclude with
an examination of the ecological and evolutionary factors
that allow more than one male mating strategy to persist
within a species.

CATEGORIES OF INTRASPECIFIC VARIATION IN BEHAVIOR

I shall distinguish between classes of behavioral variation
on the basis of whether or not they occur simultaneously in
the same population (Table 1). Either category of variation
could, theoretically at least, be caused by two different
underlying mechanisms. Variation in behavior that does not
occur concurrently in one population (Type I) might result
from either (1) the ability of individuals to practice more
than one behavioral role, depending on the conditions they
encounter, or (2) genetic differences among populations that
are separated by space or time. Likewise, variation in the
reproductive strategies of males that is expressed within one
population in one period of time (Type II) could stem from
the ability of all the members of the population to adopt
either option A or option B, with the individuals divided
into two classes--those employing A at the moment and those
employing B. On the other hand, the observed variation could
be the product of a genetic polymorphism, with the members of
the population divided into two genetically different groups
--one group rigidly programmed to perform option A and the
other programmed to perform option B.

Although it is convenient to think of the two categories

TABLE 1

Categories of intraspecific variation in behavior and the underlying causes of this variation

---

Categories of intraspecific behavioral variation

Type I   Spatially-temporally segregated variation
                  a.   Variant strategies occur in different populations
                  b.   Variant strategies occur in the same population but at different times.
Type II   Cooccurring variation
                  a.   Variant strategies occur in the same population at the same time.

Underlying causes of intraspecific behavioral variation

Mechanism I   Individual behavioral flexibility
                  a.   Individual has the capacity to adopt more than one behavioral role.
Mechanism II   Fixed behavioral polymorphism
                  a.   Individuals with different genotypes are predisposed to exhibit different behavioral strategies.

---

of variation and the two types of underlying mechanisms as completely separate entities, the division between each alternate is not absolutely clear. For example, males may search for females in different ways in a nesting area and in a contiguous location containing flowers attractive to females. The two groups of males might be considered spatially segregated by virtue of their selection of two different (but adjacent) searching areas, in which case they would be classified as an example of Type I (spatially segregated) intraspecific variation. However, the two groups of males could be considered members of the same broad-ranging population, in which case the variation would be classified as Type II (cooccurring) variation.

Similarly, distinctions between the two mechanisms of variation are not always clear. A population may consist of individuals all of whom are capable of exercising more than one behavioral option (Mechanism I). If, however, some males because of their genetic constitution are more likely to exhibit option A under certain conditions than other males, then the case would be intermediate between a completely fixed behavioral polymorphism and complete flexibility in the behavior of individuals. Moreover, as a practical matter,

distinguishing between the two mechanisms is often difficult
or impossible. Few studies of aculeate Hymenoptera have
involved marking programs with long-term observations of identifiable individuals to determine whether the same male can
adopt more than one reproductive strategy. Furthermore, even
if an individual does not change its behavioral role, this
does not prove that the individual lacks the capacity to do
so.

     With these reservations in mind, I shall first present
examples of populations separated by space or time in which
variation in behavior occurs, variation that appears to stem
from the capacity of individuals to alter their behavioral
role depending upon the conditions they encounter. Then I
shall present examples of cooccurring variation that appear
to arise from (1) individual behavioral flexibility and (2)
a fixed behavioral polymorphism.

SPATIAL AND TEMPORAL DIFFERENCES IN BEHAVIOR AMONG POPULATIONS

     Both spatial and temporal variation in behavior are prob-
ably common in the aculeate Hymenoptera, although there are
few detailed reports on this subject. Populations of the
same species, geographically separated, which exhibit behavioral variation are found in the bees *Caupolicana yarrowi*
(Colletidae) and *Protoxaea gloriosa* (Oxaeidae) (Cazier and
Linsley, 1963; Hurd and Linsley, 1975, 1976; Alcock, 1977a).
Females of these large bees forage for pollen and nectar at a
variety of flowering plants. Males search for mates at these
plants. Both species can be found at the spiny shrub *Koeber-
linia spinosa*, which grows at a site in southwestern New
Mexico as isolated bushes. The plant produces a small number
of flowers in dispersed clusters that are attractive to a
wide range of Hymenoptera. Individual males of *P. gloriosa*
and *C. yarrowi* hover near groups of flowers and pursue all
passing insects above a certain minimum size in an effort to
capture receptive conspecific females. Males of both species
are highly territorial at these plants and will strike one
another and grapple violently in disputes over ownership of a
hovering site. Hovering territorial males of *P. gloriosa* can
also commonly be found by dense patches of the Mexican poppy
Kallstroemia grandiflora, over the flowering cucurbit gourds
(Fig. 1) which often grow as well-spaced plants on desert

rangeland,[1] and by other scattered flowering species as well.

At the same time, but in different locations, other males of *C. yarrowi* and *P. gloriosa* can be found employing a totally different mate-location strategy--a wide-ranging patrol flight during which the male makes no effort to defend an exclusive territory. This is the only behavior I saw in populations of males occupying vast stands of flowering creosote bush, *Larrea divaricata,* in southeastern Arizona (Fig. 2). Far from hovering, males move so rapidly and over such great distances that they cannot be easily followed or captured. A mark-recapture study of a population of patrolling *C. yarrowi* indicates that at least some males do return to the same area over a period of several days (Alcock, 1977a). Thus, these males, although nonterritorial, do exhibit an attachment to a home range. Hurd and Linsley (1975) report intermediate behavior by C. *yarrowi* in fields of *L. divaricata,* with some males repeatedly interrupting their hovering flight to patrol a large area adjacent to the hovering station. This would seem to suggest that males can adjust their behavior in a delicate and precise manner to match prevailing conditions. A key component in making the adjustment must be the nature of the distribution of flowering plants potentially visited by receptive females. In the extreme case in which flower resources are exceptionally highly clumped and the clumps are widely separated, males hover by a patch, waiting for the arrival of females while repelling competitors from the area. At the other extreme in which flowers are numerous and evenly distributed (creosote bushes carry hundreds of flowers, and the plant may uniformly cover hundreds of acres), males patrol widely and behave nonaggressively toward conspecific males.

Temporal variation in male behavior has been recorded for a number of aculeate Hymenoptera. Linsley et al. (1963) suggest that males of the bee *Andrena mojavensis* patrol the area from which virgin females are emerging at the start of the species' flight season; later, after emergence has been largely completed, males are found patrolling flowers visited by foraging females. Basically the same pattern has been observed in the sphecid wasp *Philanthus bicinctus,* with males initially establishing waiting perches in the nesting area and

[1] The flowers of these cucurbits are not visited for pollen or nectar by females (Linsley, 1976), but may be inspected as possible food sources by freshly emerged females because copulations do occur at these plants (pers. obs.).

Fig. 1. A patch of the cucurbit Apodanthera undulata. The
lighter central region is the area of flowers. A male of
Protoxaea gloriosa hovered above the central cluster of
flowers and defended the area against intruder males.

Fig. 2. A large area covered primarily with creosote bush,
Larrea divaricata. Males of Caupolicana yarrowi and Protoxaea
gloriosa sometimes do not defend hovering territories in these
locations but instead fly rapidly from bush to bush in search
of females.

later patrolling flowers (D.L. Gywnne, pers. comm.). In
another sphecid, *Tachytes distinctus*, males wait in the midst
of an emergence area, presumably pursuing virgin females upon
emergence (Lin and Michener, 1972). After the female population has emerged and copulated once, males establish residence
by specific nests. Although Lin and Michener saw no mating
during this stage of the nesting season, it is at least possible that copulations do occur.

Perhaps the best documented example of a temporal change
in male behavior in the Hymenoptera is provided by the study
of Eickwort (1977) of the megachilid bee *Hoplitis anthocopoides*. At the onset of the flight season of this species,
males are relatively few in number and widely scattered. At
this time, individual males patrol wide areas (often 10-12 m^2)
containing the flowers (which are not yet blooming) visited
by females of their species. As the number of males increases
and competition for space intensifies, the bees restrict their
patrolling flights to smaller and smaller areas, eventually
holding strongly defended territories that embrace a single
flowering plant (0.2 m^2). As the flight season progresses
and the male population declines, flowers become more available. Territories again expand, eventually reaching sizes
associated with the beginning of the male flight season.

A fundamentally similar pattern can occur with annual, as
well as short-term seasonal, changes in the male population
density. The size of populations of the megachilid bee
Callanthidium illustre can vary greatly from year to year,
affecting the social organization of males (Alcock, 1977b).
In a year when relatively many males were competing for access
to patches of the flower *Penstemon palmeri,* individual bees
established fairly compact territories which they vigorously
defended. In a year when few males emerged, the bees traveled
broadly overlapping circuits of up to 100 m in length which
they could only weakly defend against conspecific males.

Thus temporal changes in male behavior appear to be linked
with (1) changing patterns of distribution of receptive females as the emergence season progresses and (2) variable
cost-benefit ratios associated with territorial defense. When
male competitors are rare, individual males can afford to
patrol a large area because the odds are low that a female
entering this area will be detected by another male before
the patroller locates her. As male density increases, the
long-range patroller is more and more likely to find a potential mate already taken by the time he encounters her. This
favors a reduction in the area searched and increasing emphasis on territorial defense. At some point, however, when
males become exceptionally numerous, territoriality might be
expected to break down because of the exorbitant expenditures
of time and energy required to repel a constant stream of

intruders.   Territorial breakdown has been reported for the
wasp *Sphecius speciosus* during times of very high population
density (Evans, 1966).

THE COOCCURRENCE OF ALTERNATIVE BEHAVIORAL TACTICS
WITHIN A POPULATION

More than one behavioral option may be practiced simultaneously within a population, with individuals having the
capacity to switch their tactics depending on the conditions
of the moment. At its simplest level, variation of this sort
involves males performing basically the same activity but in
different adjoining habitats.   Thus, males of a variety of
bees and wasps have been reported to search for females by
patrolling in an emergence or nesting area and, at the same
time, in adjacent foraging areas (Alcock et al., 1978).
It is probable, but unproven, that the same male can patrol
in both areas, changing its selection from day to day, depending in part perhaps on the density of competitors in the
two areas.   A somewhat more complex example involves the
halictid bee *Lasioglossum rohweri,* in which some males can be
found waiting at the nest entrances, probably for the fall
emergence of virgin queens, while others patrol widely through
the nesting site (Barrows, 1976).   Whether an individual male
can engage in both activities during its lifetime is not known
with certainty, although there does appear to be some specialization in which case the example might represent a fixed
behavioral polymorphism (see below).
In the aculeate Hymenoptera, the simultaneous occurrence
of variation in male reproductive behavior in a particular
population is most commonly observed in territorial species.
Frequently, populations contain both territorial and nonterritorial individuals. Males that cannot acquire a territory in a prime location do not necessarily establish one in
a peripheral area or constantly battle with territory owners
for possession of an already claimed area. Rather, they may
practice a totally different strategy of mate acquisition.
Among the philanthine wasps, territoriality is apparently
widespread (Simon-Thomas and Poorter, 1972; Evans, 1975;
Alcock, 1975). Commonly, but not universally, territorial
males claim a perch site in a strategic location (Fig. 3) and
add an attractant pheromone to the perch. Other males are
excluded from an area of less than 0.5 m^2 to several m^2
around the perch, depending on the size of the species. Males
without territories are abundant; this is significant because
territorial males appear to occupy only a fraction of available potential perch sites. Nonterritorial males are often
"visitors," traveling from one territory to another (perhaps

Fig. 3. A male of the philanthine wasp Clypeadon taurulus
waiting at its perch site (the leaf of a broad-leafed weed)
for females which may be attracted by pheromones applied to
the perch.

attracted by the sex pheromone applied by the perch owner),
clashing briefly with the territory holder before moving on
to the next site. Takeovers do occur, but they are very rare.
Usually clashes at a perch last fewer than 30 sec., ending
with the departure of the visitor. Thus, although visitors
may seek perches (if they can be easily obtained), it is
possible that their major goal is to inspect a large number
of territories for receptive females attracted to a perch
site by the sex pheromone signal. This hypothesis must remain
speculative without observations of visitors copulating with
females in the territories of other males. The evidence that
individual philanthine wasps can practice both territorial
and visiting tactics comes from replacement experiments in
which resident territory owners are removed. Visitors promptly fill the open perch sites. If they are removed in turn,
their places are soon taken by another set of visitors (Alcock,
1975).
    Another hymenopteran group with many territorial represen-
tatives is that of the megachilid bees. In a number of
species, males defend patches of flowers and copulate with
females that visit the areas in search of nectar and pollen.
Populations of several species of *Anthidium* contain both
territorial and nonterritorial males (Haas, 1960; Jaycox,
1967; Kurtak, 1973; Alcock et al., 1977a). Members of the
nonterritorial class fall into two groups--visitors and

satellite males. Visitors travel from one territory to
another, remaining at a particular flower patch until detected and driven away by the resident males. The visitors may
return later, having a regular circuit that takes them to a
series of territories. In contrast, satellite males remain
at one territory for periods of many hours or even days. Like
the visitors, they studiously avoid contact with the resident
male, remaining in a corner of the territory, not moving
about a great deal, and always fleeing when detected by the
territory owner, only to slip back to their position as soon
as the territory owner has returned to his patrol route
through the territory. Both groups of nonterritorial males
are clearly *not* attempting to usurp a defended patch of
flowers. When takeovers occur in these bees, they involve
intense and prolonged clashes, often over a period of several
hours, between a resident and a challenger. The visitor and
satellite strategies are practiced by nonaggressive males
that attempt to copulate with females attracted to a territory site which they do not hold or defend. They are sometimes successful because the resident territory owner may not
immediately detect female visitors to his area while feeding,
resting, copulating, or patrolling another section of the
territory. This provides opportunities for what might be
called "sneak matings" (Constantz, 1975). Thus, there are
clearly defined territorial and nonterritorial strategies,
and each strategy can lead to copulations.

Nonterritorial males can behave in a territorial manner
as shown by replacement experiments and observations of takeovers. When territory owners are removed, their places are
almost immediately taken, presumably by males previously
unable to acquire or hold a suitable area. Moreover, I
observed a marked nonterritorial male of *A. maculosum* which,
several days after marking, succeeded in replacing a territorial male after a long battle. Judging from the frequency of
takeovers at patches of flowers (Alcock et al., 1977a), desirable territories for male *A. maculosum* are in limited supply. Holding a territory must be energetically costly, eventually weakening the owner and leading to his replacement by
another male that is in prime condition. Males not able to
claim a territory immediately after emergence may employ one
of the alternatives until they locate a male which they can
overthrow.

COOCCURRING VARIATION AND FIXED BEHAVIORAL POLYMORPHISMS

Each of several cooccurring strategies in a population
may be practiced exclusively by a certain fraction of the male
population. Individuals may lack the capacity to switch back
and forth between alternative behavioral modes and instead be

programmed to pursue one behavioral role. As noted before, it is often difficult to discriminate between individual behavioral flexibility and a fixed behavioral polymorphism as sources of behavioral variation within a population. For example, it is possible that some *A. maculosum* males never acquire a territory; it would be hard to prove that such males had, but simply never expressed, the capacity to be territorial, as opposed to the possibility that from the time of emergence they were programmed to employ the satellite strategy only.

A probable but not certain case of a fixed behavioral polymorphism in male reproductive behavior in the Hymenoptera is provided by the anthophorid bee *Centris pallida* (Alcock et al., 1976, 1977; Alcock, 1977a). In this species males practice one of two very different mate-location behaviors: (1) patrolling a large home range in an emergence area in the search for sites from which a buried virgin female is about to emerge and (2) hovering in and around emergence areas or by flowering trees, waiting for receptive females to fly near them. Patrollers excavate buried preemergent females and copulate with them (Figs. 4-6); hoverers pursue, capture, and copulate with passing airborne virgin females (Fig. 7).

Size is closely correlated with the behavioral tactics of males (Fig. 8). Some males weigh three times as much as others, and head widths (which reflect body size) range over 4.5-6.1 mm. No male with a head width greater than 5.3 mm has ever been collected while hovering (N = 100), and very few males with a head width less than 4.8 mm have ever been collected as patrollers (N = 250). Thus, very large males patrol to the exclusion of hovering, and very small males strongly tend to specialize solely in hovering. Marking studies have shown that some males of intermediate size can both patrol and hover, thus exhibiting individual behavioral flexibility. Perhaps large males have the unexpressed capacity to hover, but the failure to observe this in three years of field work suggests that they are truly programmed to employ one, and only one, mate-location strategy.

Large males tend to patrol more than smaller individuals because of aggression at digging sites. When a male, using olfactory cues, finds a spot containing a preemergent female (Alcock et al., 1976), there is no guarantee that he will ultimately succeed in mating with her. The process of excavation requires about 6 min. on the average, during which time other males are likely to arrive and attempt to usurp the digging site. Violent fights are common at excavations, and the larger of two combatants almost always supplants the other. As a result, larger males are much more successful at holding sites they have personally discovered and in

Fig. 4. A male of the bee Centris pallida *beginning to remove the soil above a female waiting in her emergence tunnel.*

Fig. 5. The same male after excavating a quantity of earth.

Fig. 6. As the female scrambles to the surface, the male quickly slips onto her back and grasps her with his jaws and legs prior to courtship and copulation.

Fig. 7. A male of Centris pallida *hovering a short distance above the ground by a flowering tree.*

addition can steal sites initially found by other males. This
is reflected in the relatively large size of males captured
in copulo around dense emergence sites compared with the
distribution of male sizes in random samples of patrolling
males (Fig. 8).

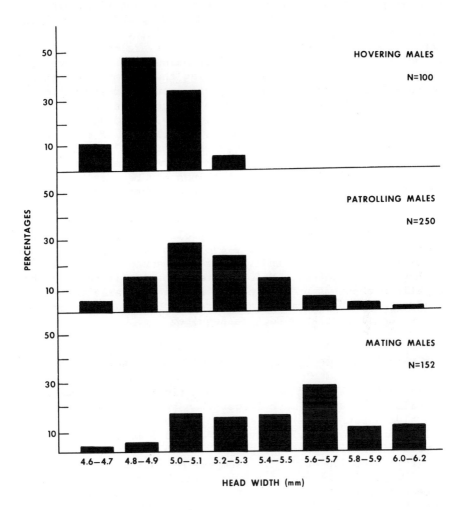

*Fig. 8. The distribution of males of different head widths
that were captured while hovering, patrolling, and copulating.
Samples were made in the years 1974-1976 at the same general
nesting-emergence area. Hovering males tend to be smaller on
the average than patrollers (very large males are never found
hovering). The mean head width of males captured* in copulo
*is significantly larger than the mean for patrolling males
(Alcock et al., 1977b).*

Given the competitive advantage enjoyed by larger males at digging sites, smaller bees may benefit by avoiding inter- actions with these males *if* they can secure an alternative source of receptive females. Some females escape from dig- gers, particularly when several males are fighting over ownership of a partially excavated digging location. In addition, other females at isolated nests probably emerge on their own and fly to flowering trees to feed. These females constitute a pool of potential mates that are more likely to be detected and captured by smaller males hovering at various heights above the ground and scanning the air overhead than by patrollers searching close to the ground for excavation sites. The adaptations that promote success in the patrolling strategy (large size, strength, fighting, and digging ability) are almost certainly handicaps in the practice of the other strategy, where aerial agility, keen vision, flying speed, and hovering endurance are paramount. Intermediate individuals with the flexibility to do both things may benefit by being able to adjust their behavior to the circumstances of the moment; on the other hand, they almost surely cannot perform either strategy with the proficiency of the small specialist hoverer or the large specialist patroller-digger. This may be the key factor favoring the evolution of a fixed behavioral polymorphism with some individuals programmed specifically to hover or to patrol. Unfortunately nothing is known of the genetic mechanisms underlying the behavioral variation in *C. pallida,* and the arguments just presented must remain specu- lative until such knowledge is acquired.

THE MAINTENANCE OF INTRASPECIFIC BEHAVIORAL VARIATION

The data collected on the reproductive success of males of *C. pallida* show that much-larger-than-average males (which are always patrollers) are apparently more fit than smaller males (often hoverers). Why then do small males, and the hovering behavior pattern, persist in this species? One can ask this question about all examples of intraspecific behav- ioral variation because one behavioral strategy might be expected to replace the alternative(s) over the course of evolution. Maynard Smith (1974, 1976) and Maynard Smith and Parker (1976) have dealt with this problem at a theoretical level, although focusing attention primarily on the various options individuals can employ in aggressive encounters. The mathematical approach of Maynard Smith has shown that under some conditions populations can exhibit what he calls a "mixed evolutionarily stable strategy"; this is to say that intraspecific variability in behavioral strategies can be the stable evolutionary condition, such that a mutant gene

linked with an altered behavioral option cannot become established in a population. Here I shall be concerned with those
elements of the natural history of aculeate Hymenoptera that
may promote the persistent expression of behavioral variation
within a population.

Intraspecific behavioral variation in male reproductive
strategies may be traced to two general factors: (1) variation
in ecological factors that affect the distribution of competitor males and receptive females and (2) escalating costs
of an evolutionarily successful competitive strategy which
may reach sufficiently high levels to favor alternative, non-
competitive strategies.

Variable ecological factors can lead to fluctuations in
population density over time and from place to place. These
contribute to variation in the number and distribution of
competing males which could influence male decisions about
where to search or wait for mates and whether to defend resources linked with mate acquisition. In particular, as
already suggested, increasing male density will tend to be
correlated with an increased rate of intrusions into patrolled
areas and an increased risk of losing potential mates to other
males for individuals searching over large areas. Thus, the
size of areas patrolled and areas defended should be sensitive
to male density, decreasing as contacts with competitors increase. Eventually, at very high densities, males may abandon
territorial behavior altogether.

Ecological variation also plays a role in temporal changes
in the location of individual receptive females and for entire
populations of females during the flight season of a species.
An individual female may be contacted immediately upon emergence *or* at flowers or nesting sites at various times after
emergence. For populations of emerging females, there is a
peak period of emergence, usually early in the flight season,
with declining numbers thereafter. In species that nest in
aggregations, males initially may be most likely to encounter
a mate at the emergence area. Later the odds may be better
at sources of nectar and pollen or at a nest. Moreover, in
many species, females may nest either as relatively isolated
individuals or in relatively compact aggregations, depending
on variable soil conditions and different patterns of food
resource availability. This creates variation in the density
of emerging females at various locations. Finally, the distribution of flowers or prey can either serve to concentrate
receptive females in space or to disperse them. Thus, in
many ways, ecological parameters can create what are, in
effect, several more or less discrete populations of receptive
females in many species of bees and wasps. In the case of
C. pallida, potential mates fall into two basic classes--the
about-to-emerge virgins buried just below the surface of the

ground and the airborne virgins that have not been captured
by patroller-diggers. In dense emergence areas, large patroller-diggers appear to enjoy a reproductive advantage; in areas
where emerging females are scattered, it may be that smaller
males hovering by flowering trees enjoy higher fitnesses.
Because there is a broad range of possible densities of emerging females for the species as a whole, males of many different sizes and different behavioral proclivities may enjoy
reproductive success, depending on the time of year and the
properties of the emergence site.

ALTERNATIVES TO COMPETITIVE RAT RACES AMONG MALES

    Gadgil (1972) noted that a striking dimorphism in male
aggressive structures (e.g., horns and antlers) exists in a
limited number of insects and vertebrates. In these species
some fully adult individuals possess elaborate combat devices,
while others lack them altogether. Gadgil suggested that
over evolutionary time males with larger and larger combat
structures in these groups enjoyed higher and higher fitness.
At some point, however, the extremely high investment required
for these structures (e.g., long developmental time, high
metabolic costs, increased conspicuousness to predators) could
favor individuals that failed to develop these traits and
refused to engage in traditional male-male contests. These
drop-outs would, however, have to be able to exploit some
alternative means to acquire mates, using time and energy
that would have been devoted to the development of horns and
antlers and to displaying and fighting with other males in
some other productive manner.
    Gadgil's arguments clearly apply to behavioral as well as
structural polymorphism. Behavioral drop-outs are known from
a variety of bird and fish species (e.g., Barlow, 1967; Hogan-
Warburg, 1966; Constantz, 1975; Keenleyside, 1972) and may
appear regularly in those insect species in which intense
male-male conflicts occur in competition for mates.
    In the aculeate Hymenoptera the visiting strategy of the
philanthine wasps, and especially satellite behavior by
megachilid males, may exemplify drop-out behavior. Satellite
males of *Anthidium maculosum* avoid the time expenditures and
energetic demands associated with the nearly continuous
patrolling and pursuing done by territorial males. It is
conceivable, although far from proven, that territorial behavior in these insects exacts a heavy toll on males as has been
suggested for a bee (Eickwort, 1977), a dragonfly (Campanella
and Wolf, 1974), and numerous vertebrates (Brown and Orians,
1970). Males that avoid territorial conflicts, at least for
a period in their lives, may tend to live longer and so

compensate for a lowered rate of copulation relative to males that continually attempt to be territorial. In *C. pallida* the question of the relative energetic expenses of patrolling as opposed to hovering does not have an obvious answer. Hoverers, however, do not run the same risk of wing wear and damage as patrollers, which frequently tumble about on the ground in fights over digging sites or in balls of grappling males that are struggling for ownership of a newly emerged female (Fig. 9). There is evidence moreover (Alcock, in prep.) that very large males may experience some disadvantageous constraints on their activity (perhaps because of problems with heat load) and possibly a higher rate of mortality (although the data on this point, based on mark-recapture studies, are ambiguous).

The avoidance of conflict is not the only solution to the spiraling costs of competitive interactions among males. Some individuals may parasitize other males that employ the traditional (and expensive) method of mate acquisition. Taking advantage of another male's investment in mate-attracting behavior is beautifully illustrated by the behavior of noncalling cricket males that gather around a singing male and intercept females attracted to the caller (Cade, this

Fig. 9. A group of four males fighting for possession of a newly emerged female (the individual with the dark gray eyes in the center of the cluster). In these fights the ball of males tumbles over the ground with much wing whirring, biting, and jostling.

volume). The silent males do not expend energy in song
production nor expose themselves to attack by predators and
parasitoid flies that use auditory cues to locate cricket
victims. Perhaps the visiting strategy of some philanthine
wasps contains elements of parasitism *if* the visitor male is
truly inspecting territories for females drawn to these locations by the attractant pheromone of the territory owners.
The visitor would in this case be saving the expense of pheromone synthesis and application, as well as the cost of the
defensive flights required to repel visiting and intruding
males from the perch area.

THE ROLE OF FEMALE PARENTAL INVESTMENT

     The costs of a competitively successful strategy may be
borne in part by the mother of a male hymenopteran as well
as by the male himself. Usually competitive success in
reproductive contests in Hymenoptera is associated with large
size. In many bees and wasps, the size of the male is directly related to the mother's investment of time and energy in
securing brood provisions for her progeny. A female can
regulate the size of her offspring by varying the number of
prey placed in the brood chamber or the quantity of nectar
and pollen provisions stored in a brood cell. Large males
cost more to produce than small males.
     If alternative methods of mate acquisition exist within a
species, maternal decisions can help an alternative persist,
even if males that practice this behavior do not on the
average enjoy reproductive success equal to that of competitors adopting a different role. In order for this to happen,
there must be a relationship between size and reproductive
strategy as there is in *C. pallida* where large males are
patroller-diggers and very small males are almost always
hoverers. Intraspecific variation in male size (and therefore
male behavior) could then be produced by variation in the
patterns of female parental investment, that is, patterns of
allocation of food resources to male offspring. For example,
variation in male size and reproductive strategy might simply
reflect the fact that the maternal strategy of producing n
males of size x, fitness y, and behavior A is equivalent to
the strategy of producing half as many males of size $2x$,
fitness $2y$, and behavior B, assuming that the total parental
investment is the same in each case. What counts from the
female's standpoint is not the fitness of any one of her male
offspring but rather the total reproductive value of all her
male progeny. Because there may be several different, and
equally costly, strategies of optimizing the summed fitnesses
of an individual's male offspring, variation may be maintained

in the size and behavioral tendencies of conspecific males.

SUMMARY

1. Intraspecific differences in male reproductive behavior
in the Hymenoptera may occur either in the same population
at the same time *or* in populations that are separated in
space or by time.

2. The mechanisms that result in intraspecific variation
in behavior include (1) the capacity of individuals to
adopt more than one behavioral role and (2) a fixed behavioral polymorphism in which individuals with different
genotypes are predisposed to behave differently.

3. Intraspecific differences in behavior are often linked
with variable ecological conditions that produce changes
in the spatio-temporal distribution of receptive females
and conspecific males. This can affect where a male may
search most productively for mates and how aggressively he
should react to competitor males in order to maximize fitness. The capacity of individuals to alter their behavioral strategy to match specific ecological conditions may
often be adaptive in these cases.

4. A second major factor in the evolution of behavioral
variation within populations may be the ever-escalating
costs of a successful competitive strategy. At some point,
drop-outs may save considerable time and energy by avoiding
male-male fighting contests and may invest their savings in
productive alternative methods of mate acquisition. When
alternative strategies are very different, requiring different attributes for their successful performance, the
result may be the evolution of a fixed behavioral polymorphism. The occurrence of some behavioral drop-outs may
be traced to the cost to females of producing very large
male offspring capable of competing for mates with other
large males.

5. Because both ecological variation and the costs of male-
male combat affect many insects, intraspecific variation
in male reproductive behavior may be the rule rather than
the exception in these animal species.

ACKNOWLEDGMENTS

I would like to thank Prof. C. D. Michener for inviting me
to present this paper at the XV International Congress of

Entomology. The article was prepared while the author was
supported by National Science Foundation Grant DEB76-04503.

REFERENCES

Alcock, J. 1975. Male mating strategies of some philanthine
    wasps (Hymenoptera: Sphecidae). *J. Kans. Ent. Soc.*
    48:532-545.
Alcock, J. 1977a. Unpublished data.
Alcock, J. 1977b. Patrolling and mating by males of
    Callanthidium illustre (Hymenoptera: Megachilidae).
    Southw. Nat. 22:554-556.
Alcock, J., C. E. Jones, and S. L. Buchmann. 1976. Location
    before emergence of the female bee, *Centris pallida,* by
    its male (Hymenoptera: Anthophoridae). *J. Zool.* 179:
    189-199.
Alcock, J., G. C. Eickwort, and K. R. Eickwort. 1977a. The
    reproductive behavior of *Anthidium maculosum* (Hymenoptera:
    Megachilidae) and the evolutionary significance of
    multiple copulations by females. *Behav. Ecol. Sociobiol.*
    2:385-396.
Alcock, J., C. E. Jones, and S. L. Buchmann. 1977b. Male
    mating strategies in the bee *Centris pallida* Fox
    (Hymenoptera: Anthophoridae). *Amer. Nat.* 111:145-155.
Alcock, J., E. M. Barrows, G. Gordh, L. J. Hubbard, L. L.
    Kirkendall, D. Pyle, T. L. Ponder, and F. G. Zalom. 1978.
    The ecology and evolution of male reproductive behaviour
    in the bees and wasps. *Zool. J. Linn. Soc. Lond.* (in press).
Barlow, G. W. 1967. Social behavior of a South American leaf
    fish, *Polycentrus schomburgkii,* with an account of recur-
    ring pseudo-female behavior. *Amer. Mid. Nat.* 78:215-234.
Barrows, E. M. 1976. Mating behavior in halictine bees
    (Hymenoptera: Halictidae): II. Microterritorial and
    patrolling behavior of males of *Lasioglossum rohweri.*
    Z. Tierpsych. 40:377-389.
Brown, J. L., and G. H. Orians. 1970. Spacing patterns in
    mobile animals. *Ann. Rev. Ecol. Syst.* 1:239-262.
Campanella, P.J., and L.L. Wolf. 1974. Temperate leks as a
    mating system in a temperate zone dragonfly (Odonata:
    Anisoptera). I. *Plathemis lydia* (Drury). *Behaviour* 51:4-87.
Cazier, M.A., and E.G. Linsley. 1963. Territorial behavior
    among males of *Protoxaea gloriosa* Fox. *Can. Ent.* 95:
    547-556.
Constantz, G.D. 1975. Behavioral ecology of mating in the
    male Gila topminnow, *Poeciliopsis occidentalis* (Cyprino-
    dontiformes: Poeciliidae). *Ecology* 56:966-973.
Eickwort, G.C. 1977. Male territorial behaviour in the mason

bee, *Hoplitis anthocopoides* (Hymenoptera: Megachilidae). *Anim. Behav.* 25:542-554.

Evans, H.E. 1966. *The Comparative Ethology and Evolution of the Sand Wasps*. Harvard Univ. Press, Cambridge.

Evans, H. E. 1975. Nesting behavior of *Philanthus albopilosus* with comparisons between two widely separated populations. *Ann. Ent. Soc. Amer.* 68:888-892.

Gadgil, M. 1972. Male dimorphism as a consequence of sexual selection. *Amer. Nat.* 106:574-580.

Haas, A. 1960. Vergleichende Verhaltensstudien zum Paarungsschwarm solitarer Apiden. *Z. Tierpsych.* 17:402-416.

Hogan-Warburg, A. J. 1966. Social behavior of the ruff, *Philomachus pugnax* L. *Ardea* 54:109-229.

Hurd, P. D., Jr., and E. G. Linsley. 1975. The principal *Larrea* bees of the Southwestern United States (Hymenoptera: Apoidea). *Smith. Contrib. Zool.* 193:1-74.

Hurd, P.D., Jr., and E.G. Linsley. 1976. The bee family Oxaeidae with a revision of the North American species (Hymenoptera: Apoidea). *Smith Contrib. Zool.* 220:1-75.

Jaycox, E.R. 1967. Territorial behavior among males of *Anthidium banningense* (Hymenoptera: Megachilidae). *J. Kans. Ent. Soc.* 40:565-570.

Keenleyside, M.H.A. 1972. Intraspecific intrusions into nests of spawning long-ear sunfish (Pices: Centrarchidae). *Copeia* 1972:272-278.

Kurtak, B.H. 1973. Aspects of the biology of the European bee *Anthidium manicatum* (Hymenoptera: Megachilidae) in New York State. Ms. Thesis, Cornell University.

Lin, N., and C.D. Michener. 1972. Evolution of sociality in insects. *Quart. Rev. Biol.* 47:131-159.

Linsley, E.G. 1976. Defensive behavior of male bees about plants not visited by their females (Hymenoptera: Apoidea). *Pan-Pac. Ent.* 52:177-178.

Linsley, E.G., J.W. MacSwain, and P.H. Raven. 1963. Comparative behavior of bees and Onagraceae. II. *Oenothera* bees of the Mojave desert. *Univ. Cal. Publ. Ent.* 33:25-58.

Maynard Smith, J. 1974. The theory of games and the evolution of animal conflicts. *J. Theor. Biol.* 47:209-221.

Maynard Smith, J. 1976. Evolution and the theory of games. *Amer. Sci.* 64:41-45.

Maynard Smith, J., and G.A. Parker. 1976. The logic of asymmetric contests. *Anim. Behav.* 24:159-175.

Parker, G.A. 1970. The reproductive behaviour and the nature of sexual selection in *Scatophaga stercoraria* L. II. The fertilization rate and the spatial and temporal relationships of each sex around the site of mating and oviposition. *J. Anim. Ecol.* 39:205-228.

Parker, G.A. 1974. The reproductive behaviour and the nature of sexual selection in *Scatophaga stercoraria* L. IX.

Spatial distribution of fertilization rates and evolution
of male search strategy within the reproductive area.
Evolution 28:93-108.
Simon-Thomas, R.T., and E.P.R. Poorter. 1972. Notes on the
behaviour of males of *Philanthus triangulum* F. (Hymenop-
tera: Sphecidae). *Tijdschr. Ent.* 115:141-151.
Williams, G.C. 1966. *Adaptation and Natural Selection:
A Critique of Some Current Evolutionary Thought.*
Princeton Univ. Press, Princeton.
Wilson, E.O. 1975. *Sociobiology, The New Synthesis.*
Harvard Univ. Press, Cambridge.

THE SURVIVAL VALUE OF COURTSHIP IN INSECTS

Robert Barrass

The Sunderland Polytechnic

INTRODUCTION

Studies of courtship are of great interest to biologists
because courtship precedes mating and the reproduction of the
species. Such studies are of particular interest to students
of behavior because courtship may be performed, as soon as
the male and female are placed together, by insects which have
had no previous contact with other members of their species.
Furthermore, since in many species courtship is completed
quickly and can be observed closely, this provides us with an
opportunity to study communication between two animals.

DESCRIPTION

The courtship and mating behavior of the parasitic wasp
Nasonia vitripennis (Walker) (syn. *Mormoniella vitripennis*)
have been described by Barrass (1960a). In courtship each
insect provides a succession of stimuli to which its partner
makes appropriate responses. There is an orderly arrangement
of stereotyped movements and postures.

Courtship Behavior

The male turns towards the female, chases, and mounts.
Once on the female's body, the male moves until its head
projects above and between the female's raised antennae
(Fig. 3A). In this position the male vibrates its wings repeatedly and beats its forelegs upon the female's head. Then
the male's head is raised and the mouthparts extended
(Fig. 1, M1), and then it is lowered as the mouthparts are
retracted (Fig. 1, M2). If the female adopts the mating
posture as the male's head is raised (Fig. 1, V1), the male
completes the head movement (Fig. 1, V2) and then moves backwards and mates. If the female does not become receptive at
the first of the male's head movements, movements of the

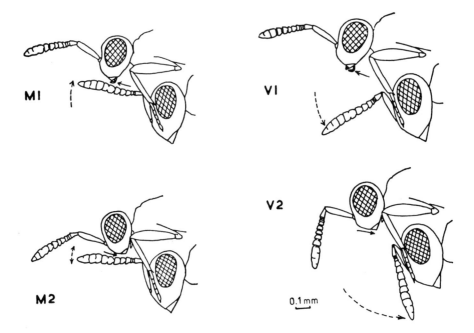

Fig. 1. (M1 and M2) Antennal movement of a courting female Nasonia and head movement of a male. (V1 and V2) Male's head movement as a receptive female stops courting and adopts the mating posture (from Barrass, 1976a).

male's antennae follow (Fig. 2), and then the head movements are repeated a number of times as a head series. After a pause in which movements of the male's wings and forelegs continue, the male's antennae are moved in a characteristic way (Fig. 2) before the head movements are repeated.

The stereotyped sequence of the male's courtship movements (the antennal movements followed by the head movements) is here called a courtship sequence, and, if the female is not receptive at the first head movement, the repetition of head movements prolongs the sequence. Because courtship comprises

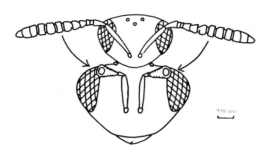

Fig. 2. The antennal movement of a courting male Nasonia (from Barrass, 1960a).

a number of courtship sequences, with a pause between the end
of each sequence and the start of the next, the head movements
are conspicuous, easy to count, and well-suited to quantitative studies.

Mating Behavior

The female stops courting as it adopts the posture in
which copulation is possible. The male completes the head
movement and then stops courting, moves backward, directs its
abdomen below the female's abdomen, and mates (Fig. 3B).

Postcopulatory Courtship

After mating, the male moves forward and courtship movements are repeated. If the female becomes receptive again,
the male does not mate twice. The encounter ends when the
male dismounts and moves away.

A

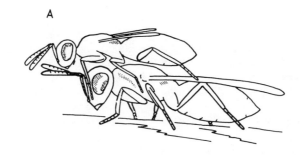

B

*Fig. 3. (A) The courtship position and (B) the mating position
in* Nasonia *(from Barrass, 1960a).*

QUESTIONS

Biologists are accustomed to asking what is the function
or adaptive value of any anatomical structure or physiological
response, and the repetition of movements in courtship has
been called courtship *persistence* and attributed to female
coyness (Richards, 1927). The male's courtship is said to
persuade the female. Tinbergen (1953) says that it may take
a considerable time to overcome the female's *reluctance*--
although he does not imply deliberate action with an end in
view.

Courtship necessitates a delay between the meeting of the
sexes and intromission. If movements have to be repeated
because the female needs to be persuaded (because of female
coyness), this introduces a further delay. Biologists have
long been puzzled by this apparent difference between what
they observe and what they expect. Once the male and female
are together, we might expect that the quicker mating is
accomplished the better it would be for the species (Richards,
1927; Manning, 1966). What then is the survival value of a
prolonged courtship?

The way in which we interpret the information available
from studies of insect courtship behavior depends upon what
problems we think we are studying: *the answers we give are
dependent upon the questions we ask*. Many scientists, assuming that the male was courting the female, have asked: What
effect does the male's courtship have on the female? Why is
the female coy? Why do some courtships take so long? In this
paper I shall ask five questions, consideration of which leads
me to a new interpretation of the survival value of courtship.

1. Does the Male Court the Female?

In courtship both insects provide a succession of stimuli.
Each of these is associated with a species-characteristic
response by its partner. This communication makes possible
cooperation. If the male is courting the female (in the sense
that the male is providing stimuli to which the female responds), then the female is also courting the male (providing
stimuli to which the male responds). Both sexes are courting,
and to observe only that the male is courting the female is
to take a one-sided view of this mutual interaction.

2. How Does Courtship Affect the Female?

Courtship affects the female in a number of ways. First,
at the start of courtship the female *either* stops other
activities *or* resumes activity. Secondly, in their first

courtship most females (96%: Barrass, 1976b) become receptive at the start of the first, second, or third head series. Thirdly, a female, having mated in its first courtship, may thereafter be nonreceptive.

In many species of insects, females that have been inseminated do not mate again (Engelmann, 1970). Cousin (1933) suggested that in *Nasonia* the presence of sperm in the spermatheca inhibits further mating. However, if the male is removed after the female has adopted the mating posture, but before mating, the female may afterwards be nonreceptive even though it has never mated (Barrass, 1965). That is to say, a courtship without mating (in which the female becomes receptive) may have a long-lasting inhibitory effect on the female's sexual behavior. A similar inhibitory effect of courtship without mating is recorded by van den Assem (1970) in *Lariophagus*, another pteromalid.

A virgin female mates early in courtship. Having mated, it can be used in experiments in which nonreceptive females are required. The behavior of the female can be predicted from its previous behavior. The receptivity of a female normally depends upon whether or not it has courted previously--not upon the duration of the courtship. The male's courting is prolonged only if the female will not mate: the repetition of courtship sequences does not cause a nonreceptive female to become receptive. Indeed, the repetition of courtship sequences does not appear to result in any change in the behavior of a nonreceptive female.

3. How Does Courtship Affect the Male?

Courtship affects the male in a number of ways. Like the female, at the start of courtship, the male *either* stops its earlier activities *or* resumes activity. *And each stage in courtship inhibits the previous stage:* chasing stops as the male starts to mount; movement over the female stops as the female stops moving; and courting stops as the male moves backwards, etc. At each stage, the new stimuli encountered not only evoke new responses but also inhibit the previous responses; that is to say, stimuli have negative as well as positive effects.

In courtship the male responds, if the female is receptive, to the absence of the female's antennae by moving backwards from the courtship position. The raised antennae provide stimuli which inhibit the backward movement, perhaps by stimulating courtship. If the female's antennae are cut off before courtship, the male moves backwards after the first head movement of its courtship. This is in keeping with the hypothesis that, normally, the female's raised antennae inhibit the male's mating behavior.

Sometimes, after mounting, a male is unable to reach the courtship position; for example, because another male is already courting, or because the female preens or raises its wings. The male may then make abdominal movements that normally precede intromission--even though it has never been in the courtship position. These observations support the hypothesis that each stage in the courtship inhibits not only the previous stage but also the next: *courtship normally inhibits the male's mating behavior.*

The aftereffects of one courtship upon the male may be observed in the interval between courtships and in the next courtship. Between courtships, if the female is removed from the observation cell, males which have courted nonreceptive females behave differently from those which have mated (Barrass, 1969). After a courtship, the male preens and dips its abdomen repeatedly. In each abdomen-dipping movement a streak of fluid is deposited on the substratum. More streaks are deposited after mating than after courting nonreceptive females (Fig. 4).

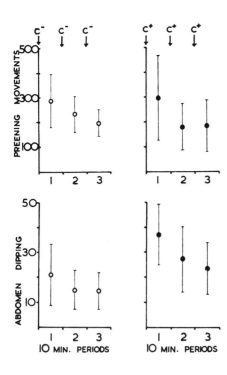

Fig. 4. The mean number of preening and abdomen-dipping movements during three 10 min. observation periods, each preceded by a courtship of either a nonreceptive (= C⁻, n = 11) or a receptive female (= C⁺, n = 6). 2S̄x on either side of mean indicated (from Barrass, 1969).

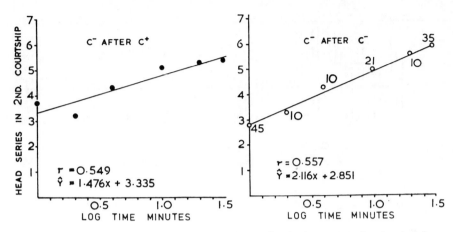

Fig. 5. Courting movements (head series) in second courtship (female nonreceptive) after courting a receptive female in first courtship (C⁻ after C⁺: each point mean for 12 ♂♂) or after courting a nonreceptive female (C⁻ after C⁻; each point mean for number of ♂♂ indicated). Regression lines from original data (from Barrass, 1969).

One courtship affects the male's behavior in its next courtship whether or not the female is receptive (Fig. 5); but if it is presented with a succession of receptive females, one male will mate many times. For example, one male mated 154 times in 4 hr. 24 min. (Barrass, 1961). Courting receptive females, and mating, clearly do not prevent further courting and mating (Fig. 6A).

If a male is presented with a succession of nonreceptive females, progressive changes may be observed in the male's sexual behavior. In the first courtship of a 24-48 hr. old male, the mean number of courtship sequences was 6.95 (n = 171; SD ± 2.09; mode = 6) (Barrass, 1960b). The second courtship is shorter than the first, and the third shorter than the second, etc. With later females the male may mount and then dismount without courting, or start to mount without mounting, or turn and chase without starting to mount (Fig. 6B).

Courtship without mating has a *cumulative inhibitory effect* on the male's sexual behavior.

4. Why Are Courtship Movements Repeated?

The word *coyness* is usually written in inverted commas to indicate that it is not a scientific term. We use such words

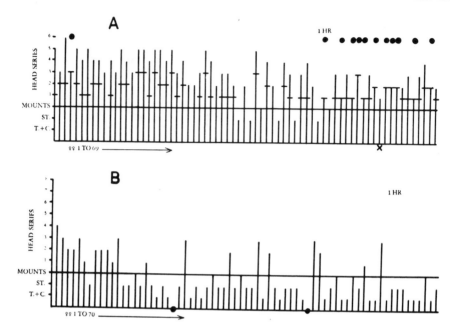

Fig. 6. Behavior of a male towards successive females presented at 30 sec. intervals. Each female was removed either
immediately after courtship or after 60 sec. if there was no
courtship. (A) Record of one male's behavior towards 69
different receptive females. (B) Record of one male's behavior towards 70 different nonreceptive females. The length
of each vertical line represents the male's behavior towards
one female, T + C = turns and chases, St = starts to mount.
A dot on the base line indicates a 1 min. observation
without turning and chasing. With the receptive females,
each horizontal line through a vertical line indicates the
point in courtship at which mating occurred. A cross below
the base line indicates a courtship in which the female
became receptive but the male did not attempt to mate. A
dot immediately above the vertical line indicates that there
was no postcopulatory courtship.

for things we do not understand: they cloak our ignorance.
The use of these terms is one of the basic problems in
studies of behavior (Lack, 1943). The words *persistence*,
coyness, reluctance, and *persuasion* are all subjective and
tell us nothing about what is happening in courtship. Unfortunately they encourage us to think that courtship has a
cumulative, stimulatory effect on the female even though
there is no convincing evidence, in any insect, that an
unreceptive female becomes more receptive in a prolonged
courtship (Kennedy, 1966; Barrass, 1976b).

Richards (1927), who used the word coyness, drew attention to a number of observations which make it impossible for us to interpret all courtship behavior in terms of its effects upon the female: (1) in some species courtship is prolonged only when the female has already mated; (2) in many species courtship is not prolonged; (3) in some species the female plays an active part or is more active than the male. Indeed, it has been suggested (Alexander and Brown, 1963) that most groups of insects passed, in their evolution, through a stage in which copulation occurred with the female mounted on the male.

Courtship may increase the male's readiness to mate (Kennedy, 1966; Chapman, 1971). Loher and Huber (1966) report that while the male *Gomphocerus rufus* (Orthoptera) may not mate with the first female courted, it is able to mate with a second female, immediately afterwards, with only a brief courtship.

However, in *Nasonia*, repeated courtships have a cumulative inhibitory effect on the male. The simplest explanation of the repetition of courtship movements is that in the courtship position both sexes repeatedly respond in the same way to the same stimuli: mutual stimulation occurs throughout. That is to say, the species-specific stimuli provided by one sex repeatedly evoke the same species-specific responses in its partner. If this is why courtship movements are repeated, then we have been asking the wrong question. The problem is not why does courtship continue for so long, but why does it ever stop.

5. What Brings Courtship to an End?

Many female insects mate only once. As a result most courtships do not lead to mating. The end of courtship, when the male moves away, may follow movements and postures of the nonreceptive female (Engelmann, 1970; Linley and Adams, 1974). However, even in the absence of such obvious responses, courtship does not go on indefinitely.

In several studies involving the repetition of a behavior pattern, waning responsiveness has been attributed to the performance of a *consummatory act* such as mating. In this consummatory act, in terms of various energy models of motivation, there is said to be a using up of reaction-specific energy (Lorenz, 1950), or a discharge of motivational impulses (Tinbergen, 1951), or drive depletion (Manning, 1966), or a satisfying of motivation (Ruwet, 1972). These terms imply that behavior comes to an end only when energy is discharged in action, but such models should not be confused with physiological reality.

The nonreceptive *Nasonia* females are like the models (dummy animals) used in many studies of animal behavior, since the termination of courtship cannot be due to the performance of a consummatory act (Barrass, 1961).

Ethologists still use the descriptive term *consummatory act* for the final act of a behavior pattern (Wallace, 1973). Hinde and Hinde (1976) say that an activity may be terminated because the animal encounters new stimuli (consummatory stimuli) as a result of the activity. It is not clear how this brings the activity to an end unless the animal stops doing one thing because it has started to do something else: each stimulus not only stimulates the next activity but also inhibits the previous activity.

The male *Nasonia* stops courting and moves to the mating position immediately after the female stops courting (i.e., becomes receptive). Here courtship stops in response to changes in the female's behavior. But mating is not the end of the encounter, since, after mating, the male moves forward and repeats courtship movements. This postcopulatory courtship is not followed by mating, so it cannot be the consummatory act (mating) that brings this behavior to an end.

The male *Nasonia* is able to mate again and again. It is not repetitive matings but courtships without mating that have a cumulative inhibitory effect on the male.

In *Nasonia* the behavior of a nonreceptive female does not appear to change during courtship. If courtship does not change the behavior of such females, then the male does not encounter new stimuli and the termination of courtship must be due to changes in the male.

When males were grouped according to the number of head series in their first courtship, Barrass (1960b) noted characteristic variations in the average number of head movements in the successive head series of a courtship. In each group most head movements were performed in the first head series and fewer in the second or third. There was then an increase followed by a decrease in the last series prior to dismounting. For example, with 39 males which performed seven head series in the first courtship, the mean numbers of head movements in successive head series were: 5.65, 4.23, 4.18, 4.74, 5.00, 5.51, and 4.85.

The inhibitory effect of courting one female may be studied by comparing the male's behavior when courting one and then a second female. Such a method of measurement is always an underestimate because, before meeting the second female, the male has time to recover from the effects of the first courtship. The longer the interval between courtships (up to 60 min.), the greater the recovery (Fig. 5). The cumulative inhibitory effect must therefore be most marked at the end of each courtship, before the onset of such recovery.

It seems logical to suggest that the repetition of courtship movements within a courtship also has a cumulative
inhibitory effect, and that this is what brings courtship to
an end.

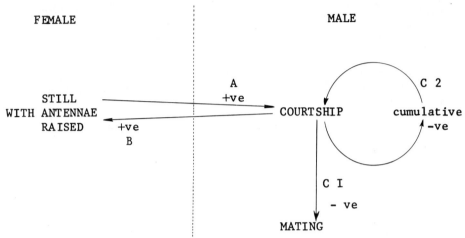

Fig. 7. Interacting influences in courtship in Nasonia
vitripennis. The male may start courting in the absence of
the female's antennae, if the female keeps still (A), but
courting continues only if the female's antennae are raised.
The female's raised antennae inhibit the male's mating
behavior, perhaps by stimulating courtship behavior. The
male's courting provides stimuli (B) to which the female
responds either by raising its antennae and maintaining the
courtship posture or by lowering its antennae and adopting
the mating posture. In view of this mutual stimulation,
courtship might be expected to continue indefinitely.
Courtship precludes mating behavior (C1). Courting may be
terminated by a change in the female's behavior to the
posture which makes intromission possible. This precludes
further courtship (the stimuli represented by A are removed)
and the inhibitory effect of courtship on the male's sexual
behavior (C1) then ceases. Intromission follows. Alternatively, if the female does not adopt the mating posture,
courtship is terminated by the cumulative inhibitory effect
of courtship on the male's sexual behavior (C2). The male
dismounts. The inhibitory effects of courtship at first
preclude mating behavior (C1) and (C2) later terminate
courtship (from Barrass, 1976b).

CONCLUSIONS

The mutual stimulation involved in courtship is in the
male opposed by an inhibitory effect of courtship upon sexual
behavior (Fig. 7). Because this inhibition is cumulative and
the stimulation is not, the male eventually stops courting,
dismounts, and moves away.

The Survival Value of Courtship

Inhibitory effects are important in courtship in several
ways (Barrass, 1976b):

1. In both sexes, courtship inhibits earlier activities
(including the male's backward movement that normally
occurs between courtship and copulation) which cannot
occur at the same time as courtship.

2. In both sexes, because courtship behavior inhibits
mating behavior, with a receptive female there is a delay
between mounting and intromission. This delay, presumably,
gives time for mutual *recognition* (of sex and species).
Another result of the adoption of the correct courtship
position is that the courting movements and the movements
which follow them, which normally lead to copulation, are
also correctly *oriented*. Furthermore, the delay involved
in courtship gives time for *synchronization* of the movements which precede copulation and so makes copulation
possible.

3. Courtship inhibits the male's courtship. Courtship is
prolonged only if the female does not mate, and, even then,
only if the male has not recently courted a nonreceptive
female. The survival value of this cumulative inhibitory
effect is that, in spite of the attraction of the male
towards the female and the mutual stimulation which occurs
in courtship, a male courting a nonreceptive female does
not court indefinitely. The termination of courtship allows
the female to resume other activities and increases the
male's chances of meeting other females--which it may
inseminate.

ACKNOWLEDGEMENTS

This paper was read at the XVth International Congress of
Entomology, in Washington, D.C., in August 1976. I thank the
Governors of the Sunderland Polytechnic, the organizers of
the XVth International Congress of Entomology, and the Royal

Society of London for travel grants. I also thank my
colleague Mr. D.W. Snowdon for his help in preparing the
illustrations, and the editors of the journals in which these
figures were first published for permission to reproduce them
in this review.

REFERENCES

Alexander, R.D., and W.L. Brown, Jr. 1963. Mating behavior
    and the origin of insect wings. *Occ. Papers Mus. Zool.
    Univ. Michigan* 628:1-19.
Assem, J. van den. 1970. Courtship and mating in *Lariophagus
    distinguendus* (Först.) Kurdj. (Hymenoptera, Pteromalidae).
    Neth. J. Zool. 20:329-352.
Barrass, R. 1960a. The courtship behaviour of *Mormoniella
    vitripennis* Walk. (Hymenoptera, Pteromalidae). *Behaviour*
    15:185-209.
Barrass, R. 1960b. The effect of age on the performance of an
    innate behaviour pattern in *Mormoniella vitripennis* Walk.
    (Hymenoptera, Pteromalidae). *Behaviour* 15:210-218.
Barrass, R. 1961. A quantitative study of the behaviour of
    the male *Mormoniella vitripennis* (Walker) (Hymenoptera,
    Pteromalidae) towards two constant stimulus-situations.
    Behaviour 18:288-312.
Barrass, R. 1965. Variations in the receptivity of the female
    Mormoniella vitripennis (Walker) (Hymenoptera, Pteromali-
    dae). *Proc. XIIth. Int. Cong. Ent., London* 1964:299.
Barrass, R. 1969. Preening and abdomen dipping by the male
    Mormoniella vitripennis (Walker) (Hymenoptera, Pteromalidae)
    after courtship. *Behaviour* 35:304-312.
Barrass, R. 1976a. Rearing jewel wasps *Mormoniella vitripennis*
    (Walker) and their use in teaching biology. *J. Biol. Educ.*
    10:119-126.
Barrass, R. 1976b. Inhibitory effects of courtship in the
    wasp *Nasonia vitripennis* (Walker) and a new interpretation
    of the biological significance of courtship in insects.
    Physiol. Ent. 1:229-234.
Chapman, R.F. 1971. *The Insects: Structure and Function.*
    English Universities Press, London.
Cousin, G. 1933. Étude biologique d'un Chalcidien: *Mormoniella
    vitripennis* Walk. *Bull. Biol. Fr. Belg.* 67:371-400.
Engelmann, F. 1970. *The Physiology of Insect Reproduction.*
    Pergamon Press, Oxford.
Hinde, R.A., and J.S. Hinde. 1976. *Instinct and Intelligence.*
    University Press, Oxford.
Kennedy, J.S. 1966. Some outstanding questions in insect
    behaviour. *In* P.T. Haskell (ed.), *Insect Behaviour. Symp.
    Roy. Ent. Soc. London* 3:97-112.

Lack, D. 1953. *The Life of the Robin*. Penguin Books, Harmondsworth

Linley, J.R., and G.M. Adams. 1974. Sexual receptivity in *Culicoides melleus* (Diptera: Ceratopagonidae). *Trans. Roy. Ent. Soc. London* 126:279-303.

Loher, W., and F. Huber. 1966. Nervous and endocrine control of sexual behaviour in a grasshopper *(Gomphocerus rufus* L., Acridinae). *Symp. Soc. Exp. Biol.* 20:381-400.

Lorenz, K. 1950. The comparative method in studying innate behaviour patterns. *Symp. Soc. Exp. Biol.* 4:221-268.

Manning, A. 1966. Sexual behaviour. *In* P.T. Haskell (ed.), *Insect Behaviour. Symp. Roy. Ent. Soc. London* 3:57-68.

Richards, O.W. 1927. Sexual selection and allied problems in the insects. *Biol. Rev.* 2:298-364.

Ruwet, J.C. 1972. *Introduction to Ethology*. International Universities Press, New York.

Tinbergen, N. 1951. *The Study of Instinct*. Clarenden Press, Oxford.

Tinbergen, N. 1953. *Social Behaviour in Animals*. Methuen, London.

Wallace, R.A. 1973. *The Ecology and Evolution of Animal Behavior*. Goodyear Publ. Co., Pacific Palisades, California.

ON THE ORIGIN AND BASIS OF THE MALE-FEMALE PHENOMENON

Richard D. Alexander and Gerald Borgia

The University of Michigan

INTRODUCTION

The terms "male" and "female" refer to alternative and complementary lifetime strategies in gonochorists or reproductive functions in hermaphrodites. In order to discuss male and female differences and similarities, therefore, it is useful first to consider certain general features of life histories which we believe require clarification.

In evolutionary terms the lifetimes of individual organisms can be viewed as comprising two kinds of "effort" appropriately termed *somatic effort* and *reproductive effort* (Williams, 1966a, b, 1971; Hamilton, 1967; Hirshfield and Tinkle, 1975; others). These two kinds of striving include, respectively, the garnering of resources and their subsequent redistribution in the interests of the reproduction of the organism's genes. With increasing tendencies to be semelparous (to breed only once or only during one very restricted period), somatic and reproductive effort come to be represented by separate periods in the organism's life, approximately corresponding to juvenile and adult. With iteroparity (repeated breeding), the periods necessarily overlap so that resource garnering and redistribution are best described as different kinds of activities that may be engaged in either alternately or simultaneously. By these usages both somatic and reproductive effort increase the likelihood of mortality, because each involves risk taking. Somatic effort, however, evolves to increase the reproductive value of the individual by rendering subsequent reproductive effort more effective, while reproductive effort evolves to increase actual reproduction, thereby incidentally reducing the reproductive value of the individual. If senescence results from unavoidable pleiotropic gene effects (Williams, 1957), the onsets of reproductive effort and senescence will therefore tend to coincide.[1]

An organism's reproductive effort can obviously be subdivided into seasonal or annual effort for long-lived, iteroparous organisms, and there are good reasons for such division since what is expended during one period is likely to
affect what is available during subsequent periods. One
expects iteroparous organisms to evolve to divide their
reproductive effort among reproductive periods or seasons,
using environmental signs indicating the relative value or
appropriateness of each period, so as to maximize the returns
from the lifetime of reproductive effort (Williams, 1966a, b).
In all such considerations the concept of effort, or striving,
avoids the erroneous view that the amounts to be expended are
predetermined and unchangeable for each individual.

Detailed comparisons of male and female activities require
further subdivisions of reproductive effort for the purpose
of analyzing mating and parental activities, gamete dimorphism, sexual selection, and the costs and benefits of
sexuality. These further subdivisions are even more difficult, and the reasons are worth a careful review.

PARENTAL INVESTMENT AND REPRODUCTIVE EFFORT

Darwin (1871) noted that "The only check to a continued
augmentation of fertility in each organism seems to be either
the expenditure of power and the greater risks run by parents
that produce a more numerous progeny, or the contingency of
very numerous eggs and young being produced of smaller size
or less vigorous, or subsequently not so well nurtured."

[1] Our distinction between reproductive and somatic effort may
at first seem not entirely consistent with the discussion of
reproductive effort by Williams (1966a, b). He exemplified
reproductive effort by the gathering of food for offspring
(i.e., the garnering of resources), an act which automatically
reduces residual reproductive value. Williams' example of a
robin deciding whether or not to forage for one more worm,
however, requires explication. Even if the worm could not
possibly be used by the parent robin except as food for its
offspring, whether or not the act of foraging for worms
actually reduces reproductive value could depend upon the
particular time of measurement. Thus, if one measured the
reproductive value of all parents just before the act of
foraging, and then again upon the return of those successful
after delivery of the worms to their offspring, the residual
reproductive value of the aggregate of parents would be
reduced. But if the second (continued on facing page)

Fisher (1958) continued the discussion, referring to an additional factor, parental care, which includes ". . . all expenditure in the form of nutriment, effort, or exposure to danger, incurred in the production and nurture of the young. In organisms in which that degree of parental expenditure, which yields the highest proportionate probability of survival, is large compared to the resources available, the optimal fertility will be low." Trivers (1972) attempted to make the concept of expenditures on progeny more operational by defining "parental investment" as "any investment by the parent in an individual offspring that increases the offspring's chances of surviving (and hence reproductive success) . . . ." This parental contribution, Trivers noted, is made at a cost--the ability of the parents to make an investment in other progeny. In the next sentence, however, Trivers exposed the problem in relating these discussions to the subdivision of reproductive effort when he excluded from parental *investment* "effort expended in finding a member of the opposite sex or in subduing members of one's own sex in order to mate with a member of the opposite sex . . ." (italics added).

Low (1978) considered the arguments of Darwin, Fisher, and Trivers, and divided reproductive effort into *parental effort* and *mating effort;* she also noted that for many species a third category involving *nepotism to relatives other than offspring* would be necessary (see also Alexander, 1977). Low evidently meant that parental effort is altered by changing

---

measurement was made while the parents were still carrying their worms, just *before* the act of feeding them to the offspring, the residual reproductive value of the parents would show an increase, unless the decision to make the last foraging trip was a reproductive mistake. The whole act of foraging for offspring would thus reduce reproductive value, but the food gathering itself would temporarily raise it, thus representing somatic effort even if the food could not be used by the parent itself. Since ordinarily a food-gathering act would predictably be embarked upon either to feed one's young or one's self, we would not usually have to consider measurements of residual reproductive value midway in the act. But especially because, as in Williams' example, worms are food for both parents and offspring, and also because robins are iteroparous, the distinction we are making seems worthwhile. We have purposely chosen for somatic effort the word "garnering" because it means to gather and store: a robin obviously gathers and temporarily "stores" (in its beak) even worms that will inevitably be fed to its offspring, and such a robin may have greater reproductive value than another one which did not make the trip and therefore lacks a worm.

the proportion of reproductive effort devoted to care of the
progeny as a whole (i.e., as opposed to mating effort), while
parental investment is altered by changing the distribution of
parental effort among individual offspring (i.e., by distrib-
uting it among greater or lesser numbers of offspring or by
furnishing different amounts to different offspring). Theoretically, at least, variations in the proportion of reproductive effort allocated to particular aspects of mating effort
could allow some individuals both to produce more gametes than
others and to invest more heavily in each. In other words,
parental effort is the sum of reproductive effort devoted to
parental investment without regard to which offspring, or how
many, received benefits. Fisher did not clearly distinguish
these two concepts in his use of parental "expenditures" (see
above), and Trivers, despite his careful definition of parental investment, subsequently used the term to mean either
parental effort or parental investment by the definitions
suggested here.

PRE- AND POSTZYGOTIC EFFORT

   Low defined mating effort essentially as Trivers (1972)
used it. As such it is always prezygotic. But not all prezygotic effort is a direct means of securing matings. Indeed,
what Low called parental effort, some of Trivers' usages of
parental investment, and Darwin's and Fisher's "expenditures"
on progeny all represent provision of resources such as nutrition or protection to *either* offspring *or* gametes. Since
females in all animal species and nearly all plant species
prezygotically couple to the gamete resources which contribute
to the success of the zygote, much prezygotic effort in females is properly regarded as parental effort (see also
Trivers, 1972). By contrast, all of the prezygotic effort of
most males, including investment in the locomotory and other
devices of sperm, and even gifts later used by the females in
parental care, are appropriately identified as mating effort
(see below). Moreover, in most species mating effort represents most or all of the male's reproductive effort, while
this is never true for females. The reason is that the female
has prezygotic control over the fates of her individual
gametes, hence of any investment in them. As a consequence,
she can optimize the pattern of expenditure on her offspring
by extending the period of investment back into the gametic
stage. The male, lacking control over the fates of his
individual gametes, is not in a position to realize gain from
investing in them in ways designed to increase their success
should they succeed in becoming part of a zygote. To some
degree, then, females may be characterized as the sex which

has retained greater control over the fates of individual
gametes, partly by holding the investment-rich eggs before
mating, sometimes by internalizing the sperm as well prior to
fertilization, and sometimes by internalizing or tending the
zygote itself after mating. This retention by females of
control over the success of individual gametes, and sometimes
zygotes, accounts for three distinctively female attributes
among modern species: (1) greater immediate control over the
process of sexual selection than the male, (2) greater ability
to regain resources from terminated gametes or zygotes through
resorption or cannibalism, and (3) (usually) greater confidence of parenthood than the male.

Our concepts of male and female, then, actually return to
the different ways in which the individuals in a sexual
species invest in their gametes. Females are, by definition,
those individuals in any gonochoristic (or dioecious) species
which have specialized to produce a smaller number of larger
and usually less motile gametes. The few exceptions are all
secondarily evolved and involve only the relative motility of
male and female gametes (Baccetti, 1970). We are aware of no
exception to the rule that females produce fewer gametes than
males and invest more heavily in each, nor to the rule that in
either gonochorists or hermaphrodites with meiotic oögenesis,
polar bodies are always formed, with most of their cytoplasm
being given over to the sister cell destined to become a
viable gamete. Assuming widespread homology of femaleness
and maleness, respectively, what is indicated is the antiquity
of the divergence between the sexes in the relative proportions of parental and mating effort, leading to an apparently
universal male-female asymmetry in the arrangement of prezygotic effort--the only universal asymmetry in regard to the
exerting of reproductive effort by males and females.

With regard to gametes, then, our attention tends to focus
on how the reproductive expenditures of either sex are divided
among them or on how numerous and how large are the gametes.
With regard to zygotes, on the other hand, because there are
two parents, we tend to be concerned with the relative amounts
of effort exerted by the two parents or with the proportions
of parental effort diverted from mating effort by males and
females, respectively (Fig. 1).

SUBDIVISIONS OF MATING EFFORT

Mating effort may be subdivided into three categories:
(1) competitive interactions with other individuals of the
same sex, (2) transfer of benefits to members of the other sex
as a part of securing matings, and (3) evidence of commitment
to parental effort to be directed at the offspring resulting

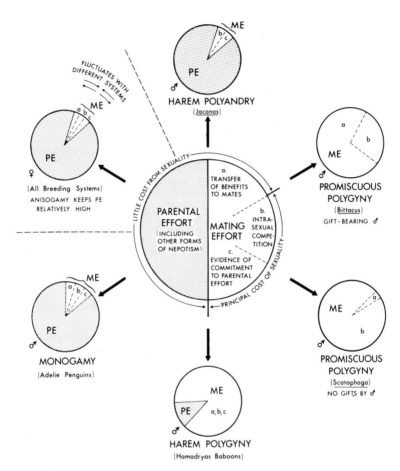

Fig. 1. Subdivisions of reproductive effort and their effects
on the cost of sexuality (large circle). Expected distributions of parental and mating effort in male and female in
different breeding systems (small circles). The different
diagrams are not intended to be quantitative except in relation to one another; variation within the breeding systems
should not change their relationships. Thus, among males, we
expect mating effort to be lowest in harem polyandry. In
monogamous systems mating effort is probably higher in males
than in females because of anisogamy. Distribution of reproductive effort varies less among females than among males,
with greatest proportions of female mating effort in polyandrous and harem-polygynous systems in which the male is parental, and least in monogamous systems. In harem-polygynous
systems female mating effort will be high when both males
and females vary greatly in ability to dispense parental
benefits.

from the mating.

The most unambiguous example of the first kind of mating effort is probably competitive interactions among males in nonresource-based leks (Alexander, 1975), such as found in the European Ruff (Hogan-Warburg, 1966) or the American Sage Grouse (Wiley, 1973). Transfer of benefits may have effects similar to parental effort in lowering the cost of sexuality (Williams, 1975; and see below) by causing a high proportion of the resources garnered by males to be converted into investment in offspring. "Gifts" of prey (Mecoptera: Thornhill, 1976), glandular secretions (Orthoptera: Alexander and Otte, 1967), or a burrow with a food cache (the short-tailed cricket: West and Alexander, 1963) may increase the amount of resources actually available for each brood of offspring and simultaneously reduce the extent of possible polygyny among males. In the case of single offspring per mating, some benefits transferred to females as part of securing matings seem to meet Trivers' (1972) definition of parental investment, but would be excluded because they are part of the male's effort to obtain matings. Some behavior by males may have multiple effects with respect to mating effort. Thus, in the course of holding territories, males may simultaneously (1) demonstrate their phenotypic vigor by direct competition with other males, (2) start nests for the female, and (3) indicate a likelihood of later investment in offspring (for example, by exclusion of predators on eggs or young from their vicinity).

MATING EFFORT AND THE COST OF SEXUALITY

Trivers' introduction of the concept of mating effort as a subdivision of reproductive effort may be coupled with the attempts of various recent authors to understand the costs and benefits of sexuality. Thus, in asexual populations reproductive effort is all expended as parental effort; by definition there is no mating effort. The existence of mating effort, then, is a consequence of sexuality, and, in turn, the so-called "costs of sexuality" (Crow and Kimura, 1965; Maynard Smith, 1971a, b; Williams and Mitton, 1973; Williams, 1975) are attributable largely to the existence of mating effort. Efforts to identify and quantify these costs have nevertheless been both controversial and confusing (e.g., Barash, 1976; Treisman and Dawkins, 1976).

Under density-independent conditions asexual clones can sometimes multiply twice as fast as similar sexual populations because all offspring are females capable of reproduction on their own. This effect, resulting from what has been termed the "cost of producing males" in the sexual population, has

been cited as the principal disadvantage of sexuality (Crow
and Kimura, 1965; Maynard Smith, 1971a; others). Williams and
Mitton (1973) also identified a "cost of meiosis," which they
defined as "the 50% loss in genetic material in meiotic
oögenesis." Williams (1975) referred to the "50% hazard per
generation" suffered by each allele as a result of meiosis,
which he contrasted with the 100% expectation of every allele
in an asexual species of being represented in every offspring.

These various costs are not always 50%, nor are they
inevitable concomitants of sexuality. None of them precisely
describes the principal costs of sexuality. Their values,
however, do change together. Thus, Maynard Smith (1971a)
pointed out that a consistently self-fertilizing hermaphrodite
largely escapes the cost of making males because only a small
proportion of the reproductive soma need be devoted to producing sperm to fertilize the available ova. Similarly,
Williams (1975) stated that the cost of making males is negligible in monogamous species in which the male and female
invest equally in the offspring. In both of these cases, the
brood size can be increased to produce almost the same potential rate of increase as in a parthenogenetic species. This
essential doubling of brood size also appears to counteract
the 50% hazard otherwise suffered by each allele, and because
male and female functions are similar, there is little or no
cost of making males (Ghiselin, 1974). The extreme contrast
would be with a gonochoristic species in which the males
contributed no parental effort and in which the cost of sexuality would be 50%.

As Maynard Smith and Williams (1976) imply, the assignment
of a principal cost of sexuality to loss of genetic material
during oögenesis is spurious since genetic material as such
is relatively inexpensive; haploidy in gametes does not
materially alter the amount of parental effort necessary to
produce a given number of gametes. The cost of sexuality thus
does not refer to the genetic materials as such, but to the
genetic materials in which the parent invests. It is the cost
of omitting genetic material from zygotes destined to receive
expensive parental investment and of having this genetic
material replaced by genetic material from a partner who does
not invest in the zygote, or who invests less. As in gamete
dimorphism, it is a result of competition among members of the
sex investing less in each offspring for mating privileges
with the sex investing more in each offspring. It represents
a diversion of parental effort--from contributions that might
enhance reproductive competition with other species or asexual
forms, to mating effort, which only affects the question of
which males within the species will be most successful in
mating. It is a diversion, however, that may help the individual carrying it out. Thus, males which devote all of their

reproductive effort to improving their mating success (by
means other than by giving the female material benefits) may
be viewed as parasites of the parental effort of their mates.
They pay no cost of diverted parental effort except through
their daughters. Yet, as a consequence, ultimately, of the
dimorphism of gametes and their specialization to unite only
with unlikes, a female in such a species cannot improve her
reproduction by producing only males if she thereby creates
a local surplus of males, reducing the number of matings
available to her sons. Nor can she win by producing males
which divert mating effort to parental effort if other females' sons which do not do this achieve sufficiently more
matings to secure a greater genetic representation among
descendants.

The cost of mating effort is thus borne by the population,
but the cost of forbearing it would be borne by the individual
through reduced success in sexual competition. A parallel
exists in the suggestion of Hamilton (1971) that tendencies
to live in groups may continue to intensify, even if they
lower the average fitness of a population, because individuals
who do not live in groups are rendered so vulnerable to
predators by those who do.

THE MALE-FEMALE INTERACTION AS RECIPROCITY

The male-female interaction can be regarded as a form of
reciprocity or as mutualism. Systems of reciprocity, however,
are generally viewed as evolving toward symmetry or balance
in the exchange (Trivers, 1971; Alexander, 1974), while the
male-female interaction seems to have evolved in a highly
asymmetrical fashion. A basic question in understanding the
male-female phenomenon is that of understanding the nature of
this asymmetry and how and why it has come about.

The implication of symmetry in reciprocal interactions is
in the value to the recipients of the resources or items
exchanged. There is no implication that the *same* items must
be exchanged. Rather, systems of reciprocity must arise and
succeed most often when the participants are specialized to
deliver, inexpensively, mutually useful but *different* items.
Presumably, symmetry in reciprocal interactions evolves because (1) each participant gains by adjusting interactions to
its own advantage, (2) participants have some choice in
accepting or rejecting interactions, or in interactions with
particular partners, and (3) participants have some ability
to alternate or exchange roles in interactions. All of these
conditions are probably met in the systems of social reciprocity that we usually envision as evolving toward symmetry.
When participants are in fact bound to a certain role (e.g.,

that of offering a specialized product that may sometimes be
overabundant) or to a certain system (e.g., are unable to
choose partners, change social groups, or escape the necessity
of engaging in exchanges), then the first of the above three
characteristics of systems of reciprocity, it seems, will
inevitably lead to inequities and asymmetry.

In the case of males and females, each is bound to the role
of its own sex in most gonochoristic forms, and we suggest
below that such asymmetry in *functions* may have preceded
gonochorism and hence preceded asymmetry between *individuals*.
Once sex is inevitable, individuals are also bound to some
kind of recombining interaction. These two facts together
mean that situations could feasibly arise in which even if
some members of one sex (say, females) are able successfully
to favor members of the other sex (males) who reciprocate
more completely than others, and to do so to their own (the
females') advantage (i.e., thereby outreproduce other females),
still, males that fail to reciprocate might so increase their
reproduction as to outrace nonreciprocating males and eventually displace entirely the reciprocating tendency in males.
This situation would lead to increased polygyny and decreased
male parental effort.

If females favor males who reciprocate or show parental
effort, then how could nonreciprocating males secure enough
matings to win as a class, reducing the extent of reciprocity
from males available to females? Aside from changes in the
extrinsic environment, the only obvious way this can occur is
through deception and desertion by males, the likelihood of
which cannot be detected or entirely avoided by females. Such
deception and desertion need not be of great magnitude in
individual cases for evolution to proceed toward lower male
parental effort against the interest of all females and the
more parental males. Indeed, across evolutionary time the
participants in any continuing system of reciprocity are
expected to improve their ability to detect and respond to
cheating, thus minimizing the amount occurring in any given
interaction and establishing a base of expectations which will
generally account for the great bulk of the actual exchange.
The notion that deception involves only a relatively small
proportion of the exchange of any long-evolved system is more
commensurate with Trivers' (1971) analysis of reciprocal
altruism than with his (1972) analysis of the male-female
interaction in which he seems to imply a much greater amount
of deception, especially on the part of the male (see also
Borgia, this volume).

Monogamy, then, and symmetry in the male-female contract--
which seems always to be secondary in higher organisms (arthropods and vertebrates)--must evolve only when parental
effort by males is so rewarded that less parental males cannot

as a class outrace their more parental fellows. These rewards, as with all nepotism, have two components: (1) degree of genetic relatedness to putative offspring ("confidence" of paternity) and (2) extent of increases in the reproductive success of assisted offspring.

We assume that evolutionary specializations involving asymmetry--for example, specializations of females to be parental and of males to be promiscuous and nonparental-- retard or reduce the likelihood of evolution toward symmetry of reproductive effort in many cases. Thus, initial male-female differences in the sizes of their gametes and later their relative amounts of parental effort and mating efforts, deriving originally from lowered likelihood of success of dispersing gametes and lowered confidence of paternity, reduce the relative likelihood of females, compared to males, gaining from additional matings. If one starts with primitive sexes in which one sex becomes more parental than the other, it is to be expected that the more parental sex will, as a result of specialization, subsequently be able to give parental care less expensively than the less parental sex. This effect, moreover, is likely to be cumulative. It increases the likelihood that females, compared to males, will evolve to invest even more heavily in offspring. As a result, females do not have as much reproductive effort left after one mating as do males, and females usually do not have the same possibility of realizing an enormously high reproductive success. Along with this long-term cumulative effect throughout the history of every genetic line, variations in confidence of maternity and paternity have continually influenced, in a proximate fashion, the differences between the sexes in their apportionment of reproductive effort.

Trivers (1972) argued that a parent's decision to invest further in an offspring depends upon the amount already contributed, considering desertion a theoretical temptation for the partner that has made the lesser investment, particularly if the difference is great. He further argues that the temptation to desert results because if no offspring are raised, the loss to the deserter is less than that of his partner. Therefore, selection would favor the partner remaining with the offspring.

Dawkins and Carlisle (1976) noted that the costs and benefits to a parent of deserting or not deserting a particular offspring actually depend, not on the amount already invested, but on the amount required to complete the investment--to make the offspring reproductive. This amount does not differ for the two parents, so it cannot account for the original male-female asymmetry in parental effort. Amounts

of past investment and required future investment correlate
inversely only when the required total investment and the
return on the investment are consistent. When these values
fluctuate extensively, as they certainly do in the rearing
of different offspring in different situations, then the
amount invested cannot be used as a reliable indicator of the
expense that will be required to make the offspring reproductive. Moreover, it is not clear that the parent which has
expended more parental effort on a brood has necessarily
expended more of its total reproductive effort--which is what
determines how much is left to be used in the production or
rearing of another brood.

In a theoretical case, if one parent in a monogamous pair
had tended one offspring and the other had tended another and
one parent were suddenly killed, the remaining parent should
arrange its parental effort so as to produce the most grandchildren without relationship to its personal investment in
the two different offspring. A real example involves marsupials, most of which start a second offspring while an older
sibling is in the pouch (Low, 1978). If the older offspring
turns out to be timed wrongly in regard to food availability
in the uncertain Australian environment, or if its mother is
hotly pursued by a predator, it is discarded and the second
offspring, held in a diapause stage before this happens,
resumes its development. The offspring with the greater investment is thus discarded in favor of the offspring with
the lesser investment, because the latter is more likely to
become a reproductively profitable investment (see also
Dawkins and Carlisle, 1976).

This argument may influence our view both of the early
stages of evolutionary divergence of the sexes and of the
reason why the female more often becomes the more parental
sex. Reasoning backwards from modern species, in an anisogametic ancestor of an organism showing no parental care to
the zygote, one might suppose that the sex producing the
larger gamete is likely to become the more parental sex if
parental care is subsequently extended to the zygote. Trivers
(1972) argues that this likelihood would stem from the differential investment of the two sexes in the gametes, leading to
the general tendency of females to be more parental than
males. But the arguments just presented suggest that a difference in the phenotypic investment of the two sexes in a
particular zygote should not in itself affect their tendencies
to be subsequently parental toward the zygote. Moreover high
male parental effort is not restricted, as Trivers' argument
would suggest, to species in which the investments of the
sexes in the gametes or in the newly formed zygote are most
nearly equal. Instead it seems to be concentrated in forms
which vary as much as possible in this regard: high-fecundity

fish with small eggs, low-fecundity birds with large eggs, and mammals with long gestation periods. What common elements, if any, exist among gibbons, songbirds, and male-brooding fish to cause their similar trends toward high male parental effort?

The adaptive significance of decisions by parents about whether or not to invest further in particular offspring appears likely to derive from cost-benefit outcomes involving three factors:

1. The likelihood that the dependent or juvenile involved is indeed the parent's own offspring--hence, its genetic relatedness to the parent.

2. The ability of the offspring to use additional parental care to improve the parent's reproduction through the offspring's own reproduction. Included will be the amount of parental investment required to bring the offspring to maturity and the offspring's likelihood of reproductive success, based on its current phenotypic attributes and physical condition, and such other factors as the season, population density, and likelihood of severe competition. Also included is the extent of the male's specialization as a parent; the most useful kind of parental investment may be very expensive or even impossible for him to provide. Thus, no male mammal has evolved to lactate despite the high probability that offspring have been lost in many species because of this inability. Nor have male birds in monogamous species evolved to contribute extensively to the food reserves of the fertilized egg, even though they may have evolved behavioral contributions which compensate for the greater early investment of the female. This fact suggests that male and female apportionments of mating and parental effort are in modern species largely divorced from the reasons for maintenance of their different regimes of investment in individual gametes.

3. The costs and benefits to the parent of alternative actions such as (a) efforts at further mating; (b) the probability of surviving to reproduce during another, perhaps better, season; (c) the presence of other dependent or needy juvenile relatives; and (d) need, relatedness, and expected success of offspring in potential subsequent broods. In general, additional matings yield more for a male than for a female, and they may be relatively inexpensive as compared to a first mating if the initial mating involved establishing a dominant position in a hierarchy or group of males or securing a good position in a lek. The number of a male's offspring may multiply as he multiplies his number of matings; while, for females, additional

matings may increase only the quality of their offspring. Such slight benefits to the female may not compensate the time, energy, and risks expended in additional matings (Bateman, 1948; Trivers, 1972).

This set of hypotheses predicts that higher parental effort by males than by females is most likely to generate in two situations: (1) in forms in which the male has more control than the female over fertilization--hence a greater "confidence" of parenthood (e.g., many fishes and some amphibians with external fertilization) and (2) in forms--like birds, reptiles, amphibians, and insects--in which (a) oviposition and fertilization are closely linked (hence confidence of paternity can remain high), (b) the eggs are relatively large (hence the female's remaining reproductive effort will likely be relatively low), and (c) the male's courtship behavior preadapts him to a continuation of parental care (hence it makes male parental care relatively inexpensive). In any of these cases it will be difficult to tell if the male actually exerts more parental effort than the female owing to the very different kinds of parental effort by the two sexes and to problems in distinguishing mating and parental effort.

To answer the question asked earlier, it is one or another combination of the following that is common to gibbons, song-birds, and male-brooding fish: (1) offspring able to benefit from additional parental care, (2) lowered likelihood of profit to males from seeking additional matings, (3) relative ease of paternal investment, and (4) high confidence of paternity.

ORIGINS OF GAMETE DIMORPHISM: AN ALTERNATIVE SUGGESTION

The origin of gamete dimorphism represents the original massive diversion of parental effort into mating effort. In modern sexual metazoans two kinds of selective action on gametes can be distinguished--those affecting their ability to become part of a zygote and those affecting their abilities to succeed once they have become part of a zygote (Parker et al., 1972). In other words, it is possible to imagine that some kinds of gametes are slightly more successful than others at locating and uniting with other gametes to form zygotes, but that this ability is incompatible with maximizing the likelihood that the resulting zygote will succeed. Similarly, those gametes with the greater likelihood of surviving and reproducing if they happen to become part of a zygote may necessarily fail to possess attributes making them most com-petitive in becoming part of a zygote in the first place. To say it another way, opposing selective forces operating before

and after zygote formation may cause the evolution of two
kinds of gametes, specifically, those that we call sperm and
eggs; the same two kinds of selective forces may lead to the
evolution of two kinds of individual organisms specialized
to produce sperm and eggs, namely, males and females. Parker
et al. (1972) have shown how these divergences and specializations might have evolved from a simple beginning involving
only variations in gamete size. They suggest that an initial
variance in the investment per offspring by different parents
would alone be sufficient to lead to a disruptive selection
on the sizes and other attributes of gametes and cause the
evolution of males and females.

Parker et al. begin with an organism which, like many
marine invertebrates today, expels its gametes in large numbers into the surrounding medium, perhaps at special times.
Any gamete may unite with any other gamete; sperm and eggs
have not yet evolved. They note that parents producing smaller gametes can make more of them, thereby, under some conditions at least, increasing the number of their gametes that
will find and unite with other gametes. Parents producing
larger gametes, on the other hand, must produce fewer of them.
At least, initially this may mean either (1) that they are
less likely to locate and unite with other gametes but more
likely to produce a surviving zygote if they are successful
in uniting, or (2) that they are less able to locate and
unite with other larger gametes and are thus less able to
produce the largest zygotes, which are most likely to survive.

Parker et al. note that if the survival likelihood of a
zygote formed by small gametes uniting with one another is
sufficiently low, and the competitive likelihood of two large
gametes actually uniting is sufficiently low, the most frequently successful zygote will be formed of one small and one
large gamete. A disruptive selection will result because of
the two alternative routes to reproductive success. The
smallest gametes will be more likely than others to locate
and unite with the largest gametes, and the largest gametes
will be likely to survive no matter with whom they unite.
Parker et al. showed that if likelihood of survival increases
with the square or cube of the volume of the zygote, the
smallest gametes are more successful than intermediate-sized
gametes, though not as successful as the largest gametes. A
frequency-dependent disruptive selection is thus generated
favoring the largest and the smallest gametes. From such a
beginning, it is easy to envision increases in gamete dimorphism, with the elaboration of locomotive and guidance devices
in sperm, until large eggs are virtually assured combination
with a sperm and are eventually afforded the opportunity of

some selection among those available. Sexual competition
among gametes, then, might be expected to lead to small
gametes aggressively locating and uniting with large gametes.
Both kinds of behavior suggest the onset of locomotion and
forced combination or penetration of other gametes, which is
now the characteristic behavior of sperm as contrasted with
that of eggs.

Conversely, large gametes may be expected to become selective once their union with some kind of gamete is virtually
assured. Perhaps they would evolve to resist union with the
first gametes to arrive in their vicinity or become available
until some kind of competition among aggressive gametes somehow indicates competitors likely to produce offspring superior
in the same competitive situation. Hence, in all probability
this led to the process of sperm "penetration" (and of the
necessity of "penetrating" the female gamete) and the production of many sperm by even monogamous males evolved. That
the general tendencies of small motile gametes and large non-
motile gametes (sperm and eggs, respectively) have been
selected in parallel to the behaviors of their respective
bearers (males and females) is apparent; in polygynous species
in which the male's parental effort is minimal, males tend to
be aggressive in courtship, females coy. It may be speculated
that both eggs and relatively sedentary females, such as
spiders on webs, which show coyness, and even all females that
encourage the attention of nearby males by forcing noisy or
obvious courtship chases, may to some extent be generating
their own private leks within which males can better be compared or must compete directly to win the female (Alexander,
1975; Cox and Le Boeuf, 1977). Such females are able to control male behavior because the female and her eggs represent
resources needed by the male and sperm, respectively (Bateman, 1948; Trivers, 1972).

Parker et al. also argue effectively that eggs (large
gametes) will be incapable of resisting the losses associated
with uniting with sperm (small gametes), since the latter will
evolve more rapidly because of their greater numbers (hence
greater variety of mutants, more intense selection, and faster
rate of adaptation) (see also Hamilton, 1967; Lewontin, 1970).
Eggs, then, will be forced to retain enough reserves to yield
viable zygotes when united with the smallest successful sperm.
It is also likely that eggs are less capable of discrimination
between sperm with reserves and those without reserves than
females are capable of choosing males on such bases, both
because of the more rapid rate of evolution of sperm (Hamilton, 1967; Lewontin, 1970; Parker et al., 1972) and because
eggs may be less able than females to evolve means of recognizing uncoupling of stored reserves in sperm from their
indicators.

Apparently, eggs also have little ability to discard an accepted sperm in favor of others that have not yet penetrated.
Perhaps this effect is best hypothesized as an evolved ability
by sperm to monopolize the egg once the sperm has entered the
cytoplasm of the egg. To say it still another way, sperm
generally lack the capability of capturing the reproductive
potential of an egg already entered by another sperm. Females,
as opposed to eggs, do however possess abilities to choose
among males, or among sperm, even after mating. Although
precedence of the sperm of the last male to mate with a female
(Parker, 1970) may be viewed as a beneficial result of certain
mating strategies by males, it is also one of many reasons
why a female is not wholly bound to produce the offspring of
a male just because she has already mated with him. Other
such mechanisms include all of the various forms of abandonment of zygotic offspring associated with "overproduction" of
eggs (for references, see Lack, 1968; Alexander, 1974).

Abilities of females to reject particular males as the
genetic contributors to the zygotes in which they will invest
extensively as parents thus appear to be considerably more
effective than eggs' abilities to reject sperm. This ability
seems concentrated in species with internal fertilization,
although high male parental effort is not.

The conclusion of Parker et al. (1972) on the points
treated here is this:

> Thus the disruptive effect noted (in the previous sections)
> over one generation could lead directly over several
> generations to the establishment of stable primary sexual
> dimorphism (anisogamy, the male-female phenomenon, and a
> 1:1 sex ratio) with the assumption only that gamete size
> is controlled by simple dominance (p. 543).

Parker et al. thus begin with something resembling a
multicellular marine organism which expels gametes into the
surrounding medium where the gametes unite to form zygotes
outside the bodies of their parents, postulating a gradual
appearance of anisogamy from disruptive selection on gamete
sizes. An alternative scenario may be constructed by beginning instead with a unicellular or acellular ancestor which--
as in some modern bacteria, diatoms, and ciliates--passed or
exchanged genetic materials during a conjugatory process.
In modern ciliates haploid micronuclei, devoid of cytoplasm
or other resources, are exchanged during conjugation in what
might be viewed as a highly evolved system in which the timing
of the exchange and the nature of the materials exchanged
probably represent a specialized minimizing of the likelihood
and extent of cheating or lopsidedness in the exchange. In a
sense, such an organism is equivalent to an anisogametic
hermaphrodite with internal fertilization. In this view, the

exchanged micronuclei function as sperm and the organism itself is equivalent to the female element or the ovum. Such "protogametes" would have developed with the appearance of sexual recombination. Because the packages of genetic information transferred during sexual recombination would likely be small relative to the receiving cell, the inequality of investment between parents may actually have *preceded* the formation of true gametes.

We assume that the basis for the transfer of investment-free packages of genetic materials during conjugation arises from the relative inability of the transferring organism to maintain the association between transferred genes and resources; this inability is to be compared with its ability to maintain the association between resources and the genes it retains within itself. We regard this situation as roughly paralleling the problem of paternity certainty in higher organisms and as crucial to understanding the early divergence of male and female functions.

If hermaphrodites mate only once, parental and mating effort are likely to be extended similarly by each individual. However, in cases where monogamy cannot be guaranteed and copulations are relatively inexpensive, hermaphrodites may gain from placing sperm in a large number of other individuals with the possibility of gaining from their parental effort. The production of large amounts of sperm, and effort expended in matings beyond what is necessary for an individual to secure sperm to fertilize its own eggs, might be considered "male" behavior by hermaphrodites. In outbreeding populations male and female effort by hermaphrodites should contribute equally to genetic representation in the succeeding generation.

Following the reasoning of Fisher (1958), this should lead to equal amounts of effort expended on each type of sexual behavior and to either specialization of individuals in one or the other type of behavior or to an equal expenditure of each type of effort by a given individual. Independently of how sexual behavior is distributed among individuals, high levels of male activities without parental effort will lead to increases in the costs of sexuality as discussed above.

We ask whether multicellular organisms which release their gametes to unite in the surrounding medium, of the sort necessary for the operation of the model of Parker et al., might not have been derived from an hermaphroditic unicellular (or acellular) ancestor like that envisioned above. Two directions for the evolution of "external" gametes could then be imagined. In one line, increasing tendencies to be non-motile or sessile may have reduced the likelihood that direct transfer of haploid nuclei could be effected; in another line, such direct transfer may have been restricted because of

tendencies toward multicellular states. In a multicellular
organism, as contrasted with a unicellular one, it would be
physically more difficult for each individual cell to conju-
gate, and tendencies of the haploid nuclei to move successfully through the surrounding medium would be favored. The same
might occur if sessile organisms were near one another but not
in direct contact; a predecessor might be very long conjugation tubes, such as are observable in some bacteria.

In the case of sessile organisms, we might envision the
evolution of alga-like forms, and, ultimately, the entire
plant kingdom. Considering modern algae, which include both
anisogametic and isogametic forms, it seems possible that
isogamety, in which all gametes are fairly large and locomotory, could evolve from the kind of unicellular "anisogamety"
just described (rather than vice versa) if the gametes, or
haploid forms, were subject to high mortality and uncertainty
in regard to the length of time and amount of effort required
to locate another gamete with which to unite. Under such
conditions the minimum effective size of the gamete could be
fairly large and determine the isogamety. The presence of
chlorophyll in the isogametes of modern algae, which in itself
imposes a certain lower limit in size, appears to support this
idea. From such organisms, or more directly from the unicellular "anisogametic" form described above, it is possible to
envision the evolution of modern anisogametic multicellular
plants--in the former case, perhaps through the kind of
disruptive selection on gamete size described by Parker et al.
(1972).

Similarly, in an "animal" line, with forms perhaps paralleling *Volvox* in some ways, one may envision specialization
of cells in certain portions of the group ("body") to produce
gametes capable of moving through the surrounding medium to
enter cells in other colonies. Such primitively multicellular
organisms would still, like ciliates, represent hermaphroditic, anisogametic, internally fertilizing forms, with the
gametes moving between them representing sperm. From such
forms the evolution of "external" fertilization would involve
release of haploid units, ova or macrogametes, into the
surrounding medium rather than acceptance of "sperm" or micro-
gametes by female elements. Presumably such release could
evolve because such "eggs" had become costly to carry, were
more effective dispersers, were safer from predators than the
parent, or because more eggs could be produced that way. In
this scheme internal fertilization in modern Metozoa, and
isogamety wherever it occurs, would be secondarily evolved,
and gonochorism would be derived from hermaphroditism.

The most important point for understanding the modern
asymmetries between male and female is that females evidently
never relinquished to the degree that males did their control

over the fates of individual gametes. The confusion of
parental investment with parental effort is more understandable in light of this consideration, since it explains why the
greater *investment* in individual gametes has enabled females
more often than males to gain by a greater overall parental
effort.

MATING EFFORT AND SEXUAL ASYMMETRY IN PAIR FORMING
AND COURTSHIP SIGNALING

There is a close correlation between the proportion of a
female's prezygotic reproductive effort expended as mating
effort and the degree to which males are able and willing to
provide resources for offspring, whether as part of their own
mating effort or as parental effort. The greatest differentials among males as desirable mates will occur when varying
amounts of resources or benefits are coupled with their
provisions of sperm to the female. Accordingly, we may expect
that when females signal males to them (as in many Lepidoptera), the expenditure and risk will be slight (as in the
production of a pheromone) unless the male brings to the
mating an ability and willingness to contribute parental
effort. Extensive searching for mates (as in silkworms and
other moths), costly signaling devices (as in acoustical
Orthoptera and cicadas), or expensive combinations of searching and signaling (as in fireflies) are likely to be restricted to males. When males provide no material benefits and
cannot defend resources useful to females, then the difference
between leks visited by females (as in the European Ruff
[Hogan-Warburg, 1966] and the Sage Grouse [Wiley, 1973]) and
stationary females visited by groups of competing males (as in
silk moths [Riley, 1895] and garter snakes [Devine, 1977]) may
simply be in whether the stationary individuals or the moving
ones undergo the greater expense (calories plus risk); in each
case we expect the males to be forced into this role. Females
seem unlikely to expend effort in seeking out lone males which
are not controlling or offering resources additional to sperm.
Males with nothing but sperm to offer, it follows, are unlikely to signal as isolated individuals, although it does not
follow that males signaling in groups necessarily are offering
nothing but sperm to females. Rather, males with nothing but
sperm to offer should be expected to locate resources important to females and should (1) either seek or call females in
the same vicinity, (2) defend from other males areas rich in
resources, or for that matter the resources themselves, (3)
control the resources so that the female is forced to modify
her behavior in favor of the males with resource control, or
(4) attempt to intercept females on their way to the resources.

If one observes males signaling in relative isolation (as in field crickets (*Gryllus:* Alexander, 1961)), it should be regarded as crucial to discover what kinds of resources important to females the males are controlling or offering.

The general tendency for long-range sexual pheromones to be concentrated in females, while long-range visual and acoustical signals are concentrated in males, we believe has two bases. First, pheromones are less likely to be perceived by a wide array of predators and parasites since they tend to evolve to a much greater degree as narrow couplings of receptor and signaling devices or even as systems involving one receptor for each signal (Kaissling, 1971; O'Connell, 1972; Roelofs, 1975). Conversely, a very wide variety of either acoustical or visual signals, respectively, can be received (though not necessarily differentiated from one another) by the same sensory apparatus because of the relatively great potential for patterning such signals without altering their carrier frequencies. This quality makes visual and acoustical signals potentially visible to a much wider array of predators, hence more dangerous to produce.

Acoustical and visual signals are also more directional and individual-specific at close range. This not only makes them more effective but increases the risk of using them. In particular, such signals would be likely to outcompete pheromones when males are clumped or densely distributed as signalers. On this basis, acoustical and visual signals should be the rule in leks. Even if males in some such species initially signaled pheromonally, we would expect them to evolve to use acoustical and visual signals at close range, eventually replacing even long-range chemical signals with visual or acoustical ones. Visual and acoustical signals also seem more likely in rapidly changing situations, such as male-male aggression, since they are both more instantaneous and more versatile.

It is testimony to the significance of the refinement of Darwinism by Williams (1966a) [causing us to ask ourselves continually what are the units of selection] that so much work on sexual behavior--including, for example, that on acoustical behavior of Orthoptera, patterning of firefly signals, lepidopteran and other sexual pheromones, and butterfly visual signals--until recently had been carried out without questions like those asked above in mind (e.g., see Alexander, 1975). What had previously been regarded as species isolating mechanisms are to a large degree evolved instead in the context of sexual selection and competition within the species.

REFERENCES

Alexander, R.D. 1961. Aggressiveness, territoriality, and
    sexual behavior in field crickets (Orthoptera: Gryllidae).
    Behaviour 17:130-223.
Alexander, R.D. 1974. The evolution of social behavior. *Ann.
    Rev. Ecol. Syst.* 5:325-383.
Alexander, R.D. 1975. Natural selection and specialized
    chorusing behavior in acoustical insects. *In* Pimentel, D.
    (ed.), *Insects, Science, and Society.* Academic Press,
    New York.
Alexander, R.D. 1977. Natural selection and the analysis of
    human sociality. *In* Goulden, C.E. (ed.), *Changing Scenes
    in the Natural Sciences 1776-1976. Phila. Acad. Nat. Sci.
    Special Publ. 12:283-337.
Alexander, R.D., and D. Otte. 1967. The evolution of genitalia
    and mating behavior in crickets (Gryllidae) and other
    Orthoptera. *Univ. Mich. Mus. Zool. Misc. Publ.* 133:1-62.
Baccetti, B. (ed.). 1970. *Comparative Spermatology.* Academic
    Press, New York.
Barash, D. 1976. What does sex really cost? *Amer. Nat.*
    110:894-897.
Bateman, A.J. 1948. Intra-sexual selection in *Drosophila.*
    Heredity 2:349-368.
Cox, C.R., and B.J. Le Boeuf. 1977. Female incitation of male
    competition: a mechanism in sexual selection. *Amer. Nat.*
    111:317-335.
Crow, J., and M. Kimura. 1965. Evolution in sexual and asexual
    populations. *Amer. Nat.* 99:439-450.
Darwin, C.R. 1871. *The Descent of Man and Selection in
    Relation to Sex,* Vols. 1 and 2. Appleton, New York.
Dawkins, R., and T.R. Carlisle. 1976. Parental investment,
    mate desertion and a fallacy. *Nature* 262:131-132.
Devine, M.C. 1977. Chemistry and source of sex-attractant
    pheromones and their role in mate discrimination by
    garter snakes. Doctoral dissertation. Univ. Mich. 67 pp.
Fisher, R.A. 1958. *The Genetical Theory of Natural Selection.*
    Dover Publ., Inc., New York.
Ghiselin, M.T. 1974. *The Economy of Nature and the Evolution
    of Sex.* Univ. California Press, Berkeley.
Hamilton, W.D. 1967. Extraordinary sex ratios. *Science*
    156:477-488.
Hamilton, W.D. 1971. Geometry for the selfish herd. *J. Theor.
    Biol.* 31:295-311.
Hirshfield, M., and D.W. Tinkle. 1975. Natural selection and
    the evolution of reproductive effort. *Proc. Nat. Acad. Sci.*
    72:2227-2231.
Hogan-Warburg, A.J. 1966. Social behavior of the Ruff
    Philomachus pugnax (L.). *Ardea* 54:109-229.

Kaissling, K.-E. 1971. Insect olfaction. *In* Beidler, L. (ed.),
  Handbook of Sensory Physiology, Vol 4. Chemical Senses.
  Springer-Verlag, New York.
Lack, D. 1968. *Ecological Adaptations for Breeding in Birds.*
  Chapman and Hall, London.
Lewontin, R. 1970. The units of selection. *Ann. Rev. Ecol.
  Syst.* 1:1–18.
Low, B.S. 1978. Environmental uncertainty and the parental
  strategies of marsupials and placentals. *Amer. Nat.*
  112:197–213.
Maynard Smith, J. 1971a. What use is sex? *J. Theor. Biol.*
  30:319–335.
Maynard Smith, J. 1971b. Evolution in sexual and asexual
  populations. *In* Williams, G.C. (ed.), *Group Selection.*
  Aldine, Chicago.
Maynard Smith, J., and G.C. Williams. 1976. Reply to Barash.
  Amer. Nat. 110:897.
O'Connell, R. 1972. Responses of olfactory receptors to the
  sex attractant, its synergist and inhibitor in the red-
  banded leaf roller, *Argyrotaenia velutinana. In* Schneider,
  D. (ed.), Proceedings of the Fourth International Symposium
  on Olfaction and Taste, Seewiesen, Germany, 1971. Wissen-
  schaftliche Verlagsgesellschaft MBH, Stuttgart.
Parker, G.A. 1970. Sperm competition and its evolutionary
  consequences in insects. *Biol. Rev.* 45:525–567.
Parker, G.A., R.R. Baker, and V.G.F. Smith. 1972. The origin
  and evolution of gamete dimorphism and the male-female
  phenomenom. *J. Theor. Biol.* 36:529–553.
Riley, C.V. 1895. The senses of animals. *Nature* 52:209–212.
Roelofs, W.L. 1975. Insect communication--chemical. *In*
  Pimentel, D. (ed.), *Insects, Science, and Society.* Academic
  Press, New York.
Thornhill, A.R. 1976. Sexual selection and parental investment
  in insects. *Amer. Nat.* 110:153–163.
Treisman, M., and R. Dawkins. 1976. The "cost of meiosis":
  Is there any? *J. Theor. Biol.* 63:479–484.
Trivers, R.L. 1971. The evolution of reciprocal altruism.
  Quart. Rev. Biol. 46:35–57.
Trivers, R.L. 1972. Parental investment and sexual selection.
  In Campbell, B. (ed.), *Sexual Selection and the Descent of
  Man 1871–1971.* Aldine, Chicago.
West, M.J., and R.D. Alexander. 1963. Subsocial behavior in
  a burrowing cricket *Anurogryllus muticus* (De Geer)
  (Orthoptera: Gryllidae). *Ohio J. Sci.* 63:19–24.
Wiley, R.H. 1973. Territoriality and non-random mating in the
  sage grouse *Centrocercus urophasianus. Anim. Behav. Monogr.*
  6:85–169.
Williams, G.C. 1957. Pleiotropy, natural selection, and the
  evolution of senescence. *Evolution* 11:398–411.

Williams, G.C. 1966a. *Adaptation and Natural Selection*.
    Princeton Univ. Press, Princeton.
Williams, G.C. 1966b. Natural selection, the costs of repro-
    duction, and a refinement of Lack's principle. *Amer. Nat.*
    100:687-690.
Williams, G.C. 1971. *Group Selection*. Aldine, Chicago.
Williams, G.C. 1975. *Sex and Evolution*. Princeton Univ. Press,
    Princeton.
Williams, G.C., and J. Mitton. 1973. Why reproduce sexually?
    J. Theor. Biol. 39:545-554.

AUTHOR INDEX

SUBJECT INDEX

A

Acanthocephala femorata, 201
Acanthocinus aedilis, 208
Achias, 221–230
   australis, 221–230
   kurandanus, 221, 222, 223, 224, 228
   rothschildi, 228
   thoracalis, 228
Agaonidae, 169, 172, 177
Aggregations, 395
   of bees, 395
   of flies, 222–223
Aggression, 391, 396–397, *see also* Fighting
   Achias, 221, 222, 223–224, 228, 229–230
   bees, 384–399
   behavioral dropouts, 396, 399
   behavioral polymorphism, 396
   effect of ecological conditions, 395–396, 399
   female, 179, 204
   fitness, 396
   structures for, 396
Alfonsiella, 177
Andrena mojavensis, 385
Andrenidae, 195
Anisogamy, 135–137, 161
   algae, 435
   ancestral form, 428, 438
   assortative fusions and, 13, 14
   cost of, 135, 136
   disruptive selection and, 135
   disassortative fusions and, 13, 14, 136, 137
   evolution of, 8–9, 433
   gamete size and, 9
   model, evolutionary, 13–15
   optimization of ovum size and, 135

   origin of, 135
   reproductive effort and, 422
   sexual selection and, 134
     role in, 13–15
   Volvocidae and, 137
Anolis garmani, 346
Anthidium, 389
   Maculosum, 390, 391, 396
Anthocoridae, 199
Antlers
   as exaggerated characters, 53
   functions, 287–288, 289
   Irish elk, 289
   resource holding power and, 287
   size selection for, 288
Anurans, 345–346
   Bufo compactilis, 345, 346
   male reproductive strategies, 345–346
   noncalling males, 345
Apodanthera undulata, 386
Arachnida, 201
Aulocostethus archeri, 268

B

Baboons, 422
Bees, 381, 382, 388, 396, 398
Behavior
   intraspecific variation, 381–399
     categories, 382
     causes, 382–384, 399
     cooccurrence in population, 388–394
     fixed polymorphism, 388–391, 399
     genetic polymorphism, 382–384, 394
     male density, 395, 396
     male reproductive, 382–399
     maintenance, 394–396